T0339776

THE TURKEY AND THE EAGLE

THE TURKEY AND THE EAGLE

The Struggle
for America's Global Role

CALEB STEWART ROSSITER

Algora Publishing
New York

Library of Congress Cataloging-in-Publication Data —

Rossiter, Caleb S.
    The turkey and the eagle : the struggle for America's global role / Caleb Stewart
Rossiter.
        p. cm.
    Includes bibliographical references and index.
    ISBN 978-0-87586-798-4 (soft cover: alk. paper) — ISBN 978-0-87586-799-1 (hard
cover: alk. paper) — ISBN 978-0-87586-800-4 (ebook) 1. United States—Foreign
relations—1945-1989. 2. United States—Foreign relations—1989- 3. United States—
Foreign relations—Philosophy. I. Title.
    E840.R64 2010
    327.73009'04—dc22

                                2010019776

Photos: Front cover, Bald Eagle Calling — Image by © Jeff Vanuga/Corbis; Male Wild
Turkey Close-up — Image by © Joe McDonald/CORBIS
    Back: Caleb Stewart Rossiter, Marissa Rauch Photography

Printed in the United States

TABLE OF CONTENTS

PREFACE: THE REAL ISSUE   1

CHAPTER 1. THE TURKEY AND THE EAGLE IN AMERICAN HISTORY   7

Hard Eagle, Soft Eagle, Turkey   12
Exceptionalism, Domination, and Cooperation   19

PART I. LESSONS FROM THE PAST

CHAPTER 2. COLONIALISM TRANSFORMS INTO ANTI-COMMUNISM: LIBERALS AND
VIETNAM, 1945 TO 1968   25

De Gaulle, Truman, and the Return of the French   28
Johnson's War, Kennedy's Men   33
The Turkeys Respond: The Rise and Self-Destruction of SDS   38

CHAPTER 3. THE SURVIVAL OF THE VIETNAM FOREIGN POLICY UNDER NIXON, FORD,
AND CARTER (YEP!), 1969 TO 1980   43

Vietnam Comes to Angola   45
Carter's Confusion: The Price for the Horn of Africa   51

CHAPTER 4. THE SACRIFICE OF CENTRAL AMERICA BY REAGAN, BUSH, AND THE "DIXIES"   59

Uneasy Allies: Soft Eagles in Congress and Turkeys in "the Groups"   64
El Salvador: The Unnecessary War   69
Nicaragua: The Manufactured War   81

CHAPTER 5. THE RESCUE OF CENTRAL AMERICA BY TURKEYS AND SOFT EAGLES   89

El Salvador: The Jesuits Case and the End of the War   90
Nicaragua: Ollie North's Petard and David Bonior's Bridge to Peace   99
Postscript on Leftist Central America: Not another Cuba   105

CHAPTER 6. AFTER THE COLD WAR: BUSH AND CLINTON'S NEW WORLD OF
DEMOCRACY...AND SAME OLD ARMS SALES TO FRIENDLY DICTATORS   107

   A Dubious Record: Clinton's Arms Sales to Dictators   111

CHAPTER 7. AFTER 9/11: BUSH, OBAMA, AND THE LONG WAR   125

   The Bush Era: "They hate our freedoms," and the War of Choice in Iraq   130
   *The Obama Program: New Respect, Old Alliances, and Wars of Perceived Necessity
   against the Talibans*   139

PART II. NOBLE DISTRACTIONS

CHAPTER 8. THE HUMAN RIGHTS TRAP   151

   Polite Dictators   153
   Phony Elections   158
   Landmine-free Wars   163

CHAPTER 9. MRS. JELLYBY AND LORD CHELMSFORD SAVE AFRICA: FOREIGN AID
AND HUMANITARIAN INTERVENTION   177

   Lord Chelmsford's Descendants: Humanitarian Intervention   191

CHAPTER 10. CLIMATE CATASTROPHE: CONVENIENT FIBS AND DANGEROUS PRESCRIPTIONS   197

   Al Gore's Movie: Apocalypse Soon   201
   The Computer Models that Captured the World   208

PART III. REFORMS AND REVOLUTIONS

CHAPTER 11. ELECTORAL REFORMS: SHACKLING THE EAGLE, FREEING THE TURKEY   217

   Choose the House through Proportional Representation   218
   Make the Senate Ceremonial, Like the House of Lords   224
   Jettison the Electors   227

CHAPTER 12. A MODEST PROPOSAL FOR DISUNION   233

   Disunion, to Disrupt Empire   240

CHAPTER 13. THE CULTURAL PUMP OF EXCEPTIONALISM   249

   How They Do It   256

CHAPTER 14. THE ROLE OF MORALITY IN DOMINATION AND ITS REJECTION   267

   Turkeys and the Moral Argument   271

CHAPTER 15. TAKING THE HANDLES: DEBATING HISTORY AND MORALITY   279

   A Media Offensive: Zinn on Steroids, in 3-D with Graphics and Music   280
   Attacking Exceptionalism, with Activism and an Anti-Imperial Party   289

ACKNOWLEDGMENTS   297

BIBLIOGRAPHY   301

   Articles, hearings, letters, and reports   301
   Books   304

INDEX   309

PREFACE: THE REAL ISSUE

In early 2007, I was sitting in a staff meeting in the palatial office of Congressman Bill Delahunt, a hulking, charming Boston-Irish lawyer who reveled in playing the part of just another guy riding the Boston "T" to work. Bill's rumpled demeanor and rambling musings were the last things hundreds of defendants remembered before being convicted during his 20 years as the district attorney. After I had watched him a few times pleasantly leading hostile witnesses in congressional hearings down a path that suddenly cornered them into contradicting their original claims, I was not surprised to learn that as a prosecutor he had at times had to apologize and arrange compensation when evidence emerged after a conviction that revealed the defendant's innocence.

I had just joined Bill's staff, returning to the congressional cockpit where I had battled for 20 years before taking a five-year sojourn as a professor. He had asked me to help him plan strategy for the foreign policy subcommittee he would chair now that the Democrats controlled the House for the first time in his 10 years in office. Settling comfortably in a puffy chair, I listened with half an ear as one of my colleagues summarized a list of other Members' bills that Bill had co-sponsored in past years and should sign onto again. Suddenly I was startled out of my lethargic state and nearly out of my seat when Bill grunted his assent to one of the bills. "Say that one again?" I asked. "That's not the real issue." Suddenly it all came back to me: liberal Democrats were still fearing national security as the rock on which their ship would break, so they were avoiding a debate on the real issue and instead seizing on tangential matters to discredit Republican policies.

The Democratic Party has lived in the valley of the shadow of fear for the 65 years since World War II, worried about the electoral consequences of being seen as weak on foreign and military policy. To defuse a constant Republican refrain of "soft on communism" or more recently "soft on terrorism," a sizable minority and at times a majority of Democrats in Congress have provided the margin of victory for votes to fund the weapons, foreign aid, and wars that have established the United States as a dominant, interventionist superpower allied with friendly dictators who supply it with military bases, covert collaboration, strategic minerals, and economic access. Liberal Democrats who are trying to minimize the damage done by this global role know that they can't gain the votes of the "Dixies" — their more conservative, mostly Southern colleagues in the party — for an alternative strategic vision, so they focus their efforts instead on tactical initiatives that constrain, rather than confront, American domination.

At its best, this practice of ducking the real issue to tie things up with side issues results in the building of a coalition that stops a misuse of American power that has become counterproductive even its own terms, like the Vietnam war, or the wars in Central America in the 1980s. At its worst, it results in bills like the one we were discussing. The "American Parity Act" required that for every dollar spent on reconstruction in Iraq, a dollar also be spent on similar projects in the United States. It had been introduced in 2005 by Rahm Emanuel, who later became President Obama's chief of staff. I said something along the lines of:

> Wait — that's just plain silly — nobody serious about foreign policy would sign up for that. If you're against the war in Iraq, if you believe that it's morally wrong or it's damaging our security, you don't want to give Bush any money to support the occupation; if you are for the war, if you believe that it's morally right or that maintaining a cooperative government there is important to our security, you're not going to condition your support on increased domestic spending. It's fine to reach out to moderates by pointing out what we could have done at home with the money we've wasted in Iraq, but it's crazy to say we should waste more as long as we get some goodies for the district! That's just not serious; it's a cheap shot to get people riled up, but it obscures the real issue that they should be riled up about.

Bill laughed and said: "That's because we're Democrats — we're not serious, and we specialize in cheap shots. OK, we'll stay off it, but tell me, what is the real issue?" This book is an attempt to answer his question.

Bill always said that he was a "samurai warrior" who fought desperate little fights on his immediate front, not a "philosopher king" who looked to the grand design of America's role in the world, but this disclaimer was just more of his blarney, a smokescreen to mask a well-developed and consistent world view. We spent the next two years, as I had spent my 20 years before, walking the fine line between being philosopher-kings trying to present a vision of a moral, cooperative US foreign policy, and being samurais coming up with cheap shots. Only slightly less transparent than Emanuel's, our cheap shots were crafty compromises that built bridges toward the Dixies in important little foreign policy fights that would distract the Bush administration and deny it a clear field for its peculiarly aggressive and unilateral version of American domination. Bill wanted to start down the harder route of being for something, speaking up for his own vision of how to achieve American security and promote American interests through cooperation. To be a credible congressional player, though, he had to take the easier path of accepting domination as an assumption but being against the unrestrained way that it was being pursued.

The Emanuel bill was a logical result of the way Democrats approached the war in Iraq: all samurai and no philosopher. In trying to stop first the invasion and then the occupation, liberal Democrats seized on any tactical issue that could discredit the administration and appeal to the Dixies, ducking the real issue of whether we have the right to dominate the Middle East and determine by force who is in its governments and what their policies are. Before the vote authorizing the invasion they hammered away on whether there was proof of programs to produce and hide weapons of mass destruction, and whether there was a workable plan to restore order, protect civilians, and rebuild Iraq. I did the same thing in my own public speeches as a professor, which lambasted claims about Iraq's nuclear program by explaining the physics used by US agencies to "sniff" the air in a region to detect and hone in on the enrichment of uranium. The case for war was so weak and fraudulent in its own terms that it was far easier and less controversial to discredit the war as stupid rather than debate its morality.

During the occupation the issues were spending levels, torture, incompetence, withdrawal schedules, the dysfunctional Iraqi parliament and regional structure, the constitutional uncertainty about whether just executive branches or legislatures as well had to approve the US–Iraq troop agreement, Iranian gains in regional power, corruption and waste in contracting, rules of engagement, length of military tours, body armor and reinforced vehicles for US troops, the failure to find weapons of mass destruction, and dozens of others that highlighted the disastrous absurdity of the situation. But by always debating tactics, opponents of the war ceded the debate on the real issue — what assumptions about ourselves and our global role made us even think we might have the right to invade in the first place?

As of 2010, the war in Afghanistan is even more mired in a debate over tactics and not assumptions, over side issues and not the real issue. The original stated goal that led Congress to approve war with the Taliban in 2001 was the worthy one of denying al-Qaeda access to a base after it had attacked the United States. Liberals in Congress who first supported the war and later questioned its length and feasibility have shied away from challenging its core assumption — that al-Qaeda's war on America is founded on an irrational hatred of America and its values, and so can only be defeated by killing all of its members and all of its Taliban hosts. In fact, like most totalitarians, al-Qaeda's leaders have been explicit about their motivations, providing us with a roadmap for defusing the threat. We were attacked for maintaining the two repressive, undemocratic allies that had been the target of al-Qaeda's *jihad*, Saudi Arabia and Egypt. Until we do what we should have done long ago for moral reasons, which is to end our support for Middle Eastern autocrats, al-Qaeda will retain its appeal and ability to recruit in the Muslim world, and we will never be safe from another attack. The reality is that the US war in Afghanistan, which has spilled over to destabilize a much more volatile country with a much larger population, Pakistan, is increasing the risk of attack; this risk is obscured by the strength of the prevailing national security paradigm.

Bill tried to challenge that paradigm by developing and broadcasting a vision of a new American global role of cooperation and mutual respect, even as we built the short-term coalitions against the worst excesses arising from the old role of domination. He held a series of hearings and issued a report highlighting polling data showing that it was the invasion of Iraq, torture, and support for repressive regimes that had led to the sharp decline in America's reputation since 2002, and not some hatred of American values. But mostly we focused on tactical questions, holding hearings and preparing legislation on the neglected congressional obligation to make the decision to go to war, a billion dollar scholarship fund for 30,000 low-income international students to attend American colleges, cutting off aid to various dictators, blocking a plan to base US troops in Iraq indefinitely, cases of rendition and torture by current covert operatives, and seeking to bring a former CIA operative, Luis Posada, to justice for airline terrorism.

Our failure to push our legislation aggressively once led me to complain to Bill, "We're not delivering on our promises." He good-naturedly replied: "We're not Domino's — we don't deliver. Anything decent we could pass, Bush would veto. All this is about creating the atmosphere for Obama to win. That is the most important thing we can do in this Congress." There is no denying that without the rebuke to George Bush's aggressive approach to foreign policy that was delivered by Barack Obama's victory over John McCain, there would be no chance to develop a new vision of the United States' role in the world. On the other hand, Obama's first year in office shows that his approach will be largely a softer, but at times even harder, version of the old approach. This book tells the story of how US politics became mired in the assumption of domination, and it offers a way for advocates of a foreign policy of cooperation to change that assumption. *That* is the real issue.

As an inside agitator, an anti-imperialist trapped in imperial Washington, I have been privileged to work with, and at times cross swords with, some remarkable people. In this book you'll meet such well-known figures as Senate Appropriations Chairman Mark Hatfield, House Armed Services Chairman Ron Dellums, House Speakers Tip O'Neill, Jim Wright, Tom Foley, and Nancy Pelosi, Students for a Democratic Society founder Tom Hayden, and Costa Rican president Oscar Arias. You'll also meet lesser known officials, congressional staff, and members of advocacy groups who are unsung heroes in the struggle for a just foreign policy: courageous non-governmental advocates like Holly Burkhalter, Cindy Arnson, and Jemera Rone of Human Rights Watch; dedicated congressional staffers like Ed King, Edie Wilkie, Cindy Buhl, Bob Browne, Kathy Gille, and Tim Rieser; and hard-bargaining worker bees among the Members of Congress like Matt McHugh, Joe Kennedy II, David Bonior, and Cynthia McKinney.

What unified these public servants, and me, as we fought for the contradictory half-loafs that inevitably emerge from congressional bargaining (like trading aid to the Nicaraguan Contras for a ban on chemical weapons, or cutting off a portion, but not all, of aid to a murderous Salvadoran Army) was that we believed in the value of reform. We were bittersweet about our victories, aware that we were only temporarily disrupting the flow of empire, but proud of them. We saw value in our defeats, arguing that things would be even worse had we not made the fight. We thought, we had to think, that the American people would force even more significant reforms if we continued to explain in Congress clearly enough and often enough that imperial behavior was hurting not just foreign citizens but their own interests. With all of these talents, why couldn't we achieve more than we did, which was essentially damage control? Why is America still dominating other countries, when so many people have worked so hard to move us toward cooperation? Why do liberal Democrats still believe they have to spend their time on side issues, and not the real issue? Consider this example.

In 1987, during Nancy Pelosi's first term in Congress, she came to a meeting in George Miller's office of the task force on El Salvador that he chaired and I staffed for the congressional Arms Control and Foreign Policy Caucus. Nancy had been hammered in her San Francisco district by the Central American "solidarity" groups for not doing more to end the war in El Salvador. As we kicked around legislative ideas for little constraints that would tie some US aid to the investigation of various murders either carried out or covered up by the Salvadoran army, she interrupted, almost shrieking in her frustration at the limited nature of our proposals: "People are dying! Children are being killed!" An awkward silence filled the room, and then George spoke tongue-in-cheek for the other ten or so Members: "Thanks for that information, Nancy — we didn't know!"

And we went right back to discussing how to frame the minimal amendments that might gain the support of Members from Kansas, Texas, and Indiana, whose only local lobbying on Central America consisted of American Legion presidents blasting them for even thinking about questioning President Reagan's wars on the communists. One of George's favorite sayings was: "Before you can save the world, you have to save your seat." He already knew what Nancy learned as she became a leader of the party and masterfully held its liberal and conservative wings together as House speaker throughout the trials of the Bush administration. Congress is fundamentally reactive — and Members need backing in their districts before they can challenge a president on national security. Opinion at home, and particularly the widely-held assumption of America's exceptional global role, goodness, and dominance, establishes the boundaries for the debate in Washington. I soon found out first-hand why that backing is so hard to obtain.

In 1997, I was angered by the opposition of a Republican Member of Congress from my part of upstate New York to some initiatives of the advocacy group I was directing, like an end to arms sales to dictators, a 50-percent cut in military spending, and a ban on anti-personnel landmines. I moved back home with my family and became his Democratic opponent in the 1998 election. My hope was to engage voters on the issues that had made me run, but I quickly found out that most of them just didn't have time to care. They had other things on their minds — their jobs, their medical needs, their kids, their communities, in short, their lives. They understood that these things were connected to foreign policy decisions, but the link was too indirect to sustain their interest.

As for asking them to support me because of the damage our policies were doing to others, I chickened out on that almost from the start. The people in my district must have missed the John Kennedy speech about asking what you could do for your country, because they mostly wanted to know what their country could do for them, in a hurry. And there sure was no clamor for doing something for the people of other countries. The longer I campaigned, the less I brought up foreign policy and the more I promised to spend my time and energy getting them their piece of the federal pie. I developed an even deeper admiration for the Members of Congress who challenged domination, even indirectly, because I saw that there was a price to pay for their activities back home.

Nearly 30 years ago, I was called back into Dean Jerry Ziegler's office at Cornell University for my celebratory glass of sherry upon having defended my dissertation on US policy in Southern Africa. Jerry and the other professors on my Ph.D. committee asked me what I was going to do with my degree. "I'm going to Washington, to make a new foreign policy," I announced. In mock horror the professors looked at each other, and one said, "I'm sorry, didn't we tell you? Foreign policy is made right here at home, in the districts. It's only ratified in Washington." Both places, of course, play a role, but my time in and around Congress has convinced me that at heart my professors were right. The boundaries of the main thrust of America's foreign policy are set through some mysterious process by the American people. Since 1945 they have chosen, or at least accepted, domination. They can choose cooperation, but as this book's examples of successful advocacy campaigns show, they won't give it a thought unless somebody brings the matter to their attention.

This book has three sections. After an introductory chapter, the six chapters of the first section review the history of US domination and citizens' efforts to control it. There are chapters covering the assumption of Europe's colonial role after World War II and the defeat in Vietnam, Nixon and Carter's reaction to it, Reagan's reassertion of power in Central America's civil wars, the liberal response that eventually forced an end to the wars, the aftermath of the Cold War, and the "war on terror." The three chapters of the second section analyze policy efforts by opponents of domination in the areas of human rights, foreign aid, and the environment that were noble in intent but served as distractions from the "real issue." Whenever possible in these two sections I tried to include tales of policy fights in which I took a personal part while working in or lobbying Congress, so that the reader can see, at least from one actor's perspective, just how choices are framed and policy gets made. These include the civil wars in Central America, arms sales to dictators, the campaign to ban landmines, and the wars in Iraq and Afghanistan.

The final section of the book contains five chapters suggesting reforms in the electoral process and a revolution in attitudes that can transform America's global role from domination to cooperation. I hope you will find the argument convincing, and join me in that effort. Frederick Douglass's advice from the 19th century struggle for black rights rings just as true today, both in Washington and throughout the country: "Agitate, agitate, agitate." You don't play, you can't win.

CHAPTER 1. THE TURKEY AND THE EAGLE IN AMERICAN HISTORY

In 1784 Benjamin Franklin played the tongue-in-cheek naturalist, and castigated the decision by the Congress of the Confederation to adopt the bald eagle as the symbol of the United States. The bald eagle, Franklin wrote, lives by "Sharping & Robbing," watching a "diligent" hawk fishing and then stealing its hard-earned booty. Rejecting this lazy thief, Franklin preferred that the national honor be borne by the proud but prudent ("tho' a little vain & silly") wild turkey, an industrious and "respectable" berry and bug eater who, while not adventurous, "would not hesitate to attack a Grenadier of the British Guards who should presume to invade his Farm Yard with a red Coat on."[1]

Franklin's juxtaposition of these two birds showed his appreciation of the potential for a struggle over the foreign policy of his new country. Eagles had long been symbols of power for European royalty as they roamed first the continent and then the globe, "Sharping & Robbing." Although he famously savored the literature and leisure of European culture during his tenure as ambassador to France, Franklin was an outspoken opponent of Europe's domination of far-flung cultures through slavery and colonialism. The turkey, native only to the Americas, was untainted by symbolic association with European expansion and indeed, with expansion of any kind. The wild turkey — unlike the flightless, heavy domestic turkey that was soon bred from it — can fly as fast as the wide-ranging bald eagle, but it spends its entire life within a few miles of its birth.

Would America be an eagle or a turkey in its relations with others? Would it Sharp and Rob, or would it mind its own Farm Yard? Would America be, as many of its found-

---

1 See Richard Patterson and Richardson Dougall, *The Eagle and the Shield: A History of the Great Seal of the United States*, Office of the Historian, Bureau of Public Affairs, Department of State, 1976, pp. 30-31. It is not true, as claimed by *Time* magazine in its July 5, 1982, issue, and often repeated in various versions, that in 1776 Franklin proposed the turkey to the first congressional committee to work on a seal, which consisted of himself, John Adams, and Thomas Jefferson. By virtue of his service as ambassador in Paris, Franklin did not serve on the subsequent committees that led to the adoption of the eagle in 1782.

ers advocated, a new kind of nation not just in its popular form of government and its religious tolerance, but also in having a foreign policy in which right made might, and neighborly collaboration replaced the interference and intervention practiced by European monarchs? As one can tell by looking on the back of the dollar bill, Franklin lost the symbolic struggle over the eagle and the turkey. He also soon fell behind in the real struggle over foreign policy. Calls for acceptance of the rights of Native American nations and neighboring governments were brushed aside by the political and economic mainstream as unacceptable weakness. The belligerent expansion of the government's zone of control continued under such imperious claims as god-given exceptionalism, racial superiority, the Monroe Doctrine, and Manifest Destiny.

There were strong and coherent arguments for self-restraint made in case after case by highly-respected commentators, including Franklin's own denunciation of slavery, Chief Justice Marshall's unenforceable rejection of Cherokee removal, and Congressman Abraham Lincoln's oration against invading Mexico. None, however, seemed able to deflect the American flood that kept surging toward the western shining sea. Individual acts of local aggression by settlers escalated into land grabs by the states they formed, and finally into federal military enforcement of large-scale rail, mining, and ranching claims that drove Indian nations onto reservations. At each step, convenient moral arguments were adopted to justify the taking of labor and land: slavery was a benefit to child-like Africans, civilization was a benefit to savage Indians, and American rule was a benefit to misguided Mexicans. Such logical contortions are, of course, not unique in the history of expanding powers. The Roman sweep into barbaric Europe under Caesar, the Muslim sweep across North Africa under the banner of Muhammed, the simultaneous sweeps at the start of the 19th century of Napoleon Bonaparte and his conscripted armies across Europe, Usman dan Fodio and his Fulani Jihad across west Africa, and Arthur Wellesley (later the Duke of Wellington) and his Scottish regiments across central India — each employed a well-reasoned message that was firmly believed by the fighting men and the folks on the home front, a message of altruism and reform. Indeed, it would be difficult to find an expansion in history that was not justified on moral grounds by those doing the expanding.

After the United States established dominance over its continental territory, it began to export its power. Perry's fleet threatened Japan into opening itself to trade in 1853, and Confederate strategists hoped to follow victory in the war of secession with the implementation of long-held plans to establish slave states in the Caribbean and Latin America. In an ironic twist on those plans, in 1869 the hero of the Union victory, President Grant, tried to annex the Dominican Republic as a home for freed American slaves. The Senate rejected the annexation but was more compliant as succeeding administrations took control of Midway Island, Guam, and Hawaii. War with Spain in 1898 was followed by American occupation of Spain's former colonies, despite the robust opposition of the elite media and the noted figures in the Anti-imperialist League, who proclaimed the occupation a classic European tactic that signaled the end of the American experiment.

These "mugwumps" (so named for sharing the grave demeanor, fatalistic world-view, and refusal to make final decisions that were allegedly characteristic of Native American sachems) deplored imperialism more for its domestic effects than for its inherent violation of other people's life, liberty, and pursuit of happiness. They believed that "jingo-ism" had lowered public discourse and narrowed the range of acceptable dissent, and they raised the specter of the pollution of America's culture and gene pool by new, non-white, non-Christian subjects.[1] The League was shattered by its failure to convince either of the major parties to adopt a clearly anti-imperialist position in the 1900 elections. Puerto Rico became a territory in name and Cuba became one in fact. Congress agreed to Rudyard Kipling's plea that it take up "the white man's burden" and funded a brutal war against the unappreciative nationalists in the Philippines. Within a decade, the Caribbean and Latin America had become an informal protectorate, with governments chosen and toppled by the United States based on their cooperation with private American economic interests.[2]

The decision to go to war with Spain, which was America's first real foray into global politics, was driven by belligerent nationalism on the part of politicians and the media. As President McKinley worked his way toward a peaceful resolution, Assistant Secre-tary of the Navy Theodore Roosevelt upbraided him for having "the backbone of a choco-late éclair." The Hearst newspapers hammered McKinley for avoiding war, and when an American battleship exploded in Havana harbor, he could hold back no more. Roosevelt resigned his office and became a cavalry colonel whose exploits led him to the governor-ship of New York, selection by McKinley as vice president, and upon McKinley's assas-sination in 1901, the presidency.

In his widely read histories, such as the four-volume *The Winning of the West*, Roosevelt combined many of the arguments that have propelled the United States into conflict, es-pecially with non-white peoples — the manliness of action, genetic and cultural superior-ity, and saintly altruism. He broadcast the popular beliefs that, "this great continent could not have been kept as nothing but a game preserve for squalid savages...The conquest and settlement by the whites of the Indian lands was necessary to the greatness of the race and to the well-being of civilized mankind...American and Indian, Boer and Zulu, Cossack and Tartar, New Zealander and Maori — in each case the victor, horrible though many of his deeds are, has laid deep the foundations for the future greatness of a mighty people."

Despite the demise of the Anti-imperialist League, public opinion soon turned against adventurism and expansion in reaction to both the war in the Philippines and Roosevelt's blustering and filibustering. He had seized the territory for the Panama Canal, protect-ing it with a new naval base at Guantanamo, Cuba, and sent 16 battleships of the "Great White Fleet" to intimidate Japan, daring a reluctant Congress to cut off funding for the journey home. It took a direct challenge from Germany to bring the United States back onto the world stage in 1917. During World War I, President Wilson invented the modern practice of using government propaganda to justify foreign policies not just on self-interest

---

1 See Robert L. Biesner, *Twelve Against Empire: The Anti-Imperialists, 1898-1900*, University of Chicago Press, Chicago, 1968, 1985, for a clear exposition of the arguments of the anti-imperialists. Modern opponents of American neo-imperialism will not find much comfort in these arguments, which were based on nativism, exceptionalism, isolationism, and racism.

2 A good example from the rich literature on American hegemony in this region is Walter LaFeber, *Inevitable Revolutions: The United States in Latin America*, Norton, New York, 1993.

but also on moral grounds. He called the practice "manufacturing consent."[1] Dramatic improvement in communications allowed Franklin Roosevelt to transform the practice into an industry when the United States was again brought into war by foreign challengers.

In both world wars, Americans learned to tell themselves, and others, that the legitimate, self-interested act of defeating attackers was also an altruistic campaign to, in Wilson's words, "make the world safe for democracy."[2] Wilson expanded on this theme of America's altruism: "We have no selfish ends to serve. We desire no conquest, no dominion. We seek no indemnities for ourselves, no material compensation for the sacrifices we shall freely make. We are but one of the champions of the rights of mankind." Wilson's words eerily presaged Secretary of State Colin Powell's mawkish statement in 2003 about the past century of US foreign combat missions, as he was making the case for invading Iraq to seize its alleged store of weapons of mass destruction: "And did we ask for any land? No. The only land we ever asked for was enough land to bury our dead. And that is the kind of nation we are."[3]

As the US-enforced settlements after the world wars showed, Wilson meant that the world was to be made safe for the European democracies, not for their colored colonial subjects. This was not surprising, or even disingenuous, given the long-standing ability of the government and media to talk of domestic freedom while accepting discrimination in law and practice against ethnic groups deemed to be outside the ruling caste, such as Indians, Blacks, Asians, Jews, Hispanics, Irish, and Italians. World War II left the European colonial enterprise bankrupt, both financially and, in the face of demands for independence, morally. Yet the United States backed nearly every attempt to retain colonial rule, from Truman's funding of France's return to Indochina in 1945 to Reagan's "constructive engagement" with the white South African regime in the 1980s. This policy was one of continuity and coincided with the strategic and commercial interests of the American elite. However, it too was presented on moral grounds as a way of helping European allies maintain their domestic popularity in the contest with opposition parties who were sympathetic to the new competitor, the Soviet Union, and so likely to impose Soviet-style repression. Lest one think that this was a crude sacrificing of African and Asian happiness to European happiness, policy-makers also told themselves and the country that gradual decolonization was better for the colonized than instant independence.

When colonialism failed (within five years for most of Asia, within 15 years for much of Africa, but not for 30 years for Portuguese Africa), the United States took over the substance of the colonial role rather than the title. For 60 years it has used covert operations, foreign aid, and military intervention to back national regimes that cooperate with the policies of the West in general and itself in particular on commerce, military and covert operations, and the diplomatic isolation of challengers. It has used the same tools to pres-

---

1 See the discussion of this operation in the book of the same name, Edward S. Herman and Noam Chomsky, Pantheon Press, New York, 1988, and reissued in 2002. A documentary on Chomsky's views, also with the same name, was released in 1993.
2 See Wilson's address to Congress in 1917 requesting a declaration of war on Germany.
3 At an MTV youth forum. See http://www.theatlantic.com/politics/nj/taylor2003-04-07. htm. Powell repeated much the same line a number of times in 2003.

sure or overthrow regimes that do not. Guatemala and Iran in the 1950s, Vietnam, the Congo, and the Dominican Republic in the 1960s, Chile, Angola, and Zaire in the 1970s, Somalia, El Salvador, and Indonesia in the 1980s, Saudi Arabia and Egypt in the 1990s, and recently Iraq and Afghanistan — these are among the scores of countries whose citizens' liberties and lives have been sacrificed on the altar of a broadly defined US security.

During the Cold War the theme used to justify these alliances and attacks was, of course, anti-communism, but despite the demise of the Soviet Union and the integration of China into the global economy, the alliances, the attacks, and the hegemony they protected continued. As the Soviet Union broke into its pieces, Colin Powell, at that time the chairman of the Joint Chiefs of Staff, revealingly joked with a congressional committee that "I need enemies" to justify the Pentagon's budget. Powell didn't have to search long, as doctrines to excuse the global reach of American power proliferated, including constraining "rogue states" and the spread of "weapons of mass destruction" under President Clinton, and "the global war on terror" and an ideological struggle between "freedom" and militant "Islamo-fascism" under President G.W. Bush. More fundamentally, both presidents reaffirmed the convenient claim that underlay Powell's ultimate proposal for a "base force" that could deter any challenges: American domination promotes a global stability beneficial not just to American citizens but to those of all countries.[1] This claim undercut public questioning of the costs in blood and treasure required to maintain hegemony by appealing to both self-interest and altruism.

The same organizations and interests that had exaggerated the threat of the Soviet Union while arguing for a global military buildup and had cited Soviet evil as moral grounds for US alliances with friendly dictators continued to exaggerate threats and argue for a buildup and unsavory alliances against a plethora of new evils, again on moral grounds. Mainstream American political opinion, while at times rejecting particular portrayals of threat and particular proposals for weapons and alliances, consistently accepted the underlying assumption that their government had the right, and indeed the moral duty to its own and other countries' citizens, to use its military and economic power to shape a "stable" international environment that is, conveniently, somehow always advantageous to both the United States and the citizens of the stabilized countries. This is the assumption that hearkens back to Franklin's day and to the choice between the turkey and the eagle — in today's terms between cooperation and domination — as the core of US foreign policy.

President Barack Obama dramatically changed the rhetoric of American purpose in his first year in office, and he was awarded the Nobel peace prize for doing so. He spoke of shared interests and mutual respect rather than asserting a unilateral right to choose governments and impose solutions, and he put an end to Bush's aggressive demand that governments stand "with us or against us" in a "global war on terror" that featured illegal renditions, secret prisons, and "enhanced interrogation techniques." Obama famously traveled to the Middle East to praise Islam as a progressive force in world history, and to

---

1 An excellent review of the development of Powell's plan and its augmentation into the Cheney-Wolfowitz Defense Planning Guidance of 1992 that became official US national security policy in 2001 can be found in David Armstrong's article in *Harpers*, "Dick Cheney's Song of America: Drafting a Plan for Global Dominance," October, 2002.

the United Nations to outline his vision of a world without nuclear weapons. However, Obama's fundamental shift in rhetoric was not matched by a similar shift in practice. He increased the size of, and the budget for, military and covert forces, and maintained Bush's arms aid and sales to dictators who provide basing and support for military and covert deployments. The two stops on his visit to the Middle East were Saudi Arabia and Egypt, where he trumpeted the cause of democratic reform without noting that the Mubarak regime and the House of Saud are authoritarian dinosaurs who treat dissent with jail and torture. He called for more cooperation in combating terrorism by Islamist militants without noting that the two leaders of al-Qaeda turned on the United States because of its military and covert support for the rule of those two dinosaurs.

Obama did quietly ease off on his campaign pledge to use military force to block Iran's development of nuclear weapons, and in a related decision which was so brilliantly complex that nobody could quite understand or criticize it, he reversed Bush's plan to place anti-ballistic missiles in Poland. However, he followed through on his pledge to step up the war against the Taliban and tripled the level of US troops in Afghanistan to 100,000 — although he bizarrely announced, before the troops could even arrive and test their effectiveness, that they would begin withdrawing within 18 months. This policy was typical of Obama's approach to America's global role: tone down the rhetoric and the excesses, and maintain the underlying alliances and military power.

HARD EAGLE, SOFT EAGLE, TURKEY

America faces a choice in its relations with the previously colonized regions between three paradigms, Hard Eagle, Soft Eagle, and Turkey, of which only the latter rejects domination and neo-imperialism. An easy way to identify these three paradigms is by their adherents' favorite news network: Fox News, National Public Radio, and Pacifica Radio. Fox and NPR may diverge in their commentary but they cover the same stories, which are announced and framed by the reigning administration. Pacifica lives in an alternative universe where the mainstream assumptions about the goodness of American power and interests do not hold sway. Pacifica has about as much overlap in world view with Fox and NPR as there is between foreign policy titles at Washington, DC's radical bookstore, Busboys and Poets, and the liberal bookstore, Politics and Prose — none. President Clinton learned this to his chagrin when he was making live calls to what he was told were sympathetic radio stations on Election Day in 2000. Instead of having the jolly get-out-the-vote chat he expected, he ended up being grilled on basic assumptions by Pacifica's redoubtable Amy Goodman.[1]

Hard Eagles, who comprise the Republican Party and a strong minority in the Democratic Party, promote a policy of military "primacy" sustained by large military forces, an extensive stockpile of nuclear weapons, and a global reach of air, naval, and ground power and technical and human spy networks at an annual cost of about $800 billion. By way

---

1 The hilarious interview is described in a book by Goodman and her brother David, *The Exception to the Rulers: Exposing Oily Politicians, War Profiteers, and the Media That Love Them*, Hyperion, New York, 2004.

of comparison, this is as much as the rest of the world's military spending; it exceeds the gross domestic product of Sub-Saharan Africa; and even accounting for inflation it is higher than during the Vietnam War, when there were three times as many US troops in a war zone as in 2009.[1] This paradigm chooses rulers of countries by unilaterally destabilizing or attacking those who do not cooperate with US military, covert, and economic policies, and by sustaining those who do with military and financial aid. It promotes predatory and protectionist economic policies that block poorer countries' transition from producing primary products to refining, marketing, and retailing. It involves much talk about promoting democracy while arming and financing repressive but cooperative regimes.

This "harder-power" paradigm is an assertive version of America's post-World War II global role of economic penetration, military alliance, and unilateral action. It has been aggressively advocated since the end of the Vietnam War by a coterie of officials, notably Paul Wolfowitz and Dick Cheney, and think-tank authors such as Norman Podhoretz, Donald Kagan, Irving Kristol, and a number of their sons and sons-in-law. Their efforts were first institutionalized in government during the Ford administration in the "Team B" attack on the CIA's modest assessment of Soviet power and influence, which laid the groundwork for the Reagan military buildup. These "neo-conservatives" then revived the non-governmental Committee on the Present Danger, which along with a coterie of right-wing think-tanks like Freedom House and PRODEMCA cited both threat and morality to promote the decade of war in Central America in the 1980s, and launched the brazenly-named Project for the New American Century, which promoted the invasion and occupation of Iraq.

This paradigm's hallmark is a belligerent personalization of foreign and domestic challenges to American power that is redolent of and related by policy to the "tough Jew" side of post-Holocaust Zionism. Both the Hard Eagles in America and the Likud Party in Israel have an elemental commitment to Jewish control of Israel — defined by its post-1967 zone of control, including East Jerusalem and parts of the West Bank — and hence Israeli military primacy in the Middle East. Both also feel a need to assert boldly their exemption from international laws, norms, and opinions for their covert operations and military actions. Like the other aspects of this paradigm, the disdain for restraint and multilateralism was enshrined in the right of "preventive" war asserted in George W. Bush's 2002 National Security Strategy, a document based on a 1992 Cheney–Wolfowitz proposal that was rejected as too extreme by George H. W. Bush.[2]

Oderint dum metuant ("Let them hate us so long as they fear us") was not a very successful policy for the Roman emperor Caligula in his aborted campaign in northern Europe in AD 39, and when it became the hallmark of the early years of the G.W. Bush administration, it again generated tremendous international resistance. Consider some of the con-

---

1 GDP is for African nations at the official exchange rate, meaning what residents can buy in convertible currencies. This method provides a fair comparison for international competitiveness. At purchasing power parity, meaning estimating the level of goods and services residents can purchase with their domestic currency, African income is at least twice as high.

2 There are many excellent treatments of the "neo-con" campaign. See, for example, George Packer, *The Assassins' Gate: America in Iraq*, Farrar, Strauss and Giroux, New York, 2005.

cepts attributed to US officials during the invasion of Iraq: the importance of using "shock and awe" as a military tactic, and the belief that "you have to understand the Arab mind. The only thing they understand is force," which led to the mantra, "the road to Jerusalem runs though Baghdad" — a prediction that a demonstration of overwhelming US power against the regime of Saddam Hussein would make it "America's decade in the Middle East," and allow the United States to cow Palestinians into accepting Israeli sovereignty over Jerusalem.[1]

If inducing fear was in fact a goal of US policy in the "W" years, international polling data show that this goal was achieved. A House subcommittee concluded after a series of ten hearings on the data in 2007 that by invading Iraq and abusing prisoners without regard for international obligations the United States created feelings of fear in other countries. In addition, the polling made clear that high-profile US refusals to complete negotiations or approve international treaties unless all of its positions were adopted created similar but less explosive feelings of irritation and resentment. Large shares of citizens of both historical allies and other nations came to consider the United States a threat to international peace and cooperation.[2]

Soft Eagles, who until the Reagan landslide of 1980 were an important part of the Republican Party, now barely control the Democratic Party. The goals of their paradigm are the same as that of their harder-power cousins — economic advantage and military primacy. However, Soft Eagles deplore the damage done to America's image and alliances by the aggressive unilateralism that led to such dramatic international eyesores as torture and abuse at Abu Ghraib prison in Iraq, the secret or foreign prisons to which "terrorism" suspects were "rendered," and the US military prison at Guantanamo Bay, Cuba. All of this they see as unnecessary to the achievement of dominance, and indeed they understand that the recent decline in America's international popularity has resulted in reduced cooperation from other governments and their citizens in the anti-terror, military, and diplomatic arenas.

While they reserve the right to use America's overwhelming military and covert power unilaterally, Soft Eagles prefer to multilateralize destabilization efforts or attacks by gaining the participation of European powers and the consent of the United Nations Security Council. They also place more emphasis on multilateral diplomacy for other policies, and opposed the Bush administration's rejection of treaties, such as the ban on anti-personnel landmines, the Kyoto Treaty on emissions of heat-trapping gases, and the International Criminal Court, that with a little compromise during negotiations could have been modified into obligations with even less actual constraint than their porous texts already permit. Soft Eagles are more comfortable than Hard Eagles with compromise, and they are less apocalyptic about the future and more philosophical about failure. Their paradigm is

---

1 For these quotes, see "The Decline in America's Reputation: Why?" a report by the Subcommittee on International Organizations, Human Rights, and Oversight of the House Committee on Foreign Affairs, June 11, 2008, pp. 5, 19. For a review of such beliefs, see Mark Lynch, "Taking Arabs Seriously," in *Foreign Affairs*, September/October 2003.
2 The hearings and reports by the Subcommittee on International Organizations, Human Rights, and Oversight of the House Committee on Foreign Affairs are available on http://foreignaffairs.house.gov.

associated with former national security advisors Brent Scowcroft and Zbigniew Brzezinski (although not during his service, but after it) and former secretaries of State James Baker and Warren Christopher, and has been extolled recently in books by Brzezinski, former national security official Joseph Nye, and "realist" scholars Stephen Walt and Michael Mandelbaum.[1]

In its never-ending battle for an electoral majority, the Democratic Party softens some of the unilateral foreign and military policy of the Republicans, but accepts its underlying assumption of America's right to dominate, its dismissal of domestic or foreign critics who dispute the assumption, and its uncritical, ahistorical view of American benevolence in purpose and impact. This is not only the stance of the neo-conservative Democratic Leadership Council, whose forebears promoted a string of wars in Vietnam, Africa, and Central America as part of the competition with the Soviet Union, and whose 2006 plan, "With all our Might: A Progressive Strategy for Defeating Jihadism and Defending Liberty," argues that larger armed forces are needed to expand benevolent American influence and promotes Pakistan as the latest unsavory and unstable regional anchor for US strategy.[2] Even the Black and Progressive Caucuses, operating on the fringe of the policy debate in Congress that is closest to an anti-imperialist critique, are reluctant Eagles. In order to be even vaguely relevant to that debate, both felt that they had to approve continued assistance to the Iraqi government during a withdrawal of US troops, and both support large military and covert budgets and overseas deployment of ships, aircraft, covert operations, and troops, with their proposed budget reductions being in the nature of a few percentage points.[3]

Rather than acknowledging that the 9/11 attacks and the resulting "war on terror" are part of a struggle for control of the Middle East between US-backed regimes and Islamists and proposing policies to address the Islamist grievances, House Speaker Nancy Pelosi often compares herself to a lioness who will be even more vigorous than Republicans: "You threaten our children — and that's America — you threaten our country, you're dead. *You're dead.*" When he served as Democratic National Committee chairman, Howard Dean presented a similar toughness and lack of introspection in his exposition of Democratic foreign policy: "We will not permit Iran to become a nuclear power, we will make the deal with the Chinese to get nuclear weapons out of North Korea, and we will catch Osama bin Laden or kill him, one or the other."[4] As a candidate and then as a president, Barack Obama similarly made it clear that his vision of American power is that of an Eagle somewhere between hard and soft.

The Soft Eagles point out that the United States has the most to gain from the essential bargain in international affairs, which is that nations must give up some specific,

---

1 Joseph Nye, *Soft Power: The Means to Success in World Politics*, Public Affairs, New York, 2004; Stephen Walt, *Taming American Power: The Global Response to US Primacy*, Norton, New York, 2005; Michael Mandelbaum, *The Case for Goliath: How the United States Acts as the World's Government in the 21st Century*, Public Affairs, New York, 2005.

2 The plan is available in full on the DLC's website.

3 The proposals for Iraq policy and military budgets can be found on the websites of the two caucuses: www.cbcfinc.org and *http://cpc.lee.house.gov/*

4 The quotations come from interviews in 2006 with *The New Yorker* magazine.

short-term freedom of action in return for a general regime that provides a longer-term benefit. They argue that negotiating mutual build-downs of nuclear weapons with Non-proliferation Treaty members China, France, Russia, and the United Kingdom would place the United States in a stronger position in negotiations with Iran to halt its attempt to acquire nuclear weapons and with the non-NPT nuclear states (North Korea, Pakistan, India, and Israel) to eliminate their weapons, and that soldiers of all countries will pay the price for the weakening of the Geneva Conventions that has resulted from US torture of suspected Islamist terrorists.

Much energy is expended by the advocates of this paradigm on what often amounts to symbolic treatment of the symptoms of domination, such as human rights violations by US allies, and poverty and civil wars in the formerly colonized countries. Funding is much higher under this paradigm for the plethora of international agencies that undertake relief, research, planning, dialogue, and peacekeeping. A particular focus is placed on boosting "development aid" as a response to global poverty, although there is little evidence that the $2 trillion in aid since the end of colonialism has reduced poverty, which is caused less by a lack of resources than by domestic and international decisions about the distribution of power, income, and opportunity. Indeed, the most destitute populations are those whose political and economic framework has been destroyed by civil wars, as in Somalia, the Democratic Republic of the Congo, and the Sudan, which result from or are exacerbated by the United States and other aid donors arming and financing dictators for strategic reasons.

Given their backing by American labor unions and working families, Soft Eagles are often more protectionist than Hard Eagles, and undercut the goals of their development aid by cutting the value of the aid in half by tying it to American goods and services, block-ing trade agreements, and supporting agricultural subsidies. The Doha trade round would have provided a substantially more open market for American and foreign products and services, but it broke down over Soft Eagles' insistence that American farmers be pro-tected as much as those in developing nations. Similarly Soft Eagles pushed to cancel a contract for American port management to a firm with ownership in Dubai and to reject a Chinese bid for an energy company, both of which undercut efforts to open up other na-tions' markets to American investment.

Turkeys hold to a paradigm of cooperation that rejects, often on pragmatic but ulti-mately on moral grounds, US attempts to determine a government's makeup and policies by threat, subversion, military and covert alliance, or force, and efforts by the Western-controlled international financial and trade institutions to enforce fiscal, investment, and trade regimes on developing countries. They vote Democratic for lack of a viable alterna-tive, and indeed one suspects that a solid minority of Democratic Eagles in Congress are Turkeys at heart. The Turkeys envision: dramatically reducing US forces to a non-nuclear, non-global core that is able to take part in major operations only in concert with others;[1]

---

1 The nuclear part of this equation has ironically been endorsed by a bipartisan coalition of leading Eagles, former secretaries of state and defense and national security advisers who have called for significant progress toward complete, mutual, verifiable nuclear disarmament. President Obama, a Soft Eagle himself, also endorses this goal, but has not taken meaningful steps to promote it. "Toward a Nuclear-Free World," George P. Shultz,

weakening the roots of anti-American terrorism by withdrawing military and financial support for repressive regimes in the Middle East and Africa; ending covert operations that bribe foreign officials and subvert foreign governments; dropping tying requirements, domestic subsidies, and other trade barriers for poorer nations and providing technical support and financing for marketing of their services and refined goods; replacing large-scale, strategically-motivated "foreign aid" programs with small-scale support for creative research and local initiatives meeting specific needs of the poor; and renouncing the role of world enforcer and adopting instead the roles of economic and educational engine, and supporter of the rule of law and citizen participation in political and economic life.

The Turkeys' perspective — that the United States is a self-serving empire masquerading as a guardian of freedom — has been persuasively presented since 1960 in books by numerous authors, notably William Appleman Williams, Richard Barnet, Howard Zinn, and Phyllis Bennis, and in interlocking campaigns by citizens' groups, of whom the Institute for Policy Studies and Peace Action are among the most prominent and the most coherent. However, this perspective has failed to penetrate the mainstream of American consciousness. Mistrusting the motivations of the system that implements US foreign policy, Turkeys engage in campaigns of resistance to various policies as opposed to campaigns to promote alternative approaches. These campaigns, in contrast to the anti-imperial perspective that guides them, have repeatedly and dramatically, although rarely, entered mainstream politics and moved US foreign policy toward their demands. Wars in Vietnam, Central America, and Iraq, and apartheid in South Africa, were severely constrained by these campaigns, and the testing and production of US nuclear weapons has been blocked since the "freeze" campaign of the 1980s reached a broader audience.

Although there are powerful strands of isolationism on both ends of the American political spectrum, this paradigm is not isolationist but rather sees the United States playing a leading role in non-violent collaborations to promote development and the rule of law. Nor is this paradigm pacifist, despite the important role of pacifist organizations in making the case for cooperation. The cooperative approach to foreign policy recognizes that the world may need to use force to maintain freedom of the seas, the skies, and communications, and to track down terrorists and roll back international aggression. Indeed, many Turkeys called more clearly than the Eagles for intervention to stop genocide in Bosnia, Rwanda, and the Sudan. They believe that there are numerous democratic nations with sufficient resources and the will to be a partner, but not an agent, of the United States in a cooperative approach to security.

Turkeys place a premium on reviving the United Nations, which has been damaged by funding cuts won by Hard Eagles in Congress and by its inability to stop the US invasion of Iraq. Like the Soft Eagles, they would increase support for the UN specialized agencies, whose many invaluable functions include controlling malaria and coordinating scientific research. However, the spectacular failures of the Security Council's hodge-podge of peace-keeping missions in Somalia in 1993 and Rwanda in 1994 and the Democratic

---

William J. Perry, Henry A. Kissinger, and Sam Nunn, *Wall Street Journal*, January 15, 2008. The authors cite 14 former secretaries of state and defense and national security advisors as supportive of their project.

Republic of the Congo and Sudan fifteen years later affirm for many Turkeys the need to remake the UN's approach to both conflict and development. Some proponents of cooperation want the Security Council to be able to deploy its own well-armed and provisioned troops to "lock down" an uncertain situation, but they recognize that as currently constituted the Security Council would not be able to create or manage such a force.[1] They want to expand the roster of permanent members to include large democratic regional actors like India, Indonesia, Brazil, and South Africa, end one-country vetoes, and give the secretary general control over the necessary forces and resources.

An important element in a policy of cooperation would be the way in which US leaders interact in international forums and with the media. Like the Soft Eagles, Turkeys believe that it is difficult to hear when one is yelling, and endorse the conclusion of a Government Accountability Office team studying US "public diplomacy" initiatives that "most of the experts who we have talked to indicate that we have a tendency to express our values and ideals from our perspective and with no real in-depth understanding of where others are coming from...."[2] Unlike the Soft Eagles, though, the Turkeys push the boundaries of accepted diplomacy by acting in solidarity not so much with foreign governments as with citizens and their organizations.

Benjamin Franklin pointed out late in his life that there were so many cases in which he had been wrong that he had become a bit uncertain about his current opinions. In this vein, Turkeys reject the Eagles' resistance to following a foreign lead. When France and Germany opposed the invasion of Iraq, they were portrayed in the media as anti-American weasels (literally, in a cover montage in the *New York Post*). The House of Representatives replaced "French fries" with "Freedom fries" in its restaurant, harkening back to 1986, when a group in Georgia burned French lingerie and broke bottles of French wine to protest the Mitterrand government's lack of cooperation in the US bombing of Libya. Yet nothing could have been better for US interests than if the United States had taken their advice.

Turkeys are, of course, not infallible. The threat by Transafrica founder and anti-apartheid hero Randall Robinson to starve himself to death over US policy on Haitian refugees galvanized liberal support for military intervention to restore President Aristide in 1994. This "humanitarian intervention" not only failed to improve life for the average Haitian and delayed internal political development but also provided a new rationale for US domination that President Bush exploited in 2002 when making the case for invading Iraq. More recently, citizen agitation on "climate change," suspiciously complemented by corporate and financial entities standing to profit from trading emission offsets and credits, has spurred the remarkable acceptance by nearly all governments of the highly-conjectural models of climate statisticians that purport to show that without reductions of heat-trapping gases, "global warming" will wreak havoc on the ecosystem. To the relief of advocates of economic growth and the resulting increase in life expectancy, particularly

---

1 Research and advocacy for this policy can be found on the website of Global Solutions, of Washington, DC: www.globalsolutions.org.
2 "Efforts to Improve America's Global Image: Are They Working?" Hearing before the Subcommittee on International Organizations, Human Rights, and Oversight of the House Committee on Foreign Affairs, April 26, 2008, p. 49.

in developing countries, this acceptance has not yet been converted into meaningful constraints on energy use because of the economic and particularly the political costs.

EXCEPTIONALISM, DOMINATION, AND COOPERATION

How does the Eagle, signifying aggression and dominance and a neo-colonial approach to US foreign policy, maintain its rule over the Turkey, signifying moderation and cooperation and an anti-imperialist approach? The answer is found in both procedure and politics, but at its heart, in American culture and self-perception. These issues are addressed in detail in the final section of the book but will be summarized here.

Members of the US House, by state laws, and the Senate, by a Constitutional amendment in 1913, are chosen under a winner-takes-all rule. This reduces the representation in government of the anti-imperialist minority that would be present under a proportional election rule. In addition, the undemocratic nature of the Senate, in which all states have two seats regardless of population, disproportionately favors the small, white states that are more interventionist than the large, multi-ethnic ones. The half million people, almost all white, in Wyoming, have as much say as the 40 million people in California, a majority of whom are not white. On average, white Americans have 35 percent more power on the Senate floor than black Americans. The casual inclusion by the Founders of the two Senate votes for each state in the Electoral College, which is otherwise weighted by population, resulted in the election of George W. Bush in 2000.

In seeking their majorities under these rules, both in individual elections and in the House and Senate as a whole, the Democratic and Republican parties naturally gravitate toward independent voters who "swing" between the two. The parties' foreign policies reflect the mood, rather than some articulated philosophy, at this center point of the electorate. The Eagles are ascendant and the Turkeys marginalized not simply because of procedural quirks that result in there being two parties at the center rather than more parties at the fringes of the political spectrum, but because American culture and self-perception have somehow made voters in the middle of the political spectrum comfortable with an aggressive, unilateral global role. The key to that comfort is a belief in American exceptionalism, promoted by a cultural pump that provides a steady stream of self-congratulation and validation in the media and at community events for its emotional foundations, which include:

- a maudlin self-perception of unappreciated benevolence, resting on historical myths that paint American history as a series of just causes;
- a belligerence in response to challenge and criticism that civil rights historian Taylor Branch calls deeply American — which is rooted in the white violence and white fears that sustained three centuries of slavery and segregation in the South, as well as in the violence of England's rule over the Scottish and Irish lands that provided so much of its global strike force in the 19th century, and so much of the population of America's Appalachian frontier; and
- a state-oriented religiosity that places a veneer of sanctity, by its nature illogical and hence unassailable, on the symbols, forces, and foreign actions of the United States.

Exceptionalism sees the United States as a leader with special rights rather than a partner with equal rights. It holds that the United States, unlike other governments, acts out of benevolence and altruism, and so has the right, indeed the duty and historical calling, to impose order on the world — over others' objections but for their benefit. Exceptionalism considers acts of self-benefit, such as forming a strategic alliance with a repressive regime, to be idealistic, because they will eventually result in American influence that will promote democracy and human rights.[1] These beliefs resonate poorly in underdeveloped nations, which have a grim history of colonization and neo-colonialism publicly justified by their perpetrators as altruism. John Tirman, director of the Center for International Studies at MIT, argued at the House hearings that exceptionalism is rooted in an historical self-image:

> The fundamental self-perception of our mission...one we have carried for centuries, is that of the frontier (in need of) "taming."...This has led us into many actions — some dangerous and violent... Many people do not share these views, many of them from ancient civilizations with their own self-referential myths and narratives.[2]

Public debate about America's global role is usually calm and guided by the Eagles' assumption of exceptionalism, but during extreme events like wars it can becomes heated and briefly involve the viewpoint of the Turkeys. Two of the best-known songs during the Vietnam War were Country Joe and the Fish's 1965 *samizdat* "Feel-like-I'm Fixin'-to-Die Rag," a bitter critique of corporate militarism that invited parents to "be the first one on your block to have your boy come home in a box," and Staff Sergeant Barry Sadler's 1966 chart-topping "Ballad of the Green Berets," a paean to a soldier who "dies for those oppressed." However, media coverage and public debate during the war was not balanced between Country Joe and Sergeant Barry — Turkey or Eagle, anti-imperialist or neo-colonialist, advocates of cooperation or dominance — but between hard and soft Eagles.[3]

The same is true for the "global war on terror," as the struggle for control of the Islamic world between theocratic Muslims and the United States and its coterie of Western-oriented strongmen was formally named by the Bush administration. Debate concerns the practicality of tactics, not the morality of goals. The media argue about what to do with global armed forces, not about whether to have them. Congress argued about whether or not Saddam Hussein had weapons of mass destruction, and over Iran's capability to build them, not over whether it is America's right to go to war to destroy them. The Democratic Party argues with the Republican Party over how to fight "the war on terror," not over whether to respond to the violent opposition of Islamist groups to America's forceful domination of the Middle East with more or less domination, and over whether the "surge"

---

1 This perspective was famously given credibility by Ambassador Jeanne Kirkpatrick in the article that led to her being picked by President Reagan as his Ambassador to the United Nations, "Dictatorships and Double Standards," *Commentary*, November, 1979.

2 See his testimony before the Subcommittee on International Organizations, Human Rights, and Oversight of the House Committee on Foreign Affairs, at a hearing on June 11, 2008.

3 For a detailed treatment of this issue, see the author's *The Chimes of Freedom Flashing: A Personal History of the Vietnam Anti-War Movement and the 1960s*, TCA Press, Washington, DC, 1996. The book can be read on-line at www.calebrossiter.com.

worked in Iraq, not over whether the United States had the right to determine Iraq's future after an illegal invasion. The harder-power Republicans have an inherent advantage over the softer-power Democrats in these arguments, because once the need for domination is agreed on and the inevitable impasses are reached, the logic for escalation of force and collaboration with repressive regimes is powerful.

The Turkeys have always been few, fragmented, and prone to anti-capitalist and pacifist sentiments that make their reasonable prescriptions on social welfare and international justice hopelessly suspect to the permanently capitalist, non-pacifist majority of Americans, and so to the electoral hopes of the Democratic party. The withdrawal of American troops from Iraq sought in 2006 by the premier anti-war coalitions, United for Peace and Justice, and International ANSWER, was not the one proposed by hawkish Democratic Representative Jack Murtha, eventually backed by liberal House Speaker Pelosi, and then implemented by centrist President Obama. Turkeys wanted a withdrawal not just of combat troops but of military and financial support for the US-emplaced Iraqi government, and a withdrawal not only from Iraq but from the Middle East, as part of a general rejection of the post-World War II foreign policy of maintaining large forces to threaten uncooperative regimes and sustain cooperative ones. In contrast, Murtha, Pelosi, and Obama, representing the overwhelming consensus in the Democratic Caucus, wanted to preserve American military power, not reduce it. Their withdrawal of combat troops would be "over the horizon" elsewhere in the region, so that air power, special operations forces, and cash and weapons could be sent back to support the "Iraq-ization" of the war and the tens of thousands of US "training" troops who would remain in Iraq.

Eagles Murtha and Pelosi opposed keeping combat troops in Iraq in large part because the war had reduced other nations' cooperation with counter-terror operations throughout the world; the Turkeys of the anti-war left regard the "war on terror" as just the latest in a long line of fraudulent excuses for alliances with despotic yet compliant regimes. This contradiction in the ultimate purposes of those who favored withdrawing from Iraq is reminiscent of similar contradictions during the Vietnam War. Senator Mark Hatfield, a leading "dove," caustically dismissed the adventure in Vietnam as damaging to American interests, saying, "This was not the way to mount geopolitics." The most potent anti-war groups, though, had no interest in mounting geopolitics. In fact, the most radical of those who opposed American power as a force for neo-imperialism actually welcomed the damage the war did to US alliances, and they joined in Che Guevara's call for "two, three, many Vietnams."[1]

Domination and cooperation are mindsets that lead to contradictory foundations for policy-making. The logic of exceptionalism dovetails with the requirements of domination: because the United States must always be prepared to achieve its goals on its own, it must maintain an overwhelming military force that need not be dependent on any allies for power projection and sustained operations; because the United States has a special responsibility to protect the world, it must avoid any treaty or program that limits its freedom of action. Until Turkeys target not just the policies of domination but the culture

1   Caleb S. Rossiter, *The Chimes of Freedom Flashing: A Personal History of the Vietnam Anti-War Movement and the 1960s*, TCA Press, Washington, DC, 1996. See "Book 2," Chapter 5.

and the mainstream self-perception of exceptionalism, Soft Eagles will continue to mimic Hard Eagles as they seek their majority. A debate solely on tactics cedes the debate on goals and assumptions. As a presidential candidate, Abraham Lincoln was asked why he supported barring slavery from new territories but did not back political rights for blacks in the free states. His response was that of a master politician, focusing not on the question of his personal beliefs but on his ability to pursue them:

> A universal feeling can not be safely disregarded...With public sentiment, nothing can fail; without it, nothing can succeed. Consequently, he who moulds public sentiment, goes deeper than he who enacts statutes or announces decisions.[1]

If Turkeys are to see a day when cooperation is the norm, they must "mould" public sentiment by targeting the "universal feeling" that exceptionalism and the domination it promotes are moral, successful, and inevitable.

---

1   Doris Kearns Goodwin, *Team of Rivals: The Political Genius of Abraham Lincoln*, Simon & Schuster, New York, 2006, p. 206.

PART I. LESSONS FROM THE PAST

CHAPTER 2. COLONIALISM TRANSFORMS INTO ANTI-COMMUNISM: LIBERALS AND VIETNAM, 1945 TO 1968

"If there is anything that makes my blood boil, it is to see our Allies in Indochina and Java deploying Japanese troops to reconquer the little people we promised to liberate. It is the most ignoble kind of betrayal." — General Douglas MacArthur, Supreme Commander of the Allied Powers in Japan, in 1945.[1]

"[To] reserve Indochina and Southeast Asia from further Communist encroachment." — President Truman's Deputy Under Secretary of State Dean Rusk, later Secretary of State to Presidents Kennedy and Johnson, explaining in 1949 the US goal in supporting France's war in Vietnam.[2]

"We've got 20 Vietnams a day to handle." — Attorney General Robert Kennedy in 1961.[3]

"[E]ven if it fails, the policy will be worth it. At a minimum, it will dampen down the charge that we did not do all that we could have done, and this charge will be important in many countries, including our own." — President Johnson's National Security Advisor McGeorge Bundy, proposing the 1965 "Rolling Thunder" bombing of North Vietnam as a way to stiffen the resolve of the government of South Vietnam.[4]

---

1 George McT. Kahin and John W. Lewis, *The United States in Vietnam*, Dial Press, New York, 1967, p. 24.

2 Stanley Karnow, *Vietnam: A History*, Viking, New York, 1991, p. 184.

3 Stanley Karnow, *Vietnam: A History*, Viking, New York, 1991, p. 265.

4 Kai Bird, *The Color of Truth, McGeorge and William Bundy: Brothers in Arms*, Simon & Schuster, New York, 1998, p. 308.

> "If you let a bully come in and chase you out of your front yard, tomorrow he'll be on your porch, and the next day, he'll rape your wife in your own bed." — President Johnson, reflecting in 1969 on why he fought in Vietnam.[1]

Throughout 1968, at the height of America's war in Vietnam, an average of 320 US soldiers died each week.[2] As public opposition to the war crept toward the majority it would finally attain in 1970, commentators on the liberal side of the American political spectrum abandoned their earlier support, and started calling the war a tragic error. Radicals, in contrast, argued that "Vietnam is no mistake." By this they meant that the assumptions about America's global role that had guided foreign policy since the end of World War II made it inevitable that the United States would end up fighting wars to keep revolutionary nationalists from taking power. To the liberals, Vietnam was a failure of tactics — too much "search and destroy," too little "clear and hold," too much resistance to a negotiated "neutralization," too little control over our ally's corruption. To the radicals, it was a failure of goals — America did not have the right to choose who would rule in other countries.

When did the slope get so slippery that there was no way but down into the infamous quagmire that killed more than a million Vietnamese? The key decision, the refusal to allow Ho Chi Minh's communist forces to rule a unified Vietnam, was made over and over again from 1940 to 1968 by the administrations of four Democratic presidents who considered themselves the epitome of liberalism (Roosevelt, Truman, Kennedy, and Johnson) and one Republican president who was firmly in the moderate wing of his party (Eisenhower).

The politically popular mission of anti-communism provided much of the rationale for this decision, but only after communist victories in China in 1949 led to Republican efforts to pin that country's "loss" on President Truman and the Democrats. The US decision to maintain a cooperative government in Vietnam was actually first made by default in the early 1940s, long before the Cold War existed, when a confused American attitude toward colonialism convinced Free French leader Charles de Gaulle that he would be able to restore the French empire. America's failure to oppose its allies' reassertion of control over Asia after Japan's defeat led directly to its own role as post-colonial enforcer in Indochina and indeed around the world. As colonialism became unsustainable, President Truman informally extended to the former colonial world the twin anti-communist initiatives that had been announced for Europe in 1947: the Truman Doctrine of military aid and the Marshall Plan of economic aid. By 1950 it was the United States, and no longer the colonial powers, taking the lead in supporting leaders who were friendly toward Western economic and military interests and destabilizing those who were not. The United States funded the French war in Vietnam until it ended with the establishment of North Vietnam in 1954 and then took on alone the role of guarantor of a non-communist government in South Vietnam.

The willingness of the US government to let its European allies regain their Asian colonies and the ease with which it then adopted the role of anti-communist enforcer

---

1 Michael Beschloss, editor, *Reaching for Glory: Lyndon Johnson' Secret White House Tapes, 1964-1965*, Touchstone Books, New York, 2002, p. 445.
2 http://www.militaryfactory.com/vietnam/casualties.asp

revealed an underlying belief in a Western right, indeed a duty, to dominate the weaker, non-white regions of the world. Something in white America's culture and history made colonialism in the 1940s seem like a well-intentioned muddle rather than an unacceptable evil. Something in white America's self-image made the revolutionary nationalists of the 1950s and 1960s rather than their Western opponents seem like the Nazi aggressors in the widely cited "Munich" parable of the dangers of appeasement. Perhaps it was an emotional identification with Europeans, or an awareness that colonial economies provided access to American capital, or three centuries of accepting slavery and segregation, or memories of driving Indian nations across the continent and sending troops into Mexico and the Philippines. In any event, when France loaded its US-armed troops onto warships in September 1945 for the expedition to retake Vietnam, US officials, usually so willing to clamp down on unilateral French military moves, and the American mainstream, who had just given so much for a war based on the Atlantic Charter's "right of all peoples to choose the form of government under which they will live," just stood by and watched.

From then until the rise of the anti-war movement to national prominence in 1965, the same year that President Johnson introduced US combat units, the American debate over Vietnam, both within the government and in public, was completely focused on tactics. The goal of maintaining a non-communist government in Vietnam had been set, and that was not up for discussion. Failure was unacceptable because it might damage America's reputation and therefore its ability to pursue its broader foreign policy goals of maintaining dozens of friendly regimes in the former colonial world — "dominoes" that could fall away in turn — and of deterring Soviet conventional attacks in Europe that might lead to nuclear war.

Even after 1965 many prominent leaders of the anti-war movement adopted the perspective of the "doves" in the administration, the congress, and the media, and argued for an end to the war not because its goal was wrong but because its cost and poor prospects had turned it into a tragic error of judgment. Rather than rejecting the right of the "hawks" to play with other countries like dominoes, they appropriated the theory themselves, arguing that the war itself was threatening US alliances. The doves sought a face-saving, negotiated, "honorable" way out, but because they validated the goal of sustaining non-communist governments in the former colonial world, they appeared defeatist and lacked credibility with both policy-makers and the public. Only groups on the fringe of American politics and indeed of the anti-war movement, like the Students for a Democratic Society and the Socialist Workers Party, rejected the goal as immoral and the war as the inevitable result of the goal. They saw that once you are debating tactics, you have lost the debate over the goal.

Whether Vietnam was an error or no mistake at all — and this chapter will provide plenty of evidence that it was both — the debate over the assumption of an American right to choose governments, which brought on the war and so might be called the Vietnam foreign policy, was certainly lost by the anti-war movement. As shown in the next chapter, the Vietnam foreign policy marched on with President Nixon "Vietnamizing" the war as part of a doctrine of logistical support for Asian armies, President Ford allying with South

Africa to try to place a cooperative government in power in Angola, and President Carter aiding African dictators in return for bases for a US intervention force for the Middle East.

DE GAULLE, TRUMAN, AND THE RETURN OF THE FRENCH

A Napoleonic self-image of greatness, promoted by an economic class that profited from colonialism, had created a political consensus within France that it must not be run out of Indochina, West Africa, and certainly not the geographically and emotionally closest colony, Algeria. For more than a decade after 1944, the irony of a country recently liberated from foreign oppression immediately re-oppressing its colonies was completely lost on voters across the French political spectrum, from communist to fascist — and certainly on ruling parties, from socialist to Gaullist. France was a great power in fact and in mind at the start of World War II, with a colonial reach from Asia across Africa to the Caribbean. The colonial vision was modified by de Gaulle in 1944 with the promise of a French Union with "free people" but not free states, in which there would be local self-government, with military, foreign, fiscal, and investment policy controlled by Paris.[1] This approach was eventually rejected by most of the nationalists in the colonies, but France was still a great power in mind if not in fact, and would not abandon its pretense to empire until 1962, after losing a seven-year war in Algeria.[2]

Franklin Roosevelt was famously anti-colonial in his sentiments, telling Secretary of State Hull in October 1944: "Indochina should not go back to France...France has had the country — thirty million inhabitants — for nearly one hundred years, and the people are worse off than they were at the beginning."[3] He mused about setting up an international trusteeship that would prepare the way for independence. His attitude percolated down to the operational level, with the OSS, the forerunner to the CIA, sharing information and supplies with Ho Chi Minh's Vietnamese resistance as they fought the Japanese who in 1940 had occupied Vietnam in an alliance with French forces of the German-controlled Vichy government. However, Roosevelt recognized, and was unsure how to handle, the political popularity his European allies won with their policy of regaining control over their Japanese-occupied colonies in Asia — the British in Malaya, the Dutch in Java, and the French in Indochina.

In the case of the French, returning to Indochina was a national mission whose achievement was believed to be crucial for any government that wished to remain in office. While the US State Department's Far East bureau was advising Roosevelt against allowing the French return, its European bureau was advising him to accept it so as not to harm relations with "the French government and people."[4] So, Roosevelt waffled and waited. In contrast to Roosevelt's uncertainty, from the very first instant that Charles de Gaulle landed in Britain in 1940 as the embodiment of the Free French, he had made it clear that his war was to regain not just France but its empire. He named his government-in-exile

---

1 Jean Lacoutre, *De Gaulle*, translated by Francis K. Price, Hutchinson, London, 1970, p. 171.
2 Martinique, the home of the most prominent anti-colonial author, Franz Fanon, ironically never caught the revolutionary fervor, and is today a department of France.
3 Lloyd C. Gardner, *Approaching Vietnam*, Korton, New York, 1988, p. 25.
4 Stanley Karnow, *Vietnam: A History*, Viking, New York, 1991, p. 148.

the Committee for the Defense of the Empire, and upon his return to Paris in 1944 explicitly rejected Vietnamese independence and readied the French fleet to return to Indochina.[1] De Gaulle was so "determined to regain Indochina" that he opposed an allied invasion of Vietnam in early 1945 because he feared the anti-colonial approach of US forces. Ho Chi Minh had hoped for the invasion for precisely the same reason, saying later that year that he could accept "a million US soldiers...but no French," and his military commander, Vo Nguyen Giap, considered the United States a "good friend...a democracy without territorial ambitions."[2] The invasion was called off after the Japanese, knowing that the forces of their former ally had now passed to de Gaulle, arrested much of the French contingent and seized complete power.[3]

At the Potsdam conference in July 1945 the United States, now under President Truman, agreed to have the British disarm the Japanese in the southern half of Vietnam and the Nationalist Chinese disarm them in the north. Upon Japan's surrender in August, Ho's Viet Minh army occupied Hanoi, where he declared a republic over all of Vietnam. His representatives then formed a coalition with other groups called the Committee of the South to administer Saigon. The Vietnamese did not resist the arrival of British and Chinese troops to repatriate the Japanese. The British immediately allowed de Gaulle's naval expedition to insert tens of thousands of fresh French troops, who then joined with British and even re-armed Japanese troops to drive the Committee of the South and the Viet Minh out of Saigon.

The British use of Japanese troops in Indochina on behalf of France and in Java on behalf of the Netherlands to "reconquer the little people we promised to liberate" was for General Douglas MacArthur, the supreme commander in Tokyo whose troops had just defeated the Japanese, "the most ignoble kind of betrayal."[4] It made his "blood boil," yet the United States did nothing to stop this tactic or block the French return in any way. This was in sharp contrast to the US reaction to the many unilateral military actions that de Gaulle ordered in Europe to demonstrate France's return as a sovereign power. In those cases, General Eisenhower and President Truman quickly cut off supplies and sent in US troops to force the French to act in concert with other allied forces. Truman was so enraged by de Gaulle's imperious, uncoordinated actions in Europe that he considered him "a psychopath."[5] Yet he allowed the "psychopath" to use his US-armed and equipped forces to recapture Vietnam, and his administration sold France $160 million worth of military vehicles and equipment to use in the attempt.[6]

What accounted for this lack of sensitivity to Vietnamese aspirations for freedom? Why was colonialism not seen as an evil, the way German fascism and Japanese militarism

1 Jean Lacoutre, *De Gaulle*, translated by Francis K. Price, Hutchinson, London, 1970, p. 171.

2 Stanley Karnow, *Vietnam: A History*, Viking, New York, 1991, pp. 159, 163.

3 Stanley Karnow, *Vietnam: A History*, Viking, New York, 1991, p. 159.

4 George McT. Kahin and John W. Lewis, *The United States in Vietnam*, Dial Press, New York, 1967, p. 24.

5 Robert J. Donovan, *The Presidency of Harry S Truman: Conflict and Crisis, 1945-1948*, University of Missouri Press, Columbia, MO, 1996. pp. 58-59.

6 J.F. Cairns, *The Eagle and the Lotus: Western Intervention in Vietnam 1847-1968*, Lansdowne Press, Melbourne, 1969, p. 50.

were? It is hard to escape the conclusion that racism played a major role in this decision. Certainly, the fear was real that the pro-American French government would perhaps lose power to a communist-led coalition if it failed to retake France's colonies. Having invested so much blood and treasure in freeing Western Europe from the Nazis and being convinced that the rapid disengagement from Europe after World War I was a strategic error that had helped bring on the next world war, US officials were interested above all in maintaining allied governments there. But why would the claims of the colonized in Asia be given such short shrift? After all, many nationalist movements, like Ho Chi Minh's, had supported America's war on Japan, and only the British among all the colonial powers had contributed much in that theater.

It seems obvious that US policy-makers and the white American mainstream and its media were comfortable with discrimination and simply did not empathize with the needs of non-white peoples forced to work in an economy controlled by whites. John Hope Franklin, the famed historian of the Negro in America, said toward the end of his life that it was still difficult for him, after all of his studying the problem, "to understand how it is that we could seek a land of freedom for the people of Europe and, at the very same time, establish a social and economic system that enslaved people who happen not to be from Europe."[1] White liberals have been willing to trade black rights for white unity throughout American history — from Benjamin Franklin in 1787 and Abraham Lincoln in 1860, who accepted slavery as the price of union, to the progressive white Southern religious leaders who were castigated by Martin Luther King Jr. in his "Letter from the Birmingham Jail" in 1963 for their call for a hiatus in agitation for civil rights.

Seeing European whites ruling non-whites in the colonies was analogous to seeing American whites ruling Negroes in the South. Feelings of superiority over child-like colored people made arguments for controlling their economic activities, at home and abroad, seem reasonable. In June 1947, Secretary of State Dean Acheson previewed the Marshall Plan for aid to Europe countries resisting "totalitarian pressures" in a speech in Cleveland, Mississippi, to the Delta Council, a coalition of business leaders. He talked without a hint of irony to this all-white group on an all-white college campus in the heart of segregation about the responsibility of and the benefit to the United States of protecting "independence and democratic institutions and human freedoms."[2]

In this context, it is not surprising that when President Truman in March 1947 responded to a formal British statement that it could not "fulfill its traditional responsibilities" with his doctrine of military aid to resist communism in Europe, he used a moral appeal that did not extend to the Asian peoples under European rule: "One way of life is based upon the will of the majority, and is distinguished by free institutions....the second

---

1 He made the remark in 2006, at age 91. It is cited in his obituary in the *New York Times*, March 26, 2009, p. B12.

2 Elizabeth E. Spalding, *The First Cold Warrior: Harry Truman, Containment, and the Remaking of Liberal Internationalism*, University Press of Kentucky, Lexington, 2006, p. 88. Acheson's remarks can be viewed on the website of the Truman Library, http://www.trumanlibrary. org/exhibit_documents/index.php?pagenumber=5&titleid=206&tldate=1947-05-05%20 &collectionid=marshallplan&PageID=1&groupid=3438.

way of life is based upon the will of a minority forcibly imposed upon the majority..."[1] Indeed, from its founding doctrine that "all men are created equal," white Americans had accepted that their moral principles need not be extended to people of color. Truman's decision to recognize Israel was explained by a biographer as proof that he "felt keenly the displacement, enslavement, and death of various peoples by tyranny, whether Nazi or Communist."[2] Colonialism, apparently, did not make the list of tyrannies.

The British left the southern zone to the French by the end of 1945, and the Nationalist Chinese did the same in the north a few months later in an agreement with the Socialist-led government that replaced de Gaulle.[3] Ho Chi Minh spent most of 1946 in Paris, unsuccessfully trying to negotiate an association with France that would phase out military, foreign policy, and fiscal control by the French Union. Full-scale war broke out in November when France took over customs offices in the port of Haiphong and shelled the areas of the city controlled by Viet Minh forces under General Giap. The war quickly became prohibitively expensive for France, which kept 100,000 troops in the field while sustaining 90,000 total casualties and supporting 300,000 Vietnamese troops. Despite receiving $24 billion in today's value in US support for the war from 1950 to 1954, France spent as much as $46 billion itself — twice as much as it had received under the Marshall Plan.[4] Other than sell arms to France and support it with aid at home, the United States did not play a significant role in its war in Vietnam until 1949, when Mao Tse-Tung's communist armies were completing their victory over their pro-Western opponents. Washington began to buzz with Republican claims that the Democrats had "lost" China, former State Department official Alger Hiss was charged with perjury based on House hearings pushed by Congressman Richard Nixon, and Senator Joseph McCarthy began his public attacks on alleged communists.

With anti-communism becoming a political touchstone in American politics, French portrayals of their colonial effort to "hold the line" rather than "abandoning Indochina to Moscow" finally began to resonate with US officials.[5] The clearest statements came from State Department official Dean Rusk, who was already predisposed to Western involvement in Asian governance from his time in the British-dominated Burma theater in World War II. In 1949, when Rusk was deputy under secretary, he said the US goal was to "reserve Indochina and Southeast Asia from further Communist encroachment," and in 1950, when he became assistant secretary for Asia, he called the war an "aggression" like those that led to World War II, "a civil war that has been captured by the [Soviet] Politburo" and "part of an international war" that the United States must win.[6] When the United

---

1 Elizabeth E. Spalding, *The First Cold Warrior: Harry Truman, Containment, and the Remaking of Liberal Internationalism*, University Press of Kentucky, Lexington, 2006, p. 223.

2 Elizabeth E. Spalding, *The First Cold Warrior: Harry Truman, Containment, and the Remaking of Liberal Internationalism*, University Press of Kentucky, Lexington, 2006, p. 95.

3 De Gaulle resigned from the weak office of the presidency, and refused to return until it was strengthened in the constitution of 1958.

4 Stanley Karnow, *Vietnam: A History*, Viking, New York, 1991, pp. 192, 199, 203. Dollar costs adjusted for inflation with the Consumer Price Index. Marshall Plan total from http://au.encarta.msn.com/media_102662701_761571105_-1_1/the_marshall_plan.html

5 Stanley Karnow, *Vietnam: A History*, Viking, New York, 1991, pp. 175, 191.

6 Stanley Karnow, *Vietnam: A History*, Viking, New York, 1991, pp. 184, 194.

States recognized the French-backed government of Emperor Bao Dai in early 1950, the State Department's Asia experts were aghast at this alliance with both the French colonial policy and their figurehead, who had played the same role for the Japanese.[1] The North Korean invasion of South Korea soon put an end to such complaints. Anti-communism was now the most potent driver of US policy in Asia, and the United States began to provide France with 80 percent of the war's costs. Senator John Kennedy may have deplored the "desperate attempt of the French regime to hang onto the remnants of empire," but he never tried to block funding for it.[2]

In the 1950 elections, the Democratic majorities in the House and Senate were whittled down, and in 1952 the Republicans took control of Congress and the presidency under a former general who made a campaign promise to go to Korea to end that war — and who did end the war, with intimations that the threat of using nuclear weapons and attacking inside China had led to concessions. Liberal Democrats like Senator Lyndon Johnson always remembered that election as the time they were punished for "losing China" and for generally being seen as soft on communism and weak on defense, despite Truman's decision to fight in Korea. They considered the Republican-dominated 1950s a lost decade for the domestic agenda they had inherited from Franklin Roosevelt, and like George Wallace vowing never to be "out-niggered" again after he lost the 1958 Democratic primary for governor in Alabama to a more blatant racist, they were determined to sound as tough as anybody when it came to Asian communists.[3]

As a result, when the French asked for direct US military intervention to stave off defeat in 1954 and a cautious Eisenhower mulled over the introduction of US combat troops and the atomic bombing of the Viet Minh forces surrounding the French Union forces at Dien Bien Phu, Democrats were careful to couch their demurral in terms of the president's own tactical concerns. They agreed with Eisenhower that the long-standing French refusal to give real power to the Bao Dai government would make foreign intervention unpopular with Vietnamese. They joined him in asking for the participation of Britain to create a multilateral sheen to the intervention, knowing that Britain would decline. Along with the British government, Army Chief of Staff Matthew Ridgway, and top State Department advisers, they resisted Eisenhower's analogy to appeasement at Munich by pointing out the dangers of a general Asian war. What they never did, though, was present to the president or the American people a principled statement that the West had no right to determine the make-up of post-colonial governments for its military and economic benefit. They argued not that the proposed intervention was wrong, but that it could not work.[4]

---

1 Stanley Karnow, *Vietnam: A History*, Viking, New York, 1991, p. 192.

2 George McT. Kahin and John W. Lewis, *The United States in Vietnam*, Dial Press, New York, 1967, p. 33.

3 *Southern Changes*, Volume 17, Number 3-4, 1995, p. 25, book review by Steve Suitts of Dan T. Carter's *The Politics of Rage: George Wallace and the Transformation of American Politics*, Simon & Schuster, New York, 1995.

4 George McT. Kahin and John W. Lewis, *The United States in Vietnam*, Dial Press, New York, 1967, p. 38-40, 44. Stanley Karnow, *Vietnam: A History*, Viking, New York, 1991, p. 213-14.

This focus on tactics meant that the United States would remain invested in finding a workable way to deny a communist victory, and as a result Eisenhower squandered two golden opportunities to disengage from Vietnam. First, in the shock of the surrender at Dien Bien Phu after years of hearing about "light at the end of the tunnel," French public opinion turned firmly against involvement in Indochina. Instead of letting France take the lead, and the blame, for Ho Chi Minh's forces taking over all of Vietnam, Eisenhower's representatives adopted a tough stand at the Geneva negotiations in 1954, which created a French military zone in the south and a Viet Minh one in the north, and set national elections under international control for 1956. The United States refused to sign the accords and immediately set up and aided a new government in Saigon under President Ngo Dinh Diem that was finally fully independent of the French Union.[1]

Second, believing that Ho Chi Minh would win 80 percent of the vote, Eisenhower supported Diem's refusal to hold the elections, effectively establishing South Vietnam as a separate, capitalist nation with an American guarantee against integration with the communist north.[2] Ho protested the canceling of the elections and, after concentrating for the next few years on consolidating his rule in the north, began the campaign to regain the south, first through logistical support to southern cadres known as the Viet Cong, or communists, and then through advisers, and finally, in the mid-1960s, combat units from his army. The Diem regime was corrupt, linked in the public mind to colonialism, and only sporadically present in the countryside; the Viet Cong were disciplined, linked to the national liberation struggle, and omnipresent. This was the deteriorating situation bequeathed to President Kennedy in 1961.

JOHNSON'S WAR, KENNEDY'S MEN

The story of how Kennedy, Johnson, and their chosen advisers struggled not to lose a war that they knew could not be won has been well told by David Halberstam in *The Best and the Brightest* in 1968 and by Kai Bird in *The Color of Truth* in 1998. One can justly criticize the Cold War liberals for their naïve historical analogies, their fanciful future scenarios, the false certainty they caustically displayed in public, and the devastation they visited on the people of Indochina. However, there is no denying the moral motivations behind their convenient belief that what was good for America was good for the world. Both in public and in their internal memorandums and private conversations that were revealed in the Pentagon Papers or by archival research, they spoke of Vietnam as the latest in a series of noble efforts to help people resist totalitarian control. Usually this resistance could be accomplished with bluster, foreign aid, and covert operations, but sometimes, like in World War II, Korea, and finally in Vietnam, it required military action. Ironically, these liberal warriors agreed with their radical opponents that the war was no mistake.

Like the colonial administrators who preceded them in managing the colored world, the best and the brightest had been propagandized by school and culture to conflate their nation's foreign power with human progress. Victory over Germany and Japan reinforced

---

1 Kahin, pp. 47, 51, 66-67.
2 Dwight D. Eisenhower, *Mandate for Change, 1953-1956*, Doubleday, Garden City, NY, 1963, pp. 337-38. The 80 percent statement can be found on page 372 in the 1994 edition.

this belief, and then the Korean War turned it into an assumption that guided the group's every deliberation. The unpopularity of North Korean leader Kim Il Sung even among the most ardent opponents of the US-backed South Korean dictatorship seemed to these liberals to confirm that American had a moral duty to fight for any non-communist government, no matter how repressive, if the alternative was a communist one. When pressed to defend the Vietnam War in public, McGeorge Bundy did not cite strategic and economic imperatives as he would have done in government discussions, but fell back on morality: "None of us wants other men to be forced under a totalitarian political authority."[1] The final refuge of moral motivation was the need to forestall nuclear annihilation. The liberals argued that despite Kennedy's demonstration of willingness to use force and risk war in Berlin in 1961 and the Cuban missile crisis in 1962, a lack of resolve in Vietnam might encourage the Soviet Union to attack Western Europe, and lead to nuclear war, and China to engulf Asia, while an unpredictable use of military force there might give the Soviets pause.[2]

Cock-eyed and self-serving as these judgments appear today, at the time they helped create the consensus that it was not just a right but a moral duty of the United States to make the thousands of interventions, little and big, in other peoples' affairs that were constantly required to enforce America's vision of a capitalist, democratic world. As Robert Kennedy said when asked about Vietnam in 1961, when it was just another post-colonial country where the United States was trying to maintain a friendly regime, "We've got 20 Vietnams a day to handle."[3] In fact, it was Vietnam's neighbor, Laos, that departing President Eisenhower told John Kennedy might well require US military action to deny power to a communist movement.[4] The weakness of the communist rebels, though, allowed Kennedy to fashion a face-saving coalition settlement in 1962 that accepted and in fact guaranteed Laos' neutrality in the Cold War.

This was precisely the sort of settlement that Kennedy refused to consider for Vietnam. When President Diem began to edge toward it, US officials signaled that they would welcome Diem's removal in favor of military leaders opposed to any coalition with communists and any neutrality in the Cold War.[5] Kennedy's advisers told him that Diem's corruption and lack of appeal and Ho's determination and popularity could quickly lead to unification under the communists. Since that would be portrayed by Republicans as a defeat, most analysts agree that Kennedy accepted a coup, in which Diem was murdered, as part of a general intention to get through the 1964 presidential election without "losing" Vietnam and then seek a face-saving solution. He indicated that intention to an adviser:

---

1   Kai Bird, *The Color of Truth, McGeorge and William Bundy: Brothers in Arms*, Simon & Schuster, New York, 1998, p. 320.
2   Francis X. Winters, *The Year of the Hare*, University of Georgia Press, Athens, 1997, pp. 6, 131; Kai Bird, *The Color of Truth, McGeorge and William Bundy: Brothers in Arms*, Simon & Schuster, New York, 1998, p. 338.
3   Stanley Karnow, *Vietnam: A History*, Viking, New York, 1991, p. 265.
4   Kai Bird, *The Color of Truth, McGeorge and William Bundy: Brothers in Arms*, Simon & Schuster, New York, 1998, p. 217.
5   Kai Bird, *The Color of Truth, McGeorge and William Bundy: Brothers in Arms*, Simon & Schuster, New York, 1998, p. 253; Francis X. Winters, *The Year of the Hare*, University of Georgia Press, Athens, 1997, pp. 88.

"If I tried to pull out completely now from Vietnam, we would have another Joe McCarthy scare on our hands, but I can do it after I'm re-elected."[1]

Indeed, domestic politics was as omnipresent as morality in the minds of the Cold War liberals as they made decisions about Vietnam. Fairly typical was the justification National Security Advisor McGeorge Bundy gave to President Johnson for the Rolling Thunder bombing campaign over North Vietnam in 1965: "[E]ven if it fails, the policy will be worth it. At a minimum, it will dampen down the charge that we did not do all that we could have done, and this charge will be important in many countries, including our own."[2] Johnson's fear of being seen as being soft on communism was evident in his decision to send US marines to the Dominican Republic in 1965 to deny power to Juan Bosch, who had been fairly elected but ousted by a military coup: "If I let them fall, you know what the [Republican Party's] Dirksens are going to do to us. They're going to eat us up if I let another Cuba come in there."[3] His decision was all politics and no knowledge. When Robert White, a junior State Department officer in the Dominican Republic, picked up Bundy at the airport during the US occupation, he bravely asked him, "Sir, have you considered the possibility that we're on the wrong side?" Bundy replied, "Young man, it's a little too late for that now."[4]

From the start of his presidency, Johnson's telephone tapes show that he was obsessed with not permitting "another China in Vietnam," by which he meant another "who lost China" campaign launched against Democratic candidates.[5] Even after his 1964 election, in which he won what is still the biggest share of the vote in history, garnering 61 percent of the popular vote to Goldwater's 38 percent, Johnson was convinced that "losing Vietnam" when "85 percent of the people in this country" supported the war would reduce his majorities in the 1966 mid-term elections and thwart his ability to pass his domestic health, education, anti-poverty, and civil rights legislation.[6] Looking back on Johnson's escalation from Kennedy's 14,000 advisers to full-scale combat with 500,000 troops, his attorney general Nicholas Katzenbach said, "[I]t would not have made any difference what anybody advised him...It was fear of the right wing..."[7]

Kennedy, Johnson, and their advisers were constrained by the assumptions that they had the right to determine Vietnam's future, and the duty to maintain a non-communist

---

1 Kai Bird, *The Color of Truth, McGeorge and William Bundy: Brothers in Arms*, Simon & Schuster, New York, 1998, p. 261.

2 Kai Bird, *The Color of Truth, McGeorge and William Bundy: Brothers in Arms*, Simon & Schuster, New York, 1998, p. 308.

3 Michael Beschloss, editor, *Reaching for Glory: Lyndon Johnson' Secret White House Tapes, 1964-1965*, Touchstone Books, New York, 2002, p. 300.

4 White later became ambassador to a number of Latin American countries, including El Salvador, and has served as president of the Center for International Policy, a Washington advocacy group, for 25 years. Personal conversation with Ambassador White.

5 Kai Bird, *The Color of Truth, McGeorge and William Bundy: Brothers in Arms*, Simon & Schuster, New York, 1998, p. 272.

6 http://www.usconstitution.net/elections.html, Michael Beschloss, editor, *Reaching for Glory: Lyndon Johnson' Secret White House Tapes, 1964-1965*, Touchstone Books, New York, 2002, pp. 356, 445.

7 Kai Bird, *The Color of Truth, McGeorge and William Bundy: Brothers in Arms*, Simon & Schuster, New York, 1998, p. 337.

government and a capitalist economy in the South. Within those assumptions, they labored mightily, bloodily, fruitlessly, and increasingly illogically and in contradiction to their own information about the situation on the ground. Johnson's only in-house critic, Under Secretary of State George Ball, wrote of McGeorge Bundy's proposal in 1965 to respond to deterioration, incompetence, and illegitimacy in South Vietnam's government by bombing North Vietnam that he "marveled at the way ingenious men can, when they wish, turn logic upside down."[1] Bundy did not hope to force Ho Chi Minh to stop sending supplies and troops south, but argued bizarrely that the bombing might stiffen political resolve within the South. Johnson approved this "Rolling Thunder" campaign and later that year rejected Ball's memorandum recommending a face-saving withdrawal in which South Vietnam would invite the United States to leave. Instead, he accepted Defense Secretary Robert McNamara's plan to send in US combat units to forestall South Vietnam's collapse.[2] Based on the assessments he was being provided, Johnson did not expect that plan to convince North Vietnam to negotiate away its goal of a unified Vietnam. He told a congressional supporter, "They spit in our faces...They wouldn't even open the letter...I don't blame them. I defeated Goldwater [by] 15 million [votes]. Now why would I want to give Goldwater half my Cabinet? They're winning. Why would they want to talk?"[3]

The apparent illogic of Johnson throwing all his chips into what he knew was probably a losing hand was due primarily to domestic politics, but he expressed it, and clearly agonized over it, in terms of morality. However, with the South Vietnamese government now so patently unable to protect most of its citizens and so unwilling to govern fairly over this it could protect, Johnson's moral concerns were focused on people in other countries. He worried, without any evidence, that Thailand was a domino, likely to fall to communism if he permitted another "Munich" in Vietnam.[4] With much encouragement from Secretary of State Dean Rusk and assorted "wise men" gathered from previous administrations, he decided that US credibility in Europe demanded escalation rather than accommodation. "You've got to go in," counseled John McCloy, the informal chairman of the Establishment, simply because the United States had to be seen as keeping its commitments. Turning on its head the French president's argument for a Yugoslavian neutrality that would allow overextended US forces to return to Europe, the wise men concluded that if South Vietnam fell, "De Gaulle would find many takers for his argument that the US could not now be counted on to defend Europe."[5]

Later in the 1960s both Bundy and McNamara became opposed to escalation, but only because it was shaking the consensus in Europe and at home for America's dominant role

1 Kai Bird, *The Color of Truth, McGeorge and William Bundy: Brothers in Arms*, Simon & Schuster, New York, 1998, p. 303.

2 Kai Bird, *The Color of Truth, McGeorge and William Bundy: Brothers in Arms*, Simon & Schuster, New York, 1998, p. 339.

3 Michael Beschloss, editor, *Reaching for Glory: Lyndon Johnson' Secret White House Tapes, 1964-1965*, Touchstone Books, New York, 2002, p. 355.

4 Kai Bird, *The Color of Truth, McGeorge Bundy and William Bundy: Brothers in Arms*, Simon & Schuster, 1998, New York, p. 311.

5 Kai Bird, *The Color of Truth, McGeorge Bundy and William Bundy: Brothers in Arms*, Simon & Schuster, 1998, New York, pp. 256, 338.

in the world.[1] Cold War liberals never renounced the goals of the war, and even bizarrely claimed as a positive side-effect of Johnson's resolve the slaughter of hundreds of thousands of ethnic Chinese and legal communist party members by the Indonesian Army in late 1965, which inaugurated 30 years of military dictatorship. The CIA called the slaughter, which US officials assisted and applauded, "one of the worst mass murders of the 20th century."[2] The Cold Warriors acknowledged mistakes in judgment, but not in purpose, and apologized for failing, but not for trying. McNamara used this approach with Johnson when pushing him to send combat troops in 1965: "...we were wrong not because we did what we did. We were wrong because we failed."[3] Johnson responded, "That's right," and when he dramatically announced his decision to seek peace rather than re-election in 1968, his speech was a categorical restatement of America's military, logistical, and moral commitment to South Vietnam.[4]

Liberal critics of the war, whether within the administration like George Ball, in Congress like Senators Mike Mansfield and Mark Hatfield, or even in the wing of the anti-war movement represented by liberal groups like SANE and the Moratorium committee, were themselves trapped by the Cold Warriors' assumptions and goals.[5] Ball had directed Kennedy's task force on Vietnam in 1961, which proposed ways to maintain the Diem government without US combat troops.[6] His 1965 proposal did "not suggest that the United States should abdicate its leadership in the Cold War." It called the Vietnam War un-winnable at any reasonable cost and judged any US combat commitment to be a "catastrophic error" that should be avoided because "any prudent military commander carefully selects the terrain on which to stand and fight."

In contrast to McNamara, who was proposing to forestall defeat, Ball was proposing that the United States package and manage it, and move on to similar challenges elsewhere where our ally would be "a stable, viable government."[7] Johnson was not convinced. Having ceded the debate on goals, Ball was in an inherently weak position in the debate on tactics. Mansfield similarly tried to talk Johnson out of escalation by proposing less-

1 Caleb S. Rossiter, *The Chimes of Freedom Flashing: A Personal History of the Vietnam Anti-war Movement and the 1960s*, TCA Press, Washington, DC, 1996, p. 221; Kai Bird, The Color of Truth, *McGeorge Bundy and William Bundy: Brothers in Arms*, Simon & Schuster, 1998, New York, p. 371.

2 Kai Bird, The Color of Truth, *McGeorge Bundy and William Bundy: Brothers in Arms*, Simon & Schuster, 1998, New York, pp. 352-354, 371. William Bundy constructed a particularly fanciful version of events, in which the alleged pro-communist plotters within the Indonesian Army, whose attempted coup provided the excuse for the Army's mass murders, rushed into action because they believed that Johnson's stand in Vietnam was weakening their position. Historians have found no evidence of a linkage between events in Vietnam and either the plotters' decision or the Army's fervor in the massacre.

3 Michael Beschloss, editor, *Reaching for Glory: Lyndon Johnson' Secret White House Tapes, 1964-1965*, Touchstone Books, New York, 2002, p. 377.

4 http://www.lbjlib.utexas.edu/Johnson/archives.hom/speeches.hom/680331.asp

5 For a detailed examination of the strains of the anti-war movement, see Caleb S. Rossiter, *The Chimes of Freedom Flashing: A Personal History of the Vietnam Anti-war Movement and the 1960s*, TCA Press, Washington, DC, 1996, pp. 191-266.

6 Stanley Karnow, *Vietnam: A History*, Viking, New York, 1991, p. 267.

7 Kai Bird, *The Color of Truth, McGeorge Bundy and William Bundy: Brothers in Arms*, Simon & Schuster, 1998, New York, pp. 333, 339.

er actions, not by questioning the assumption that there was a legitimate entity called South Vietnam that the United States had the right and duty to preserve.[1] As noted above, Hatfield believed that the war was so obviously tarred with French colonialism that it was "not the way to mount geopolitics," and SANE called for negotiations as a prelude to withdrawal, yet was willing to reprint articles concluding that US credibility ruled out withdrawal so long as the articles criticized US bombing and combat operations.[2] Johnson was contemptuous of these critics who disputed his escalation and its human toll but wouldn't take responsibility for rejecting the goal of preserving friendly governments or admit that a communist victory would be the most likely result of de-escalation: "[Mansfield] came down...[saying] 'Oh, my God, don't send any resolution up here!' They don't want to *vote* against doing it. They just want to talk and *whine* about it..."[3]

THE TURKEYS RESPOND: THE RISE AND SELF-DESTRUCTION OF SDS

While the administration, Congress, and the public mainstream were hearing murmurings about tactics in Vietnam in 1965, that year also saw the honing of a critique of US goals not just in Indochina but around the world that would set the tone for the nation-wide protests that eventually helped end the war. The vanguard thinkers were in the Students for a Democratic Society (SDS), a white "new left" group that had no interest in "mounting geopolitics" and indeed wanted to disrupt what it saw as America's assumption of the colonial powers' role of allying with repressive regimes who allowed access to foreign capital. The Socialist Workers Party, which provided much of the logistical support for the massive demonstrations of the next five years, held a similar view, but it focused so singularly on moving the coalition of sponsoring groups from calling for negotiations to demanding "Out Now!" that SDS was unchallenged as the intellectual leader of the white youth movement.

SDS had its roots in a complex critique of American politics, economics, and society drafted by Tom Hayden in 1962. The Port Huron statement called for "participatory democracy," arguing, as SDS's name itself implied, that the passive receipt of advertising and slogans during elections fueled by cash from business interests did not constitute a meaningful democracy. Like the Cold War liberals, Hayden was motivated by the moral imperatives to help people live in freedom and to reduce the risk of nuclear war, and he acknowledged that countering communism was a morally worthy objective. From his perspective, though, the policies of the Cold War liberals were protecting segregation at home, allying with dictators abroad, and threatening other nations with nuclear destruction. Anti-communism, he wrote, was being used as cover for both American hegemony and rule at home by the "power elite" identified by C. Wright Mills. The Port Huron state-

---

1 Michael Beschloss, editor, *Reaching for Glory: Lyndon Johnson' Secret White House Tapes, 1964-1965*, Touchstone Books, New York, 2002, p. 347.
2 Caleb S. Rossiter, *The Chimes of Freedom Flashing: A Personal History of the Vietnam Anti-war Movement and the 1960s*, TCA Press, Washington, DC, 1996, pp. 209-210, 228-230,
3 Michael Beschloss, editor, *Reaching for Glory: Lyndon Johnson' Secret White House Tapes, 1964-1965*, Touchstone Books, New York, 2002, p. 351.

ment sought an explanation for these problems and found it in the apathy induced by post-war American life.[1]

The statement identified "egotistic" individualism and repetitive, "stultifying" work — in the factory, the office, and the university — as alienating factors that kept people from combining to control their political and economic lives. The result was, in the words of the statement, estrangement, helplessness, doubt, isolation, depersonalization, and indifference to human affairs. Echoing Franz Fanon, the psychiatrist who catalogued mental illnesses caused by the degradation of colonialism, the statement asserted that there were public sources of these "private troubles." In turn, the "national doldrums" meant that people did not discuss values and how they could be reflected in government, so the military-industrial complex and big corporations were able to control both domestic and foreign policy. Port Huron argued that the Democratic Party would never be able to promote corporate regulation, "public sector spending," anti-poverty programs, nuclear disarmament, and dramatic cuts in military forces until it expelled the "Dixiecrats" who opposed civil rights and used anti-communism to wreck social movements at home and justify military intervention abroad. The only way to build such a party would be for average citizens to come out of their shells at work and in the community, and form alliances that would push aggressively for economic and political control at the local level.[2]

SDS members went out to implement this strategy as civil rights workers and community organizers, and the group stayed under the national and even campus radar until Johnson's plans for escalation brought the war to the forefront in 1965, just as black nationalism was making it more difficult for white activists to work on civil rights. Pacifist and socialist groups had been holding tiny demonstrations against the war for a few years, but SDS was the fresh face of the left, and its April call for a march on the Pentagon drew 20,000 people, including the black nationalist Student Non-violent Coordinating Committee, who because of the draft had quickly come to see a link between oppression of people of color at home and abroad.[3] More importantly, the speech of SDS president Paul Potter at the march became an underground campus classic, quickly whisked about the country by mimeograph and word of mouth to many of the students who had been attending the numerous "teach-ins" on the war that spring.

Potter applied the Port Huron critique to the war, which he called no mistake but rather a "symptom of a deeper malaise." He asked people to "name...[and] overcome" the system that could oppress blacks at home and Asians abroad, and still claim to "police the world." The system was not capitalism, as many of the socialist groups in attendance

---

1 Hayden's description of the document and its influences can be found in his *Reunion: A Memoir*, Random House, New York, 1988, pp. 73-102.

2 The text of the final statement is at http://coursesa.matrix.msu.edu/~hst306/documents/huron.html

3 Deferments for college students meant that blacks were being drafted disproportionately, and low skill levels meant that they were going into combat units even more disproportionately, even before the Pentagon started Project 100,000, which waived induction standards for people who scored below permitted levels on IQ tests, 41 percent of whom were black. Caleb S. Rossiter, *The Chimes of Freedom Flashing: A Personal History of the Vietnam Anti-war Movement and the 1960s*, TCA Press, Washington, DC, 1996, pp. 214, 256-257.

hoped he would say, but a particular corporate variant that had come to control the American government, economy, media, and universities. Potter said that because "the war has its roots deep in the institutions of American society," the task of the anti-war movement must be to "build a democratic and humane society in which Vietnams are unthinkable." He called for the "implementation of the values that would have prevented Vietnam" and made it clear that one of those values was the principle that America did not have the right to determine for other peoples whether they would be communist or held in "subjugation" by a US-backed regime.[1]

Potter's speech inaugurated a political movement whose leaders, and many of their followers, not only rejected US hegemony but considered it as evil as the Nazi war machine that the Cold War liberals used as motivation. Both sides were now seeing German analogies. SDS told the anti-war movement not to be like the "good Germans" of the 1930s who went about their pleasant lives as Hitler consolidated power, bullied Jews, and seized Austria and Czechoslovakia, well before his total control made it suicidal to denounce the invasions of France and Russia and the slaughter of Jewish civilians. In their frustration over the next five years with the violence they saw arrayed against both the Vietnamese and the Black Panther Party, and the lack of response to the violence from the Democratic Party, SDS went many steps farther and came to see the average American as the good German, American culture as the source of hegemony, and capitalism as the root of all the evil.

This transition was a double-edge sword. By equating the culture with the war, it convinced a legion of activists to reject all authority and customs. They disrupted sporting and community events, refused to salute the American flag (or flew it upside down and even burned it), threw dollars onto the floor of the stock exchange, occupied campus buildings, chanted "the whole world's watching" as Chicago police attacked them at the 1968 Democratic convention, shouted down liberal politicians at the growing anti-war marches, refused induction into either the Army or corporate roles after college, and generally showed contempt for white America and its institutions. All this had a cumulative effect in convincing first the electorate and then the guardians of the "system" that the domestic cost of continuing the war in Vietnam was simply too high.

The angry protests, however, also brought an end to the reasoned debate and engagement with the average American that was envisioned by SDS in Port Huron in 1962 and Washington in 1965. Such an engagement had been endorsed by as able a social tactician as Martin Luther King Jr., who in 1967 warned against even peaceful civil disobedience over Vietnam because there was so much education of the mainstream still to be done.[2] Education was overwhelmed by denunciation, and there was little progress made toward Potter's goal of building a society whose values would make "more Vietnams unthinkable." The unpopularity of the war and of the anti-war movement rose in lockstep.

---

1 http://www.hippy.com/article-130.html
2 Caleb S. Rossiter, *The Chimes of Freedom Flashing: A Personal History of the Vietnam Anti-war Movement and the 1960s*, TCA Press, Washington, DC, 1996, p. 231.

By 1969 SDS had gone from leading to overreaching when it identified capitalism and American culture as evil, decided to use violence as "armed propaganda" to make that point, and labeled as racist anyone who disagreed with their diagnosis and prescription.[1] Lyndon Johnson and amenable commentators "red-baited" the anti-war left long before speechwriters Pat Buchanan and William Safire wrote their memorably alliterative assaults for the Nixon administration, and SDS took the bait. It was not long before communist dictators like Fidel Castro, Ho Chi Minh, and Mao Tse-tung were, as enemies of SDS's enemies, being held up as friends and role models. For most of the anti-war movement, these weren't the good guys but rather just guys who should be left alone, so by the beginning of its bombing campaign in 1969 SDS had become alienated from even its closest allies.

In essence, SDS had extended its argument that Vietnam was no mistake from the political realm to the cultural one. SDS's singular contribution to the anti-war movement had been in developing and publicizing the thesis that American acceptance of the post-colonial mantle after World War II had brought with it a commitment to maintain pro-capitalist, anti-communist governments, which then led to a series of tests of US resolve that left developing countries subjugated or devastated. SDS now wanted to know why Americans had accepted the commitment and then persevered through the tests. Was it an understandable combination of the unexpected global reach of America after World War II, the barrage of anti-communism and American exceptionalism to which people had been subjected, and legitimate concern about America's credibility, or evidence of elemental racism and greed in the American character? The former could be changed, through the sort of education and moral appeal favored by Martin Luther King Jr.'s generation of civil rights leaders. The latter could only be forced into surrender, by the disruptive anger favored by the Black Panther generation of black militants.

It was easy for SDS and its followers to see distasteful traits in the American character that could explain public support for Johnson's escalation in Vietnam. Many leaders and followers throughout white American and especially Southern history have openly exhibited the traits described in the previous chapter: a maudlin self-perception of unappreciated benevolence, a quasi-religious homage to the military, and a belligerence that is spurred by criticism from anybody perceived to be of a higher social class. Indeed one had to go no farther than Johnson himself to find all of these traits. He said of his Vietnam critics, "They'll never approve of what I do — I didn't go to their fancy colleges."[2] He personalized the war, considering Ho Chi Minh's refusal to give in an insult, telling Martin Luther King Jr., "I don't want to pull down the flag and come home running with my tail between my legs," and turning it into a sex crime: "If you let a bully come in and chase you

---

1 A number of the SDS members who formed the Weather Underground have written memoirs about its cult-like operations. A good example is Cathy Wilkerson, *Flying Close to the Sun*, Seven Stories Press, New York, 2007.

2 http://www.americanheritage.com/articles/magazine/ah/1972/4/1972_4_4.shtml

---

out of your front yard, tomorrow he'll be on your porch, and the next day, he'll rape your wife in your own bed."[1]

The genocide of America's Indians also hung over the war, further convincing activists who were painfully aware of the violent resistance to black rights that a virulent racism at the core of the character of white America was to blame for the war in Vietnam. Military orders and explanations to the press were full of references to Indian country, scouts, and reservations. Johnson famously told US troops in Vietnam to "come home with that coonskin on the wall," as if they were Daniel Boones, hunters on the fringes of civilized society. The first unit to face major combat, in Ia Drang in 1965, was the 7th Cavalry, the same regiment George Custer led to disaster against the Sioux at the Little Big Horn in 1876. Far from disclaiming the dubious heritage of the Indian displacement, on parade the 7th's troopers wore the same wide-brimmed, gold-tasseled hats as Custer's, and they used as a motto and password the name of the marching song, Garryowen, that Custer had introduced.[2]

The hopelessness that SDS had pledged to attack now overwhelmed SDS itself. The Americans who had been seen as potential allies trapped by the system were now seen as willing collaborators in the system's crimes. They were no longer, as Bob Dylan sang, sympathetic "pawns" in the system's game, but wicked knights who needed to be unhorsed. The best and the brightest of the protest generation had been driven off-track by their refusal to lose, much as their namesakes in the establishment had been. As the movement they had started grew so powerful that the war had to be ended, they were fugitives, on the run, and so focused on their own survival that they could not help plan its post-war agenda. As a result, the assumption at the heart of the Vietnam foreign policy — that it was essential to national security that the United States maintain in the former colonial world repressive anti-communist governments who cooperated economically and militarily — survived the defeat in Vietnam.

---

1 Michael Beschloss, editor, *Reaching for Glory: Lyndon Johnson' Secret White House Tapes, 1964-1965*, Touchstone Books, New York, 2002, pp. 389, 445.
2 http://www.us7thcavalry.com/legend.htm

CHAPTER 3. THE SURVIVAL OF THE VIETNAM FOREIGN POLICY UNDER NIXON, FORD, AND CARTER (YEP!), 1969 TO 1980

The Vietnam War effectively ended in late January 1968 during the Tet, or New Year's, holiday, when General Giap launched a risky body blow at the American occupation, throwing most of his irregular southern units into assaults in every city and sending regular northern divisions against Hue city and the US base at Khe Sanh. More Americans, and many more Vietnamese, were killed after Tet than before it, but the war was over because the American commitment to it had dissolved. Giap's gamble paid off because President Johnson, elite opinion-makers, and the American public were stunned when the claims of victory they had heard in preceding months were contradicted by a month of combat in the cities. The Tet offensive was defeated only by bombardment of enemy-controlled areas, the most publicized being the destruction of the town of Ben Tre "in order to save it."[1] US fatalities jumped to over 500 in one week from an average of 220 per week in 1967. Faced with continued strong infiltration of PAVN troops and the unreliability of South Vietnam's troops, the Pentagon requested the addition of up to 207,000 troops to the existing 525,000. In March, with his popularity falling and credible primary challengers emerging over Vietnam, Johnson rejected the request, suspended the bombing of North Vietnam, called for negotiations, and decided not to seek re-election.[2]

For seven years after the Tet offensive Presidents Johnson, Nixon, and Ford continued the violent search for a non-communist government that de Gaulle had started with Truman's acquiescence in 1945, bombing at will throughout Indochina and invading Cambodia and Laos as fitful negotiations dragged on in Paris. They were playing a losing hand, and both the Pentagon and Giap knew it. He had raised the ante with Tet and the contin-

---

1 Stanley Karnow, *Vietnam: A History*, Viking, NY, 1991, pp. 558-561, 575-577; Caleb S. Rossiter, *The Chimes of Freedom Flashing: A Personal History of the Vietnam Anti-war Movement and the 1960s*, TCA Press, Washington, DC, 1996, pp. 215-216.
2 Stanley Karnow, *Vietnam: A History*, Viking, NY, 1991, pp. 562-564, 573, 580.

ued infiltration of northern units, showing that he would accept any casualty level to win the war, and Johnson had folded. Political conditions in America required the withdrawal of US troops, who had become dispirited and less willing to engage in offensive combat in any event.[1] This took the war back to early 1965, when Johnson had sent in the troops to avoid the collapse of South Vietnam to lightly-armed irregular units. Now the North had 150,000 regular troops in the South, including tank and rocket battalions and mobile anti-aircraft units, and the collapse was all the more unavoidable.[2]

Under his 1969 doctrine of aiding Asian nations to resist communism with their own rather than US troops, Nixon convinced Congress to pump almost as much aid into South Vietnam as it raised with its own taxes, a dubious mark of the weakness of a US client state that was not exceeded until El Salvador's civil war in the mid-1980s.[3] "Vietnamization" fielded a million troops out of a population of less than 20 million, a share historically matched only by North Korea, and built the world's fourth-largest air force.[4] However, the government's corruption and neo-colonial relationship with its citizens were fundamentally unchanged since the days of Bao Dai and Diem. The troops were rarely paid, and they were no match for their opponents. Nixon signed a face-saving agreement in 1973 that he called "peace with honor," even though it expelled US forces while leaving Giap's troops in the field. Ford and the Republicans blamed the Democratic Congress in 1975 for not following through on Nixon's hollow pledge to "respond with full force" on behalf of South Vietnam, but the charge of losing Vietnam that had so terrified Democratic presidents from Truman to Johnson turned out not to be very potent. Swing voters no longer seemed to care, and they replaced Ford with Governor Jimmy Carter of Georgia a year after the fall of Saigon.

The presidents had been constrained in their tactics by the shift in public opinion against the war and congressional reaction to the shift, but their goal remained the same, both in Vietnam and elsewhere in the former colonial world. The foreign policy of backing cooperative regimes that led to the war in Vietnam survived it handily. The anti-war movement's first big legislative victory was the 1970 Cooper–Church ban on US combat troops in Cambodia, but it became law only as part of a bill funding the repressive government there.[5] Even as the last US helicopters lifted off from Saigon in 1975, Secretary of State Henry Kissinger was readying a plan to join the civil war in Angola that would follow Portugal's departure.

---

1 Caleb S. Rossiter, *The Chimes of Freedom Flashing: A Personal History of the Vietnam Anti-war Movement and the 1960s*, TCA Press, Washington, DC, 1996, pp. 256, 308.

2 Stanley Karnow, *Vietnam: A History*, Viking, NY, 1991, p. 671.

3 Mark Hatfield, Jim Leach, and George Miller, *Bankrolling Failure: United States Policy in El Salvador and the Urgent Need for Reform*, Arms Control and Foreign Policy Caucus, US Congress, 1987, p. 5.

4 For troops per capita, see the State Department's *World Military Expenditures and Arms Transfers* series at http://www.state.gov/t/vci/rls/rpt/wmeat/; for South Vietnam's Air Force, see Robert Mikesh, *Flying Dragons: The South Vietnamese Air Force*, Schiffer, Atglen, PA, 2005.

5 Caleb S. Rossiter, *The Chimes of Freedom Flashing: A Personal History of the Vietnam Anti-war Movement and the 1960s*, TCA Press, Washington, DC, 1996, p. 258.

Like the last seven years of the 30-year American war to control Vietnam, the war in Angola was fought almost exclusively for strategic credibility abroad and political advantage at home. Kissinger was advised that the US-backed factions had little chance of winning, but he convinced Ford to make the pro-Soviet forces pay for their victory, to send a message of US firmness to friends, foes, and voters in the wake of the defeat in Vietnam.[1] Later in the 1970s Carter would find his dream of a moral foreign policy shattered by a perceived need for strategic credibility and political popularity. Somalia's Siad Barré was just one of a dozen dictators he funded and armed in return for US access to natural resources or military bases. Carter threatened the use of force to guarantee access to Middle Eastern oil, and he supported combat operations to support a tyrant in Zaire and unseat one in Afghanistan. Millions of people died in the wars spurred by Ford and Carter and millions more continued to live under dictators they armed. Vietnam looked more and more like no mistake.

Newly-energized citizens' groups with expertise in various regions of the world emerged from the anti-war movement and pushed for a moral foreign policy to match Carter's rhetoric on human rights. However, the public's exhaustion with Vietnam cut both ways. Citizens may not have been ready to send troops to back repressive friends, a phenomenon that became known as the Vietnam Syndrome, but they were also not interested in asking why these regimes deserved any form of US support. Much of the citizen activism generated by the anti-war movement was diverted into new causes, like environmentalism and campaign finance, that looked inward at the quality of life for Americans rather than outward at the impact of US policy on the world.

VIETNAM COMES TO ANGOLA

From its revolution until the end of the Cold War and Soviet subsidies, tiny Marxist Cuba, an impoverished Caribbean island of less than 10 million people, played an improbably outsized role in Africa. From Algeria's independence struggle in 1961 and its border conflict with Morocco in 1963 through the Congo's trials in the 1960s and wars in Angola and Ethiopia in the 1970s to Angola's defeat of South Africa's invasion in 1988, Cuba was the only outside power willing to support its African allies not just with cash, weapons, and military advisers, but with thousands of soldiers in combat units. Fidel Castro's risky policy was driven by an ideological identification with anti-colonial movements and Marxist regimes, and it was often as surprising to the Soviets as it was to US officials.[2] The addition of the insult of Cuban combat operations to the injury of Soviet material support

---

1 John Marcum, "Lessons of Angola," *Foreign Affairs*, April 1976. See also Caleb Rossiter, *The Bureaucratic Struggle for Control of US Foreign Aid: Diplomacy vs. Development in Southern Africa*, Westview Press, Boulder, 1985, p. 53, and Piero Gleijeses, *Conflicting Missions: Havana, Washington, Pretoria*, Galago, South Africa, 2003, pp. 287-291, 353-358.

2 The first 20 years of the Cuban story are covered in admirable detail in Piero Gleijeses, *Conflicting Missions: Havana, Washington, Pretoria*, Galago, South Africa, 2003. Cuba's very first forays into Algeria risked strategic relations with France and economic relations with Morocco, but Castro seems to have never wavered. See pp 32, 42. US officials were well aware that Cuba was not a simple Soviet proxy, even as they called it one in public. See p. 392.

for governments and liberation movements led US policy makers to view Africa as a zero-sum chess board where any enemy of a Soviet or Cuban-backed state or group was a friend, even in the case of the pariah state of South Africa or the Marxist dictator in Somalia. In Angola, the result was a 25-year civil war with a death toll of a million.[1]

Portugal's rightist dictatorship had refused to join the European decolonization of Africa in the 1960s, and was fighting wars with persistent but small-scale liberation movements in its five colonies. As a NATO ally with a key air base in the Azores, Portugal received US weapons and transport aircraft that it used openly in Africa, in violation of a ban contained in the arms agreements.[2] Far from sanctioning Portugal, Kissinger proposed ending the ban as a reward for its help in shipping US arms to Israel during the 1973 "Yom Kippur" war, when other NATO members had refused. Aghast at the impact this would have on US relations with African countries, his assistant secretary for Africa, Donald Easum, fought the proposal. Easum focused on the tactical question of US relations and not on the morality of the goal of helping a colonial power rule Africans. This left Kissinger free to turn Easum's tactical argument against him, saying that the less cooperative NATO members would be impressed by the price he was willing to pay in Africa to back a cooperative ally in Europe. His plan was only thwarted by a military coup in Portugal in April 1974 by a left-leaning junta that announced its intention to leave Africa.[3]

In Angola three separate rebel movements had been fighting Portugal and often each other for a decade. The Soviet Union and Cuba favored the multi-ethnic MPLA that was popular around Luanda, the coastal capital, deciding like most foreign observers that the FNLA in the north was a tool of Zaire's dictator Mobutu, who coveted Angola's oil-rich Cabinda enclave, and that UNITA in the inland south was tainted by collaboration with Portugal. The Soviet Union had been providing small amounts of training and weaponry to the MPLA; the CIA had been keeping the FNLA's leader, who was linked to Mobutu by tribe and family, on its payroll for two decades; and China had backed UNITA.[4] As the factions fought for control of the capital in 1975, Kissinger decided that an uncontested MPLA victory would be seen internationally as a sign of weakness on the part of the United States, particularly because Vietnam had just been unified under communist rule. He proposed arming and backing the FNLA and UNITA through a covert CIA program.

Kissinger was not dissuaded by the nearly universal opposition of the foreign policy bureaucracy. Nathaniel Davis, the new assistant secretary of state for Africa he had moved in to replace the suspect Easum, informed him that these factions were unlikely to win and that an MPLA victory would pose no particular threat to US interests in Angola, or indeed in the region. Davis took the position that George Ball did when trying to talk Johnson out of escalation in Vietnam in 1965. He accepted the goal of emplacing friendly

---

1   20th Century Atlas, Death Tolls and Casualty Statistics, at http://users.erols.com/mwhite28/warstat3.htm.

2   Caleb Rossiter, *The Bureaucratic Struggle for Control of US Foreign Aid: Diplomacy vs. Development in Southern Africa*, Westview Press, Boulder, 1985, p. 52.

3   Piero Gleijeses, *Conflicting Missions: Havana, Washington, Pretoria*, Galago, South Africa, 2003, pp. 230-232.

4   Piero Gleijeses, *Conflicting Missions: Havana, Washington, Pretoria*, Galago, South Africa, 2003, pp. 235-245, 281.

governments, but called Angola a poor place to pursue it and warned that a loss would damage US credibility: "If we are to have a test of strength with the Soviets, we should find a more advantageous place."[1] Davis proposed encouraging the Angolan factions to settle their differences. He was missing Kissinger's point, which was not to win but to show governments around the world that the United States would make the Soviets pay for any advances. As in Vietnam, US officials actively discouraged their allies from pursuing a negotiated solution that would include Soviet-backed forces in the government.

Kissinger argued that with the fall of South Vietnam, the Soviet Union would see "the US as weak and unwilling to stand up for its commitments anywhere in the world," even though he could not identify for President Ford any particular place where this was true.[2] Publicly he told a congressional hearing: "The Soviet Union must not be given any opportunity to use military forces for aggressive purposes without running the risk of conflict with us."[3] Privately, he told Ford that resisting the MPLA would maintain US influence with Zaire's Mobutu, a long-time CIA ally who made strategic minerals available to the West.[4] Strategic credibility, as always, was tied up in domestic politics. A White House aide had remarked in 1964 that permitting a victory by Congolese rebels whom Secretary of State Rusk had judged to be communists would be "hard to explain politically" for Johnson, who already faced charges from Goldwater that he was "soft on communism."[5] The same concern that a lack of resolve in a little-known African country might come back to haunt him appears to have influenced Ford's decision on Angola. The "Watergate" election of 1974 had devastated the Republican Party, giving the Democrats two-thirds of the House and 60 votes in the Senate. The moderate wing of the party was facing a revolt from the Goldwater wing against the policy of "détente" and compromise with the Soviet Union, and neo-conservative activists who were gaining traction in the American media were pushing President Ford to conduct a "Team B" evaluation of the CIA's assessments of Soviet power and intentions.

Although Ford had escaped identification with détente, Kissinger, who was both his secretary of state and his national security advisor, was its architect. Former California Governor Ronald Reagan was reprising his strong run for the presidential nomination in 1968, and indeed almost won the 1976 nomination. Ford feared, accurately, that opposition to détente and to any hint of weakness toward the Soviet Union would feature heavily in Reagan's primary challenge, and Reagan did include Angola in his 1976 speeches attacking Ford.[6] Kissinger's plan, though, undercut Reagan, who could complain that Ford had

1 Piero Gleijeses, *Conflicting Missions: Havana, Washington, Pretoria*, Galago, South Africa, 2003, pp. 266, 291.
2 Piero Gleijeses, *Conflicting Missions: Havana, Washington, Pretoria*, Galago, South Africa, 2003, p. 389.
3 John A. Marcum, "Lessons of Angola," *Foreign Affairs*, April 1976.
4 Piero Gleijeses, *Conflicting Missions: Havana, Washington, Pretoria*, Galago, South Africa, 2003, pp. 287-289.
5 Piero Gleijeses, *Conflicting Missions: Havana, Washington, Pretoria*, Galago, South Africa, 2003, p. 385.
6 Melvin Small, *Democracy and Diplomacy: The Impact of Domestic Politics on Foreign Policy, 1789-1994*, Johns Hopkins University Press, Baltimore, MD, 1996, p. 131.

not won, but had to acknowledge that he had at least tried: "We gave just enough support to one side to encourage it to fight and die, but too little to give them a chance of winning."[1]

When deciding what to do in Angola in 1975, Ford also had to worry about the possibility of being attacked on détente in the 1976 race by a Democrat. Strident anti-Soviet Senator "Scoop" Jackson had run well in some 1972 primaries and had announced his very credible candidacy in February 1975. Known as the senator from Boeing, and staffed at times by neo-conservatives Richard Perle and Paul Wolfowitz, Jackson had attacked Eisenhower in the 1950s for not building more nuclear missiles, lobbied for the anti-ballistic missile system to be put in his state and opposed Nixon's ABM treaty, backed the war in Vietnam, and most recently enacted, over Kissinger's vehement objections, a law blocking tariff preferences for the Soviet Union until it permitted an increase in Jewish emigration. If Jackson were the Democratic nominee and Ford had simply watched the MPLA take power in Angola, he would find himself in the uncomfortable position of being portrayed as soft on communism in the general election, as Nixon had been in 1960 by Kennedy on both the "missile gap" and Cuba.

Despite substantial CIA military aid, Zaire's logistical help, and the invasion of a South African armored column, the MPLA and a first small contingent of Cuban troops quickly won the civil war in November 1975. The CIA and Zaire ferried FNLA troops in to try to take the capital from the north, and South Africa bombed the MPLA's defense lines for them, but 120 Cuban special forces with truck-carried multiple rocket launchers caused a rout, and the FNLA fled back to Zaire. South Africa's 1,000 troops were advancing with UNITA from the south, so the Cubans wheeled toward them next, burned bridges to force them into an ambush, and again used the rocket launchers to send the column reeling.[2] The introduction of 4,000 Cuban troops before the end of 1975 convinced Zaire to leave Cabinda alone and South Africa to retreat with its by-then 3,000 troops back into Namibia, bitterly blaming the United States for betraying an alleged promise to support its invasion.[3]

As the dissident US officials had predicted, the formal collaboration with Zaire and particularly the informal collaboration with South Africa damaged America's standing in Africa. South African liberation had become a public goal throughout the continent, so much so that 24 countries, joined by Saddam Hussein's Iraq, boycotted the highly-anticipated 1976 Olympics over the participation of New Zealand, whose rugby team had played in South Africa. Kissinger had already displayed a tin ear on apartheid, approving a security strategy in 1970 that accepted the white regimes of Rhodesia and South Africa as anti-communist allies who could eventually be guided to political settlements with their black majorities. This decision was made against the wishes of the State Department's

---

1 See Reagan's March 31, 1976, radio speech in *The Cold War*, a collection of documents edited by Jussi Hanhimaki and Odd Arne Westad, Oxford University Press, 2004, p. 533.
2 Piero Gleijeses, *Conflicting Missions: Havana, Washington, Pretoria*, Galago, South Africa, 2003, pp. 310-317.
3 Piero Gleijeses, *Conflicting Missions: Havana, Washington, Pretoria*, Galago, South Africa, 2003, pp. 299, 320, 327.

regional experts, who leaked the strategy and called it a "Tar Baby" option that would attach the United States to the white regimes.[1]

The collaboration with South Africa spurred into action both Democratic Senator Dick Clark of Iowa, who chaired a subcommittee on Africa, and the small but vocal left-leaning advocacy groups who focused on US policy in Africa, such as the American Committee on Africa (ACOA) and its new Washington Office on Africa.[2] ACOA prodded and supported Clark in holding hearings and offering an amendment to block a replenishment of the CIA's military aid in the fall of 1975. Known today as Africa Action, ACOA was founded in 1953 in New York City by a small group of social activists who saw their work on African liberation as complementing their work on black civil rights in America.[3] Whether having baseball legend Jackie Robinson lead its fight against South Africa's readmission to the Olympics in 1968, or asking municipal workers to push cities to remove pension funds from banks who were lending to South Africa, ACOA could count on the outrage that black Americans felt about white rule in southern Africa to give its campaigns a special resonance in American politics and with the media that no other foreign policy lobby enjoyed. Kissinger was oblivious to this resonance until it blindsided him in Angola.

Arguing that military aid could lead to "another Vietnam" and calling for an "ethical" foreign policy in contrast to the secrecy of CIA funding and Kissinger's anti-Soviet focus, Clark and his ally John Tunney of California refused to back down in the face of pressure from not just Kissinger and Senate conservatives, but liberal anti-communists like Hubert Humphrey and the *Washington Post*.[4] They easily won passage of amendments that barred further funding for the CIA's program in Angola.[5] Fearing that both Congress and Cuba would turn their attention to other countries in the region, Kissinger reversed course on Rhodesia in early 1976. He traveled to Lusaka, Zambia, to announce an offer of a billion dollars of aid to compensate white farmers for their land if a transitional government emerged. The shift in policy was for tactical, not moral, reasons. Kissinger argued to conservative members of Congress that putting the United States on the side of managed transition would "limit Soviet influence."[6] These members, with the lobbying help of Christian evangelical groups, had kept in place since 1971 an amendment by Senator Harry

---

1 Excellent sources on the policy include Mohamed El-Khawas and Barry Cohen, *The Kissinger Study of Southern Africa: National Security Study Memorandum 39 (Secret)*, Lawrence Hill, Westport, CT, 1976, and Anthony Lake, *The 'Tar Baby' Option: American Policy Toward Southern Rhodesia*, Columbia University Press, New York, 1976.

2 For a history of the American Committee on Africa, see the memoir of its founder, George M. Houser, *No One Can Stop the Rain*, Pilgrim Press, New York, 1989.

3 George M. Houser, *No One Can Stop the Rain*, Pilgrim Press, New York, 1989, p. 63.

4 Robert David Johnson, "The Unexpected Consequences of Congressional Reform: The Clark and Tunney Amendments and US Policy toward Angola," *Diplomatic History* 27 (2003): 215-243, available on the web at *http://academic.brooklyn.cuny.edu/history/johnson/clark. htm*

5 George M. Houser, *No One Can Stop the Rain*, Pilgrim Press, New York, 1989, pp. 290-291; Caleb Rossiter, *The Bureaucratic Struggle for Control of US Foreign Aid: Diplomacy vs. Development in Southern Africa*, Westview Press, Boulder, 1985, p. 54.

6 Caleb Rossiter, *The Bureaucratic Struggle for Control of US Foreign Aid: Diplomacy vs. Development in Southern Africa*, Westview Press, Boulder, 1985, p. 55-57. See also Kissinger's speeches at the time, which show his desire to achieve a workable settlement in Rhodesia before Cuban troops can get involved, in Hanes Walton Jr., Robert Louis Stevenson, James Bernard

Byrd of Virginia permitting the importation of Rhodesian chrome for industrial and military purposes, in violation of the United Nations economic embargo on Rhodesia.

The Clark amendment came at the tail end of a brief period of assertion of congressional power over foreign policy that was driven by congressional revulsion over the human cost of aggressive anti-communism in Indochina, and over revelations of CIA covert operations. This period lasted roughly from the enactment of the War Powers Resolution in 1973 to the creation of the Church committee that revealed covert operations and the enactment of the Harkin amendment barring aid to human rights violators in 1975. Politically chilling proof that the period was ending came quickly. Although the MPLA had won the war well before the Clark amendment barred a renewal of funding for the US-backed forces, the Ford administration and neo-conservative commentators hammered at the Democrats for "losing" Angola to the Soviet Union. United Nations Ambassador Patrick Moynihan predicted that due to this "Soviet neo-colonialism...Europe's oil routes will be under Soviet control, as will the strategic South Atlantic," with Brazil as the next target.[1] Tunney was able to use his Angolan effort to defuse a challenge from the left by former SDS leader Tom Hayden in his 1976 primary, but he lost in the general election to San Francisco State University President S.I. Hayakawa, who made the Soviet "victory" in Angola a prominent part of his campaign. Under pressure from Hayakawa, who had made his reputation by taking tough stands against student protestors, Tunney shied away from "the awakening" he had proposed, a new policy in Africa that was not founded on great power politics. He chose instead to muddy the waters, bizarrely attacking Kissinger's vision of détente for allowing a Soviet advance in Angola, and supporting military aid to Zaire's Mobutu to contain it.

After the MPLA solidified its victory and became an open ally of the Soviet Union, Clark too chose not defend his "ethical" foreign policy in Angola and Africa. He recognized that by 1977 "the mood of America has changed" after a brief period of exhaustion and perhaps embarrassment over the defeat in Vietnam during which charges of being soft on Soviet advances, in Africa or elsewhere, had little traction. In almost identical language to assistant secretary Davis's internal dissent in 1975, he praised Kissinger's efforts to counter Soviet influence, and said that he had opposed the covert program for practical reasons. His said his goal had been simply "keeping Americans out of war," and he promised to back "an action that we can succeed with." In his 1980 re-election bid he was defeated by conservative Republican Roger Jepsen, who accused him of promoting "the exact thoughts of Russia" in Angola. The electoral fates of Tunney and Clark provided liberal members of Congress with two more good reasons not to get in the path of foreign policies that could be portrayed as strong and anti-Soviet.[2]

Rosser Sr., eds., *The African Foreign Policy of Secretary of State Henry Kissinger*, Lexington Books, Lanham, MD, 2007.

1 Piero Gleijeses, *Conflicting Missions: Havana, Washington, Pretoria*, Galago, South Africa, 2003, p. 332.

2 Robert David Johnson, "The Unexpected Consequences of Congressional Reform: The Clark and Tunney Amendments and US Policy toward Angola," *Diplomatic History* 27 (2003): 215-243, available on the web at *http://academic.brooklyn.cuny.edu/history/johnson/clark.htm*

CARTER'S CONFUSION: THE PRICE FOR THE HORN OF AFRICA

The presidency of Jimmy Carter was a maddening period for hawks, doves, turkeys, eagles, and any other breed of foreign policy bird. Carter's fundamental approach to both the purpose and the domestic politics of international relations and military spending vacillated, not day to day or issue to issue or between speeches and actions but within a single day on a single issue, within a single speech or act. He appointed the softest and hardest of eagles not just at the top of his foreign policy team but throughout it. The high-profile combination of cautious détentist Cyrus Vance as secretary of state and aggressive anti-Soviet Zbigniew Brzezinski as national security adviser was no less explosive than the lower-level pairings of Assistant Secretary of State for Human Rights Patt Derian, a civil rights activist, and Assistant Secretary for Asia Richard Holbrooke, a noted Cold Warrior, or of Derian's deputy Mark Schneider, a fierce critic of Chile's junta in the office of Senator Ted Kennedy, and Assistant Secretary for Latin America Terry Todman, a career foreign service officer.[1]

Some speculated that Carter simply wanted to make sure he received sound arguments on both sides before making decisions, but in practice his decisions often included both sides' proposals. In 2008, a bemused scholar with excellent access to Carter's papers called this practice of including contradictory approaches in a single policy decision "paper clipping," and found that it was a defining characteristic of Carter's administration.[2] Like a Turkey, Carter wanted a moral foreign policy that supported human rights and democracy, but like a Soft Eagle he wanted it in order to weaken the Soviet Union at home and discredit it internationally. Like a Soft Eagle, he wanted to reduce arms transfers and military training to repressive regimes that might implode and leave radicals in charge, but like a Hard Eagle he wanted the cooperation of those same regimes on military bases, covert operations, and access to oil and other strategic minerals.

The result was an administration that started the Conventional Arms Transfer talks and ended up with record arms sales; created a human rights bureaucracy that approved "human rights" abstentions on World Bank loans for power projects yet ignored the protests of that bureaucracy and provided the sanctioned governments with weapons; castigated dictatorship yet armed dictators from Morocco to Egypt, the long way around the world, through Sudan, Zaire, Pakistan, the Philippines, Nicaragua and El Salvador; and hoped to cut Cold War tensions and nuclear arsenals through the Strategic Arms Limitation Talks (SALT II), yet ended up starting a rapid military buildup that included the multi-warhead MX missile. All of Carter's contradictory impulses collided in the Horn of Africa, a region of dictatorship, tenuous agriculture, poverty, civil conflict, and Cold War

---

1 Some of the explosions are detailed in Caleb Rossiter, with Anne-Marie Smith, *Human Rights: The Carter Record, the Reagan Reaction*, International Policy Report, Center for International Policy, Washington, DC, September 1984, and in Scott Kaufman, *Plans Unraveled: The Foreign Policy of the Carter Administration*, Northern Illinois University Press, DeKalb, 2008, pp. 32-36, 212.

2 Scott Kaufman, *Plans Unraveled: The Foreign Policy of the Carter Administration*, Northern Illinois University Press, DeKalb, 2008. A summary of a number of important analyses of Carter's foreign policy can be found in the introduction to Donna R. Jackson, *Jimmy Carter and the Horn of Africa: Cold War Policy in Ethiopia and Somalia*, McFarland, London, 2007.

rivalry. His record there shows clearly that, far from making human rights "the soul of our foreign policy," he continued the Vietnam foreign policy of supporting repressive governments in return for military access and other forms of cooperation.[1]

Orthodox Christian Ethiopia, with a population of 30 million in 1977, had a history of 2,500 years of organized feudal government. Until the five-year Italian occupation after Mussolini's invasion of 1935, which can well be considered the beginning of World War II, it was the only polity in Africa that had never been colonized. The Amhara, a complex ethnic entity accounting for roughly a third of the population, dominated the other main ethnic groups. Under Emperor Haile Selassie (who, as Ras ["prince"] Tafari, had unwittingly given his name to the Jamaican cult of Rastafarians), Ethiopia was a reliable US ally, providing military bases and covert communications facilities. A military coup in 1974 by a "Derg," or council, of Marxist officers led by Haile Mengistu resulted in a change in foreign orientation, with the Soviet Union taking over the US role as both arms supplier and occupant of the bases, but the domestic domination by the Amhara continued. The Derg immediately faced four ethnic rebellions among the Tigray, Eritreans, Oromo, and, in the southern desert region of Ogaden, the Somalis.

In contrast to Ethiopia, with its large population and feudal stability, Muslim Somalia was a shifting confederation of nomadic clans totaling no more than three million people. The clans' territories had been divided after the Berlin Conference of 1885 between Britain, France, and Italy. When Somalia was recreated as a state in 1960, the government chose a five-pointed star for its flag, signifying its claims not just to the former British and Italian Somalilands that constituted its legal territory but to three other places where ethnic Somalis lived: the French colony of Afars and Issas (now Djibouti), the Ogaden, and northeastern Kenya. A military coup in 1969 brought to power Marxist officers led by Siad Barré. Somalia became an ally of the Soviet Union and allowed it to build air and naval bases in Berbera in return for a massive aid program that created a large and mobile army, which Barré hoped to use to regain some of the points on the Somali flag.

When Somalia invaded the Ogaden in July 1977, the Soviet Union had to choose between its two clients, and it chose Ethiopia. Somalia quickly seized most of the region, but in November the Soviets flew in 12,000 Cuban troops who led a counter-offensive that drove the Somali army out by March 1978 before pointedly stopping at the border.[2] Like Ford in Angola, Carter had to decide how to respond to a Soviet and Cuban policy of using military force to settle an African dispute. In Angola, that intervention had come on behalf of a movement, but in Ethiopia it came at the request of a recognized government and in defense of its borders. The world feared the chaos that would emerge if it became acceptable to redraw Africa's crazy quilt of illogical colonial lines by force. The United Nations had established the principle in 1960 that decolonization was not to change existing lines,

---

1   Aryeh Neier, *Taking Liberties*, Public Affairs, New York, 2003, p. 152.
2   Donna R. Jackson, *Jimmy Carter and the Horn of Africa: Cold War Policy in Ethiopia and Somalia*, McFarland, London, 2007, pp. 68, 100.

and all African states except Morocco and Somalia had signed a 1964 declaration on the integrity of African borders.[1]

Brzezinski later argued that détente in general and the SALT II talks in particular were "buried in the sands of the Ogaden" when the Soviets ferried in the Cuban troops.[2] He certainly did his best to make this argument true, although the Soviet invasion of Afghanistan to support a Marxist government against militant Islamists was far more lethal to SALT II than the Cuban airlift to support one in Ethiopia. The SALT negotiations were indeed slowed by the Ogaden crisis and became less ambitious, but they were completed in 1979.[3] The agreement was opposed by Democratic Senator Jackson and the Senate Armed Services Committee, who believed that it gave too much to the Soviets, and when the Soviet Union invaded Afghanistan in December, efforts to ratify it were shelved.

Brzezinski told Carter that continuing business as usual in the SALT talks was unwise, not to mention politically risky, because it would appear to the Soviets, other nations, hawkish senators, and swing voters that there was no price to pay for Soviet "adventurism" in Africa.[4] He cited a "growing domestic problem involving [the] public perception of the general character of [our] policy, [which is] seen as 'soft'," and he warned that "our critics...will ask for examples of 'toughness,' and exploit against us such things as...the current Cuban activity in Africa."[5] Vance disagreed with highlighting the Cuban effort and linking it to SALT, and deflected Brzezinski's proposal to send a carrier battle group to the area as a show of force.[6] However, pressure began to build as conservative Republicans, looking to gain seats in the mid-term elections, hammered on Carter, claiming that he was allowing the Soviets to turn Africa into "a communist enclave," and a solid majority of Americans agreed.[7]

Spurning the advice of his special emissary on Soviet affairs, the legendary diplomat Averell Harriman, in March 1978 Carter gave a speech in which he called the "projection of Soviet proxy forces" in Africa an "ominous" development that could block cooperation on other matters.[8] By defining a Soviet-bloc intervention in Africa as a threat to US security, Carter, like Ford in Angola in 1975, set himself up for failure and a perception of weakness. There was nothing he could do about Cuban help to Ethiopia, help which actually did

1 Mark W. Zacher, "The Territorial Integrity Norm: International Boundaries and the Use of Force," *International Organization*, March 2001.

2 Donna R. Jackson, *Jimmy Carter and the Horn of Africa: Cold War Policy in Ethiopia and Somalia*, McFarland, London, 2007, p. 2.

3 Scott Kaufman, *Plans Unraveled: The Foreign Policy of the Carter Administration*, Northern Illinois University Press, DeKalb, 2008, pp. 138, 180.

4 Samuel M. Makinda, *Superpower Diplomacy in the Horn of Africa*, Routledge, New York, 1987, p. 127.

5 Scott Kaufman, *Plans Unraveled: The Foreign Policy of the Carter Administration*, Northern Illinois University Press, DeKalb, 2008, p. 123; Donna R. Jackson, *Jimmy Carter and the Horn of Africa: Cold War Policy in Ethiopia and Somalia*, McFarland, London, 2007, p. 82.

6 Scott Kaufman, *Plans Unraveled: The Foreign Policy of the Carter Administration*, Northern Illinois University Press, DeKalb, 2008, pp. 122-124.

7 Donna R. Jackson, *Jimmy Carter and the Horn of Africa: Cold War Policy in Ethiopia and Somalia*, McFarland, London, 2007, pp. 65-67, 115-117.

8 Scott Kaufman, *Plans Unraveled: The Foreign Policy of the Carter Administration*, Northern Illinois University Press, DeKalb, 2008, pp. 117, 125.

more for African stability than the Cuban presence in Angola that Carter's UN Ambassador Andrew Young had famously, and largely accurately, called a stabilizing factor.[1] Ford, of course, could and did blame the Democrats for letting the Soviet Union "win" in Angola. Carter had only himself to absorb the defeat he defined.

While détente was only temporarily sidelined by the Cuban troops in Ethiopia, another of Carter's signature policies — human rights — did indeed die in the sands of the Ogaden, or more accurately on the runway and in the port that the Soviets had built in Berbera, Somalia. To gain access to those facilities for the US Rapid Deployment Force after the Soviet invasion of Afghanistan, in 1980 Carter provided $40 million in weapons and training to the Marxist government in Somalia, fueling a ten-year civil war that has been followed by 20 years of chaos. This decision was part of the Carter Doctrine: "An attempt by any outside force to gain control of the Persian Gulf region will be regarded as an assault on the vital interests of the United States of America, and such an assault will be repelled by any means necessary, including military force." Repressive governments in Kenya, Oman, and Morocco also saw their military aid increased in return for bases for or cooperation with the Rapid Deployment Force, which later became the US Central Command.[2] In addition, the Pakistani dictatorship, which had been barred from military aid because of its pursuit of nuclear weapons, was provided with weapons and cash in return for being the conduit of US and Saudi aid to the anti-Soviet rebels in Afghanistan.

Carter had certainly armed dictators before. From the very start of his administration he had accepted the argument of his regional and military specialists that concerns about democracy were trumped in Marcos's Philippines, the Shah's Iran, Tolbert's Liberia, and Mobutu's Zaire by the need to continue arms transfers in return for cooperation with military and covert operations and access to strategic minerals. Indeed, just before the Somali invasion of the Ogaden in 1977, Carter had informed Barré that the United States would counter Soviet support for Ethiopia by asking other countries to give him arms, and perhaps by providing him with "defensive" weapons.[3] After the introduction of the Cuban troops, Carter again used arms transfers as the currency of international relations, demonstrating US resolve by approving substantial sales of military aircraft to the dictatorship of Gaafar Nimeiry in neighboring Sudan.[4]

Similarly, Carter had started a two billion dollar annual security aid program for Egyptian strongman Anwar Sadat in return for his recognition of Israel in the Camp David agreement, helped China arm the Khmer Rouge against Soviet-backed Vietnam, gave

---

1 "A Muzzle for 'Motor Mouth'?", *Time*, April 25, 1977.

2 David Isenberg, "The Rapid Deployment Force: The Few, the Futile, the Expendable," Cato Policy Analysis No. 44, Cato Institute, Washington, DC, November 8, 1984. Available on the web at http://www.cato.org/pubs/pas/pa044.html

3 Some have argued that this decision gave a "green light" to the invasion by convincing Barré that the United States would back, or at least not oppose, it. However, the planning for the invasion preceded Carter's decision. Donna R. Jackson, *Jimmy Carter and the Horn of Africa: Cold War Policy in Ethiopia and Somalia*, McFarland, London, 2007, pp. 70-71; Scott Kaufman, *Plans Unraveled: The Foreign Policy of the Carter Administration*, Northern Illinois University Press, DeKalb, 2008, p. 122.

4 Scott Kaufman, *Plans Unraveled: The Foreign Policy of the Carter Administration*, Northern Illinois University Press, DeKalb, 2008, p. 122.

North Yemen $400 million in arms because of a dubious report of Soviet pressure, and supported the Nicaragua and Salvadoran military dictators because of the alleged communist leanings of their opponents.[1] Throughout Carter's presidency Brzezinski, with the support of the Defense Department, much of Congress, and a surprising share of Vance's own State Department, had been pushing him into alliances with anti-Soviet dictators despite the obvious human cost to their people.

Carter provided CIA aid to the Afghan rebels against their pro-Soviet government six months before the Soviet invasion, and then failed to tell the American people of the US role when he denounced the invasion.[2] He provided logistical support to the dictator Mobutu in Zaire to defeat incursions into resource-rich Shaba province by Lunda rebels in 1977 and 1978. When Brzezinski advised him in 1979 that "the country craves, and our national security needs, both a more assertive tone and a more assertive substance to our foreign policy...for international as well as domestic political reasons," Carter must have wondered what more he needed to do to shake the "soft on communism" label. Historians agree that well before 1980 Carter knew he had failed to "sell" the country on his original vision of "soft power" or provide an "overarching vision that would give his foreign policy meaning," and in response to low approval ratings had become almost as instinctive a Cold Warrior as any president before him.[3] Still, beginning a new relationship with the brutal Somali dictator in an explicit trade of arms for bases and arming nuclear pariah Pakistan to aid rebellion in Afghanistan signaled that whatever struggle had taken place in Carter's soul between the Turkey and the Eagle was over. For Democrats in general the combination of strategic and domestic political fears about the Soviet invasion of Afghanistan and the continuation of the Iranian hostage crisis pushed human rights and democracy to the side. It was telling that the only objection Soft Eagles in Congress raised to Carter's aid-for-bases plan was that Somalia might use the weapons in its continued destabilization of the Ogaden.[4]

Carter's decision, when the chips were down, to favor military collaboration over human rights in his policies and within his bureaucracy, was mirrored by his propensity to favor diplomatic over development concerns in the allocation of foreign aid. The State Department had overseen the Agency for International Development (AID) when its programming was dominated by counter-insurgency efforts in Vietnam and by infrastructure projects requested by cooperative heads of state. In the post-Vietnam era pressure was building, ironically with the help of former Defense Secretary McNamara at the World Bank, to focus foreign economic aid on the "basic human needs" of the poor.

---

1 Scott Kaufman, *Plans Unraveled: The Foreign Policy of the Carter Administration*, Northern Illinois University Press, DeKalb, 2008, pp. 85, 164-165, 163-164, 168-170, 230.

2 Scott Kaufman, *Plans Unraveled: The Foreign Policy of the Carter Administration*, Northern Illinois University Press, DeKalb, 2008, p. 163.

3 Donna R. Jackson, *Jimmy Carter and the Horn of Africa: Cold War Policy in Ethiopia and Somalia*, McFarland, London, 2007, pp. 136, 180-181; Scott Kaufman, *Plans Unraveled: The Foreign Policy of the Carter Administration*, Northern Illinois University Press, DeKalb, 2008, p. 55.

4 Donna R. Jackson, *Jimmy Carter and the Horn of Africa: Cold War Policy in Ethiopia and Somalia*, McFarland, London, 2007, pp. 156, 160-164.

Carter pledged his support for this morally-based effort and established a cabinet-rank International Development Cooperation Agency (IDCA) whose director was also the head of AID. Under this arrangement, which Britain and Canada also use, foreign economic aid would be distributed based on the judgment of development experts and not on the strategic and diplomatic demands of the State Department. The reform existed only on paper, though, and the allocation of both "security supporting assistance" for cooperative governments and development aid to combat poverty remained under the effective control of the State Department's regional bureaus. When IDCA director Thomas Ehrlich forced the issue by proposing to end programming in a few countries where dictatorship and corruption made development aid unlikely to succeed, Deputy Secretary of State Christopher firmly rejected the proposal — masterfully citing development goals and principles to mask his successful power play.[1]

The transition to democracy in Zimbabwe provided an example of the struggle over using foreign aid for development or diplomacy. Carter won a repeal of the Byrd amendment in 1977, but there was pressure for its renewal in 1979 when Rhodesia announced an "internal settlement" that placed a black minister at the head of government but excluded the rebel groups, such as Robert Mugabe's ZANU, and left whites in charge of military forces and the economy.[2] Carter and the "front-line" African leaders rejected this neo-colonial arrangement, and helped the combatants hammer out the democratic Lancaster House agreement that ended the war and white rule.[3] Acting through front-line leaders he had provided with substantial aid, Carter was able to pressure Mugabe into accepting the agreement. Having seen the utility of foreign aid as a diplomatic tool in the settlement, Carter hoped to use it to establish a strong rapport with Mugabe, who became president of the new country. AID proposed that its aid start with long-term developmental programming to support the health system in Zimbabwe, but the State Department insisted instead on the cash assistance requested by Mugabe.[4] Unfortunately, the amount of money Carter provided in 1980 and Reagan provided in 1981 in another cash-like import program totaled only a tenth of the "Kissinger billion," which could have eased Zimbabwe's future decades of conflict over land reform.

Non-governmental advocacy groups with roots in the anti-war movement tried to stop Carter's slide from Soft to Hard Eagle. On balance they had little impact, because Carter's slide was the result of a far more powerful shift of public opinion back to a Cold War mindset after the brief aberration of opposition to the high social costs of the war in Vietnam. In addition, as is often the case during Democratic administrations, the advocacy groups were relieved to have a vague ally in the White House and some access to policy-makers at the State and Defense Departments. As the conservative assault on Carter be-

1 Caleb Rossiter, *The Bureaucratic Struggle for Control of US Foreign Aid: Diplomacy vs. Development in Southern Africa*, Westview Press, Boulder, 1985, pp. 223-225.

2 George M. Houser, *No One Can Stop the Rain*, Pilgrim Press, New York, 1989, pp. 335-336.

3 Aleyiwola Abegunrin, *Nigerian Foreign Policy under Military Rule, 1966-1999*, Praeger, New York, 2003, p. 86; Caleb Rossiter, *The Bureaucratic Struggle for Control of US Foreign Aid: Diplomacy vs. Development in Southern Africa*, Westview Press, Boulder, 1985, p. 63.

4 Caleb Rossiter, *The Bureaucratic Struggle for Control of US Foreign Aid: Diplomacy vs. Development in Southern Africa*, Westview Press, Boulder, 1985, pp. 153-156.

came louder and more vicious, they were careful not to be seen as piling on, and in fact had to take on the role of Carter's defender. Finally, new movements for environmental protection and campaign finance reform absorbed a great deal of progressive energy and legislative effort that had previously been expended on foreign policy. The Environmental Defense Fund (founded in 1967) and Greenpeace (1971) stimulated millions of Americans to demand respect for public health and natural "ecology," and Common Cause (1970) spurred both transparency in government and complex legal challenges to campaign spending.

The advocacy groups were probably least successful in the area of military spending and arms control, where they were overwhelmed by well-funded and well-reported portrayals of Soviet power and intentions by the Coalition for a Democratic Majority, the Committee on the Present Danger, and the Coalition for Peace through Strength, which had been endorsed by over 200 members of Congress.[1] Carter began to increase the military budget in 1978 and pressured allies to increase theirs. In July 1980 he announced a presidential directive on nuclear targeting that implied the major buildup of both nuclear and conventional forces that was soon implemented by President Reagan.

The advocacy groups had a mixed record in southern Africa, helping Carter repeal the Byrd amendment and pushing him to reject a settlement in Rhodesia that excluded the main rebel groups, but failing to overcome his opposition to sanctions on South Africa to promote an end to apartheid — in part because Carter thought of South Africa as an ally in convincing Rhodesia to accept majority rule.[2] They were most successful in South America, where the human rights abuses of dictators in Chile, Argentina, Paraguay, and Uruguay were both spectacular and well reported, and there was little danger of nations being taken over by arguably pro-communist or at least anti-American rebel movements, as was the case in Central America. Left-leaning think-tanks like the Institute for Policy Studies and the Washington Office on Latin America called for foreign aid sanctions on South American dictators while working in virtual partnership with the State Department's Human Rights bureau. When Deputy Secretary Christopher proposed that Carter demonstrate a stronger anti-communist profile by providing military aid to Argentina, Assistant Secretary Derian blocked the move by threatening to resign.[3]

Both the African and Latin American-oriented advocacy groups received an unexpected boost from the 1975 Helsinki Accords, under which the Soviet Union and the other Warsaw Pact members gained recognition of their borders in return for agreeing to guarantee a broad array of human rights for their citizens. Helsinki undercut the prevailing belief that governments had no right to monitor and criticize other governments' internal activities. With the US government and the non-governmental Helsinki Watch cataloguing and complaining about politically-motivated detentions of human rights activists by

---

1   Scott Kaufman, *Plans Unraveled: The Foreign Policy of the Carter Administration*, Northern Illinois University Press, DeKalb, 2008, pp. 182-183.
2   Scott Kaufman, *Plans Unraveled: The Foreign Policy of the Carter Administration*, Northern Illinois University Press, DeKalb, 2008, p. 64.
3   Scott Kaufman, *Plans Unraveled: The Foreign Policy of the Carter Administration*, Northern Illinois University Press, DeKalb, 2008, p. 212.

Warsaw Pact members, other advocacy groups gained legitimacy in the policy debate by adopting the same tactics and language. As noted by Aryeh Neier, a founder of Helsinki Watch who oversaw the expansion of its mission to every region of the world as executive director of Human Rights Watch, the "instrumental" use of human rights by anti-communists legitimized the cause for the entire political spectrum and allowed activists to turn US officials' words in one context against them in another.[1]

Longstanding arms control groups like the Council for a Livable World and the Quakers' Friends Committee on National Legislation received their boost from insurgent offices within the Congress that provided analysis, procedural information, and help with legislation to the groups' congressional allies. The House Democratic Study Group and the bicameral Members of Congress for Peace through Law (later renamed the Arms Control and Foreign Policy Caucus) were funded by dues from the offices of members of Congress. Their staff were inside agitators, loyal to a progressive view of foreign policy rather than to the party leadership. They helped members who had little seniority on the powerful military and foreign policy committees coordinate their opposition to committee initiatives, which were usually quite favorable to the Defense and State departments. During Carter's presidency these legislative organizations spent much of their time supporting Carter's modest arms control agenda against conservative efforts to derail it. During Reagan's presidency they would serve as nerve centers for progressive members of Congress and reinvigorated citizens' groups in their bitter struggles over nuclear weapons and wars in Central America with the conservative "Dixie" Democrats. The Hard Eagles were ascendant by the time Reagan defeated Carter in the 1980 landslide, but the Soft Eagles in Congress and the Turkeys outside would find their wings again, in resistance to the Republican revolution.

---

1 Aryeh Neier, *Taking Liberties*, Public Affairs, New York, 2003, pp. 156, 185-188.

CHAPTER 4. THE SACRIFICE OF CENTRAL AMERICA BY REAGAN, BUSH, AND THE "DIXIES"

Out of the political and physical wreckage of the Vietnam War, Jimmy Carter began the rebuilding of a foreign policy based on the very premises and policies that had led to it. He rehabilitated the idea that the United States had the strategic right, the moral duty, and the electoral necessity to deploy forces and provide funding around the world to sustain repressive governments and movements who were friendly to US interests. Yet Carter's foreign policy is thought of today as having been focused on human rights and peace, because the imperial resurgence he started was so tentative compared with the way it was pursued with a vengeance by Ronald Reagan.

Aid to African dictators in return for strategic minerals, military bases, and collaboration on covert programs? Somalia, Sudan, Liberia, Zaire, and Kenya all started small with Carter and boomed with Reagan, becoming the five largest recipients of US military and economic aid in sub-Saharan Africa in the 1980s. Four of the five were brutal dictatorships that collapsed into civil wars and state chaos, leaving millions dead and their economies ruined.[1]

A rapid buildup of the armed forces and the military budget, and new nuclear weapons and multiple-warhead missiles on land and in submarines? Carter started them, and Reagan boosted them, on the way to a "real," meaning inflation-adjusted, 50 percent increase

---

1 Only Daniel Moi's Kenyan kleptocracy, which was aided in return for the Rapid Deployment Force's naval base at Mombasa, avoided civil war. "Is There a Human Rights Double Standard? US Policy Toward Equatorial Guinea and Ethiopia," Hearing before the Subcommittee on International Organizations, Human Rights, and Oversight, House Committee on Foreign Affairs, US Congress, May 10, 2007, statement of Chairman Bill Delahunt. Available on the web at *http://foreignaffairs.house.gov/110/dela051007.htm*. As the statement acknowledges, this focus of aid on friendly African dictators was noted at the time by Holly Burkhalter, of Human Rights Watch.

in spending.[1] Arms and training for the armed forces of Asian dictators, as in Indonesia, Pakistan, and the Philippines, and aid to the fundamentalist Afghan rebellion? Carter got them going, but Reagan dramatically expanded them.

Nowhere was the turn from Soft to Hard Eagle more pronounced, and more deadly to societies, than in Central America. When Carter left office in 1981, a fractious coalition was muddling by in Nicaragua under the leftist Sandinistas who had just upended the 42-year rule of the US-backed Somoza family, and the Contra ("anti"-Sandinista) rebels consisted of a few hundred of Somoza's former National Guardsmen being trained by the Argentine dictatorship. A rightist junta ruled El Salvador with minimal US assistance, and its armed forces and related death squads had killed a few thousand civilians suspected not so much of collaboration with the FMLN rebels as with opposition to the oligarchic social order. The Guatemalan army's brutality in what was then a low-level campaign of repression against Indian villages that were allegedly sympathetic to leftist rebels had led to a cut-off of US military aid. When Reagan left office eight years later, all three countries were smoldering ruins from drives for military victory fueled by massive infusions of congressionally-approved aid (El Salvador and Nicaragua) or encouraged by US policy and covert operations and aided by US allies (Guatemala).[2]

The first President Bush accepted a negotiated solution rather than military victory for the Contras in Nicaragua in 1989 because Congress had cut aid in reaction to the 1986 "Iran-Contra" scandal and its revelations of illegal aid and lying to Congress by administration officials. In response the Nicaraguan government held the fair election that Reagan had claimed could never occur, which was won by the US-backed civic opposition. However, Bush fought on in El Salvador, only to see Congress shocked into cutting aid when the premier US-trained brigade murdered the rector of the University of Central America, five of his fellow Jesuit professors, and two witnesses. The operation had been ordered by a panicked Salvadoran High Command during a rebel offensive that, like Tet in Vietnam, had discredited US claims of victory in the ten-year war. The aid cut triggered a negotiated settlement based on a purge of the army and the integration of the rebels into the police force, the very deal that the rector, Father Ignacio Ellacuría, the Soft Eagles in Congress, and the Turkeys in the advocacy groups that backed them had said was possible before Congress voted full funding for a military victory in 1984.

In Guatemala the army's campaign against Indian villages escalated into such a slaughter that there was little left to fight over, and a peace settlement soon followed those in Nicaragua and El Salvador. President Bill Clinton felt constrained in 1999 to apologize for the US role there after the Guatemalan Truth Commission issued its report, which found that the campaign had verged on "genocide." He offered a carefully-worded statement in Guatemala City that could have applied to any of the three conflicts in Central America:

---

1 Jeffrey Record, "Reagan's Strategy Gap," The New Republic, October 29, 1984, p. 18.
2 Israel, Argentina, and the CIA have been credited with crucial support to the Guatemalan counter-insurgency campaign, and US-backed forces committed "acts of genocide." See Point 13 of Section I of the Conclusions in the Report of the Guatemalan Historical Clarification Commission, 1999, http://shr.aaas.org/guatemala/ceh/report/english/toc.html, and Linda Haugaard, "Admissions and Omissions: the CIA in Guatemala," In These Times, July 22, 1996, which reviews the report of the president's Intelligence Oversight Board.

"It is important that I state clearly that support for military forces or intelligence units which engaged in violent and widespread repression of the kind described in the report was wrong. And the United States must not repeat that mistake." As will be seen, Clinton was at that very time doing just that in other regions of the world, setting records for arms transfers to non-democratic governments.

The human toll of US policy was staggering. Perhaps a quarter of a million people, nearly all civilians, with best estimates of 60,000 in Nicaragua, 70,000 in El Salvador, and 140,000 in Guatemala, were sacrificed to US national security, American domestic politics, and the imperial paternalism that confuses morality with domination and takes up Kipling's "white man's burden" to protect another people from one of their factions. More than two million people were driven from their homes, and most of those made their way to the United States.[1] Like the European colonial powers, America became socially entangled in the countries it dominated and saw its own complexion broadened as a result through immigration.

Reagan energetically portrayed military victory in each country as the only way to prevent the establishment of "another Cuba" that would provide the Soviet Union with a military foothold in America's back yard and repress the human rights of its citizens. His administration used an unprecedented and in some cases illegal publicity campaign that set the terms of debate in the elite media and Congress, even if it never convinced a majority of Americans.[2] Reagan also made it clear to Congress that allegiance on this issue was his priority, and would be rewarded on other policy fronts. The combination of Cold War politics and presidential powers proved irresistible to both moderate northern Republicans and the conservative, mostly southern Democrats whom liberal Democrats disdainfully called "Dixies," from Dixiecrats, the informal name of the segregationists who left the Democratic party in protest over Harry Truman's modest civil rights platform in 1948 and ran Governor Strom Thurmond of South Carolina for president.[3]

The Republican Senate that came in with Reagan's victory and held power through 1986 easily passed all of his proposals on Central America and bargained firmly in confer-

---

1 Robert S. Kahn, *Other People's Blood: US Immigration Prisons in the Reagan Decade,* Westview Press, Boulder, CO, 1996, pp. 2, 11; Susanne Jones, *The Battle for Guatemala: Rebels, Death Squads, and US Power,* Westview Press, Boulder, CO, 1991 pp. 204-205.

2 The illegality was alleged by the General Accounting Office and documented in detail in a report by the House Foreign Affairs Committee that was largely authored, in a historical irony, by the person whose office at the Democratic National Committee was one of the targets of the 1972 Watergate break-in, chief counsel Spencer Oliver. Cynthia Arnson, *Crossroads: Congress, the President, and Central America, 1976-1993,* Pennsylvania University Press, University Park, PA, 1993, pp. 177, 190-191.

3 The media often used the term "Boll Weevils" to refer to the conservative Democrats. In response, some in the Republican leadership used the mocking and matching Northern infestation "Gypsy Moths" to refer to insufficiently conservative Republicans. The conservative Democrats preferred to be known by the older label of "Yellow Dogs," meaning a Southerner who would vote for a yellow dog before he'd vote for a Republican. The label had historical connotations of loyalty to the working man — so long as he was white. The Democrats' Franklin Roosevelt had brought in the New Deal, but the Democrats had also been the party of secession and then segregation. The Dixies changed their label to Blue Dogs in the 1990s, complaining that the liberal party leadership was "choking them blue" by limiting their access to national campaign funds.

ence committees with the Democratic House. There was a lot of truth in an April Fool's issue of "The Week Ahead," the listing of upcoming hearings and votes that the congressional Arms Control and Foreign Policy Caucus sent out to its 140 liberal members. Titled "Weakly Ahead," the spoof claimed that the Foreign Relations Committee would hold a hearing on declaring war on a long list of countries at 10 a.m., with a vote on the Senate floor scheduled for noon. The House was nominally controlled by the Democratic Party's liberal leadership, but the balance of power was held by the roughly 60 Dixies. They had bolted to the Republican position in 1981 on Reagan's proposal to cut taxes and social spending, and Speaker "Tip" O'Neill, Majority Leader Jim Wright, and Whip Tom Foley had to tread carefully and accommodate the Dixies' views or risk losing control again. Complicating this task was the fact that two powerful party leaders, Wright (a Texan) and Appropriations Committee deal-maker and military bellwether Jack Murtha of rural Pennsylvania, were energetic advocates of funding the entirety of Reagan's aid requests for El Salvador.

Soft Eagles in Congress disputed neither Reagan's goal of blocking another Cuba nor his assumption that the United States had the right, and indeed the moral duty, to do so. Instead they fought Reagan on tactical grounds, arguing that the oligarchic societies favored by US allies were unsustainable, and that these allies' human rights abuses were unacceptable. The Turkeys in the many advocacy groups who very effectively kept the Soft Eagles engaged and armed with facts and horror stories could argue all they wanted for the right of countries to work out their own futures, without the self-interested American interventions that had cemented the brutal back yard oligarchies in the first place. The folk music trio Peter, Paul, and Mary could sing all they wanted about a policy in El Salvador that would "kill the people to set them free" and ask the moral question, "who put this price on their liberty?"[1] Liberal Members simply could not join in with the Turkeys' suggestion, through these bards, that it was "time to leave El Salvador," because they felt they could not dispute widely-believed national security imperatives and still be credible participants in the policy debate, both in their districts and in the capital.

The Soft Eagles cited the words of President Kennedy, who had said that "those who make peaceful revolution impossible make violent revolution inevitable," but they were also guided by his actions, and so did not renounce the threat and, when necessary, the use of violence to bar unfriendly regimes from taking power in America's "back yard." From the subversion of Guatemala's democracy in 1954 through the Bay of Pigs invasion in 1961, the Cuban missile crisis in 1962, the intervention in the Dominican Republic in 1965, the destabilization of Chile's democracy in 1973, and the invasions of Grenada in 1983 and Panama in 1989, liberals were overwhelmingly unwilling to defend the sovereignty of anti-American regimes. Like the Turkeys, they argued for conditioning aid to repressive gov-

---

1 From Peter, Paul, and Mary's song, "El Salvador," written by Noel ("Paul") Stookey and Jim Wallis in 1983. The singers might have been particularly angry because the type of US aerial gunship provided to the Salvadoran Air Force, the Armed Cargo (AC)-37, was nicknamed "Puff, the Magic Dragon," as had been the larger version, the AC-130 gunship, in Vietnam. "Puff" was named for the blasts of smoke that were emitted by its coordinated automatic machine guns, which blanketed a large area with bullets placed every few inches.

ernments on strict human rights protections, but they did so for reasons of strategy as well as morality. They portrayed the use of conditions as a way to guide those governments to the popularity they would need to prevent leftist movements from gaining popular appeal and taking power.[1] It was just as "instrumental" an approach to human rights as the Reagan administration's decision to use human rights "in the contest with the Soviet bloc" by arguing that communist dictatorship as an outcome of cutting aid to rightist dictators would be the ultimate abuse.[2]

The legendary French foreign minister Talleyrand is known, probably apocryphally, for referring to a certain execution ordered by Napoleon as being "worse than a crime — a blunder." Most of the Turkeys saw the US effort to win rather than settle the Central American wars as a crime, and most of the soft Eagles saw it as a blunder, while the Reagan and Bush administrations and their Dixie allies saw it as a noble mission. "Conditioning" Reagan's aid requests for the Salvadoran and Guatemalan armies and the Nicaraguan Contras on improvements in their human rights record was a superficially sound strategy for the liberals. The human rights records of protectors of the old social order were inherently atrocious, and Dixies who strongly supported Reagan's assumption that America has the right to ban unfriendly regimes in its back yard were still troubled by those records. However, by ceding the debate on Reagan's goals and assumptions, the liberals made themselves the weaker party that lacked a coherent reason to oppose aid when aggressive publicity by the administration highlighted left-wing abuses.

Liberals did have one powerful tactical arrow in their quiver with which to demonstrate congressional opposition to letting Reagan have his way in Central America — Vietnam. That single word, with its connotations of slippery slopes, of advisers becoming combat troops, and of humiliating defeat, still resonated powerfully in Congress and with its constituents. Nixon's policy of Vietnamization may have failed in Indochina, but it had succeeded in one sense at home. As long as foreign troops did the fighting and dying, Americans were not too agitated about taking sides in a civil war. The flip side, as top House strategist Kathy Gille recalls, was that they were easily agitated about the involvement of US troops, making that issue, simply coded "another Vietnam," the "template" that overlay debate about Central America.[3] Soft Eagles took pains to raise the specter of US troops in combat, and hard Eagles had to react to an early misstep by Secretary of State Alexander Haig by renouncing any such possibility.[4]

1 For example, Senator Frank Church argued against aiding the Somoza dictatorship in the 1970s because its abuses would make a "Castro-type revolutionary government" more likely. Cynthia Arnson, *Crossroads: Congress, the President, and Central America, 1976-1993*, Pennsylvania University Press, University Park, PA, 1993, p. 31.

2 Quote from the "Clark–Kennedy" memorandum establishing the Reagan administration's human rights policy, cited in Caleb Rossiter and Anne-Marie Smith, "Human Rights: The Carter Record, the Reagan Reaction," International Policy Report, Center for International Policy, September 1984, p. 23. See also pp. 11, 90.

3 Gille was an aide to Congressman David Bonior, who ran the House leadership "whip" task force on Nicaragua from 1985 until the end of the war. Interview, June 2009.

4 Cynthia Arnson, *Crossroads: Congress, the President, and Central America, 1976-1993*, Pennsylvania University Press, University Park, PA, 1993, p. 92. For specific examples of members of Congress citing fears of Vietnam-style combat, see p. 59 (Rep. Clarence "Doc" Long), p. 122 (Sen. Daniel Inouye), and p. 134 (House Intelligence Committee Chair Eddie Boland).

In 1982 Haig had publicly refused to rule out the use of US troops, so crusty constitutionalist Senator Robert Byrd introduced a bill barring troops without congressional approval. After George Shultz replaced Haig, the administration defeated amendments based on the bill in both Houses in 1983 only by renouncing any intention to use troops. In May 1984 House Whip Foley unexpectedly offered the ban on troops during late-evening consideration of the bill authorizing the military budget, and Congressman George Miller craftily called for a recorded vote that Foley had promised he would not demand if the leadership of the Armed Services committee quietly accepted the amendment.[1] The House was suddenly on record, 341-64, and while Foley's amendment was whittled down to an advisory opinion in conference with the Senate, it set an important boundary for the administration. As a fitting measure of the Democrats' sensitivity to charges of being soft on Soviet military power in the hemisphere, when Foley won House passage again in 1985 and 1986, he accepted a Republican modification waiving the amendment if Nicaragua obtained MiG fighter planes.[2]

UNEASY ALLIES: SOFT EAGLES IN CONGRESS AND TURKEYS IN "THE GROUPS"

In 1984 a staffer for House deputy whip Bill Alexander strategized with other congressional staff after a visit to El Salvador. Looking over his shoulder in mock fear and speaking in hushed tones, he said, "We're on the wrong side — has anybody told the Members?" He was reprising Robert White's 1965 query to national security adviser McGeorge Bundy about the Dominican Republic, described in Chapter 2, or Bobby Kennedy's observation as a senator in 1965 when emerging from a Chilean mine organized by a communist union, one that did not jibe with his actions as attorney general: "If I had to work in that mine, I'd be a communist too."

The United States was indeed on the wrong side of a confrontation between oligarchies and peasant masses, and between the oligarchies' brutal enforcers and the advocates of a fair society. Repression had driven intellectuals and social leaders to armed struggle in Central America, just as it had in South Africa, where Nelson Mandela was jailed for commanding the African National Congress's "Spear of the Nation." But while Soft Eagles were sympathetic to the South African rebellion, and Turkeys, including pacifist groups and churches, funded it, very few wanted or pushed for a victory by the armed leftist movements in Central America. Republicans and Dixies in Congress and their neo-conservative cheerleaders took the side of the Contras and the Salvadoran and Guatemalan armies, pushing for US funding and military victories, but only a fringe of Turkeys in "solidarity" groups called for victory by the Sandinistas and the Salvadoran and Guatemalan rebels and raised funds for communities under their control. Most of the Turkeys in the advocacy groups and all of the Soft Eagles in Congress buried their differences about US

---

1   There was an informal rule that the Whip didn't offer amendments, but the Arms Control and Foreign Policy Caucus suggested to Foley that he do so. His sponsorship added about 150 votes to a similar amendment offered previously by junior Member Ed Markey.

2   The modification was approved 377-45, leading 14 of the most liberal members to oppose the new Foley amendment for sidestepping Congress' constitutional duty to approve combat by US forces. "Foley Amendment" files of Edith Wilkie and Caleb Rossiter, Arms Control and Foreign Policy Caucus, Legislative Records, National Archives.

strategic rights and together took the side of cease-fires and negotiated settlements so that the people of Central America would not have their lives destroyed by a Cold War bludgeoning.

On Central America, more than on most issues, the Soft Eagles in Congress were prodded and guided by a coterie of their staff. Greg Craig, Senator Ted Kennedy's foreign policy staffer who later became White House counsel for President Obama, would welcome his colleagues from roughly 20 congressional offices with Shakespeare's line from *Henry V*, "we few, we happy few, we band of brothers" when they came together regularly to plot in 1984.[1] In Congress, knowledge of proposals and their timing is the currency of the realm, and Members and staff tend to hoard it. This was especially true among Democrats in the 1980s, when the lack of party discipline lived up to the old joke: "I'm not a member of an organized political party — I'm a Democrat." This was largely due to the Dixies, who could rally to protect each other from the leadership, or just switch parties. When the House Republican leadership threatened Olympia Snowe with losing her seniority if she didn't back aid to the Contras, she caved in. When the Democratic leadership took Phil Gramm's seniority away for sponsoring Reagan's 1981 budget cuts, he simply quit Congress, became a Republican, and won his seat back. In this vacuum of party power, Democratic Members acted like entrepreneurs trying to corner a market. On Central America, though, there was a sense that the staff were engaged in an important mission of ending wars, and the band of brothers, and sisters, kept working together and sharing information even when their bosses were at loggerheads.

Part of the glue that bound the Soft Eagles together and then bound them to the Turkeys in the advocacy groups was the Arms Control and Foreign Policy Caucus, led by Edie Wilkie. Wilkie came to Washington after college in 1968 to spend a summer ending the Vietnam War and stayed to become a Member's chief of staff and then executive director of the Caucus. The Caucus was an internal goad on Central America, a counter-weight to the pounding by the Reagan administration. It flooded Members with strategy memos, drafted amendments, organized task forces to "whip" them, wrote and publicized reports to provide material and motivation for committee and floor fights, and sponsored speakers from the region for private meetings in which Members honed their public arguments.

---

1 The band included, from the Senate, Bob Dockery and Janice O'Connell with Chris Dodd, Rick Rolf and later Julie McGregor with Mark Hatfield, Ed King and Dick McCall with Robert Byrd's leadership committee, Barry Sklar and Gerry Connelly (later a congressman from Virginia) with Foreign Relations Chairman Claiborne Pell, and Janet Breslin and later Tim Rieser with Pat Leahy. In the House it included George Kundanis with Whip (and then Majority Leader and Speaker) Tom Foley, Billy Woodward with Gerry Studds, Kathy Gille with David Bonior, Vic Johnson and Rob Kurz with Western Hemisphere Subcommittee Chairman Mike Barnes, Cindy Arnson with George Miller, Mike Marek with appropriator Dave Obey, Jan Shinpoch with Mike Lowry, Gary Bombardier with Matt McHugh, Ed Long with Ted Weiss (and then Senator Tom Harkin), and Laurie Schultz with Jim Jeffords. Other key staff were part of the conspiracy but for various reasons of protocol and other duties rarely came to these informal sessions, like Mike O'Neil and Bernie Raimo from the House Intelligence Committee, Jim McGovern (also later a congressman) with House Rules Chairman Joe Moakley, and Richard Collins with Senate Foreign Operations Appropriations and then Defense Subcommittee Chairman Daniel Inouye.

Although the Caucus was studiously bipartisan and bicameral in its officers and its initia-tives, in practice its primary function was to assist House Members in supporting and at times spurring on the Democratic leadership. It was therefore a natural partner of the reform-minded House Democratic Study Group, which most non-Dixie Democrats, the core of the Caucus's 140 members, also joined. Wilkie and DSG Executive Director Dick Conlon roamed through the Congress as super-staffers representing the interests of a large number of Members. They could gather information and foment plots knowing that their officers would back them up. Wilkie was much closer to the advocacy groups than Conlon was, and her staff regularly attended the groups' strategy sessions as partners.

During the early 1980s the most potent advocacy groups with the greatest mainstream constituencies threw their energies into two remarkable and successful challenges to the usual presidential domination of national security issues, the nuclear "freeze" and finan-cial sanctions on South Africa. Boston arms expert Randy Forsberg encouraged arms con-trol, religious, and reform organizations such as Common Cause to build a nationwide campaign based on Senator Mark Hatfield's 1979 amendment calling for a common-sense "moratorium" by the Soviet Union and the United States on building nuclear weapons and their missiles. Taking advantage of citizens' concerns over aggressive comments by the Reagan administration about winning a nuclear war, by 1983 the Freeze had passed voter initiatives in hundreds of communities, won the endorsement of the House and the Demo-cratic party, galvanized congressional opposition to the MX missile and nuclear testing, and forced the administration into detailed negotiations with the Soviets over global and European arms levels.[1]

The other, almost miraculous, success for advocacy groups was the enactment in 1986 over Reagan's veto of Congressman Ron Dellums' cutoff of American investment in South Africa. This "Anti-apartheid Act" played a crucial role in spurring the beginning of the ne-gotiations that brought multi-ethnic democracy in South Africa in 1994.[2] On November 21, 1984, TransAfrica founder Randall Robinson was arrested for refusing to leave the South African embassy. It was not a propitious moment for a protest.[3] After 20 years of national and international sniping at South Africa's segregated sporting teams, visitors, and arms and oil imports, the apartheid government had been only symbolically isolated. It was under such little pressure economically that it could easily spend the extra premium for making rather than importing its weapons — including a phenomenally expensive seven atomic bombs with which to discourage its "front-line" black-ruled neighbors from ever attacking.

Nelson Mandela and other top African National Congress leaders, who had been im-prisoned after adding bombing of infrastructure to their previously non-violent resistance campaign, were entering their third decade of life sentences on Robben Island. The ANC leadership and the ragtag force it was training in the "front-line" countries were infil-

---

1 Glen Harold Stassen and Lawrence S. Winters, eds., *Peace Action: Past, Present, and Future*, Paradigm, Boulder, CO, 2007, pp. 8-9, 69, 82.
2 Nelson Mandela himself made this argument, at an award ceremony in Houston sponsored by the Rothko Chapel, in 1991.
3 Also arrested were Washington, DC's non-voting Congressional Delegate Walter Fauntroy, and US Civil Rights Commissioner Mary Frances Berry.

trated and militarily ineffectual, and South Africa raided its neighbors and assassinated ANC cadre with impunity. The Afrikaner elite was well on its way to implementing a grand strategy of designating the African majority as citizens of ten new countries in iso-lated tribal "homelands." To top it all off, the Reagan administration, which had just been strengthened by Reagan's overwhelming victory over Walter Mondale, vigorously op-posed putting pressure on South Africa, under a policy called "constructive engagement."

Yet Robinson's arrest sparked a conflagration. Over 4,000 people, notably Rosa Parks of Birmingham bus boycott fame and members of the Congressional Black Caucus, were arrested at daily marches at the embassy. South African "shanty towns" sprang up on col-lege campuses, and labor unions, universities, and even cities reversed their decades-long resistance to "divesting" their endowments or pension funds from banks and businesses investing in South Africa. Senator Mitch McConnell was typical of conservative Republi-cans who switched their position and voted to override Reagan's veto. He opposed sanc-tions, but the turmoil when he tried to go through the shanty towns at the University of Kentucky to attend a football game led to his conversion. Senate Majority leader Robert Dole, in a last gasp of opposition that brought what threatened to be a last gasp of life from outraged minority leader Robert Byrd, locked the President's veto message in his safe. Admitting that the apoplectic Byrd probably had the more persuasive case under the Senate rules, Dole simply said, "I did not become majority leader in order to lose." He finally traded the vote that overturned the veto for the Democrats ending a filibuster on some other item.[1]

Despite strenuous organizing that produced a great deal of grassroots pressure from church members and city councils, the dozens of smaller groups that specialized in human rights and Central America were not able to achieve anything near the clout of the Freeze or the anti-apartheid movement. They did, however, play a crucial role in the debate, tak-ing liberal members of Congress on trips to the region to give them credibility and motiva-tion, sponsoring briefings on the Hill, providing reliable information from district lobby-ing that Soft Eagles could use in "whipping" their assigned swing Members, and feeding the media stories that kept the issue alive. Like the Members of Congress, the "lobby" groups cooperated remarkably well on Central America, despite being inherently in com-petition for funding, publicity, and survival.

The diversity of the groups that were part of the weekly meetings chaired by Cindy Buhl, the formidable director of the Coalition for a New Foreign and Military Policy's Central America Lobby Group, was at times overwhelming. There were religious lob-bies: Catholics, Baptists, Jews, Presbyterians, Methodists, Unitarians, Quakers, and more. There were human rights groups: Americas Watch, Amnesty International, and the Law-yers Committee on Human Rights. There were groups with expertise in Latin America,

---

1 The anti-apartheid act came at a time when the price of gold suddenly collapsed, causing international commercial banks to hold off on rolling over the government's loans. See Terry Crawford-Browne, *Eye on the Money*, Umuzi Press, South Africa, 2007, for the remarkable tale of how he used his banker's acumen first to aid the ANC's campaign to block commercial lending to South Africa in the 1980s and then to investigate ANC's corruption in the international arms deals its leaders signed in the 1990s after taking power. An upsurge in street demonstrations in South Africa also helped convince the government to start discussions with Mandela over a new political system.

like the Washington Office on Latin America, the Council on Hemispheric Affairs, and the Center for International Policy. There were peace groups, notably SANE/Freeze, Veterans for Peace, and Women Strike for Peace. There were even constitutionalists: the American Civil Liberties Union had a Washington office, run by former and future National Security Council staffer Mort Halperin, which opposed the Contra war solely because it was funded through the CIA's secret appropriations. This was also the position of the powerful "good government" group Common Cause. In addition to lobbying in Washington and home districts, a number of groups specialized in sponsoring regular trips to Central America, including the Unitarian Universalist Service Committee, the Commission on US-Central American Relations, and the Arca Foundation.

The "solidarity groups" that funded left-leaning communities in Central America had little direct impact on the Washington debate, but they spread the word in thousands of church and community meetings, spurring others to lobby Congress.[1] Far from accepting the goal of blocking another Cuba, the solidarity groups were largely partisans for the existing Cuba. Far from accepting the half a loaf that Soft Eagles fought to win, they occupied those Members' district offices in protest. Activists in these groups often had met Central Americans who were later killed by US-aided forces, and so their commitment was charged with anger. When Gus Newport, the mayor of Berkeley, testified in 1986 before a House committee that he knew that US-supplied aircraft were bombing villages and strafing peasants because he had been there on a solidarity trip when it happened, conservative committee member Dan Burton gleefully claimed to have been present on the other end of the firepower, observing the Salvadoran air force at work. Outrageous as his callous dismissal of aerial bombardment was to those who had seen its results firsthand, Burton's support for tough military action to win the war represented the majority opinion in Congress.

After crushing losses in 1984 on El Salvador and 1986 on Nicaragua, Soft Eagles in Congress wrote amendments to limit and try to settle the wars, but they usually lacked the votes to win even modest conditions on US aid. At some point each year, there would have to be a decision to "cave in."[2] Deciding just what that point should be occasioned constant disappointment and at times bitter recriminations between the groups and the Members who had to make the call. Leadership aide George Kundanis, whose frequent presence the groups knew provided exceptional benefits to and access for their efforts, was savaged by the solidarity groups for announcing the compromises. Cindy Buhl recalls that the solidarity groups reneged on an agreement not to do the same thing in a later meeting with George's boss, Whip Tom Foley, which resulted in all the groups having their access to the

---

1 These included the Committee in Solidarity with the People of El Salvador, Neighbor to Neighbor, the Nicaragua Network, Witness for Peace, and the Network in Solidarity with the People of Guatemala.

2 Staff called this the "Maalox" moment because they wanted the Members to show more calcium in their backbones. As noted in the Preface, at her first meeting with George Miller's Salvador task force in 1987, new Member Nancy Pelosi, juiced up by the solidarity groups in her district, implored the members not to consider compromise legislation when "people are dying, children are dying!" Of course, she quickly became a master of the art of the possible in legislation, and eventually Speaker of the House, earning the enmity of the same groups.

leadership suspended. This phenomenon of the militant left taking its frustration out on its allies was, of course, not limited to Central America. The *Village Voice*'s James Ridgway similarly savaged Congressman Ron Dellums and SANE/Freeze lobbyist Laurie Duker in a column for supporting an amendment to cut "Star Wars" missile defense spending — because spending any money at all was absurd and dangerous.

On a lighter note, in addition to the groups, there were the stars. Jackson Browne raised money for Central American advocacy in his concerts. Unfortunately, the beneficiary was the loopy Christic Institute, which filed and lost lawsuits relating to the Iran-Contra network. Lobbying on Central America, Bonnie Raitt actually made George Miller blush by sitting in the barber chair in his office and raising her legs, saying that it reminded her of a gynecological exam. Richard Gere caused a screaming stampede of publicity in Rochester, New York, going door to door for the successful campaign of contra aid opponent Louise Slaughter. Actors Ed Asner and Mike Farrell sponsored trips by American doctors to assist wounded Salvadoran rebels.[1] "MASH" star Farrell put on an elegant lunch in the Capitol as a way of thanking the "happy few" congressional staff for their work. A staffer was seated next to a woman who was dressed far too fashionably to be a colleague, and asked her which group she was with. She laughed and said, "You're kidding, right? I'm one of Charlie's Angels." Living in an intense bubble of politics with little access to popular culture, the staffer replied: "Who's Charlie?"[2] That's a decent metaphor for the uneasy alliance between Congress and the groups: they didn't really understand each other, but they knew they were comrades in a sacred struggle.

EL SALVADOR: THE UNNECESSARY WAR

Talleyrand, who managed to serve in turn a revolution, an emperor, and a king, did in fact say, "treason is a question of timing." For poor El Salvador, its devastation was the result of bad timing. Had it been the first rather than the second of the rightist dictatorships in America's "backyard" to be threatened by a leftist insurgency in the 1970s, it might have escaped the US-backed civil war that killed 70,000 of its citizens and drove a million, one fifth of the country, from their homes. When Nicaragua's cartoonish Somoza family was tottering in 1978 and 1979, President Carter made only a half-hearted attempt to help it stave off this one of the "inevitable revolutions," as Cornell professor Walter LaFeber titled his book on the struggle between poverty and privilege in Central America. When El Salvador's military rulers began to lose control to a leftist uprising in 1979 and 1980 that was aided by the new Sandinista government and its Cuban and Warsaw Pact allies, Carter responded to a growing consensus in Washington that things were spiraling out of control, and that it was a strategic, moral, and political imperative to keep the FMLN from taking power.

A Carter adviser said, "The domino theory lives...No President wants to lose something to communism on his watch." Another affirmed that it was now considered "unac-

---

1 A top staffer at Medical Aid to El Salvador was Jody Williams, who would later coordinate the International Campaign to Ban Landmines.

2 Speaker Tip O'Neill was similarly insulated from popular culture. When Robert Redford introduced himself to Tip in an airport, Tip cluelessly replied, "Nice to meet you, Bob."

---

ceptable to the United States" for the extreme left to take over in El Salvador.[1] In the spring of 1980, Carter was reeling from the firestorm of criticism generated the previous fall by the CIA's reclassification of a Soviet logistical unit in Cuba as a "combat brigade." Not even the horrific assassination of popular Archbishop Oscar Romero at mass in March in retaliation for his call to soldiers not to obey commands to kill civilians could convince Carter to withdraw his request to Congress for additional military aid. Despite their quite accurate belief that the murder was carried out by "death squads" who were either in or allied with government security forces, in an appalling moment of truth three of the most liberal House members provided the margin of victory for a subcommittee "reprogramming" of $5.7 million that laid the groundwork for a $6 billion war. David Obey, Matt McHugh, and Bill Lehman were caught in the classic political trap of liberals who have risen to positions of authority in committees but cannot command a majority on the floor. If they defeated the request, the administration would simply find other ways to pursue it, either by breaking tradition and ignoring their decision, which occurred in a gray area of the law, or by inserting the funds in other pieces of legislation. Then the Members would be seen as irrelevant, and they would lose whatever meager amount of congressional limitation existed, as oversight of the program was passed on to other, less liberal actors.

The three liberals were also caught in the classic ideological trap of Soft Eagles. While they did not buy the Pentagon's claim that the aid would "help strengthen the army's key role in reforms," they were concerned that an end to aid might lead not to a negotiated settlement but to the collapse of the Army and a slide to a left-wing "tyranny." That was a risk they were not willing to take. Agreeing with an argument advanced by Ambassador Robert White, Obey reasoned that since he was asking conservatives to take "a chance on affecting the conduct" of the left-wing government in Nicaragua with US aid programs, he should be willing to take a chance on affecting the conduct of the right-wing government in El Salvador.[2] Soft Eagles simply were not, politically or ideologically, in the business of suggesting that it was high time to renounce the right to "affect the conduct" of Central America countries.

Another horrific slaughter in December 1980, this time of four American nuns by the National Guard, also did not deter the Carter administration from providing military aid during the FMLN's offensive just prior to Reagan's inauguration. Carter and Reagan were both Eagles who assumed America's right to block unfriendly governments from taking power, and indeed, the continuity of the goal of barring the emergence of "another Cuba" can be traced through every president back to Eisenhower — and even beyond, as a US "Milgroup" commander indicated when remarking that El Salvador had been within "our traditional sphere of influence since the Monroe Doctrine, in 1823."[3] As a Soft Eagle, though, Carter perceived the internal roots of the conflict, and was seeking a negotiated settlement at the lowest possible cost in human life, while Hard Eagle Reagan saw the

1 Cynthia Arnson, *Crossroads: Congress, the President, and Central America, 1976-1993*, Pennsylvania University Press, University Park, PA, 1993, pp. 38, 40.

2 Cynthia Arnson, *Crossroads: Congress, the President, and Central America, 1976-1993*, Pennsylvania University Press, University Park, PA, 1993, pp. 42-43.

3 Cynthia Arnson, *Crossroads: Congress, the President, and Central America, 1976-1993*, Pennsylvania University Press, University Park, PA, 1993, p. 7.

conflict as a Soviet power play and was seeking victory at virtually any price. The very first official act of Reagan's new secretary of state, former NATO commander Alexander Haig, was to remove White as ambassador. Haig portrayed the unrest in Central America as a Soviet challenge akin to the invasion of Afghanistan, announced that the United States was "drawing the line" in El Salvador, and initiated a decade of downplaying human rights abuses by incorrectly claiming that the raped and murdered nuns may well have triggered the crime because they had "run a roadblock."[1]

As former House staffer Cindy Arnson has shown in her authoritative *Crossroads: Congress, the President, and Central America, 1976-1993*, both congressional opposition and the reality of the situation ironically, and quickly, forced the Reagan administration to use Soft Eagle tactics to achieve its Hard Eagle goal of military victory. Much effort was expended by the administration on addressing the internal roots of the conflict, such as human rights abuses, impunity of the perpetrators from prosecution or even inconvenience, control of the land by a tiny minority, the lack of a forum for negotiations. In return, Congress appropriated increasing amounts of money for the war both as military aid and "economic" aid that was used in counter-insurgency programs. Certainly much of the administration's effort to promote superficial reforms was cynically motivated to gain support for funding, as shown by this portrayal of dissenting Members by Assistant Secretary of State for Latin America Tony Motley: "Take away their lily pads [and] the croaking stops." However, Arnson concludes that there was a real struggle waged within the administration by human rights "instrumentalists" who actually wanted to press the Salvadoran government and Army to reduce the rebels' appeal by making meaningful reforms — like not murdering dissidents.[2]

Perhaps unwilling to make, and certainly lacking a floor majority for, a judgment that El Salvador's performance in these areas had already warranted a cut or an end to US aid, Soft Eagles led by Steve Solarz, a member of the House Foreign Affairs Committee's Western Hemisphere subcommittee, enacted legislation in 1981 requiring the administration to "certify" that the government was making progress in them. A strange ballet took place in hearings from 1982 to 1984, with the administration's representatives reporting sufficient progress to justify releasing the next tranche of aid, and human rights groups and liberal Members expressing shock that they could make such phony claims with a straight face. Of course, both sides knew full well that for the certification process, as for most of the dozens of similar certifications with vague conditions that are enacted each year, if Congress was not willing to cut off aid at the time it wrote the legislation — and an amendment in the full Committee by Representative Gerry Studds to do just that was defeated 22-9 — the administration would certainly not do so itself.[3] The certification process was

---

1 "Nuns Believed Killed Trying to Run Roadblock, Haig Says," AP wire story, Toledo Blade, March 19, 1981.

2 Cynthia Arnson, *Crossroads: Congress, the President, and Central America, 1976-1993*, Pennsylvania University Press, University Park, PA, 1993, p. 139.

3 Cynthia Arnson, *Crossroads: Congress, the President, and Central America, 1976-1993*, Pennsylvania University Press, University Park, PA, 1993, pp. 69-73. President Carter's "certification" in March 1980 that Nicaragua was not assisting the FMLN is a good example of the shoe being on the other foot — Republicans who had achieved that certification process to

by its nature one of "weakness and deceit," as journalist Raymond Bonner titled his book on US policy-making toward El Salvador.

The administration at first tried to deny the unpleasant reality that government forces were engaged in or allowed the brazen murders by death squads. Like the Carter administration, it blamed the killings on either the leftist rebels or far-right private forces with no connection to the government. The reporting by human rights groups and the press that Congress used in the certification hearings made this stance so untenable that two consecutive ambassadors gave prominent speeches in El Salvador warning the Army that if it did not, as it clearly could, stop the death squads, US aid would be in jeopardy. Vice President Bush even visited in 1983 and handed the president a list of suspected death squad supporters in the officer corps who should be taken out of positions of authority and sent abroad as defense attachés. Similarly, when supporters of aid to El Salvador such as Senate Foreign Relations Chairman Chuck Percy prepared legislation tying US aid to the continuation of a land reform opposed by the large farmers who backed the powerful ARENA party, the administration convinced the Salvadoran Assembly to reverse its plans to end the program.[1]

In 1982 and 1984 the administration had its eye very much on Congress when it arranged for presidential elections and then interfered in them to ensure that Major Roberto D'Aubuisson, the former director of the national secret police who became a death squad leader and then founded ARENA, would not win. The 1982 election was held in the Assembly, where D'Aubuisson controlled a working majority for his candidacy. Both the administration and its leading congressional supporters, such as Percy and House Majority Leader Jim Wright, made it clear that a D'Aubuisson presidency would result in Congress significantly cutting US aid. D'Aubuisson deferred to the High Command of the Army, which insisted on a centrist caretaker who was on the US ambassador's short list of acceptable candidates. D'Aubuisson instead became president of the Assembly, and when he and Christian Democrat José Napoleón Duarte squared off in a nationwide run-off in 1984, the administration successfully weighed in with more threats, overt aid to the election process that favored Duarte, and financial assistance to him and his campaign from the CIA.[2]

Around this time, as if to affirm this book's thesis of continuity in the US foreign policy of domination, the proverbial bad penny, Henry Kissinger, turned up. At the start of 1984 Congress was preparing for the release of the report of the Kissinger Commission on Central America. This "national bipartisan" commission, like most of the presidential commissions that were proliferating at the time, was intended to disarm public and con-

---

slow down US aid to Nicaragua were every bit as outraged at Carter's justification as any Democrat was at Reagan's certifications — and with just as good reason. See p. 49.

1 Cynthia Arnson, *Crossroads: Congress, the President, and Central America, 1976-1993*, Pennsylvania University Press, University Park, PA, 1993, pp. 43, 50, 99, 100.

2 Cynthia Arnson, *Crossroads: Congress, the President, and Central America, 1976-1993*, Pennsylvania University Press, University Park, PA, 1993, pp. 96, 98, 148. See also José Napoleón Duarte, *Duarte: My Story*, Putnam, New York, 1986, pp. 183-185. For the claim of CIA funding, see Howard Jones, *Crucible of Power: US Foreign Relations since 1987*, Scholarly Resources, Wilmington, DE, 2001, p. 465. Ironically, both candidates were credibly alleged to have been CIA "assets" earlier in their careers.

gressional opposition to administration policy. Like chairman Kissinger, nearly all the 12 commissioners were public figures who knew next to nothing about Central America. The few with foreign policy credentials were hardened Cold Warriors: Kissinger, Boston University President John Silber, and AFL-CIO President Lane Kirkland. As the drift of the report became clear during its drafting — more economic and military aid to El Salvador, vaguely conditioned on attention to human rights, and continued but unspecified pressure on Nicaragua — the only hope for dissent was the one of the eight congressional counselors to the Commission who had opposed both wars, House Western Hemisphere Subcommittee Chairman, and Caucus member, Mike Barnes.

At the strong urging of his staff director, Vic Johnson, Barnes toyed with the idea of writing a dissent that would challenge the "bipartisan consensus" that such reports were intended to portray. Johnson warned Barnes that the report "had the sole purpose of legitimizing what they wanted to do." Barnes had Johnson prepare a dissent but at the last minute, feeling isolated on the Commission and disarmed by the report's inclusion of language ceding the liberals' argument that aid should be conditioned on respect for human rights, he decided not to submit it.[1] Like the liberals who approved the reprogramming funds after the assassination of Archbishop Romero, Barnes was trapped by politics and policy. While he had been put into his chairmanship in a rare coup against a more conservative Democrat precisely because liberal leaders wanted someone to stand up to the administration, he was not going to place himself out past the fringe of the consensus cited by the report: "The United States cannot accept Soviet military engagement in Central America." And once he accepted that premise — that any step was justified to block the emergence of a government that might choose to call on the Soviet Union for its military needs, as Cuba did after the Bay of Pigs invasion — the haggling over the precise wording of the trade-off of human rights for aid did not seem to justify a formal dissent.

Issued in mid-January, the Kissinger report was used as expected to support Reagan's request for a significant increase in economic and military aid to El Salvador, which was to be packaged inside a regional plan for Central America in the annual foreign aid authorization. However, because funds for that bill could not be appropriated before the fall, the administration kept the heat on by requesting $93 million in military aid as part of an emergency appropriation for African famine relief. The Senate quickly approved $63 million, but in April the money ran into a formidable roadblock on the House floor in the person of George Miller, the chair of the El Salvador task force of the Arms Control and Foreign Policy Caucus. Unlike a surprisingly large number of legislators, Miller knew how to legislate. He grew up observing his father's 20-year career in the California Senate and worked on the staff of its majority leader after he lost a bid for the seat left open by his father's death in 1969. A "Watergate baby" who came to Congress at 29 in the reform class

---

1 Interview with Victor C. "Vic" Johnson, July 22, 2009. Johnson was not surprised, telling the author at the time that "95 percent of what we write up here ends up in the waste basket." Unfootnoted claims and conversations that follow in this chapter and the next for the period 1984 to 1990 come from the author's recollection, enhanced by the Rossiter and Wilkie boxes in the Caucus files at the National Archives, in the files for Legislative Service Organizations.

of 1974, Miller was supremely comfortable roaming the House floor, trading unspoken commitments and using arcane parliamentary tools.

Most liberals would have gotten out of the way of Majority Leader Wright, who was shepherding the Salvador aid through the House. Unlike the Dixies, they didn't fear the administration's promise to portray aid opponents as "Pontius Pilates" washing their hands of Central America as it fell under Soviet control, because nearly all of them came from the 90 percent of congressional districts that have been gerrymandered to perpetual electoral safety. It was taking on Wright, who held so much sway over so much of the House business, that was the risk. For Miller, who had already been told by the administration of credible right-wing plots to kill him hatched in both El Salvador and Guatemala, taking on Wright was no big deal. He piped up, "I object!" to routine motions designed to bring the aid package swiftly to the floor, and walked out, leaving the request in parliamentary limbo. This forced Wright to go looking for him in the hallways outside the chamber to ask him to withdraw his objection.

"You're not talking to me," Miller said. "Tell me what's going on." As other Members gathered around, Wright launched into a forceful depiction of soldiers being down to one bullet. Miller's Caucus task force had prepared an analysis of the military purpose of the actual list of items being requested, which the staff of the committees of jurisdiction, instinctively preserving their bosses' institutional power, were typically not interested in either sharing or summarizing in a useful manner. The memo, which Miller had sent around to Congress and the press, had concluded that, contrary to the constantly recycled administration claims that without the aid the Army would have to "go back to the barracks," the aid would be used to build completely new units as the Army was expanded. Miller probably wished that the soldiers really were down to one bullet, since then they couldn't massacre so many civilians, but he interrupted Wright and caught him on liberals' safest, and therefore favored, ground: winning an argument on the other person's own terms. "Jim, stop, stop," he said. "This aid is for new units. New units! This has nothing to do with an emergency. We'll deal with it in the regular aid bill."

Wright, known for his flowery and dramatic speaking, started to portray the aid as crucial to the survival of democracy in El Salvador, but Miller just snorted, "save it for the floor," and walked away, his tone indicating that he considered it pap and would say so in the debate. Wright had heard Miller's unspoken warning shot loud and clear, as had the other members. He knew that he probably had the votes to win, but that Miller was threatening to make it a messy and public intra-party fight. Speaker Tip O'Neill, who had opposed helping the government of El Salvador since the murder of the nuns, two of whom who were Maryknolls like his aunt, prevailed upon Wright to hold off consideration of the emergency bill until after the foreign aid bill — ignoring the supposedly starving Africans — and the administration uncovered an emergency authority to draw down $32 million from existing funds for the Army.[1]

The fight on the main Kissinger request for El Salvador took place first in Mike Barnes' subcommittee. Liberals controlled the votes there, but Barnes and Steve Solarz were wary

---

1 Cynthia Arnson, *Crossroads: Congress, the President, and Central America, 1976-1993*, Pennsylvania University Press, University Park, PA, 1993, pp. 121, 155, 157.

of becoming irrelevant by passing something that would be rejected by the full Foreign Affairs Committee, which was less liberal. The full House was even less liberal, and the Senate could be counted on to approve whatever Reagan requested and bargain hard for it in conference with the House. In contrast, the Caucus' strategy was to achieve as tough a "mark-up" as possible in the Subcommittee, rejecting the Kissinger report's goal of building a bigger Salvadoran Army to defeat the rebels, and then fight each step of the way. Despite pressure from Miller's 40-member task force, which met frequently and in a rare move interfered in the Subcommittee mark-up by lobbying its members and pushing a resolution in the House Democratic Caucus, Barnes and Solarz decided not to support Gerry Studds' proposal to delay any consideration of military aid until the administration reported that the security forces had been purged of death squads. Instead, the Subcommittee passed a variety of porous barriers to the use of economic aid in the military effort, and divided the openly military money into "tranches" that could only be released with the approval of the House and Senate.[1]

The administration promised to veto any bill containing even that modest a constraint, and Republicans made it clear that they would not support the full foreign aid bill in the House Foreign Affairs Committee unless the tranches were dropped. Democratic chair Dante Fascell of Florida desperately wanted to enact the foreign aid bill, and needed Republican and administration support to do so. He cannily set about engineering to lose on El Salvador without obviously betraying Barnes, which would cost him liberal support for the overall bill.[2] Fascell first convinced the Committee to pass the bill without the contentious Central American section, which would be taken up on the floor by the full House. Then during floor consideration he became what a staffer angrily called "the dog who didn't bark," in a reference to the Sherlock Holmes story where the criminal is revealed by the dog's familiarity with him. Fascell should have been much in evidence before and during the floor action, using his institutional clout with other Members to promote the stance of Barnes' subcommittee, which the Rules committee had reinserted in the bill as the "Democratic Caucus" position. Instead, Fascell sat out the fight on replacing Barnes' provision with the Kissinger package, in the form of an amendment by the Committee's top Republican, Bill Broomfield, and noted Democratic Hard Eagle Jack Murtha.[3]

---

1 Foremost among the economic conditions were restrictions on the "cash transfer" that committee Member Sam Gejdenson and his staffer Kathleen Bertelsen had developed following the leaking, though the Center for International Policy, of an internal AID audit revealing corruption in the program.

2 Vic Johnson, interview, June 17, 2009. This was a systematic practice on Central America for Fascell and his staff director Jack Brady. Johnson recalls that whenever the Committee's differences between the two house's versions of the annual foreign aid bill would be narrowed by Fascell's staff and their Republican Senate counterparts in the "pre-conference" meeting to work out differences, the Central American sections would come back irrevocably weakened, with no involvement of the subcommittee staff. When Johnson would have Mike Barnes "feign surprise" at this in the Democratic members' meetings before the formal conferences, Fascell would with equal disingenuousness turn and chew out one of his staffers for having failed to consult with the subcommittee.

3 In addition, in a maddening breach of protocol Richard Peña, a member of Fascell's staff with connections to Jim Wright, had given Fascell's purported opponents the Committee's "whip" list of Members who were still on the fence. This allowed the Republicans and the administration to court them with legislative and executive branch favors.

The outcome of the floor fight on May 10 was pretty clear after the administration engineered Duarte's election as president over D'Aubuisson on May 6. In vain Miller's task force members organized "one-minute" speeches at the start of House business every day comparing the mania for elections in El Salvador that would validate a heroic, democratic figure-head for the military and right wing to the repeated use of elections to gain congressional support for the war in Vietnam. In vain they tracked down their assigned targets on the floor to make the argument personally. With Duarte's election as an excuse to "give him a chance," the Dixies were simply not going to be able to withstand the public hammering on communism and freedom and the private goodies for their districts that Reagan and his team were giving them, and moderate Republicans were under institutional pressure to stick with the party position. Rejecting a request from the rest of the leadership, Jim Wright gave an emotional floor speech against the Committee provision, and 56 Democrats, almost a fifth of the caucus, went with him, 53 of them from the South or Southwest. Only eight Republicans voted against the Broomfield–Murtha amendment, and it recorded a narrow four-vote victory.[1]

Barnes' decision in January not to dissent from and discredit the Kissinger Commission came back to haunt him in that vote. The Kissinger trade-off was enough aid to win the war in return for "certain minimum standards of respect for human rights." Barnes had joined a majority of the Democratic caucus in voting down Gerry Studds' floor amendment to bar all military aid, so he could not argue that current conditions in El Salvador already voided the deal. He had to argue that Congress needed to keep the pressure on by voting every few months to release tranches of aid, but few members like to take repeated tough votes when they can take one and be done with an issue. Buffalo congressman and former Bills quarterback Jack Kemp closed the floor debate for Broomfield–Murtha. Like Barnes, he had been an official counselor to the Kissinger Commission. He ended by quoting from the report, stressing that the amendment was consistent with the report's recommendation that military aid "should, though legislation requiring periodic reports, be made contingent upon demonstrated progress" on ending the death squads and taking action against past violators. Barnes leapt to his feet, and on a point of order was given permission to add the next sentence in the report: "These conditions should be seriously enforced."

It was a dramatic moment, which implied that Kemp had deviously omitted these words and that only Barnes' provision had an enforcement mechanism, and so was the true embodiment of the Kissinger deal. Barnes had boxed himself into accepting Kissinger's goal of defeating, rather than settling with, the rebels, while arguing that his provision would help Duarte keep the Army in check on human rights. Unfortunately for him, both Kissinger and Duarte were openly advocating passage of Broomfield–Murtha. As a congressional aide says in Cindy Arnson's book, the Dixies and the Republicans knew they were voting to fund a military victory that day.[2] Congressional opposition on El Salvador

1 Cynthia Arnson, *Crossroads: Congress, the President, and Central America, 1976-1993*, Pennsylvania University Press, University Park, PA, 1993, p. 140.
2 Cynthia Arnson, *Crossroads: Congress, the President, and Central America, 1976-1993*, Pennsylvania University Press, University Park, PA, 1993, p. 163.

collapsed after the vote and the conviction of the nuns' murderers in the National Guard (although not their superiors) later in May, which released the 30 percent of previous military aid that Congress had tied to a trial in that case. Nicaragua took center stage and the administration began applying the same sort of pressure to the Dixies on aid to the contras. Aid to El Salvador quadrupled over the next three years along with the size of the Army, as Peter, Paul, and Mary's hyperbolic prediction in their song came true, almost to the exact dollar of annual funding: "They say for half a billion they could do it right; bomb all day and burn all night."

A few members, under the prodding of the Arms Control and Foreign Policy Caucus, kept the flame burning during the Duarte presidency by sponsoring research reports that generated some media coverage and a few modest amendments. First came a 1985 report on aid to El Salvador sponsored by Miller, and moderate Republicans Jim Leach, the Caucus chair, and Senate Appropriations chair Mark Hatfield. The authors evoked a "haunting reminder" of the fraudulent "cheerleading" by US officials in Vietnam as it catalogued cases of the administration's "insufficient, misleading, and even false" statements about attacks on civilians, roles of US military advisers, and AID's use of economic aid for counterinsurgency. Willie Blacklow, Miller's press secretary, offered the report as an "exclusive" to a *New York Times* reporter, with the result being a front page picture of Hatfield and the headline: "Lawmakers say US is Misusing Aid for El Salvador."[1] The rebels wrote a letter to the authors exploring the idea of a cessation of their attacks on the economy during negotiations. For constitutional reasons, the sponsors felt that they had to turn the letter over to the State Department to pursue — which meant the end of the initiative.

The administration was concerned that the spate of follow-up stories — including an editorial cartoon by Conrad in the *Los Angeles Times* that showed a landmine labeled "beach ball," a tank labeled "tractor," and a US soldier labeled "agricultural adviser" — would hamper their efforts to increase economic aid and continue shuttling in short-term military advisers to evade an informal "cap" of 55 personnel. Both the State Department and AID issued vigorous, detailed attacks on the report's examples of misleading information and its analytic reversal of their claimed three-to-one ratio of economic to military aid to a similar ratio of war-related to reform-related aid. Jim Bond, the staffer for Senator Bob Kasten, the chair of the foreign aid subcommittee on Hatfield's Appropriations Committee, prepared a memorandum disputing the report's claims of insufficient consultation with Congress. The *Wall Street Journal* attacked the report in a lead editorial titled "Ghostbusters" that accused Hatfield, Leach, and Miller of raising the false specter of Vietnam. The authors welcomed the attacks for keeping the debate alive, and gleefully sent responses to the media and all congressional offices.

The Caucus tried to rally resistance to the administration's 1986 effort to waive for Central America the "section 660" ban on US aid to police forces, which had been spurred by revelations in the 1970s about AID's police training programs in dictatorships, and particularly by House staffer and future Senator Tom Harkin's discovery of Vietnam's "tiger cage" prisons. The tenor of the administration's request and the Caucus report on it was encapsulated in an exchange between State Department point person Jim Michel and

---

1 February 12, 1985.

Miller staffer Cynthia Arnson in a House briefing.[1] Michel was trying to appeal to liberals, bemoaning the fact that an infamous massacre could not be solved because the ban on police aid kept the investigators from having the necessary forensic skills. Arnson replied that the investigators for that case were in fact from the Special Investigative Unit that Congress had specifically funded to handle high-profile cases: "I was actually there when they raised the bodies from the well. They concluded that the Army did it, but the judges were too scared to pursue the case. The problem is still political will, not technical skill." In keeping with the administration practice when caught out in a lie, Michel did not acknowledge the point and simply continued with his briefing.[2]

Leach, Hatfield, and Miller published a follow-up report on El Salvador in November 1987 titled "Bankrolling Failure," which contrasted the happy predictions in 1984 of US officials describing the progress that could be expected if the Kissinger Commission's aid levels were funded with the severe deterioration that was apparent from Salvadoran and US government data.[3] The report also alleged that the Iran–Contra network used fuel from the Salvadoran Air Force's US-filled tank, which would constitute an illegal transfer of funds, and used airline terrorist and former CIA asset Luis Posada as its local logistics director.[4] As a result, in perhaps the only true act of accountability for the entire Iran–Contra deception, Colonel James Steele, the commander of the US military group, had his promotion to general blocked by Senator Harkin.[5]

---

1 The report accused the administration of already having broken the 660 ban with numerous dubious legal rulings. Arms Control and Foreign Policy Caucus, "Police Aid to Central America: Yesterday's Lessons, Today's Choices," August 13, 1986.

2 The administration was largely successful in its request for an end to the 660 ban, but the problem of political will was never solved. The SIU never became a formal part of the judicial system, which meant that its work in solving the Army's 1988 San Sebastian massacre went unused. It was also blocked by the Army from investigating the Jesuit murders in 1989. See the El Salvador section in Human Rights Watch's "World Report 1990."

3 The Caucus staff unearthed detailed data on combat losses and the use of economic aid in military campaigns from the colorful Army Chief of Staff Adolfo Blandon, who also was eager to provide quotes on forced induction into the armed forces for low-income men trapped at soccer games ("Thank God for your trucks — before we just lassoed them and brought them in.") and the effect of human rights conditions on military behavior ("Though some don't want to admit it, the conditions the US placed on us helped"). Less productive was a meeting with Colonel Lopez-Nuila, the head of the National Police, who was stunned when asked by the researchers how he would change his methods from the time when he headed the Treasury Police during their murder of thousands of political opponents without a single investigation of misconduct. "It is hard to say who was killing whom back in 1981," was his response.

4 Former CIA operative Posada was wanted by Venezuela for escaping from prison before a final verdict could be rendered in his trial for killing 73 civilians by bombing a Cubana flight in 1976.

5 Harkin staffer Ed Long used Harkin's authority to block the promotion, generating a news story that scrolled along the screen during the Superbowl broadcast in 1988 before Long had a chance to tell Harkin about it. The General Accounting Office later found that the fuel had indeed been transferred and that the State Department's internal inquiry spurred by the Caucus report had been weak and cursory. See GAO report NSIAD-89-186, December 1989. Steele later surfaced as a private military training contractor in Iraq during the US occupation.

The US embassy was so enraged at previous Caucus reports that the researchers had to organize their visit through human rights groups, such as Americas Watch and the Salvadoran Archbishop's *Tutela Legal*, or Legal Protection, office.[1] Maria Julia Hernandez was the lead investigator for *Tutela Legal*. She roamed the country, recording the complaints of peasants whose relatives had been taken and killed by armed men, usually from the Army. In a humorous example of the priorities of the American media, a profile of her courageous work that was to run in the Style section of the *Washington Post* in 1987 was spiked to make room for an exclusive interview with a figure in the sex scandal of televangelist Jim Bakker, Rocco Riccobono, *aka* the "Italian stallion."[2] Jemera Rone, the counsel for Americas Watch, was a sort of an alternative US ambassador, fulfilling the traditional duties of embodying American values and assisting visiting delegations.

Rone's tenure in El Salvador was proof of the adage, "Be careful what you ask for; you just might get it." In a rhetorical flourish in about 1984, US ambassador Thomas Pickering said to Americas Watch founder Aryeh Neier, "Come down, open an office here; you'll see we tell the truth." Pickering may have been expecting the typical young human rights researcher, but instead he got a star mergers and acquisitions lawyer who was casting about for a more meaningful job. Rone quickly concluded that, "The US embassy, all they said was lies. I don't know where they got it all."[3] Rone investigated murders and the Salvadoran and US authorities' responses to them, stating her facts in her reports as carefully, and working the press as assiduously, as she had in her previous position, when millions of dollars were riding on her accuracy. Rone's cause was helped in a Latin, male-dominated culture by her striking appearance — tall, beautiful, with shock-red hair. Army officers and judicial and government officials took it as a challenge not to avoid her and her questions, which would have been far smarter for them.[4] US embassy and military personnel could not avoid her calls for another reason: Pickering's invitation. Americas Watch used it to act as if Rone were somehow a guest of the US Embassy and would call the ambassador and the State Department the second there was resistance to her work. What would have taken Congress months of calls and letters to uncover, such as the status of a case in court, Rone could unearth in a minute by calling the right officer in the embassy.[5]

---

1 The researchers were stunned at the vehemence of the refusal to assist and in particular charges of treason leveled by Deputy Chief of Mission David D'Louhy. He had already resisted and insulted someone far more powerful, and he had his promotion to senior rank blocked by Senator Chris Dodd and his legendarily long-memoried staffer Janice O'Connell.

2 Riccobono, who had been unearthed by sexual misconduct investigative reporter Michael Isikoff, claimed to have had an affair with the supposedly virginal Jessica Hahn, who alleged that she had been raped by Bakker, who then paid her $265,000 of church money for her too-brief silence. See Jeffrey Toobin, *A Vast Conspiracy*, Random House, New York, 1999, pp. 29-30.

3 Interview, June 17, 2009.

4 The same phenomenon was true for Tina Rosenberg, who interviewed death squad leaders and assassins in El Salvador and Colombia for her 1991 book *Children of Cain: Violence and the Violent in Latin America*. She reported that they acted as if not meeting her challenge would be a blow to their self-image.

5 Despite her gilded status in San Salvador, out in the war zones of the countryside where she did much of her research Rone was no safer than the typical peasant. Claiming the protection of the embassy or accreditation by the United Nations human rights office was

The 1987 Caucus report generated far less press than the one in 1985. Duarte's reputation as a reformer had curbed the American media's appetite for taking on the Reagan administration in El Salvador. The authors exchanged editorials in the *Washington Post* with warrior-editor Stephen Rosenfeld, but more significantly they laid the groundwork for rebuilding a consensus among soft Eagles: that the policy of pursuing military victory had failed and should be replaced by a policy of promoting a settlement. As a result, in 1988 Hatfield almost won a stunning victory in the Appropriations Committee for placing 50 percent of Salvadoran military aid under "reprogramming" controls that allow foreign policy committees to delay, cut, and even block aid, depending on the prevailing political winds. The Committee was more liberal than the Senate as a whole, and as the ranking Republican Hatfield had great sway. Republican New York Senator Al D'Amato offered his vote in return for a "transportation demonstration" project, meaning a section of New York highway. When Senator Kasten almost went apoplectic on learning this during the mark-up, D'Amato showed why he was such a lovable rascal, saying for all to hear, "I'm an honest politician....Once bought, I stay bought."

Kasten read out a maudlin letter from Salvadoran President Duarte — ostensibly from his deathbed at the US Army's hospital in Washington but actually written by Kasten staffer Jim Bond in his office just down the hall from the meeting — asking that all the aid be approved, as a tribute to his memory. However, enough moderate members lined up behind Hatfield that the final decision came down to the 86-year-old committee chairman, John Stennis of Mississippi, a conservative dinosaur from the Democratic Party's segregationist past. Stennis was quite ill with a disease that had already taken one of his legs and confined him to a wheel-chair, and his mind was cloudy, at best. Hatfield was his best friend and a frequent presence at his bedside when he was in the hospital. At first he voted "aye," giving Hatfield the victory, but the scurry of staff aides to his side made him aware that he had just reversed his 41-year record of supporting every war and every aid package to repressive but cooperative regimes. "Mark," he said plaintively, "what do I want to do?" Hatfield was too much of a gentleman to take advantage of the older man's confusion, and told him that he should vote "no" on the amendment, and it was defeated 15-14.[1]

In 1989 the Bush administration aggressively continued to promote the Reagan policy of military victory. The election in March of ARENA's Alfredo Cristiani to replace Duarte gave Caucus members in both Houses an argument to use to revive the debate about the need for a settlement. In the House Western Hemisphere subcommittee member Peter Kostmayer pushed for a suspension of half of El Salvador's military and cash aid for six months to encourage Cristiani to negotiate. The aid would be held under "reprogramming" requirements. During the mark-up in the House subcommittee, though, Chairman George Crockett suddenly agreed with a Republican amendment to drop Kostmayer's reprogramming provision. He may have been influenced by the announcement by liberal Senators

---

as likely to get you killed as protected at the frequent military roadblocks. As she says in retrospect, "I didn't have a good sense of danger."

1 With the assistance of mercurial Pennsylvania Senator Arlen Specter, Hatfield would have won, but in a classic example of the vagaries of lobbying, a lobbyist in the liberal Jewish advocacy community who might well have been able to deliver him simply forgot to follow through on his assignment.

Dodd and Kerry that they would support unconstrained aid so as to give Cristiani, who they rightly perceived as being in the moderate wing of the proto-fascist ARENA, a chance to show his commitment to peace and human rights.[1]

Crockett's move caught Kostmayer by surprise since he was expecting a challenge to his amendment from the Republicans, not from his own chairman, and he decided not to fight it. Former Caucus chair Matt McHugh, who had cast a crucial vote in 1980 for aid to the Salvadoran army, decided to reverse Crockett's move on the floor. Working with the lobby groups and Miller's El Salvador task force, McHugh achieved a surprisingly strong vote of 185 (62 votes more than a similar but unpromoted amendment by John Conyers had achieved earlier in the year). In the Senate the fight was led by Hatfield, Harkin, and Patrick Leahy.[2] They came up 10 votes shorter than expected on the floor, at 33, because Cristiani had dramatically agreed to meet with the rebels and the defection of Dodd and Kerry gave other liberals some cover.[3] The war would continue. The Soft Eagles and Turkeys were no closer to winning than they had been the day Broomfield and Murtha won House backing for the Kissinger commission's aid package.

NICARAGUA: THE MANUFACTURED WAR

Jimmy Carter and liberals in Congress played a role in the formation of the Contras, in the sense that they responded to the Sandinista military victory over the US-created National Guard in 1979 by making it clear that the composition and actions of the new coalition government were of concern to US national security. Despite accepting Somoza's demise, Carter had tried to keep the Sandinistas from taking power, backing various schemes to force power-sharing and approving CIA aid first to extract Somoza's leadership and then to fund media, unions, and opposition parties who were not allied with the new government.[4] When the soft Eagles finally overrode ferocious Republican and Dixie opposition in 1980 and passed Carter's proposal for a small loan program oriented toward the Nicaraguan private sector, they made it clear that they were promoting general oppo-

---

1   In addition, Cold Warriors in the media were making a major push to keep El Salvador's military effort going, as it became clear that Secretary of State Baker was going to settle the Nicaraguan conflict, first with Congress and then in the region. Columnist Mort Kondracke's March 1989 prediction in the *New Republic* was typical of this perspective. Kondracke said that "we've made a good beginning" and that any cut in aid to El Salvador for the human rights abuses that might follow ARENA's victory would lead to "communist victory."

2   Leahy was not a member of the Caucus, although his staff were ironically the Caucus' most important collaborators in the Senate.

3   Cynthia Arnson, *Crossroads: Congress, the President, and Central America, 1976-1993*, Pennsylvania University Press, University Park, PA, 1993, p. 245. A few solidarity groups had decided not to support Hatfield on the floor — for not cutting enough aid. Prominent among these was Neighbor-to-Neighbor, a San Francisco group that was leading a boycott of Salvadoran coffee. Its lobbyist Shelly Moskowitz showed an admirable level of *chutzpah* by trying to attend a strategy session in Harkin's office with the groups who were supporting the amendment.

4   John Booth, Thomas Walker, *Understanding Central America*, Westview Press, Boulder, CO, 1999, p. 77, and Cynthia Arnson, *Crossroads: Congress, the President, and Central America, 1976-1993*, Pennsylvania University Press, University Park, PA, 1993, p. 75.

sition to the Sandinistas — and specifically the presence of liberal banker Arturo Cruz in the government. Jim Wright, halfway from a Soft to a Hard Eagle, took an intense interest in the matter, portraying US aid as a tool to use in a struggle between "Marxism and freedom." Presidential candidate Ronald Reagan's platform calling "another Cuba" unacceptable was unexceptional, because that was the liberals' assumption as well.[1]

The Soft Eagles had a hard time grasping why they infuriated the new Nicaraguan government as much as the Hard Eagles. Congressional liberals who believed they were trying to help the new government were taken aback by the vehemence with which even their mildest criticism was rejected. They were repeatedly embarrassed and angered when visiting Nicaragua by the government's aggressive descriptions at public events of US imperial history. This nationalist need should have been no surprise. The very name of the ruling party recalled a hero who led an uprising against US occupation in the 1920s, and any implication that the United States had a right to guide Nicaragua's choices was an insult to the nationalist pride of these "Sandinistas." In particular, they were enraged by the Carter administration's insistence that Nicaragua repay debts incurred by Somoza's regime or lose access to international credit. Right-wing Members of Congress railed against what the Sandinistas saw as fully justified expropriations of the properties of American businesses and individuals who were supporters of the Somoza regime.

The lengthy congressional debate that directed most of the new loan to the private sector rather than the government irritated the Sandinistas all the more, and the rumors — true, as it turned out — that CIA money was being distributed to their opponents sent them over the edge. After Reagan's election, the Sandinistas hunkered down, with visions of US-backed invasions in Guatemala in 1954 and at the Bay of Pigs in 1961, and of the CIA-spurred public destabilizations in Chile in the 1970s, dancing their heads. They were not surprised when reports of Argentinean training of Somoza's old officer corps reached them in 1980, or reports of American training camps in 1981.

The Reagan administration seized on Nicaragua's support for its Salvadoran comrades as the basis for the CIA program to arm and train the former National Guardsmen. Carter's loan program had included a Republican amendment that would cut off the loan program if he found that Nicaragua was aiding the Salvadoran rebellion, but he danced around the requirement by certifying that the aid was not significant. Reagan immediately certified that it was, and CIA director William Casey informed the Intelligence Committees that former Guardsmen would be sent into Nicaragua to disrupt the flow of weapons to El Salvador. This fiction was transparent from the start — the much-disputed flow of weapons was of no concern to the Contras, who simply wanted to seize power again.

House Intelligence committee chair Eddie Boland, a respected moderate from Massachusetts who bunked and strategized with Speaker Tip O'Neill, craftily used the disingenuous finding against the administration. Reflecting O'Neill's dictum that "timing is everything," he marched methodically toward his goal of killing the program. In 1982 he defused the prospect of the defeat of a straight-forward cut-off amendment by Tom Harkin by writing into law the administration's own pledge that it was not trying to overthrow the

---

1 Cynthia Arnson, *Crossroads: Congress, the President, and Central America, 1976-1993*, Pennsylvania University Press, University Park, PA, 1993, pp. 47, 49-51.

Nicaraguan government. Then, in July 1983, with the evidence of the Contras' own words as his shield, he and Foreign Affairs committee chair Clem Zablocki used a rare closed session to convince the House to end the Contra program and replace it with an overt plan for interdicting weapons. Jim Wright provided important support for the Boland–Zablocki amendment, and a well-publicized set of US navy maneuvers with Honduras helped Boland make his case that Reagan was on a slippery slope into another Vietnam. George Miller, though, believed that the deciding factor for many Democratic members who did not care much about the issue was that the administration had "lied to Eddie Boland." In a year-ending deal, the House leadership accepted half a loaf on the Contras, or $24 million of the $48 million approved by the Senate, in return for a whole loaf on chemical weapons, or none of the Senate's $106 million.[1]

Boland's victory in the House contained the seeds of the trouble that lay ahead for opponents of Contra aid. The White House managed a nationwide publicity campaign that raised the specter of Soviet domination of the region, and Republicans openly accused Democrats of acting as agents of that domination. Southern Democrats, who had seen their nearly 100 percent control of congressional seats reduced to 70 percent since the passage of Johnson's civil rights legislation, ran from this line of attack. According to Arnson, 41 of the 50 Democrats who opposed Boland were from the former Confederate states. To try to stem this tide, Boland had asked a second-term Dixie from Oklahoma, Dave McCurdy, to write a letter to the House endorsing his amendment.[2] He thought that having someone who won his first race by supporting school prayer and the public display of a statue of Christ would help inoculate him from charges of liberalism. He was right this time, but in elevating McCurdy he was helping create a monster that two years later broke the back of House resistance to Contra aid.

Soft Eagles were at pains to show that their dispute with Reagan was on tactics, not goals. Mike Barnes argued that military intervention was a prescription for disaster, and would only push Nicaragua toward Cuba and the Soviet Union, and then organized an open letter to Nicaraguan president Daniel Ortega castigating his crack-down on the opposition and his connections with Cuba. Liberal stalwart Howard Wolpe agreed with President Reagan that Central America could never host "a base for Soviet operations."[3] In October 1983 the continuing popularity of the US right to block "another Cuba" was confirmed when little public or congressional protest accompanied the US invasion of Grenada during a power struggle within the leftist ruling party. A runway that Cuba was building for Grenada's tourism sector provided part of the pretext for the invasion. When Congress in 1984 enacted a complete ban on funding the Contras — the famous "Boland amendment" that even barred US officials from arranging contributions from others — it did so not from some new recognition that the Contra policy was an immoral intrusion

---

1 The House also dropped its ban on testing anti-satellite weapons. Cynthia Arnson, *Crossroads: Congress, the President, and Central America, 1976-1993*, Pennsylvania University Press, University Park, PA, 1993, pp. 128, 132-136, 145.

2 Cynthia Arnson, *Crossroads: Congress, the President, and Central America, 1976-1993*, Pennsylvania University Press, University Park, PA, 1993, pp. 19, 135.

3 Cynthia Arnson, *Crossroads: Congress, the President, and Central America, 1976-1993*, Pennsylvania University Press, University Park, PA, 1993, pp. 107, 129-130.

on another country's sovereignty, but from a combination of congressional pique and CIA blunders.

January 1984 brought news reports that the Contras had mined Nicaragua's main harbor and bombed its airport. It quickly became clear that the attackers were in fact not Contras, but CIA personnel and contractors. Republican Intelligence committee members were "pissed off" — to quote Senate chairman Barry Goldwater — but not because the attacks constituted acts of war under international law or might cause problems in relations with countries like the Soviet Union and the Netherlands whose ships were damaged.[1] They were angered because they felt that the CIA had slipped the plans for the attack by them, in particular the plan to use CIA personnel. Congressman David Bonior sponsored a resolution condemning the mining, which passed both Houses, giving a hint that the president's request for more aid was in trouble. Casey's deputy director, Robert Gates, sent him a sycophantic note blaming the mix-up on "chicanery and scoundrels on the Committee staffs," and urging him to undercut the complaints by being more transparent with the Committees.[2] The administration redoubled its public campaign for Contra aid, with House Intelligence committee member Dick Cheney presaging his performance as vice president by claiming on the floor that he had seen secret information confirming outlandish administration allegations about the power projection capabilities of the feeble Nicaraguan army. Soviet MiG fighters were frequently, and erroneously, reported to be on their way to Managua.

In October 1984, a CIA training manual for the Contras that encouraged various forms of torture and assassination was exposed, adding to the mood of disgust with the CIA, even among the adherents of Contra aid.[3] Casey's continued minimal mumblings in closed committee sessions did little to calm congressional fears that the CIA was incompetent and rudderless in Nicaragua. At the end of the year conference meeting the House this time held firm for the Boland amendment, and the Senate surrendered the aid it had approved. The Senate did extract a commitment from the House to give Reagan a right to a floor vote on providing $14 million in aid in April 1985, but as a legal matter the program was dead. As a practical matter, Reagan, Casey, Assistant Secretary of State Elliott Abrams, and the National Security Council were just getting warmed up with their secret

---

1 International law was even less of concern. The Arms Control and Foreign Policy Caucus distributed a report titled "Against the Law," which offered 30 US and US-incorporated international laws that the administration appeared to be violating in Central America. No standing committees investigated the charges, just as none challenged the patently illegal decision of State Department legal adviser Abraham Sofaer simply to "withdraw" from a Nicaraguan suit on the mining in the International Court of Justice. By treaty the United States had agreed never to withdraw from a pending case. A State Department official argued to the Caucus at the time that by passing aid to the Contras in the past, Congress had effectively superseded the treaty — a dubious proposition, given that treaties are, under the Constitution, the "supreme" law of the land. The Court found against the United States, but its judgment was ignored. In 1986 Sofaer solved the conundrum for future cases by having the United States formally terminate from the Court's jurisdiction.

2 *Robert M. Gates, From the Shadows: The Ultimate Insider's Account of Five Presidents and How They Won the Cold War*, Simon & Schuster, New York, 2007, p. 309.

3 Tim Weiner, "CIA Taught, then Dropped, Mental Torture in Latin America," *New York Times*, January 29, 1997.

efforts to coordinate aid from such diverse dictatorships as Saudi Arabia, Brunei, Honduras, and even, through surcharges for illegal US arms, Iran.

Political scientists and Members of Congress agree: when a president really wants something in foreign policy, and wants it more than anything else, he can usually get it. It may take a while, and he may have to ignore other initiatives while he expends a tremendous amount of time on the effort, molding congressional opinion and buying congressional votes, but he will succeed. The period from the legal end of Contra aid in December 1984 to the House vote in June 1986 providing $100 million in military aid is a classic case in point.[1] To entice the swing Dixies, President Reagan conducted a nearly non-stop barrage of speeches and meetings in which he announced supposedly major reforms of the Contra leadership and US negotiating strategies. At the same time, Reagan's aides coordinated bitter attacks on the Dixies in their districts for abetting the "Soviet–Cuban connection" in Central America or ignoring Nicaragua's alleged mistreatment of Jews.

Most importantly, the Dixies were offered the locally-important bureaucratic favors that only presidents can deliver, and northern Republican swings lost those favors just as their House leaders were threatening their seniority and appropriations. One by one the Dixies were blessed with an Oval Office meeting with Reagan, who would make his pitch and then send them into the next room to take up their local needs with cabinet members like Agriculture Secretary John Block. The North Carolina Democratic delegation waited happily for each of the many rounds of Contra aid votes so it could put itself in the middle of a bidding war of tobacco subsidies between Reagan and Tip O'Neill, which Reagan, of course, usually won.

The House decided by just two votes in April 1985 to limit the administration's $14 million request to resettlement aid. This vote was the first test of Reagan's campaign to portray the Contras as "freedom fighters" and the "moral equal of our Founding Fathers." Staff at the Arms Control and Foreign Policy Caucus interviewed Contra defector Edgar Chamorro and produced a report just prior to the vote called "Who Are the Contras?" that identified 46 of the 48 top military posts as being held by former National Guardsmen. This claim — and the great Spanish *noms de guerre* like *El Toro* (the bull), *El Invisible* (the invisible one), and *El Bestia* (the beast) that were revealed for the leaders — got wide play in the press and in the floor debate.[2] After the apparent Democratic win, Republicans who wanted to continue the war and liberal Democrats who feared the result of a conference with the Senate voted to defeat the overall bill that included the resettlement aid.

---

1 The legislative moves and counter-moves on Contra aid from 1985 to 1989 are staggeringly complex and overlaid with multiple possible interpretations. A good chronology of the many floor votes is provided in William LeoGrande, "The Controversy over Contra Aid, 1981-1990: A Historical Narrative," in Richard Sobel, editor, *Public Opinion in US Foreign Policy: the Controversy over Contra Aid*, Rowman and Littlefield, Lanham, MD, 1993.

2 Arms Control and Foreign Policy Caucus, "Who Are the Contras: An Analysis of the Makeup of the Military Leadership of the Rebel Forces, and of the Nature of the Private American Groups Providing them Financial and Material Support," April 18, 1985. The administration's response was a study by the State Department claiming that only half of the senior political and military positions were held by former *Somocistas* — itself not exactly a description of "Founding Fathers."

A number of Dixies, flummoxed by this surprise move and angered by a trip Nicaraguan president Daniel Ortega took to Moscow after the vote, coalesced around a proposal by Dave McCurdy to have another vote in June on a $27 million aid package that would keep the Contras alive as a bargaining chip and force more political openness in Nicaragua.[1] More than 30 Dixies and moderate Republicans switched their votes and passed McCurdy's amendment, as offered and modified by Republican leader Bob Michel. McCurdy's package included only "humanitarian" aid — meaning every logistical need of the Contras except ammunition and weapons, which news articles at the time by Joanne Omang of the *Washington Post* and Bob Parry of the Associated Press revealed were being delivered from other sources, through the coordination of Oliver North of the National Security Council.[2] The urgency with which the administration sought, and received, the weakening of an amendment by Senator Pell that constrained US promotion of aid from other sources made it clear even to McCurdy's supporters that the Contras would use his aid not just to stay alive, but to keep on fighting.[3]

Having gotten its bridge from McCurdy, the administration soon tossed him over the side of it. Despite the promise of Secretary of State George Schultz that the aid would help a new civilian leadership negotiate with the Sandinistas, the administration told the mili-

---

1 This concern with a foreign leader's travel plans recalls the outrage of US diplomats in 1962 when President Ben Bella's first trip after victory in the Algerian revolution was to thank his long-time military backer, Castro's Cuba. McCurdy was advised in this effort by a self-styled "gang of four" nominal Democrats — an ironic but perhaps telling reference to the leaders of the murderous Cultural Revolution who tried, and failed, to seize power after the death of Chairman Mao. Indeed, two of the gang called themselves former Marxists and anti-imperialists who had come to see American intervention abroad as a force for good: author Robert Leiken, who had created a Washington buzz with his 1984 description in the neo-conservative *New Republic* of tough Sandinista electoral tactics, and human rights lobbyist Bruce Cameron, whose off-again, on-again positions on the Contras followed those of his hoped-for Nicaraguan savior, Arturo Cruz. The other two were longtime Scoop Jackson hawk Penn Kemble and recent convert Bernard Aronson. They wrote speeches for McCurdy, drafted moderate letters for Reagan to sign in return for Dixie votes on Contra aid, and even wrote a military strategy titled "How to Build a Proxy Force into a National Liberation Movement." Superb detail on and tortured justification for their role can be found in Cameron's book, *My Life in the Time of the Contras*, University of New Mexico Press, Albuquerque, 2007.
2 Congressmen Mike Barnes and Lee Hamilton wrote to and Barnes met with North's boss, National Security Advisor Robert McFarlane about these press reports, and he denied them, leading to his eventual conviction in the Iran-Contra affair.
3 Bruce Cameron, *My Life in the Time of the Contras*, University of New Mexico Press, Albuquerque, 2007, pp. 64-67. Reagan's intense campaign had a spillover effect favoring a general toughness in foreign policy. When the annual foreign aid authorization came to the House floor a few weeks after the approval of McCurdy's $27 million, it led to a piling on of votes to aid "Contras" in Afghanistan, Angola, and Cambodia that journalist Stephen Rosenfeld labeled "The Guns of July" in a play on the title of Barbara Tuchman's history of the reckless posturing that started World War I. See "The Reagan Doctrine: The Guns of July," *Foreign Affairs*, Spring 1986. A Hard Eagle whose views were reflected in Washington Post editorials, Rosenfeld probably did not intend the title to be derogatory. As of 2010 this militant bill, passed by a coalition of Republicans and Dixies with most of its traditional liberal supporters opposing it, was the last foreign aid authorization ever enacted.

tary leaders to keep pursuing a military victory.[1] In 1986 the administration asked for $100 million, largely in military aid, to step up the war. Again it started its round of publicity about reforming the Contras, and again the Caucus gained its own publicity for reports casting doubt on these claims.[2] McCurdy signed on to a deal with Dave Bonior, who had been appointed by the Democratic leadership to lead the whip group on the Contras that would provide a lesser amount of logistical aid with the intent of keeping the Contras alive in their Honduran bases to spur negotiations. The administration sandbagged Mc-Curdy in April by using another parliamentary trick to derail his victory, and then by June had weaned away enough of his supporters to win a 221–209 vote for all of its aid.[3]

Bonior was in a dicey situation throughout this period, having to give McCurdy enough to keep him from going over to Reagan completely but not giving him so much that the more liberal Democratic caucus wouldn't revolt. He was successful, but he and his staff incurred the wrath of many of the lobby groups and the left flank of the Democratic Caucus, who believed strongly that dancing with the devil in the form of some support to the Contras was a prescription for losing the entire debate.[4] Day after day, meeting after meeting, he made the case to the dozens of members in his liberal whip group that losing McCurdy would lead to a far more devastating war. He kept his charges on task with assignments both to become expert and speak out on particular aspects of the Contra policy and to whip their closest friends among the wavering Dixies, and he looked to the future, forming Pax Americas, which gave money and celebrity support to congressional candidates who might displace Contra supporters.[5] In the end, the administration simply wore down the swings with its repeated attacks and enticements. Bonior was the better strategist, but he could not match the power of the president. As with El Salvador, the Hard Eagles won, and the Soft Eagles and Turkeys lost.

---

1 Cynthia Arnson, *Crossroads: Congress, the President, and Central America, 1976-1993*, Pennsylvania University Press, University Park, PA, 1993, pp. 203-204.

2 "The Contra High Command," March 1986; "Contra 'Reforms': Are the Miami Agreements Significant?", June 18, 1986.

3 McCurdy later became chair of the both the Intelligence Committee and the neo-conservative Democratic Leadership Council. He was removed from the Intelligence chair after urging President Clinton to pick him, and not Les Aspin, as Defense Secretary, to keep leftist congressman Ron Dellums from replacing Aspin as chair of the Armed Services committee. See "Oklahoman who Opposed Foley to Lose Intelligence Post," *New York Times*, January 23, 1993. McCurdy lost a Senate race in Oklahoma and later served as the head of industry groups like the Electronics Industry Alliance.

4 For example, the Arms Control and Foreign Policy Caucus helped Congressman Ed Markey oppose the McCurdy proposal by sending around to the House a series of photographs of cargo aircraft that could be provided to the Contras under it, titled "Humanitarian Aircraft."

5 One such candidate was Louise Slaughter, who as mentioned previously won a seat in Rochester with the door-to-door campaigning of actor Richard Gere.

CHAPTER 5. THE RESCUE OF CENTRAL AMERICA BY TURKEYS AND SOFT EAGLES

After the election of a liberal president in El Salvador in 1984 led Congress to vote a massive aid increase in search of a military victory, Congressman George Miller met with the staff of the Central American task force he chaired for the Arms Control and Foreign Policy Caucus to discuss legislative strategy. "We just have to wait for some bodies to turn up," he said with grim humor, suspecting with good reason that they would, because the Salvadoran Army was its own power, independent of the charming civilian. The bodies did turn up, in the tens of thousands, and when eight of them caught the public's attention in the Jesuit slayings of 1989, the groups and Members who had kept the flame burning on El Salvador with reports, meetings, publicity, lobbying, and amendments were in a position to take advantage of it and quickly achieve a majority favoring an aid cut-off and an end to the war. The same was true in Nicaragua after a cargo "kicker" named Eugene Hasenfus from the Ollie North network fell out of the sky, leading to the Iran–Contra revelations, a cut in aid to the Contras, and a peace settlement. Good generals make their own luck, said Buonaparte, and both wars ended faster, saving thousands of lives and building a sounder peace, because advocacy groups and their allies in Congress persevered in the darkest days and were ready to strike when the bodies turned up.

This conclusion is not universally shared. At a reception in 1990 the State Department's desk officer for El Salvador and the neo-conservative writer Joshua Muravchik expressed amazement at the assertion, which seemed self-evident to Soft Eagles in Congress and Turkeys in the advocacy groups, that the recent progress toward a settlement of the war in El Salvador that would purge the Army and bring the rebels into the police force had resulted from the aid cuts. The assertion obviously vindicated the liberal strategy throughout the 1980s of cutting aid to the Salvadoran army so that it would accept the fact that a military victory was impossible. These armchair warriors believed quite the opposite, namely that progress toward the settlement of the war was the result of the massive US expansion of the army, achieved over the strenuous protests of the liberals, which had forced the rebels to renounce military victory and make a deal.

This dispute about the causes of the Salvadoran settlement has, if anything, hardened over time. Former Assistant Secretary of State for Latin America Elliott Abrams responded to the UN Truth Commission's listing of army massacres whose existence he belittled while in office by saying: "The [Reagan] Administration's record on El Salvador is one of fabulous achievement."[1] This assessment has been ratified by Pentagon analysts, who argue that: "The primary objective of keeping El Salvador from becoming a communist state was realized."[2] In contrast, Jemera Rone, the Americas Watch counsel in El Salvador during the civil war, was nearly rendered speechless when informed of such conclusions in 2009. The same debate has taken place over Nicaragua. Those who opposed the Contra war tend to believe that it was settled because the aid cut-off after Iran–Contra ended the Contras' hope of military victory, and that an earlier aid cut-off would have achieved much the same result. Those who supported the war say that it was the US aid that helped the Contras force the Sandinistas to open up the political process and hold a fair election.[3] The review in this chapter of how both wars ended resolves the dispute largely in favor of the Soft Eagles and Turkeys. Without them, the wars in Central America might well still be blazing 20 years later, as is the case in Colombia.

EL SALVADOR: THE JESUITS CASE AND THE END OF THE WAR

Most people fantasize about being able to say to a bully or a cheater, "You've picked on the wrong person" — and then make the boast come true. In both his life and his death, Father Ignacio Ellacuría played that role to perfection with the Salvadoran Army and the oligarchs it maintained. Alive, he pushed the Salvadoran polity toward the settlement that the Army feared; when the Army killed him, it set in motion an inexorable movement toward that very settlement. Ellacuría's intellect and tenacity made him a rising star in a group full of people who had both those qualities: the Catholic Church's Society of Jesus, or Jesuit priests. Having come to El Salvador from the Basque region of Spain as a teenaged Jesuit, he had been there for 30 years when the civil war erupted in 1980 and was known

---

1   David Corn, "Elliott Abrams: It's Back," *The Nation*, June 14, 2001, Cynthia Arnson, *Crossroads: Congress, the President, and Central America, 1976-1993*, Pennsylvania University Press, University Park, PA, 1993, p. 290. The report itself if available in English on the website of Human Rights Watch, http://www.hrw.org/reports/pdfs/e/elsalvdr/elsalv938.pdf.

2   James S. Corum, "The Air War in El Salvador," *Air Power Journal*, Summer, 1998. http://www.au.af.mil/au/cadre/aspj/airchronicles/apj/apj98/sum98/corum.html.

3   In interviews in June 2009 Cindy Buhl, who served as coordinator of the Central America Lobby Group, and Kathleen Gillie, who was one of Congressman David Bonior's strategists, affirmed as obvious the hypothesis that the groups and the liberals helped end the war. A contrary opinion is implied in the title of a chapter, "The Limits of Lobbying: Interest Groups, Congress, and Aid to the Contras," by Cynthia Arnson and American University professor Philip Brenner in Richard Sobel, editor, *Public Opinion in US Foreign Policy: The Controversy over Contra Aid*, Rowman and Littlefield, Lanham, Maryland, 1993. However, the chapter itself largely describes the lobbying and offers no systematic analysis that would demonstrate the limits of its impact.

throughout the country for his role in founding and eventually leading the University of Central America.[1]

Ellacuría was recognized in El Salvador as a key intermediary in the beginning of formal peace talks between the government and the FMLN rebels in September 1989. The rebels unilaterally suspended economic sabotage and agreed to talks aimed at purging the military so that they could take part in elections, but the Army showed its independence from Cristiani by responding with increased combat activity. When someone, and of course the Army and its death squad allies were the prime suspects, bombed a union building at the end of October, the FMLN withdrew from the talks. Cristiani asked Ellacuría to serve on a commission investigating the bombing, but before he could start that task the FMLN launched a major offensive on November 11 that succeeded in seizing a number of the poorer areas of San Salvador. The High Command of the Army, led by Air Force General Rafael Bustillo and Chief of Staff Colonel René Emilio Ponce, decided to bomb the rebel-held areas, which drove out both the rebels and 50,000 refugees, and to kill Father Ellacuría.[2]

The Bush administration had been arguing for a few months before the offensive that the current class, or *tanda*, from the Salvadoran military academy that had ascended to leadership was composed of a new breed of US-trained officers who understood the importance of respecting human rights and confronting corruption. This class was known as the *Tandona*, meaning "big class," because of its unusual size. Obviously, the American medicine didn't take, since the *Tandona* gave the orders to eliminate Ellacuría, and the top US-trained and formed brigade, the *Atlacatl*, was selected for the task, which was carried out on November 16. Just days before, US Army special forces had been training the brigade in night operations and weaponry. Congress only found out about that training because the press reported during the week or so of urban combat that the training team was trapped by rebels for a few days in the hotel where they were staying. In response to congressional complaints that the "Green Berets" were not included in the limit of 55 US military personnel the administration claimed it was observing, the Pentagon argued that such training by mobile teams was primarily considered training not for the Salvadorans, but training for the teams in "how to train." The massacre and the bizarre rationale for violating the 55-man cap confirmed for congressional critics their main claims about administration policy in El Salvador — that the Army was not "reforming" under US tutelage and that the administration was misleading Congress on US aid.[3]

Ellacuría had gathered five of his top administrators and professors to stay near him for their safety, so the Army also killed them and a cook and her daughter so as to leave no witnesses. As with many of its murders, the Army tried to blame the FMLN, using a cap-

1 Ellacuría was also well known in Congress. He spoke twice at strategy sessions for members of the Arms Control and Foreign Policy Caucus.

2 Tom Barry, *Central America Inside Out*, Grove/Atlantic, New York, 1991, pp. 156-158. See also the definitive account of the Jesuit case, Teresa Whitfield: *Paying the Price: Ignacio Ellacuría and the Murdered Jesuits of El Salvador*, Temple University Press, Philadelphia, 1994, the various reports of the House Democratic ("Moakley") task force, and the Truth Commission's report.

3 Cynthia Arnson, *Crossroads: Congress, the President, and Central America, 1976-1993*, Pennsylvania University Press, University Park, PA, 1993, p. 249.

tured AK-47 and scrawling FMLN slogans as it left, and US Ambassador William Walker stoked this perception for a few days as well, but the deceptions quickly unraveled under the glare of international visitors and press. The bodies that George Miller had predicted would embolden Congress to challenge administration policy had indeed finally turned up. It would be up to two determined Catholics, Congressman Joe Moakley and Father Paul Tipton, the president of the Association of Jesuit Colleges and Universities (of which the UCA was an affiliate), to use the case to turn Ellacuría's dream of a settlement into a reality.

Moakley, the avuncular but iron-willed chairman of the Rules committee, had become an unlikely expert on El Salvador because of his work on behalf of the refugees who were flooding his Boston district. Moakley quickly offered an amendment withholding some aid until the murders were investigated, on which he improved Matt McHugh's 185 votes earlier that year to 194 in defeat, and was appointed by Speaker Tom Foley to chair a Democratic task force to investigate the murders. Cindy Buhl of the Central America Working Group and staff director Vic Johnson of the House Western Hemisphere subcommittee both describe the choice of Moakley as brilliant. Johnson was irritated at first with yet another of many usurpations of his subcommittee's jurisdiction, but soon saw that Moakley would be believed and followed in his conclusions from the investigation in a way that policy-oriented Members who already had a profile on the issues would not be. Buhl focused on the leadership's comfort level with an old and careful hand: "The Speaker trusted Moakley politically...not to lead the leadership out on a limb."[1]

In running the investigation, Moakley relied heavily on his long-time staffer and alter ego Jim McGovern and on McGovern's friend and confidant Bill Woodward of Gerry Studds' staff. Indeed, it was Woodward who had originally suggested the idea of a task force to handle the investigation.[2] It was a testament to the ineffectiveness on Central America of the lead committees on foreign policy that the initiative that ended the war was coordinated by staff who were from the Rules committee (McGovern) and the committee on Merchant Marine and Fisheries (Woodward). Foreign Affairs committee chair Dante Fascell was a Dixie on El Salvador, as he had revealed in the Broomfield–Murtha vote of 1984. The Western Hemisphere subcommittee of his committee had been bludgeoned into weakness by Barnes' continual losses on the House floor even before he made an unsuccessful run for the Democratic nomination for the Senate in Maryland in 1986 and was replaced by lethargic George Crockett. David Obey's Foreign Operations subcommittee of the Appropriations committee suffered from the Obey problem. Personally and jurisdictionally prickly, Chairman Obey refused to open up his deliberations to other Members and groups, and so could not build coalitions on Central America when he needed them.

The gregarious, rambling McGovern and the saturnine Woodward were an unlikely pair. McGovern would greet all callers with "How ah ya" in his broad Massachusetts brogue. In contrast, Woodward would sit quietly in a meeting, looking a bit like a wispy Beat poet in a black shirt and black tie, before offering a short and sardonic take on the

---

1 Interview with Vic Johnson, July 22, 2009, and Cindy Buhl, draft paper for presentation at a 1991 conference, unpublished.
2 Interview with Bill Woodward, September 29, 2009.

absurdity of the situation. Both went on to bigger if not better things, McGovern as a congressman and Woodward as a top aide to and author with Secretary of State Madeleine Albright. They were joined on the first staff trip to the murder site by Vic Johnson, who had important contacts and expertise in El Salvador, and Mike O'Neil, Speaker Foley's representative and the former Intelligence committee counsel. These four staff helped Moakley transform his technical investigation of a crime into a reversal of a policy. They were guided through the underworld of the Army and the death squads by Leonel Gómez, an unlikely upper-class Salvadoran land reformer who had fled to Washington to escape assassination.

Moakley had the power of the Rules committee and indeed of the House leadership behind him, and he used it. He set his own agenda for his equal branch of government and simply ignored or overrode the Bush administration's many attempts to disrupt the investigation. At one critical stage Defense Secretary Dick Cheney denied the task force an interview with a US Army major who had revealed conversations with a Salvadoran officer who had told him, accurately, that the High Command had given the order for the massacre. Moakley got his old House colleague Cheney on the phone and roared at him: "Dick, you cut out this [expletive] and get him down here now, or the next time you want the Rules committee to report out the Defense bill, you are [expletive]....[expletive]!" Cheney caved in, and the major came for the interview.

In February 1990 Moakley took a delegation of Members, including a few Republicans who were not formally part of the task force, to El Salvador, where they met with the High Command. It was a surreal session, given that the High Command had ordered the killings and now had to pretend that they were vigorously pursuing the investigation of the supposedly renegade battalion that had carried them out. This was the first time that most of the Members had been exposed to officers who believed both that they were beyond civilian control and that anyone who criticized them was a communist worthy of death. What experts on Latin America had been trying to explain to Congress for years — that the armed forces were not comparable to the US armed forces that Members knew and respected — came through loud and clear. The Salvadoran officers simply could not contain themselves in their disgust for the Jesuits as dupes of the FMLN, and assumed that these reasonable Members of Congress agreed, given the US aid that had been approved despite the tens of thousands of murders they committed, facilitated, or left uninvestigated — from Archbishop Romero and the nuns in 1980 through the death squads and the El Mozote massacre in 1981 and the Las Hojas massacre in 1983 to human rights commissioner Herbert Anaya in 1987 and the San Sebastian massacre in 1988.[1]

Far from showing the remorse or horror that the Members expected, some in the High Command forcefully expressed the attitude, as if among understanding men of the world, that the meddling Jesuits were communists who had got what they deserved. It was clear that the investigation was going nowhere and that's what the High Command wanted. According to McGovern, when the members of Moakley's task force came out of that first

---

1 This was not an isolated incident. Teresa Whitfield recounts other portrayal of the Jesuits as "communists" who "needed killing" that shocked congressional staff and other Americans. *Paying the Price: Ignacio Ellacuría and the Murdered Jesuits of El Salvador*, Temple University Press, Philadelphia, 1994, pp. 271-272.

meeting with the High Command, one of them turned to him and said, "[Expletive], Joe, you were right all these years — these people are [expletive] crazy, they're killers." According to other members, the performance had been perceived as "insulting" and Ambassador William Walker had been perceived as "lying."[1] The crucially enlightened member, though, was not on the trip: Jack Murtha, the hawk of hawks who had sponsored the Kissinger Commission amendment back in 1984 and supported aid to the Salvadoran Army ever since. As a Catholic who respected the Jesuits and as someone who had his own long-standing relationships with key members of the *Tandona*, Murtha felt betrayed by the obvious roadblocks that Moakley was telling him were being thrown in the way of the investigation. "These guys lied to me," said Moakley. "Yeah, they lied to me too," replied Murtha.[2] That was when Moakley knew he would be able to win a vote in the House.

The first report of Moakley's task force was a caustic critique of the "virtual standstill" in the investigation and the inability or failure of investigators to explore whether superior offices had ordered the operation. In the new, post-Cold War context, in which the cry of communism and Soviet domination no longer resonated in Washington, the report sealed the fate of the *Tandona* when it was released on April 30, 1990, three weeks before a vote on a Moakley–Murtha amendment. The amendment was patterned on a proposal by a suddenly reconverted Senator Dodd that proposed cutting military aid in half and making the other half contingent on the government's progress in the Jesuits' case and in negotiations to end the war. In a creative twist dreamed up by Dodd staffer Bob Dockery, all the withheld aid would be released if the FMLN tried to win the war during the negotiations. The administration, which had sent Assistant Secretary of State Bernard Aronson to testify that "the armed forces have cooperated fully" and that one unit's atrocity should not reflect on the whole Army, had suddenly lost credibility and control over the debate.[3]

The other Catholic who made a major contribution to turning the tide in El Salvador was Father Paul Tipton, a bombastic Jesuit priest whose inherent and well-displayed social conservatism set him apart from the church leaders who usually lobbied Congress on Central America. A son of the South, Father Tipton had for 17 years been president of Spring Hill, a Jesuit college in Mobile, Alabama. He had recently come to Washington to become president of the association of all 28 American Jesuit colleges and universities, which supported the UCA as a sister institution. Tipton became a whirlwind of action, taking it as a personal mission to rally the potent Jesuit network in America first to punish the Salvadoran Army for the murder of his brothers and their staff, and then perhaps to get lucky and have that punishment lead to the peace that the murdered Jesuits had been promoting for so long.

Before Tipton could even turn to thinking through what policies he should promote, he had to deal with a crisis within the crisis — the administration's attempt to discredit the testimony of the Jesuits' housekeeper, Lucia Cerna, who at a time when the administration and the Salvadoran Army were still trying to point the finger at the FMLN for

1 Teresa Whitfield, *Paying the Price: Ignacio Ellacuría and the Murdered Jesuits of El Salvador*, Temple University Press, Philadelphia, 1994, pp. 167-168.
2 Interview with Jim McGovern, October 2, 2009.
3 Cynthia Arnson, *Crossroads: Congress, the President, and Central America, 1976-1993*, Pennsylvania University Press, University Park, PA, 1993, p. 253.

the murders was the only witness to have seen soldiers on the campus at the time of the murders. After giving her testimony under the protection of the Spanish embassy and rightfully fearing for her life, Cerna was escorted under French protection to Miami, only to be held in custody and browbeaten for eight days by US and Salvadoran interrogators until, fearing deportation to El Salvador, she recanted her testimony.[1] She was finally re-leased to Tipton, who hid her away in his home in Alabama until Moakley needed her. He then turned his formidable anger on the administration, including, by chance, Republican Party Chairman Lee Atwater, his seatmate on the flight back to Washington.

The vehemence of Tipton's lobbying seemed to arise as much from the administration's treatment of Cerna as from the murder of the Jesuits. He distributed a letter in which he accused Ambassador Walker of a "shocking betrayal" of his duties and American values in trying to discredit Cerna, setting the tone for what became a bitter conflict between Jesuit colleges and the administration. By losing Tipton so early in the investigation, the administration had entered a public relations war they could not win. He arranged for 4,000 American colleges to sign a letter condemning the murders, and then followed up by turning the presidents of major Catholic universities like Georgetown, Boston College, and Gonzaga loose on the administration and, more importantly, the press and Congress. Coming fresh to the debate on El Salvador, Tipton did not worry about the ins and outs of previous approaches or the wording of conditions. He simply decided that there had to be a price paid for the murders, the cover-up, and Cerna's treatment, and he roamed the halls of Congress, buttonholing all the Members to whom his association's members gave him access and pressing them to commit to supporting whatever Moakley proposed.[2]

To complement Moakley's work, Democrat Howard Berman used his position as the new chair of the Arms Control and Foreign Policy Caucus to start an investigation of the *Tandona*. Caucus staff, working with Lise Hartman in Berman's office and Julie McGregor in Hatfield's, identified the 15 officers who made up the High Command, 12 of whom were from the *Tandona*, and requested from the US Defense Intelligence Agency a list of their assignments during their careers, as reported by successive US defense attachés. Caucus staff also scoured contacts in El Salvador to find human rights abuses that occurred dur-ing those deployments. The Pentagon initially sent a form letter refusing to provide the listings. Berman was not a senior Member of Congress like Moakley, but he was legendary for tenacity and retribution as part of the "Waxman–Berman machine" through which he, his political consultant brother Michael, and Congressman Henry Waxman dominated California politics. He fired back an angry letter, saying "surely this is a joke" and "this borders on the flippant," went off to talk to higher-ranking Members, and somehow soon got his post-by post listing of the career assignments.

1 Teresa Whitfield: *Paying the Price: Ignacio Ellacuría and the Murdered Jesuits of El Salvador*, Temple University Press, Philadelphia, 1994, pp. 86-88.
2 Teresa Whitfield: *Paying the Price: Ignacio Ellacuría and the Murdered Jesuits of El Salvador*, Temple University Press, Philadelphia, 1994, p. 168. Tipton also worked with the staff of the Caucus and Senators Hatfield and Kasten on a successful act of atonement for the American role in the slaughter of the Jesuits: an appropriation to pay off the UCA's $10 million building debt to a US-backed regional aid agency.

Caucus staff visited El Salvador, where Maria Julia Hernandez gave them access to *Tu-tela Legal*'s files of complaints of human rights abuses, which were easily matched up with the dates from the Pentagon's records of the High Command's earlier assignments.[1] In the early 1980s peasants were scared to report abuses for fear of another massacre in retribution, so the entries were anonymous, general, and obscure, on the order of, "A peasant told a visiting investigator that the military came through and took three men from the village, who never returned." As the war and the killing dragged on, peasants became either bolder or more fatalistic, traveling to San Salvador to see the near-mythical Maria Julia and describe in great detail the designation of the Army unit, the commander's name, the names of the victims, and the requests they had made to the Army for information on their whereabouts. A surprising source of information was Colonel Milton Menjivar, Steele's successor as commander of the US military group. Menjivar's assistance reflected a split among US officials about how to respond to the Jesuit killings. Some wanted to hunker down and support the *Tandona*, but Menjivar saw them as corrupt and incompetent, and wanted to discredit them and move them out.[2]

The Caucus report on the High Command, "Barriers to Reform," authored by Berman, Hatfield, and Miller, was released at a press conference the day before the May 22 House vote on the Moakley–Murtha amendment. It included a detailed listing of killings of non-combatants, torture, and disappearances under the command of these supposed reformists, and concluded: "14 of the 15 officers in El Salvador's primary commands have risen to their positions despite having had documented abuses of human rights carried out by troops under their command...In *none* of the over 50 cases listed have even junior officers been brought to trial, even though nearly every case would seem to point to officers either ordering the abuse, concealing it, or failing to investigate it." The press and Members were hungry for simple numbers that made a case, and "14 of 15" was in great use in the news and on the floor the next day. Reflecting its own confusion, the administration never undertook its usual tactic of disputing the report. A Salvadoran newspaper ran the Caucus report as a front page story titled "*Obstaculos a la Reforma*," and included pictures of the officers who were accused of condoning human rights abuses. The story was the first public challenge to the *Tandona*'s inevitability. The newspaper office was bombed and burned to

---

1 The staff also reviewed transcripts from the CIA's Foreign Broadcast Information Service and military records previously dislodged with Freedom of Information Act requests by the private National Security Archive, and interviewed experts on the Salvadoran armed forces like journalist Joel Millman, who had just published a devastating portrayal of the *Tandona*'s financial corruption in "El Salvador's Army: A Force Unto Itself," *New York Times Magazine*, December 10, 1989. The research trip itself was sponsored by a human rights group in Houston, the Rothko Chapel, and its founder, Dominique de Menil. The Chapel's focus on El Salvador came from board member Frances Tarlton ("Sissy") Farenthold, a legendary "reform" Democrat in Texas.

2 The Salvadoran army was also confused about its future during Moakley's initial investigation. Some offices were ready to jettison the *Tandona*, but most of the battalion commanders were holding firm. In March 1990 Colonel Colorado tried to disrupt the informal cease-fire that Cristiani had established as a prelude to negotiations, by sending his war-painted battalion across the Rio Torola into rebel territory during a ceremony at which FMLN supporters who had returned from Honduras where naming their camp after one of the murdered Jesuits. Cristiani's control over his Army was becoming less and less evident to Congress.

the ground, but the message lingered on, and the negotiations were largely about the purging of the armed forces to guarantee the rebels' safety in taking part in politics.

Moakley's amendment won in a landslide with 250 votes, with most Dixies and even 31 Republicans supporting it. Murtha was probably the person the most responsible for the addition of 60 votes since the McHugh and Moakley amendments in 1989. He first demanded that only he and Moakley speak for the amendment so as not to scare off the Dixies with liberal rhetoric and speakers. Then he used his considerable clout as the top defense appropriator to gain commitments. When a Dixie asked him if he was going to "close debate," meaning deliver the final speech, Murtha replied: "I don't close debate. I close military bases. Are you with me or not?" In a turnabout of the Republican tactic that so enraged him when it was used against him on Contra aid in 1985, Dixie Dave McCurdy, who had been on the task force but opposed the Moakley–Murtha provision, then organized a coalition of Dixies to join with Republicans in voting down the entire foreign aid bill.[1] The die, though, was cast. The administration quickly resolved its internal debate and began pushing the *Tandona* out as fast as it could in an effort to salvage future military aid. In contrast, war-like to the bitter end, the *Washington Post* bemoaned the Moakley–Murtha victory for emboldening the rebels and spurring the Army to remove its restraints. George Miller respond a few days later with a piece recounting the Army's history of slaughter up to the murder of the Jesuits, and asking "what restraints?"

The *Tandona* and the rest of the Army leadership realized that funding would be cut in the appropriation later in the year and began preparing their financial futures in exile as the UN-sponsored peace negotiations moved forward. The Senate ratified the House action, with a stunning 74–25 victory for Dodd's amendment, now cosponsored by chair Pat Leahy of the foreign operations subcommittee. A conversation on the floor between two Southern Democrats during the vote on an amendment by John McCain to waive the Dodd–Leahy aid cuts if the rebels did not agree to a cease-fire showed how the murder of the Jesuits had become the most important factor in the voting. Bennett Johnston of Louisiana asked Jim Sasser of Tennessee: "How did you vote?" Sasser replied: "I voted no. When they killed those priests, that was it for me." Johnston reversed his long-time support for aid to the Salvadoran Army and voted to defeat McCain's amendment. Murtha went to El Salvador in January 1991 to tell Ponce that as a long-time friend of the Army he wanted it clear that the authors of the murders "had to be found."[2] Ironically, it would turn out that by talking to Ponce he had already found one of the authors. Ponce's revealing claim in the meeting with Murtha that the Army should be applauded because "we allow there to be elections" was all it took for Murtha to realize that there was no hope for the *Tandona*, and he told McGovern, who was staffing the trip, to take them straight to the airport.[3]

---

1 Robert Pear, "House Moves to Free Nicaragua and Panama Aid," *New York Times*, May 24, 1990. The amendment was originally intended to be "Moakley-McCurdy," but Moakley went to Murtha after McCurdy insisted on weakening it. Interview with Jim McGovern, October 2, 2009.

2 Cynthia Arnson, *Crossroads: Congress, the President, and Central America, 1976-1993*, Pennsylvania University Press, University Park, PA, 1993, p. 258.

3 Interview with Jim McGovern, October 2, 2009.

There were many bumps and turns in the road to the January 1992 peace treaty, and Congress, more than the administration, kept up the momentum by stressing to both sides the new congressional reality, which was that US aid for reconstruction was contingent on the *Tandona* leaving and the rebels coming in. The settlement was aided by the intimate, daily involvement in the peace talks of Moakley, McGovern, Woodward, and Gómez, who had returned to El Salvador to guide Moakley's investigation.[1] By 1991 Moakley had reported publicly his conclusion that the High Command had not only covered up but also ordered the hit on Ellacuría.[2] He once said to a State Department official: "I know nothing about El Salvador, I've got two staff who don't speak Spanish and one crazy Salvadoran. You have all these intelligence people and you know the area perfectly. How come I found the truth and you didn't?"[3] The UN Truth Commission affirmed Moakley's findings in 1993 and also found that in a sample of roughly one third of all political murders and after-combat massacres, 85 percent were reported to have been committed by US-backed security forces.

Cindy Buhl noted in 1991 that opponents of aid to the Salvadoran war effort "were lucky," because Assistant Secretary of State Bernard Aronson failed in his efforts in 1990 to reach a "bipartisan consensus" of trading a military purge for more military aid only because he continued to have a Cold Warrior's tin ear for what was happening both in Congress and on the ground.[4] The administration even intended to restore all the withheld aid in 1991 when the FMLN murdered downed US pilots, despite the law's standard for restoration of an offensive that threatened the government's survival. An awareness somewhere above Aronson in the department that such a move would only bring tougher aid cuts the next year and disrupt the suddenly inevitable settlement convinced the administration to back down.[5]

House Foreign Affairs staffer Vic Johnson recalls the surprise of Aronson aide Peter Romero in 1992 when Johnson agreed in a heartbeat to his request to hold off on considering the Salvador section of the foreign aid bill to allow delicate negotiations to move forward. "You haven't believed us for eight years, and you still don't believe me now," Johnson said. "All we ever wanted you to do was push negotiations to end the war." When Johnson checked with his new chairman, Bob Torricelli, and the other Democrats on the subcommittee, they all agreed to leave the Salvador section blank. The Soft Eagles in Congress — and most of the Turkeys in the groups — had always wanted a negotiated revolution, not an FMLN victory, and that is what they finally achieved.

Cindy Arnson concludes in her book that liberal Members of Congress "tried to have it both ways" — to block full-scale war while not being "soft on communism." She thinks

---

1 Ambassador Walker made the surprising and courageous decision to put him on the embassy staff. Interview with Bill Woodward, September 29, 2009.

2 See "Statement of Representative Joe Moakley, Chairman of the Speaker's Task Force on El Salvador, November 18, 1991," at http://www.cja.org/downloads/Final_Task_Force_ElSalvador-1.pdf

3 Interview with Jim McGovern, October 2, 2009.

4 Cindy Buhl, draft paper for presentation at a 1991 conference, unpublished.

5 University Press, University Park, PA, 1993, p. 257.

---

that they often didn't say what they believed, but what they felt they could say.[1] But Soft Eagles were, and are, not "soft" on perceived threats to US security — like Soviet MiGs, "another Cuba," and, in a later era, governments who provide sanctuary to terrorists who attack American citizens. That is why they vote overwhelmingly for the CIA budget and unhappily accept US aid to repressive governments that provide bases and support to US military and covert missions and strategic minerals to the American economy. Only a handful of Members, like Gerry Studds, were aligned with the Turkeys in the groups who wanted the United States to leave El Salvador alone, even if that resulted in the rebels taking power. When liberal Members of Congress said that they were trying to help Duarte with their conditions, or trying to reform the Army, so that there could be a balanced settlement of the war, they meant it.

If there was anybody saying what they didn't believe about El Salvador, it was the string of administrations who knew from their deep penetration of the Salvadoran security forces just how endemic their culture of violence was, but told Congress and the public that it had been arrested by US aid. As Arnson notes, from the Carter to the Bush administrations, top officials, entrusted by the American people to be their representatives to the world, lied systematically, as if by instinct, about the Salvadoran security forces' brutality and resistance to investigation of that brutality. A similar farce was illustrated every year in the annual congressional testimony of Americas Watch's Holly Burkhalter on Guatemala. Burkhalter would simply compile the administration's annual testimonies for the 1980s, in which each one negated the previous year's claim of progress by conceding that there had been horrible abuses a year before, but that the situation was now much improved.

The tragicomedy of US policy toward El Salvador reached its nadir in 1993, with Secretary of State Warren Christopher's claim of being "deeply shocked" by the report of the UN Truth Commission. Having chaired the inter-agency group that first implemented US human rights policy under President Carter, and having access to classified intelligence reports, let alone the often more accurate and timely news reports from massacre sites in El Salvador, Christopher was no more shocked than the French prefect in the Bogart film *Casablanca* when he was informed that gambling was occurring in Rick's American bar. Why did this softest of Eagles have to dissemble, and why did he accept the report of the internal investigation he ordered, when it absolved State Department personnel of lies that were as knowing and systematic about Salvadoran government murders as Robert McNamara and McGeorge Bundy's were about South Vietnamese military prowess? It is hard to avoid the conclusion that Christopher wanted the State Department to be able to retain its credibility, and its ability to be taken seriously when lying, for other days.

NICARAGUA: OLLIE NORTH'S PETARD AND DAVID BONIOR'S BRIDGE TO PEACE

There should be a statue in Managua of Michigan Congressman David Bonior, surrounded by his staff — Kathy Gille, Jerry Hartz, Steve Champlin, and Sarah Duffendach, and their inside strategist and confidant on the House leadership staff, George Kundanis.

---

1 Cynthia Arnson, *Crossroads: Congress, the President, and Central America, 1976-1993*, Pennsylvania University Press, University Park, PA, 1993, p. 276.

Without their work, it is highly likely that the war that devastated Nicaragua would have continued a lot longer, and to no better ending. It is true that for all his effort, Bonior lost the big test of 1986, as the House approved $100 million and a wider war. However, when a Contra cargo plane carrying weapons was shot down in October, and Eugene Hasenfus became Reagan's Gary Powers by falling into the custody of the Nicaraguans, Bonior's work in that losing effort was rewarded. The administration had been caught cheating, and even worse began to look foolish after White House staffer Oliver North's "neat" idea of selling arms to Iran and giving the proceeds to the Contras was revealed in November. Bonior and his whip group were well-positioned to use this as the foundation stone to fashion a bridge back for the Dixies. North was, to use Shakespeare's metaphor from Hamlet, hoist with his own petard.

Some historians would put House Speaker Jim Wright on that pedestal, because he daringly filled the constitutional void left by President Reagan's effective abdication during his last, lost two years in office. Wright took over the executive branch' s job of pushing Costa Rican president Oscar Arias' regional agreement to a workable conclusion. President Bush's Secretary of State James Baker certainly gets some votes for nailing down a deal with Congress in the spring of 1989, for which he had to bulldoze through the objections of executive and legislative advocates of untrammeled presidential foreign policy power who retained Reagan's commitment to total victory over both Congress and the Sandinistas. But Wright and Baker were reaping in a warm spring a crop that had been tended by Bonior over the course of a long, cold winter.

Bonior was a thirty-six-year-old congressman in 1981 when CIA director William Casey started funding the Contras. Almost immediately he began speaking out against US support for civil war in Nicaragua by exposing military training camps in Florida.[1] For the rest of the decade, and especially after he convinced the leadership in 1985 to let him lead a whip group on the Contras, Bonior devoted most of his time and congressional chits to ending the war in Nicaragua. This commitment was a bit surprising, since his district was heavy with working-class, anti-communist Polish-Americans who expected him to focus on bringing a bit of bacon home, he was not on any foreign policy committees, and his primary national security focus had been on supporting health and employment for Vietnam-era veterans, of which he was one. Through dozens of pieces of legislation, hundreds of meetings, and thousands of whip assignments Bonior served as the connection between the Dixies and the Democratic Caucus, trying to address the concerns of the Dixies without losing his liberal base, and eventually bringing most of them back over a legislative bridge to support an end to the war.

As the Iran–Contra scandal spiraled out of control in late 1986, the stars were suddenly aligned for peace in Nicaragua, even as the fully-funded Contra army Reagan had always wanted made its way onto the battlefield from its Honduran sanctuary. A synergy developed between the efforts of Bonior, Speaker Wright, and Costa Rican president Oscar Arias to promote a settlement in which the Contras would disband and take part in elections with guarantees for their ability to campaign. All of this was only made pos-

1 Cynthia Arnson, *Crossroads: Congress, the President, and Central America, 1976-1993*, Pennsylvania University Press, University Park, PA, 1993, p. 77.

sible by the consistent success of the Nicaraguan army against the Contras. Driven back into Honduras and even attacked and routed there in 1988, the Contras failed to become militarily more than a nuisance. Of course, the same can be said for many eventually successful rebel forces like the FLN in Algeria and the ANC in South Africa, but they had the overwhelming backing of the populace who destabilized the government with strikes and shut-downs. There was no such outpouring of popular support for the Contras.

Using information gleaned from his expanding army of whips, Bonior used the hysteria over the continuing revelations from Iran–Contra to win a provision in March 1987 that he considered a "bridge" to allow Dixies to vote against the Reagan administration without directly taking on its goal of ousting the Sandinistas. By bridge, he meant that once they had started walking away from Reagan on a procedural issue, they would find it possible to keep on walking and eventually arrive on the Democratic leadership's side and openly reject him on substance. The amendment was disingenuously called a "moratorium," which implied a pause rather than the cut-off the leadership hoped it would portend. It was presented as an exercise in good government, and would have withheld the final $40 million from the 1986 aid package until the administration provided an accounting for all the contra aid it had coordinated from foreign sources. The 1986 congressional elections had been good to the Democrats, who had regained control of the Senate by defeating six of the ardent conservatives who had come in with Reagan in 1980, and had expanded their House majority by five seats to a 40-member margin. When the moratorium passed the House by 34 votes in March and received a majority in the newly-Democratic Senate in April, but not the 60 votes needed to end a Republican filibuster, leaders of both parties publicly warned the Contras that Congress was unlikely ever to approve significant amounts of aid for the war.[1]

When Bonior was introduced to the crowd at a fund-raising concert for Countdown '87, a campaign to pressure swing Members on the Contras, the "Washington" half of the crowd cheered a hero who had found a way to use the Iran–Contra revelations to get the Dixies on record against military aid. The "solidarity" half booed an enemy who had promised the bridge-walkers a vote later in the year on aid to sustain the Contras in camps during peace negotiations. Liberal Democrats, under pressure from the lobby groups, argued that based on the administration's track record any aid would allow the Contras to carry on the war, but Bonior convinced them that a far wider war would result if the logistical aid were defeated and Reagan regained the initiative.

Supporters of the Contras were encouraged by the easy treatment the Democratic leadership decided to give the Reagan administration in the Iran–Contra hearings. NSC staffer North, resplendent in his Marine uniform and rows of medals, was lionized by the Republican members of the joint committee, who justified his secret violations of the Boland amendment by comparing them to Abraham Lincoln's open suspension of some Constitutional rights as emergency measures in the 100 days before Congress met to address the question of secession. Unlike Frank Church in his hearings on the CIA ten years before, Democratic co-chairs Lee Hamilton and Daniel Inouye were at pains to keep the

---

1 Linda Greenhouse, "Washington Talk: Congress; Contra Debate Is Over, For Now, but It May Really Be Over Next Fall," *New York Times*, March 27, 1987.

investigation focused on previously-known tactics and subordinates rather than use it as a fishing expedition to uncover and weaken US interventionist capabilities, or dislodge the administration.[1] Senate staffer and future congressman Gerry Connelly fumed at House majority leader Tom Foley's public statement that he hoped that the Committee would find no "smoking gun" implicating Reagan in the impeachable offense of diverting Iranian arms revenues to the Contras. To Connelly, this revealed the Democratic leadership's refusal to fulfill its duty to follow evidence wherever it led, even if that could lead to a politically riskier course than the current one that offered modest short-term advantage.

Whatever temporary benefit Contra backers got over the summer from the hearings was negated by Bonior's use of sticks as well as carrots on the Dixies. Countdown '87, hatched at Democratic donor Smith Bagley's retreat in the Georgia islands, raised money through its high-profile concerts and ran targeted advertising campaigns in swing districts. Rosa DeLauro, who had been Senator Dodd's chief of staff, ran Countdown like a public relations firm, not a lobby group of grassroots volunteers, and the Dixies for the first time felt the public sting from the left in their district that they had been feeling from the government-coordinated and at times government-funded Republican right. It was unprecedented for Democratic leaders to be conspiring with groups to attack their own members, but Bonior's coordination of Countdown's target list was a salutary warning to Dixies that they could stay on the bridge if they wanted without ever completely crossing over to the side of opposition to any aid to the Contras, but would be punished if they ever turned around and went back to Reagan's side.

The chances of attaining a negotiated settlement improved in 1987. Oscar Arias revived the Central American presidents' "Contadora process" that had been rendered pointless by Reagan's 1986 victory on Contra aid, and won the Nobel peace prize for getting them to sign his related plan for increased political openness and an end to outside aid to rebels. Speaker Wright stepped into the vacuum of the administration's confusion in the fall and openly negotiated with both Nicaragua and the Contra leadership on an agreement for the Contras' return to politics. While the Contras eventually refused to sign on, a sense of inevitability was spreading. Bonior had kept up his intense pace of whip assignments throughout the Iran–Contra hearings. For example, a single meeting in July two months before any floor action was expected attracted a remarkable 32 Members, who reported on previous contacts and their demands, "took names" of the members they were to contact in this round, and were assigned themes for research and publicity. With the House

---

1 John D. Saxon, an associate counsel on the Iran-Contra committee, charges that lead counsel Arthur Lyman decided not to call national security adviser Colin Powell to testify because he did not want to derail the career of a leading black officer. See *Birmingham News* post by Saxon, August 26, 2007. Investigative journalist Robert Parry notes that Hamilton, as a respected Democratic moderate, was often chosen to lead panels that calmed rather than roiled the political waters, such as those investigating the alleged "October Surprise" by Reagan advisers trying to delay the release of Iran's American hostages in 1980, the "Iraq-gate" financing of Saddam Hussein by the first Bush administration, the causes of the 9/11 attacks, and the conduct of the war in Iraq. In 2008 Hamilton also lent congressional credibility to a panel led by former secretaries of State Christopher and Baker that proposed repealing the War Powers Act and its requirement that US troops be withdrawn from foreign combat within 60 days unless Congress approves the mission.

whip count running against him, Reagan withheld his intended fall request for $270 million in new aid. The House provided a dribble of logistical aid in December, setting up a final confrontation in February 1988. The White House cranked up the machine again for a final orgy of publicity, accusations of treasonous promotion of communism, and government favors.

Still showing its masterful manipulation of the leading media, the administration orchestrated a blast of publicity for a defector from Nicaragua's general staff, Major Roger Miranda. His dubious claims of a planned doubling of Nicaragua's army and, again, the coming delivery of MiG fighters, were provided to a small group of outlets, including the *New York Times*, the *Washington Post*, and ABC News, but only on the condition that the articles be printed the next day, leaving no time to investigate the claims before they were reported. Miranda's claims dissolved under independent investigation over the next few months, but the size of the initial media "hit" ensured that his claims would be central to the coming vote on the Contras.[1] Still, in February, Bonior's work came to fruition as the House rejected Reagan's request for a greatly reduced $36 million aid package, by a vote of 219–211.[2]

Bonior had led just enough Dixies across the bridge to win a real vote, not a symbolic one like the "moratorium." Again, to win he had to promise the Dixies that he would deliver enough liberal votes to keep aid coming to maintain the Contras in their base camps. By the time he arranged that vote, in April, the Contras had been beaten so badly in a border raid by the Nicaraguan army that Reagan sent 3,000 US troops to Honduras to guarantee their safety. Liberals could see that the logistical aid posed little risk of sending the Contras back into Nicaragua, and supported Bonior in a 215–210 victory. As usual, Republicans united with liberal Democrats to defeat the bill on final passage, but after a few months they realized that this time there would be no Dixie-led reversal and agreed to enactment of the aid plan. Wright then stepped into the vacuum again and maneuvered the president into signing a proposal with him that envisioned an end to the fighting in return for open elections.

When James Baker became President Bush's Secretary of State in 1989, he wanted to end the distraction of the continual congressional bickering over the Contras. He came up to Capitol Hill in March and simply did the deal with Speaker Wright, brushing to the side the neo-conservatives and the advocates of presidential authority who had dominated the Reagan White House. The Democrats agreed to appropriate monthly funds to keep the Contras alive in base camps during negotiations, and Baker agreed to give each of four Congressional committees veto power over releasing succeeding portions of the aid. If the Contras went back to war, Congress would cut off the funds.[3] Baker's pragmatism

---

1 Americas Watch executive director Aryeh Neier debated Miranda for the Arms Control and Foreign Policy Caucus, identifying serious discrepancies in his account. The Miranda affair is recounted and analyzed in Barry D. Adam, "Nicaragua, the Peace Process, and Television News," *Canadian Journal of Communication*, vol. 16, no. 1, 1991.

2 The Senate, despite its new Democratic majority, approved the aid, as it did every one of Reagan's Contra requests throughout his presidency.

3 Cynthia Arnson, *Crossroads: Congress, the President, and Central America, 1976-1993*, Pennsylvania University Press, University Park, PA, 1993, p. 233.

enshrined the "reprogramming" powers of the committees, which had been of dubious constitutionality since the 1983 "Chadha" decision by the Supreme Court had held that only the full Congress, overriding a veto if necessary, could take an action that had the effect of changing law. Baker's open sharing of power with Congress was vigorously but unsuccessfully opposed by White House counsel C. Boyden Gray.[1]

The deal with Baker was Jim Wright's last triumph. Republican insurgent Newt Gingrich had responded to Wright's unprecedented involvement and success in pursuing a diplomatic agenda in Nicaragua in 1988 by forcing an inquiry by the Ethics committee into Wright's financial dealings. The committee reported in April 1989, that Wright had a sweetheart book deal that amounted to a gift to Wright from a union, and that his wife had a job that amounted to a gift from a developer. The Speaker's position was further damaged by a *Washington Post* story in its "Style" section in May recounting a crime against a former Post staffer by his top aide, John Mack, who as a 19-year-old clerk had inexplicably attacked and badly injured a customer named Pamela Small 16 years before. Wright had given Mack, the brother of his daughter's husband, a low-level position so he could be released on parole after he served two years in jail, and Mack had risen by his perseverance and loyalty. Liberal women in Congress, usually ardent advocates of rehabilitation for prisoners, called for Mack's head, and he resigned.[2] By the end of the month, Wright had resigned as well.[3]

As part of the Arias peace plan, the Nicaraguan government had agreed to move up its next election and permit international observers to monitor the campaign and the vote-counting. Soft and Hard Eagles alike voted to fund newspaper owner Violetta Chamorro's UNO opposition party through one of Reagan's anti-communist legacies, the quasi-governmental National Endowment for Democracy, but the Sandinista party was confident that it would prevail in the February 1990 election. Contrary to pre-election polls, UNO won the presidency and a majority in the parliament. Left-leaning American observers attributed the result to the threat of a renewed war and economic embargo; right-leaning observers attributed the result to the arrogance of the Sandinistas. Nicaraguans seemed simply to be exhausted by the war and were ready for a new chapter. Ironically, the prospects for economic recovery were stunted by a campaign by conservative Members of Congress to reduce foreign aid to Chamorro's government because she had invited the Sandinistas to be a junior partner in the ruling coalition and to retain Ortega's brother Humberto as her top military adviser.[4]

---

1 John Broder, "Nicaragua Accord No Bush Retreat, Baker Says," *Los Angeles Times*, March 27, 1989.

2 Michael Oreskes, "Wright Aide's Past Shocks Capitol," *New York Times*, May 5, 2009.

3 A loyal warrior with a long memory, David Bonior pursued the new Speaker as Gingrich had pursued the old. As a result, in 1996 Gingrich was sanctioned by the Ethics committee for dubious financial arrangements relating to his politically-oriented "course" at Kennesaw State College in Georgia. Weakened by the Ethics case, a 1987 House vote to reprimand him for it, and the poor results of the 1988 elections, Gingrich too resigned from the speakership and the House.

4 Cynthia Arnson, *Crossroads: Congress, the President, and Central America, 1976-1993*, Pennsylvania University Press, University Park, PA, 1993, pp. 241-242.

In the run-up to the Nicaraguan election, the US invasion of Panama provided a devastating display of the continued vitality of the assumption, shared by Soft and Hard Eagles alike, that led to the Contra war: unfriendly governments in Central America pose an unacceptable threat to American security and an unacceptable affront to American credibility. Like the invasion of Grenada in 1983 in the midst of a liberal–conservative dispute over how to neutralize the leftist threat in El Salvador, the deposing of Manuel Noriega's dictatorship did not become a political issue in the United States. The average American did not necessarily understand how dictator Manuel Noriega had made such a rapid transition from valued partner in the Contra war to indicted drug-running embarrassment, but had been told that US military personnel and their families were being treated brutally in random encounters with Noriega's forces, and that he would pose a threat to the use of the Panama canal once the on-going transfer was completed. America was clearly comfortable with President Bush delivering the same message Queen Victoria did in the 19ᵗʰ century when she would respond to every mistreatment of her trade emissaries in West Africa by sending a punitive expedition at some point in the next few years. An empire demands respect, and respect demands that those not showing it pay a price. Turkeys protesting the invasions of Grenada and Panama were invisible in the mainstream media, their argument that America should live with its neighbors' choices as a moral matter as disconnected from the debate between Soft and Hard Eagles as their belief that Nicaragua should have been able to have its mythical MiGs.

POSTSCRIPT ON LEFTIST CENTRAL AMERICA: NOT ANOTHER CUBA

On June 1, 2009, Mauricio Funes was escorted to a podium by an Army honor guard to take the oath of office as president of El Salvador. Funes was the candidate of the FMLN, the rebel movement that the Army had fought for twelve years. He was also a graduate of the UCA, whose leadership, of course, had been murdered by the Army's elite US-trained brigade on the order of the Army's High Command. Sandinista Daniel Ortega, Nicaragua's elected president, joined Funes for the celebrations later that day. US Secretary of State Hillary Clinton represented President Obama at this surreal moment for US foreign policy. Presidents Carter, Reagan, and Bush had sacrificed over 130,000 Salvadorans and Nicaraguans to keep their countries from falling under the control of these quasi-Marxist parties.

Even under the new US regime, the old assumption of the right to direct other governments in the American back yard lingered. Elliot Engle, the chairman of the House subcommittee covering Latin America, told reporters that Clinton had come to El Salvador because of her deep concern over the trend toward leftist governments in Latin America, such as Ecuador's election of a candidate who fulfilled his campaign promise not to renew the lease on a US military air base. Of Clinton's presence, Engle said: "I think it means we want to engage with El Salvador because we don't them drifting all the way left."[1] This remark indicates that just as ending the war in Vietnam did not end the Vietnam foreign policy, ending the wars in Central America did not end the foreign policy that led to them.

---

1 "US, Cuba Ties in Spotlight as Clinton Visits Central America," *Agence France Presse*, June 1, 2009.

CHAPTER 6. AFTER THE COLD WAR: BUSH AND CLINTON'S NEW WORLD OF DEMOCRACY...AND SAME OLD ARMS SALES TO FRIENDLY DICTATORS

The unexpected collapse of the Warsaw Pact in 1989 and the fragmentation of the Soviet Union in 1991 forced a redefinition of America's global role. For more than 40 years the fear of advantage for the Soviets and their communist system had been the primary justification for every major military, covert, and foreign policy decision of the United States — and suddenly the Soviet Union was gone. President George H. W. Bush, his advisers, and the public at large were understandably stumped, unsure how to characterize the purpose of global US military deployment and alliances. Francis Fukuyama, a leading neo-conservative thinker, grabbed elite and even public attention with his 1989 article, "The End of History?", which argued that a trend toward liberal, market democracy was a logical, global development that would eventually encompass all nations.[1] China's crackdown on calls for democracy in Tiananmen Square in 1989, Saddam Hussein's invasion of Kuwait in 1990, and an outbreak of ethnic conflict in previously-stable African states and the former Yugoslavia dispelled the hope that Fukuyama's thesis would be vindicated in the short term, but the article still reinforced the sense of victory over communism as an ideology and amplified the Turkeys' call for a "peace dividend" from dramatic cuts in unneeded military spending.

In his speech to Congress in March 1991 after he had forged a coalition that drove Iraqi troops out of Kuwait, Bush announced that the purpose of his foreign policy would be to create a "new world order," which he properly credited to British Prime Minister Winston Churchill. Rejecting the unilateralist disdain of the Reagan administration, Bush looked to "the United Nations, freed from cold war stalemate...to fulfill the historic vision of its founders: a world in which freedom and respect for human rights find a home among all

---

1 *The National Interest*, Summer 1989.

nations." National security adviser Brent Scowcroft, a retired Air Force general who had held the post under Ford as well, had to defend this cooperative vision against Secretary of Defense Dick Cheney and his neo-conservative under secretary for policy Paul Wolfowitz, who had led the Ford administration's "Team B" attack on the CIA's modest view of Soviet capabilities and intentions.

Cheney and Wolfowitz developed a draft Defense Planning Guidance in 1992 that cautioned against multilateral action, and called for the use of military force to prevent the rise of a challenger in any region and maintain US access to mineral resources. Like Bush's new world order, and Churchill's, Cheney's vision was couched in moral terms trumpeting the benefits to the world of stability and prosperity under benevolent US dominance and American values. Rejected by the White House, the draft was turned into a Pentagon document as the "Zone of Peace" Regional Defense Strategy.

Presidential candidate Bill Clinton, with no experience on national security issues, campaigned almost exclusively on the domestic economy. Reducing trade barriers to boost growth was his only real foreign policy proposal. Clinton's instincts were all Dixie, though, as shown by his recent chairmanship of the Democratic Leadership Council, which was founded in 1985 by Al Gore and other Southern senators to promote a tougher, centrist, "New Democrat" line both on domestic issues like welfare and on foreign and military policy. Gore and his long-time national security aide Leon Fuerth filled the foreign policy vacuum in Clinton's campaign and his early presidency with a consistently neo-conservative and technocratic approach. The neo-conservativism had shown in Gore's 1988 campaign for the Democratic nomination for president, in which he attacked his opponents for being insufficiently supportive of Israel and not backing aid to maintain the Contras.[1]

Gore's technocratic side had shown in his support in Congress for various arcane elements of the nuclear deterrent that he justified on grounds of even more arcane strategy, such as the neutron bomb, the Trident II submarine-based missile, and, most notably, the MX missile. In 1983 Gore was the leader of a "gang of four" Democrats who signed onto a deal crafted by Scowcroft that, to the outrage of liberal Democrats, provided the votes needed to rescue the multi-warhead MX missile in return for Reagan backing the single-warhead "Midgetman" missile.[2] As vice president, Gore played a crucial role in both of Clinton's rapid surrenders to the Pentagon on arms control, successfully urging him to continue nuclear testing and the deployment of anti-personnel landmines. The decision on nuclear testing was quickly washed away in a storm of Democratic protest in Congress, but as will be discussed in Chapter 8, the position on landmines was maintained up to and past the 1997 agreement of 135 countries to the Ottawa "ban" treaty.

---

1 Gore also challenged Massachusetts Governor Michael Dukakis' furlough program for prisoners, which led to Republican investigations that resulted in the infamous commercial featuring a black convict who had raped and murdered after failing to return to prison after a furlough.

2 Bill Turque, *Inventing Al Gore*, Houghton-Mifflin, New York, 2000, p. 143-150. As vice chairman of Henry Kissinger's international door-opening firm, Scowcroft, like Kissinger, was called upon at times to lead bipartisan presidential commissions designed to obtain congressional majorities.

After his election Clinton tasked his national security adviser Tony Lake with identifying a unifying theme for his foreign policy. Lake came up with "democratic enlargement," which he and Clinton presented in speeches in 1993. US security would be enhanced by the expansion of the reach of democratic and free-market institutions, which of course would be a moral good for the rest of the world.[1] Both Wolfowitz and Clinton, then, were envisioning an encouraged and perhaps enforced "End of History." Indeed, by the time the neo-conservatives founded the Project for a New American Century in 1997, its general vision of global alliance with cooperative regimes and its specific purpose of "regime change" in Iraq were different only in nuance from Clinton's views and policies. Predictably, Clinton's Churchillian claim that stability imposed by the United States would bring happiness to others was applauded by national security pundits like columnist Thomas Friedman, who applauded the "gatekeeper" status this plan accorded the United States.[2] "Enlargement" also encompassed Clinton's first major foreign policy decision, which was to react to the dissolution of the Warsaw Pact not by closing down the expensive NATO military alliance that had countered it, but expanding it by admitting former Soviet allies.

NATO expansion was a project of first Hard and then Soft Eagles. It was opposed by Turkeys in arms control groups as well as by some Eagles, including Friedman, who were also concerned about irritating Russia and risking progress in reducing Russia's nuclear arsenal.[3] In 1993 future UN ambassador and former Wolfowitz staffer Zalmay Khalilzad, who like him had studied under neo-conservative godfather Albert Wohlstetter at the University of Chicago, wrote a paper for the RAND Corporation advocating NATO expansion.[4] In 1994 a few former Warsaw Pact members were invited into a loose "Partnership for Peace" that could have been the end of the project had not Clinton's assistant secretary of state for Europe, Richard Holbrooke, and the non-governmental US Committee to Expand NATO, taken up the cause. Led by the vice president of Lockheed Martin, a major arms contractor that hoped to and did sell government-funded fighter aircraft to new NATO members, the Committee operated out of the American Enterprise Institute and its Albert Wohlstetter conference room.[5] Wolfowitz was, of course a member of the Committee. Less predictably, former Ted Kennedy staffer Greg Craig and other prominent Soft Eagles signed up. By 1997 three Central European countries had been invited into NATO, and in 1998 Congress and the other national parliaments ratified the decision.

In addition to enlargement, Lake in 1994 began to develop a new purpose for US foreign policy: the taming of "recalcitrant and outlaw states." Based on a line from a 1990 Pentagon study, the "rogue state" doctrine provided a basis both for economic and military pressure on Iraq and for continued alliance with regimes cooperating with US military

1 Douglas Brinkley, "Democratic Enlargement: The Clinton Doctrine," *Foreign Policy*, Spring 1997.

2 http://www.chomsky.info/articles/199312—.htm

3 See James M. Goldgeier, *Not Whether, but When: The Decision to Enlarge NATO*, Brookings Institution Press, Washington, 1999, pp. 138-155.

4 "Extending the Western Alliance to Eastern Europe: A New Strategy for NATO," RAND IP-107-AF, 1993.

5 Bruce Jackson, the arms executive, surfaced again in 2003, successfully pushing some of the nations of "new Europe" (as secretary of Defense Donald Rumsfeld called them) to becoming part of the "Coalition of the Willing" in Iraq.

and covert activities.[1] It found some resonance in a 1993 article by Samuel Huntington, "The Clash of Civilizations," that disputed Fukuyama's confidence and identified "alien" non-European cultures that would reject and conflict with liberal democracy.[2] Turkeys too were not unaware of the historic opportunity to replace the Cold War vision of national security, and flooded their allies in the Clinton administration and Congress with proposals for fifty percent cuts in world military forces and spending and the redirection of these resources to human development under more democratic and progressive international financial institutions.[3]

The foreign policy debate within the Clinton administration was disconnected from the potential tasks, structure, size, and weapons systems of the US armed forces. Neither Lake nor Secretary of State Warren Christopher had the vision or the stature to corral the Pentagon. They also knew that Clinton was skittish about any confrontation in the aftermath of the "Pentagon's successful resistance to his promise to end a ban on gays in the military." Nor did the administration have anyone in the Pentagon who could align military strategy with the purported foreign policy. Cerebral Secretary of Defense Les Aspin was out in a year because of public reaction to the deaths of 18 soldiers in a confusing peace-keeping mission in Somalia. He was replaced by Bill Perry, who was a technocrat rather than a strategist. Fire-breathing neo-conservative Jim Woolsey might have given some guidance as director of the CIA, but in his two years there he had an oddly arms-length relationship with Clinton.

While the Pentagon lacked a strategy, it still had a budget that brought contracts to virtually every congressional district. As chairman of the Joint Chiefs of Staff in 1992, Colin Powell could only make an inchoate appeal for funding to the Senate Budget Committee on the basis of an undefined global stability: "We are the pre-eminent force for stability in the world....We have to remain engaged, it's expected of us. It's the role that history has given us as a superpower. And so, we have to keep forces in Europe, in the Pacific, in Southwest Asia, in the Mediterranean."[4] During the hearing he joked with the senators that to justify the Pentagon's budget request: "I need enemies!" With the end of the Soviet challenge, Pentagon planners could see how the "primacy," or dominance of the battle space, that the Navy had traditionally sought could be extended to the land and air as well. In 1993 they produced a congressionally-mandated "bottom-up review" that posited the need for forces sufficient to fight and win two major wars simultaneously. Few in Congress took the requirement seriously, but it did provide a rationale for the jettisoning of serious discussion of the Turkeys' peace dividend. After a 50 percent real increase in the 1980s, military spending fell by just a fifth in the 1990s, despite the completion by 1990 of

---

1 Michael T. Klare, "The New 'Rogue State' Doctrine," *The Nation*, May 8, 1995.
2 *Foreign Affairs*, Summer 1993.
3 See, for example, Citizens' Commission for a New US Policy Toward the Developing World, "Fulfilling the Promise," coordinated by the Institute for Policy Studies, 1994; and Coalition to Rethink US Aid to the Middle East, "Toward a Safer Future for the Children of Abraham: A Proposal for Restructuring US Aid to the Middle East," January 1995; and the call of the Nobel Peace Laureates' Year 2000 campaign, coordinated by Demilitarization for Democracy (absorbed in 2000 by the Center for International Policy), 1995.
4 See the transcript of the Center for Defense Information video featuring this statement. http://www.cdi.org/adm/Transcripts/526/

purchases of a generation of new weapons and the disintegration of the Warsaw Pact and the Soviet Union.[1]

In the end, all the promises of the promotion of democracy by all the Eagles in both administrations at the end of the Cold War would hypocritically bump up against the reality of long-standing alliance with the most reliable partners for military and covert cooperation in the developing world, dictators. That these alliances were then cemented with record levels of arms transfers confirms that the Cold War was more a convenient excuse for US power projection after World War II than a moral struggle over the right of people to choose their way of life.

A DUBIOUS RECORD: CLINTON'S ARMS SALES TO DICTATORS

After the invasion of Kuwait in 1990 there was a great deal of discussion in Washington of the unfortunate fact that Saddam Hussein's armed forces had been armed by many of the countries that were now preparing to evict them. Iraq had obtained modern weaponry from France, Russia, and even the United States, through both the diversion of government agricultural credits and the approval of transfers from US-armed neighbors during the Iran-Iraq war.[2] Even as the war to drive Iraq out of Kuwait got underway, Secretary of State James Baker and other administration officials pledged to constrain the level of sophistication of US arms sold to the Middle East and to negotiate an international agreement that would constrain other supplying countries. However, the demand for weapons as the oil-rich region restocked in the aftermath of the war proved too lucrative a target for American arms manufacturers to miss, particularly as deliveries of the weapons the Pentagon had ordered during the Reagan buildup came to an end. Democratic leaders in Congress called on the Bush administration to live up to its pledge, but as Bill Clinton became first their candidate and then their president, their resistance to arms sales ebbed.[3]

Turkeys in the arms control groups began a dialogue with Clinton's director of national security issues Tony Lake on the arms trade almost as soon as Clinton formally locked up the nomination in June 1992. The Project on Demilitarization and Democracy (PDD) couched its memorandum to Clinton in terms of the benefits to the American economy and US security of helping developing countries reduce their military spending and arms imports and the political power of their armed forces. Titled "Demilitarization of the Developing World: How to make 'foreign' policy a domestic issue in your campaign," the proposal argued first from economic self-interest:[4]

---

1 The decline was arrested late in the Clinton years, and his and the younger Bush's new weapons and higher readiness levels drove spending up 75 percent in the 2000s, even without counting the cost of operations in Afghanistan and Iraq. All figures in real, inflation-adjusted dollars. Center for Defense Information, *CDI Military Almanac 2007*, p. 85.

2 A series of investigative reports by Murray Waas and Douglas Frantz in the *Los Angeles Times* revealed the US role in Iraq's rearming. See "Abuses in US Aid to Iraqis Ignored," March 22, 1992, "Iraq Got US Technology After CIA Warned Baker," July 22, 1992, and "Kuwait, Saudis Supplied Iraq with US Arms," September 12, 1992.

3 Federation of American Scientists, *Arms Sales Monitor*, Issue 1, March 1991.

4 Many of the memorandum's points echo those made in testimony by the group's director, the author of this book, before the Subcommittee on Foreign Operations, House Appropriations Committee, May 1, 1992.

- Our economic future lies in trade with the developing world...one of the greatest drains on the economic growth in developing countries that we and they so badly need is their militarization:
  - $200 billion in annual military spending (four times its foreign aid from all sources), spurred by $40 billion in annual arms imports from the developed world (nearly 90 percent from the five permanent members of the UN Security Council);
  - the dozen or so wars at any one time (e.g., Peru, Somalia, Sudan) that destroy infrastructure, drive out investment, and spread refugees through neighboring countries; and
  - the continued political power of armed forces that maintain half of the developing world in dictatorship (e.g., China, Indonesia, South Africa, Saudi Arabia, Haiti) and keep another quarter from moving to full democracy despite the presence of elections (e.g., Colombia, Honduras, Egypt, Philippines).

After a brief foray into morality — noting that violations of human rights go hand in hand with militarization and that the indirect death toll from 40 years of civil wars taking place on the "ideological chessboard" of the Cold War was 40 million people — the memorandum reverted again to American self-interest:

> If we accept business as usual as the Bush administration does...we will see more Panamas and Iraqs, countries where military-backed regimes with whom we pragmatically played ball descended into lawlessness, leading to wars that killed American soldiers and devastated regional economies for decades to come.

This theme was expanded in the next few years into a publicity campaign called "arms sales are boomerangs," which contrasted demilitarized democracies like Botswana that boosted the American economy with their growth and high demand for imports with US-armed and financed dictatorships like Somalia whose civil wars ended up requiring US troops and relief aid.[1]

PDD warned Lake about a particularly egregious example of a costly and dangerous proposal for the sale of 72 advanced fighters to Saudi Arabia by the McDonell Douglas Corporation, and urged Clinton to oppose it and separate himself from Bush, who was wavering on giving his approval. A union and company-run public relations campaign called "US Jobs Now" had set out to overturn the position of both the State and Defense Departments, which regarded the sale as unnecessary and destabilizing. The campaign's claim of 40,000 jobs being "saved" by the sale was taken up by the congressional delegation from Missouri, where the line where the fighters had been made for the US Air Force was being terminated. The delegation, including two usual congressional proponents of human rights and democracy abroad, Republican senator and Episcopal priest John Danforth and Democratic House majority leader Dick Gephardt, actively promoted the sale.

---

1 Scott Nathanson, the creative deputy director of PDD, made spandex superhero costumes and giant boomerang head-pieces for a phalanx of activists who wore them to demonstrations.

Similarly, the sale was backed by liberal Senator Chris Dodd because the engine for the fighter was made in his state of Connecticut.[1]

The claim of 40,000 jobs, which obviously ignored the jobs that would be generated elsewhere in the economy by Saudi purchases of other goods and services, let alone the cost of giving Israel even more advanced fighters to offset the Saudi version, became a constant refrain in the debate. The MacNeil-Lehrer Newshour used the figure as fact, despite a detailed dissection of it at a press conference featuring Congressman Howard Berman and conversion economist Greg Bischak. Indeed, opponents of the sale like Berman were portrayed by the Newshour and the sale's promoters as being motivated solely by support for Israel, rather than by concern over the escalating cost and sophistication of a spiraling arms race in the Middle East.[2] As a result, most reporters treated the debate as a replay of the fight during the Reagan administration over the sale of early warning aircraft to Saudi Arabia, rather than a first round in a post-Cold War struggle over the use of arms exports to keep factories, and profits, going as Pentagon orders dropped.[3] To the horror of the arms control groups, Clinton did precisely the opposite of what PDD asked him, using economic grounds to justify not his opposition but his support for the proposed sale and coming out in favor of the sale even before Bush did in an attempt to win Missouri in the general election. Rather than take the argument that "if we don't sell, the British will" as an opening for a multilateral agreement to restrain arms exports, Clinton took it as a spur to make sure America got the sale. Bush quickly fell in line and also reversed the State and Defense Departments' position against the sale of F-16 fighters to Taiwan, in an attempt to lock up the vote in Texas, where they were made.

After Clinton's election, but before his inauguration, another large arms deal was foisted on the Pentagon. Liberal Senators Howard Metzenbaum of Ohio and Carl Levin of Michigan warned the Army that if it did not support the sale of 256 of its most sophisticated tank to Kuwait, it would include a requirement in defense bills that the Army buy enough itself to keep the lines open in Lima, Ohio, and Warren, Michigan. With its limited procurement budget and no need for the additional tanks, the Army checked off on the sale. However, the 30-day period for making the sale official had not expired by the time Clinton took office. PDD again asked Clinton, through Lake's staff director Nancy Soderberg, to reverse Bush's decision. As a foreign policy aide to Senator Ted Kennedy, Soderberg had worked to limit and in some case block sales of jet fighters to Honduras and transfers of armed helicopters to El Salvador. Her response as a Clinton aide, though, was muted. Noting that it was difficult to turn around a sale that was already so far down the

---

1   Anne Detrick and Caleb Rossiter, "Guess Who's Selling Deadly Arms Now? Liberal Democrats Enter the Weapons Biz," *Washington Post*, Outlook Section, May 16, 1993. Dodd's support for arms exports to repressive regimes was also the subject of a book by John Tirman of the Connecticut-made Blackhawk helicopter, *Spoils of War: The Human Cost of the Arms Trade*, Free Press, New York, 1997.

2   An extensive correspondence developed between the Newshour and advocacy groups over their complaint that the segment had been aired with the 40,000 figure with no discussion of arguments by dissenting economists.

3   The "AWACS" sale resulted in the defeat of the chairman of the Senate Foreign Relations committee, Chuck Percy in 1984, though an independent campaign on behalf of congressman Paul Simon by a pro-Israel Californian.

---

pipeline, she said: "Oh, they won't let us do that." The "they" Soderberg was referring to was the Pentagon — although "they" was now actually "her" because she worked for the Pentagon's boss, the president.[1]

The advocacy groups who had come together after the Gulf War to constrain the arms trade called themselves the Arms Transfer Working Group (ATWG, which was pronounced "A-twig"). ATWG comprised 45 arms control, development, religious, scientific, veterans, and human rights groups, who met weekly to plot strategy and divide tasks. While unable or unwilling to challenge the specific sales to Saudi Arabia and Kuwait, Soderberg agreed to meet with a delegation from ATWG as part of an NSC review of arms trade policy. The March 1993 meeting in the White House was at first a genial reunion of former compatriots. The delegation found Soderberg receptive to its claim of the benefits for US security and the lives of people in developing countries of a concerted demilitarization. She affirmed the argument put forward by John Isaacs of the Council for a Livable World, the dean of arms controllers in the advocacy community, that the real lesson of the Gulf War was that externally-fueled regional arms races can lead to devastating conflict. Similarly, Soderberg agreed with Joanne Carter of the development advocate RESULTS that militarization was slowing economic growth and draining US resources for relief that should have been going into development, and with Daryl Fagin of Americans for Democratic Action that the conversion of arms-exporting factories to civilian activities would be popular with Clinton's Democratic base. However, when the delegation offered its specific proposal for a six-month moratorium on arms exports to countries failing to meet a "Code of Conduct" that would bar sales to regimes with excessive military spending or that denied "significant popular participation in government," the fissure between Clinton and the Turkeys became clear.

"Would that include the Arab states?", Soderberg asked. Told that it would, she frowned dubiously as Steve Aoki, her aide on loan from the State Department's bureau that approved arms transfers, responded that "our regional interests sometimes clash with our interest in arms restraint...Restraint would create an enormously contentious domestic problem that Clinton will want to avoid." Isaacs refocused the discussion on the policy reasons for a moratorium by noting that no matter how difficult it would be to explain short-term job losses, "the alternative is unacceptable." Soderberg, though, cut to the heart of the domestic political reality: "The President wants to know immediately, 'who will lose their job?' You must address this." The delegation tried to compare the situation to a speech Clinton had given on California base closings and the budget deficit, in which he argued that conversion to civilian uses would turn a short-term contraction into a long-term benefit, arguing that: "Only Clinton can paint the picture of a world at war being against our interests. And this can be tied to help for democracy, which is one of his visions." Soderberg responded positively, saying: "You must make this politically and economically attractive to him, and if you do, I'll get it in his options."

---

1 For the details on the sale, see Project on Demilitarization for Democracy, "Abrams Tanks for Kuwait: A Sale in Search of a Mission," January 15, 1993. Primary research was performed by a PDD fellow who was a graduate student on active duty, and could easily get into the Pentagon and interview the Army desk officer who had to approve the sale to save the procurement budget from the Democratic senators' threat.

A few days later a similar delegation met with Mort Halperin, the former Washington director of the American Civil Liberties Union, who had been nominated to a new position as assistant secretary of defense for democracy and peacekeeping.[1] Halperin agreed with ATWG's analysis of the importance for democracy of reducing the size and political power of armed forces in developing countries. He, rather than the delegation, said in the meeting that in many countries "their role has never been to defend from another country, but to repress, torture and murder their internal opponents." When it came to major US arms sales to those armed forces, though, Halperin clearly had smaller fish to fry. Although he was heading a new office that by definition could take on any issue relating to the promotion of democracy, he said that "arms transfers is not my portfolio, although I'll be at the table," and that he intended to use his small budget to support demilitarization in small countries, "where it is easier," citing the "Costa Rican model." In meetings later in the Clinton administration with Harold Koh, a noted legal theorist in the area of human rights who became assistant secretary of state for human rights and democracy, John Holum, a staffer for liberal Democrat Dave Obey who became director of the State Department's Arms Control and Disarmament Agency, and Lee Feinstein, an ATWG stalwart himself who became deputy director of policy planning at the State Department, ATWG's natural allies continued to make it clear that they were shying away from confronting arms sales to dictators because they sensed that Clinton would not back them up. In Koh's case, an ATWG delegation pointed out that US arms sales to dictators was inconsistent with the right to free and fair elections that was listed on the wall-mounted version of the Universal Declaration of Human Rights in his office.

In April ATWG submitted a lengthy paper outlining for Clinton a speech making the case for the proposed moratorium on arms to dictators and subsequent multilateral negotiations, but his continued approval of controversial sales convinced PDD by the end of May that, as it said in a note to Soderberg, "his campaign pledge to halt destabilizing arms transfers has collapsed in a pile of dangerous arms races (Saudi–Israeli; Greece–Turkey; East Asia) driven by domestic politics." ATWG did follow up on Soderberg's suggestion at the March meeting to "get Congress to write Clinton on it. He reads and answers quickly everything Congress sends him." By July it had generated a letter from 111 Members of Congress, including Berman and Ben Gilman, the top Republican on the House Foreign Affairs Committee, making the case for Clinton to promote a demilitarized vision of the world and a multilateral regime for the control of arms sales to developing countries. By this point, though, the letter was a way to start organizing Congress to confront the administration, because ATWG had finally accepted that the Democratic president that it had been so pleased to see defeat Bush had politically aligned himself with the desire of arms-makers to continue Cold War levels of production and profits through exports.

There were no more helpful approaches to the administration on arms sales in the Clinton years. ATWG spent its time trying to enact laws to constrain its former soulmates who had "gone downtown" to serve Clinton. Soderberg told ATWG that conven-

---

1 A former Kissinger staffer, Halperin had a lengthy history as an outspoken opponent of US support for repressive governments, and conservatives in the Senate blocked his nomination. However, he continued to handle the "democracy" portfolio for Clinton in a variety of positions that did not require confirmation.

tional arms control was an issue that Clinton might be able to take on "in the second term," but ATWG's experience was that once Clinton blinked on confronting the arms industry's argument that exports meant jobs — and that was during the 1992 campaign, as well as throughout his first term — there would never be good time to confront it. Clinton personally promoted sales to Saudi Arabia and a number of other non-democratic governments, and arms exports to dictators soared to record levels throughout the 1990s, constrained primarily by the financial limitations of the purchasers.

ATWG promoted a plethora of failed legislative initiatives during Clinton's presidency, such as blocking military participation in "air shows" where dictators flocked to watch weapons-makers demonstrate their wares and barring US Export–Import Bank financing of arms sales, a proposal that was fiercely opposed by Senator Dodd, who wanted Connecticut-made Black Hawk helicopters sold to Turkey. ATWG did succeed in enacting legislation forcing the international financial institutions to audit not just the civilian but the military budgets of loan recipients for corruption (an effort led by Congressman Joe Kennedy), banning the export and briefly the use of anti-personnel landmines (an effort led by Senator Patrick Leahy), and conditioning fighter sales and military training for the Suharto dictatorship in Indonesia on progress toward free elections and an end to its occupation of East Timor (an effort led by Congressman Patrick Kennedy). Most of its work, though, was devoted to a systematic challenge to US arms transfers, the Arms Trade Code of Conduct

In early 1992, as ATWG was casting about for a legislative campaign that John Isaacs had suggested was needed to rally public support for restraint in the arms trade, the director of a British advocacy group, Saferworld, visited Washington. Raj Thamotheram had dreamed up a "Code of Conduct" for European governments under which they would pledge not to export weapons to unstable regions or to governments not meeting international obligations on human rights. Under the leadership of PDD's Anne Detrick, ATWG sharpened Thamotheram's largely hortatory and loosely-defined categories into four standards that governments had to be certified by the administration as meeting in order to receive US weapons and training: "promotes democracy," including a specific, measurable requirement that the government was chosen in free and fair elections, "respects human rights," including vigorous investigation and prosecution of violators, "not engaged in armed aggression," and "full participation in UN Register of Conventional Arms." The language on human rights and armed aggression largely restated existing law, and participation in the UN Arms Register would be a simple matter for any country, so the real impact of the Code would be in aligning US arms sales with the oft-proclaimed policy of promoting democracy.[1] ATWG's publicity campaigns always referred to it as the "No Arms to Dictators" Code of Conduct.

ATWG took a draft of the Code legislation to Republican senator Mark Hatfield and Democratic House arms control expert Berman to ask them to be the bipartisan sponsors. As a pacifist who believed that both US and global militarization invariably damaged

---

1 The State Department's annual report on human rights practices already had a section for each country that judged whether citizens had an effective right to choose their government through free and fair elections, so the Code of Conduct was effectively inviting the administration to use that standard in determining which countries would be eligible.

American interests, Hatfield gladly accepted. Berman demurred, and ATWG moved on to a junior member, Cynthia McKinney of Georgia, an anti-imperialist who hoped one day to succeed Ron Dellums as the expert foreign and military conscience of the House. To make the bill bipartisan in both Houses, ATWG soon recruited Senator Brian Dorgan of North Dakota and Congressman Dana Rohrabacher of California as lead cosponsors. The unlikely pairing of McKinney and former Reagan speech-writer Rohrabacher behind a "no arms to dictators" Code of Conduct gave ATWG hope that meaningful legislation could be passed by the "moralistic" left and right over the "responsible" center. In the 1970s the key piece of legislation on human rights, which barred US support at the World Bank for "gross" abusers, was enacted over the strenuous objections of the foreign policy establishment and its adherents in Congress by a left-right coalition led by Congressman Tom Harkin and Senator Jesse Helms, who both hated the World Bank, but for entirely different reasons.

On the positive side, the alliance against dictators by the "odd couple" of McKinney and Rohrabacher certainly boosted the attention paid to ATWG's initiative. It was compelling theater to pair someone who spoke from the hip about communist repression and tried to fight alongside the Afghan rebels against the Soviets with someone who also spoke from the hip, but about imperialist oppression, and backed the Lumumbist rebel Laurent Kabila, who dethroned Joseph Mobutu in Zaire. On the negative side, neither had a reputation as a consensus-builder and legislator, McKinney because she was a freshman just out of the Georgia legislature, where she had made a reputation when her denunciation of the invasion of Iraq led to a walk-out by many of her colleagues. However, for the first few years of her tenure, McKinney proved to be an able legislator, learning parliamentary rules and floor practices and taking the time to "whip" possible co-sponsors. Rohrabacher, in contrast, did little more than lend his Republican name and his incessant invocations of Ronald Reagan at press conferences.

ATWG turned its grassroots members such as Peace Action and religious lobbies loose on their representatives to co-sponsor the bill, and its Washington members published reports and testified at hearings and briefings on the arms trade and the Code.[1] Lora Lumpe of the Federation of American Scientists, Natalie Goldring of the British American Security Information Council, Scott Nathanson of PDD, and Bill Hartung of the World Policy Institute took the lead in producing reports and appearing in the media. PDD's specialty was an annual compilation of US arms transfers called "Dictators or Democracies?" that totaled up the value of weapons deals with countries that were acknowledged as not freely elected by the State Department human rights report. Typical was its 1995 finding that "non-democratic governments received 85 percent ($47.1 billion) of the $55.2 billion of American weapons that were transferred to developing countries through sales or foreign aid during the past four years."

By 1995 ATWG was ready for a test, and asked McKinney to take the rare congressional step of pushing for a floor vote on an amendment she knew would lose rather than

---

1   See, for example, the transcript of a hearing titled "US Policy on Conventional Weapons," held by the House Committee on Foreign Affairs, November 9, 1993, US Government Printing Office, 1994.

bargaining to find a symbolic compromise. This step is rare because a losing test vote can discredit both a concept and its sponsor, and force potential supporters into perpetual opposition. Congress respects winners, even if the win is not for a significant policy change, so the institutional pressure for making a deal if faced with losing is enormous. At times, though, there is an overwhelming need to put people on record on a clear policy choice so that a grassroots movement can go after them back home and try to convert them for the next vote. Thus McKinney agreed to the fight, totaled a respectable 157 votes of the 218 needed to win, and told the groups to get to work, thanking their supporters and identifying and winning over the swings.

In the Senate, despite the standing joke that as a devout Baptist "Saint Mark" Hatfield was happiest when he lost 99–1 on a moral question, he was no more eager to force a losing test vote than McKinney had been. At the unanimous request of the 300 groups, nationwide, who were now lobbying for the Code, and after a last-minute appeal by a long-haired male lobbyist who promised to accede to the socially-conservative Hatfield's routine request that he cut his hair, Hatfield finally agreed to force a test vote in 1996. First, though, ATWG had to survive a potential break with Hatfield's Democratic cosponsor, Byron Dorgan, over the third rail in US foreign policy, Israel. From the start of the Code movement, Democratic support for Israel had been the elephant in the room. The administration would have probably determined that Israel met the Code's standards, but as a practical matter, even if it didn't, Congress would have funded its weapons anyway. By positively naming Israel and its Camp David partner, Egypt, in the foreign aid appropriation every year, Congress had already made it clear that it wanted them to have US weapons regardless of their compliance with particular standards.[1]

Not satisfied with the reality, as outlined in an ATWG memorandum to Congress, that Israel would not be affected by enactment of the Code, former Berman staffer Brad Gordon asked Dorgan to modify the Code to exempt any country taking part in the Middle East peace process — meaning Israel, Egypt, and probably Jordan. ATWG told Dorgan and Hatfield that it would denounce and oppose any bill that made an exception for any country or region, and AIPAC showed it probably agreed that the Code was no threat by backing down. Ironically, ATWG was attacked from the left for "exempting" Israel from the Code with its memorandum, despite having forced Dorgan to drop his modification and despite the participation of some of its members in a much-publicized proposal for a moratorium on arms transfers to the Middle East and the redirection of Camp David aid from military to peace-building purposes.[2] The Hatfield–Dorgan amendment received

---

1   More generally, enacting the Code of Conduct could not permanently bar arms transfers to dictators as its name implied, because with a subsequent law Congress could always make an exception. What was really new about the Code was that non-democratic governments who received weapons through cash sales, rather than from congressionally-approved foreign aid, would have to receive a positive affirmation in law each year. Under the Supreme Court's 1983 "Chadha" decision on presidential powers, opponents of an arms sale had to enact a law in 60 days, over the president's veto — a nearly impossible task logistically and politically. The Code would have reversed the burden of action, forcing supporters of arming a dictator to enact a waiver.

2   See "Bringing Israel up to Code," *Counterpunch*, October 16-21, 1996, and "Toward a Safer Future for the Children of Abraham: A Proposal for Restructuring US Aid to the Middle

only 35 votes, the same proportion as McKinney–Rohrabacher. As was the case in the 1995 House vote, a number of Democrats from arms-producing states renounced their reputations as human rights leaders to show their labor and corporate supporters and local media that export jobs came first, and many more were ready to oppose the amendment had it come closer to passage. Connecticut senators Dodd and Lieberman reprised the opposition in the House vote of the entire delegation from the state of Sikorski helicopters and Pratt & Whitney jet engines.

ATWG agreed to focus all its effort for the next year on winning a vote in 1997 during the mark-up of the foreign aid authorization in the House International Relations Committee, which would force the administration to try to strip the amendment out on floor. Armed with the whip list from the McKinney vote, the Washington-based groups worked on having Code supporters in Congress line up the swing votes on the Committee, and the district-based groups worked on the swings back home. ATWG was optimistic about its chances in the committee. The test votes on both floors that had been achieved by this poorly-funded coalition of arms control and religious groups had brought the dangers of the arms trade to the fore for the first time in mainstream foreign policy debates since Bush and Baker reversed their Gulf War pledge to constrain sales to the Middle East. A congressionally-mandated study group of Soft and Hard Eagles chaired by defense analyst Janne Nolan issued a report to Clinton that detailed the risks to US security from the pace and sophistication of the arms sales race between supplying countries, recognized that the profit motive rather than strategic rationales was driving the race, and called on the National Security Council to take over the approval process from the compromised State and Defense Departments and promote vigorous negotiations with other suppliers for mutual restraint.[1]

Despite these favorable signs, the ATWG effort did not go well. McKinney was starting to develop a reputation for flakiness and extreme statements, and her ability to round up the Democratic votes she needed to win in the committee was fading.[2] In addition, the aggressive appeal to corporate interests that House Whip Tony Coelho started in 1980 as head of the Democratic Congressional Campaign Committee had paid off. Bernard Schwartz, president of the Loral arms-maker, had become one of the party's key donors, and arms makers' political action committees and their lobbying coalition, the Aerospace Industries Association, or AIA, had made millions of dollars of campaign contributions to the Democratic National Committee, to Clinton's re-election effort, and to Members of

---

East," Coalition to Rethink US Aid to the Middle East, January 1995.

1 "Report of the Presidential Advisory Board on Arms Proliferation Policy," pursuant to executive order 12946.

2 Her view that the Bush administration set up or allowed the 9/11 attacks led to her defeat in the 2002 Democratic primary, which was actually, under Georgia law, an open primary in which Republicans could vote. National Jewish donors gave heavily to her challenger, because of her evolving position against Israeli occupation and her father's reputation for anti-Semitic statements. She returned to Congress in 2005, but a confrontation with a Capitol policeman gave credibility to another primary challenger, and she lost again in 2007.

Congress.[1] The AIA and its affiliated unions lobbied committee members whose constituents' jobs depended on arms exports, and Defense and State Department officials made the strategic case for US weapons rather than European ones, with no mention of mutual restraint. While ATWG's grassroots groups generated a lot of publicity in their districts for the endorsement of McKinney's Code by a coalition of Nobel Peace Prize winners put together by former president Oscar Arias of Costa Rica, they could not win enough firm commitments. When the amendment was offered in June 1997, it was defeated 23–21. Amory Houghton, a moderate New York Republican who local groups thought had committed to the Code, and indeed had voted for it on the floor in 1995 when its failure was apparent, provided the deciding vote against it. However, Republican committee chair Ben Gilman also had a few commitments available to switch votes had he needed them.

Disappointed that the result of a year's grassroots work should be so minimal, McKinney worked out a compromise with Gilman that she would add to the foreign aid bill during floor debate. The compromise retained the entire Code amendment, including its requirement that the administration annually submit a list of countries not meeting the Code that it still wished to arm, but switched the burden of action on this list to the congressional opponents of an exemption, who would have to enact a bill rejecting it. While this process simply reaffirmed the existing reality, ATWG's Washington offices agreed to the compromise, so as to have a good chance of enacting at the least the presumption of "no arms to dictators," and setting up a process for liberal Members to force votes on exempted countries. However, 11 grassroots chapters of ATWG member Peace Action went over the head of their national director, Gordon Clark, and wrote McKinney directly to ask her to offer, and obviously lose on, the original bill on the floor.

The incident showed how difficult it was for even the most locally-bred and oriented Washington leader, in this case Clark, to keep a finger on the pulse of local activists. At about the same time AWTG leaders brokered a compromise between Congressman Joe Kennedy and Father Roy Bourgeois, the leader of a grassroots movement to close the US Army's training center for Latin America, the School of the Americas in Ft. Benning, Georgia. Kennedy was nowhere near having the votes needed to close the center, but had surprisingly gained the agreement of senior members of the Armed Services committee to turn it into discussion center for civilian and military leaders. Father Bourgeois returned home to spread the good news, but a day later had to send this note back to Washington: "Accept nothing less than *CLOSE THE SCHOOL OF THE AMERICAS*. We can do it! Any... reform of the S.O.A. will only hurt our cause." Kennedy had to back out of the deal, and the military training at the center went on as before.

McKinney rejected the plea by Peace Action's local chapters, and after getting over her irritation at being portrayed as a sell-out by the very groups that had asked her to compromise, played a smooth parliamentary game to win the weakened Code's approval

---

1 ATWG developed a friendly adversarial relationship with the AIA and its top Washington lobbyist, former Democratic Senate Foreign Relations staffer Joel Johnson. Sporting buttons that read, "AIA=NRA: Pushing Weapons at Home and Abroad," ATWG members demonstrated at the AIA offices and debated Johnson in hearings and in the media. Off-camera, Johnson was a good sport, once asking his debating partners: "No arms for dictators? Who else are we going to sell to?"

by voice vote on the floor. However, when the conference meeting with the Senate on the underlying bill stalled, McKinney and ATWG were unable to break the Code amendment out along with some other items that were placed in another bill and became law. ATWG did manage to block House consideration of what it called a "faux Code" calling for multilateral, rather than US action, which was offered by Connecticut congressman Sam Gejdenson in 1998. McKinney won House approval of an amendment in 1999 that instructed the administration to explore an international Code, but all of this was a feeble aftershock to the disastrous Committee vote in 1997. One ATWG leader took a leave to run unsuccessfully for Congress against Houghton, and others broke off relations with McKinney as her public stances became increasingly bizarre, because, as one said, "it was as if a brick fell on her head around 1996." In the Senate Hatfield's retirement in 1998 forced ATWG to find a new leader, since few in the group wanted to entrust the Code to Dorgan after his dance with AIPAC. John Kerry agreed to sponsor the Code, but he, like Dorgan, made a compromise deal to weaken the Code without consulting ATWG, and the grassroots effort simply faded away.

Some groups in ATWG were drawn into an effort promoted and funded by Tony Blair's Labor Party and then government in Britain to establish a symbolic, and toothless, European Union Code of Conduct. The EU Code was drawn up under the direction of the international office of Amnesty International in London, which unlike the American office in Washington had a position of not supporting the US Code's broad bar of "no arms to dictators." The London office believed that Amnesty's governing mandate required a focus not on how a government was chosen, but on physical abuses by its forces; in short, not on democracy but on human rights. In 1999 Amnesty revised the international code proposed by Oscar Arias and his band of peace-prize winners, dropping the ban on arming dictators and replacing it with a requirement that exporting countries determine whether particular small arms might be used in specific acts of torture and repression. British arms control groups followed the lead of Paul Eavis, who had replaced the more strident Raj Thamotheram as head of Saferworld, and took Amnesty's side against ATWG.

The formal adoption of Amnesty's Code by the European Union had no impact on arms exports, and European heads of state continued to lobby Middle Eastern autocrats and South Africa's democrats alike to win contracts for major weapons systems. Bribery to close arms deals, both as illegal cash payments and as legal pledges to "offset" arms payments with economic incentives like building factories or importing goods, continued to be practiced at the highest levels of European government. Tony Blair's government was caught making billions of dollars in payments to Saudi leaders, but closed down the investigation on grounds of national security. A number of European governments were caught making payments to the African National Congress and individual South African politicians, including Deputy President Jacob Zuma and his financier Shabir Shaik. The French government refused to cooperate with the investigation by the South African anticorruption police, fearing the sting of the "Scorpions," whose charter placed them beyond the control of the South African cabinet.

The Code movement rallied Soft Eagles to a new standard in US foreign policy, at least those Soft Eagles whose districts did not host arms manufacturers looking to replace Cold War procurement with foreign sales. On balance, it must be judged a failure. The failure was not in falling short in the Herculean task of enacting a binding Code barring arms transfers and training for dictators. That would have been perhaps too much of improvement to expect on legislation banning aid to military regimes that seized power from democratic governments during the previous year, which Patrick Leahy had placed in annual Senate appropriations bills since the late 1980s. Considering the power of the AIA, their allied unions, and a president and leading members of Congress who were tied to them by politics and campaign contributions, the Code's founders in ATWG and leaders in Congress knew that this was always an unlikely outcome. The failure was not even that Clinton continued to export record levels of arms to dictators. His commitment to short-term stimulation of the arms industry was obvious from the time he supported the fighter sale to Saudi Arabia as a candidate. The real failure of the Code movement was that it never achieved its underlying purpose of stigmatizing authoritarian rule and militarization on moral grounds, for both Turkeys and Eagles, the way that acts of murder and torture had been stigmatized by the human rights movement of the 1970s. The great victory of that movement was enshrining in the foreign policy mainstream the concept that it was wrong to aid the abusers. US policy-makers still decided at times to do so, but the onus was on them to justify the aid, and on the repressive regimes to minimize their egregious acts of violence.

The Code movement never broke through to a mainstream understanding of the immorality of backing regimes that denied free elections. The Turkeys in ATWG had decided to try to reach Eagles in the Congress and the public with the broadly appealing notion of the "boomerang" effect of arms transfers on US interests, more than with the moral claim that it was wrong to help repress people in other countries. When ATWG was trying to block the foreign operations appropriation in 1998 that had added a Senate provision reorganizing the State Department but not the House-passed McKinney's compromise Code, its appeal to Members of Congress used precisely that order in its argument: "Why reorganize the State Department without changing its most dangerous policy: arming dictators and human rights abusers? Stand up for our troops, who in Panama, Somalia, and Haiti faced troops we had armed. Stand up for their citizens' human rights and their right to choose their leaders in free elections." Not only did the US troops come first, but the differentiation of human rights and free elections in the last sentence was an acknowledgement the movement had failed to elevate free elections to the status of a human right.

Even Turkeys, with Amnesty International and Human Rights Watch as leading examples, never accepted the notion that a lack of democracy in developing countries was as dangerous to their people as outright human rights abuses, because it created the conditions for protest, conflict, and the resulting abuses. In 1997 ATWG member PDD, recently renamed Demilitarization for Democracy, published "Fighting Retreat," a lengthy study of the role of military political power in thwarting the transition to free elections and other democratic practices in Africa. However, many human rights advocates were at that time supporting Clinton's African Crisis Response Initiative, which armed and trained dictators' armies to take part in peace-keeping operations in other African countries, despite the risk of their using their arms and new skills to maintain military rule at home. This was in keeping with some Turkey's and many Soft Eagles' new-found interventionism, in which they hoped to use US military power in the uncertain new world to protect citizens from their governments. In Haiti, Bosnia, and Kosovo, interventions by American troops were hailed by Soft Eagles and even some Turkeys with the same fervor they would have been criticized during the Cold War. Refueling, overflight, rear area logistical support, and covert operations were needed as much for "humanitarian" interventions as for Carter's Rapid Deployment Force or Reagan's aid to Angola rebels, and dictators who provided them might reasonably have expected an exemption from the Code of Conduct, even if it had become law. The stated purpose of US foreign policy was in a confusing transition, from world enforcer to world protector. It was hardly a rallying cry for public support, but it would justify increased budgets until something better came along.

CHAPTER 7. AFTER 9/11: BUSH, OBAMA, AND THE LONG WAR

President George W. Bush and Vice President Dick Cheney did not start the long war for control of the Middle East, although these Hard Eagles and their neo-conservative advisers certainly prosecuted it with gusto. When Bush defeated Al Gore in 2000 because of a quirk of constitutional bargaining in Philadelphia two centuries past — in which each state was given an extra two electoral votes regardless of the size of its population — Paul Wolfowitz, Richard Perle, Doug Feith, David Wurmser, David Addington, and Elliott Abrams finally had the chance to test fully the proposals they had promoted only fitfully in secondary positions in the Reagan and first Bush administrations, and as members of the 1970s Committee on the Present Danger and its 1990s counterpart, the Project for a New American Century. Bush and Cheney eagerly adopted their "with us or against us," "gloves-off," unilateral program of torture, assassination, reprisal, and "preventive" war and "regime change," all with pointed disdain for both congressional authority and international laws or organizations that saw America as just another country rather than an exceptional global actor.

Bill Clinton had provided something of a starting line for Bush and Cheney when he responded to an alleged Iraqi plot to assassinate the first president Bush and to al-Qaeda's bombing of two US embassies in Africa not with indictments and international legal pressure, but with missile attacks without congressional or UN authorization. He also started the CIA practice of "rendition," kidnapping members of the Egyptian Islamic Jihad in Eastern Europe and flying them to Egypt for prison and torture, and started an air war on Serbian troops in Kosovo and economic targets in Belgrade on his sole authority. However, it was not Clinton who the neo-conservatives were emulating, but Israel. Israel has at times felt that its survival has hinged on such a program, and indeed some of these advisers — Perle, Wurmser, and Feith — had advocated elements of it for Israel in a memorandum to the Likud party in 1996 that advocated a "Clean Break" with the restraints of the past.[1] After 9/11, Bush and his band justified US exemption from international law and opinion by taking a similarly apocalyptic view of the threat posed by al-Qaeda's attacks on civilians and the potential for Saddam Hussein to unleash "weapons of mass destruction." Al-Qaeda's attacks, though, were more pretext than motivation, since neo-conservatives had always held this view and advocated this program. Over three decades, since the end of the Vietnam War, they had consistently argued that US national security, indeed national existence, justified unilateral action unconstrained by domestic Constitution and dissent or international law and opinion. As noted in Chapter 5, they had likened the Reagan administration's violations of both domestic and international law in the Contra war to Lincoln's extra-constitutional steps to protect the nation at the start of the Civil War.

President Barack Obama was similarly not the first American leader to fight the long war more judiciously. While he paid far more attention than Bush to opinion in the Muslim world, multilateral initiatives, and the self-defeating limits of Western military action, Obama did so as a Soft Eagle in pursuit of a policy, accepted by both Soft and Hard Eagles, that Franklin Roosevelt had set firmly in place when large-scale oil was discovered in Saudi Arabia in the 1930s. That policy was to maintain Western access to Middle Eastern oil by backing cooperative dictators and kings through arms transfers, training, covert support, the forward deployment of US military forces, and the use of those forces when needed to achieve pro-Western outcomes to regional conflicts. Most notable among these alliances have been those with the House of Saud, the House of Pahlavi in Iran, the East African autocrats who hosted the Rapid Deployment Force in the 1980s, and the traditional rulers of Bahrain, the United Arab Emirates, and Qatar who have provided basing rights since 9/11. Osama bin Laden dates the US policy even earlier, and calls it a continuation of the Crusades that started in 1096, but despite Bush's unfortunate use of "crusade" in a speech soon after 9/11, there is no religious overtone to US military penetration of the Middle East. The better historical analogy is the Great Game, the struggle for control of Central Asia's export wealth between Britain and Russia in the 19th century.

A complicating factor for the oil-based US policy in the Middle East has been the existence since 1948 of a Jewish state in Israel. Truman's decision to reject the advice of Secretary of State George Marshall and recognize the new state has since cascaded, as Marshall feared, into a guarantee of Israeli survival and a major irritant in US relations with the Muslim rulers and subjects of the Middle East. Eisenhower forestalled the collision of these competing trains with his threat to intervene on Egypt's behalf during the French, British, and Israeli seizure of the Suez Canal in 1956, but they met head on during the 1973 Yom Kippur War. US resupply of Israel's forces provided the justification for the effective embargo that the Organization of Petroleum Exporting Countries, or OPEC, had failed to achieve during the previous Arab-Israeli war in 1967.

OPEC blocked all sales to American firms, cut production by 20 percent, and raised its prices for European firms. Facing the damage of the OPEC embargo, as well as a Soviet threat to intervene to protect Egypt's army after it had been encircled by Israel's, Secretary of State Kissinger leaked plans for a US invasion and ten-year seizure of Saudi oil fields

---

1 The memo was prepared for the Institute for Advanced Strategic and Political Studies. It can be found at http://www.israeleconomy.org/strat1.htm.

and successfully pushed Arab countries and Israel to negotiate an end to the war, which provided a pretext for the end of the five-month embargo.[1] All this led to a rapid, inflation-adjusted doubling of world oil prices, a global economic slow-down that persisted throughout the 1970s, a doubling of the US inflation rate to 11 percent, and frustratingly long lines at gas pumps. Carter was assisted in his election in 1976 by the OPEC oil malaise and was hampered in his reelection bid in 1980 by the further doubling of these higher oil prices after the Iranian revolution and the start of the Iran–Iraq War, which again doubled the inflation rate, this time to 13 percent, and led to a global recession.[2]

This volatile mixture of oil, international security, and domestic politics has been engrained in the memory of American officials, making any consideration of a fundamental change in policy unthinkable. When former Foreign Affairs committee chairman Lee Hamilton met with a group of Democratic House members in 2008 to develop a strategy on the Middle East and the topic turned to the contradiction of the United States backing the oil autocrats while talking about promoting democracy in the Middle East, his assessment was blunt and dismissive. "We can, and should" talk about American values, he said, but "we simply are going to back them. They have the oil." Soft Eagles hold much the same attitude about US military, economic, and covert support for the Mubarak government in Egypt, not because of oil but because of its continuation of Anwar Sadat's recognition of Israel under the Camp David agreement of 1978. Support for Israel is a mantra for Soft Eagles, and indeed, they largely followed Hamilton's approach with Iran under its repressive Shah Pahlavi in the 1970s, both because of its oil and because of the Shah's close collaboration with Israel on trade and military matters.

With so much of the oil wealth and Camp David aid being used to purchase American-made weapons, Eagles accept, if not openly cheer for, the continued rule of the Middle Eastern authoritarians. They comfort themselves with the accurate argument that a policy of demanding free elections as the basis for close relations would probably bring to power Islamist governments like Iran's. Hard Eagles fear that such governments would not cooperate with the West militarily, Soft Eagles fear that they would be even more conservative than the current rulers on recognizing Israel and women's rights, and both fear that they would make access to oil less predictable. Day to day, though, and even year to year, it is not access to oil that drives specific administration decisions. In that sense, Secretary of State James Baker's justification of the 1991 Gulf War as required by "O-I-L" and historian Michael Klare's thesis that both the 1991 and 2003 wars were cases of "blood for oil" are misleading.[3]

---

1 Stephen J. Cimbala, *Military Persuasion: Deterrence and Provocation in Crisis and War*, Pennsylvania State University Press, University Park, PA, 1994, p. 279; Robert Bryce, *Gusher of Lies: The Dangerous Delusions of Energy Independence*, Public Affairs, New York, 2009, p. 96.

2 Oil prices returned to their pre-embargo base in the early 1980s, only to rise even farther with the invasion of Iraq, before the recession of 2008 brought them back to pre-embargo levels again. WTRG Economics, "Crude Oil Prices," at http://www.wtrg.com/oil_graphs/ oilprice1947.gif. All inflation figures are from the US consumer price index of the Department of Labor.

3 Baker made his comment when asked by the press to justify US military action to drive Iraq out of Kuwait. Klare explores his thesis in *Blood and Oil: The Dangers and Consequences of*

It is true that US involvement in the long war is rooted in the region's oil, but it was challenges to US credibility, and not to American access to oil, that triggered the US response in the two wars. Similarly, the invasion of Afghanistan in 2001, Bush's support for Ethiopia's invasion of Somalia in 2005, and Obama's continuing wars against the Talibans of both Afghanistan and Pakistan were only indirectly related to oil. These wars were undertaken to disrupt havens for al-Qaeda, and al-Qaeda's leaders had attacked American citizens and US forces over US maintenance of the Egyptian and Saudi regimes they hoped to replace, and the maintenance was indeed linked to oil and Israel. However, the immediate purpose of these wars was to retaliate for 9/11 and discourage future attacks. As was the case for the British Empire under Queen Victoria, whose "little wars" required the dispatch of troops into combat somewhere in the colonial world in literally every year of her 64-year reign, a global power almost by definition must meet any challenge to its dominance.

There was no oil at stake in Indochina, nor in Central America, nor even in oil-rich Angola, whose Cabinda enclave has continued to sell its oil to the West throughout all the wars and changes in governance, yet administrations felt the need to demonstrate US resolve with military action. It was Saddam Hussein's seizure of Kuwait that led to the first Gulf War, and it was his chafing under the US-led and UN-backed military and economic pressure that eventually led to the second. Hussein had become unruly, and like Panamanian dictator Noriega after the Contra War and Zairean dictator Mobutu after the Cold War, Hussein was no longer needed by the United States after Iraq's war with Iran ended. His invasion of Kuwait threatened the predictability of the region, just as the looming electoral victory of an Islamist party, the FIS, did in Algeria a year later. In that case the Algerian army, with French backing and US acquiescence, stepped in with a coup, triggering a civil war in which 100,000 civilians died.[1] The New World Order required order, and US policy supplied it.

The Hard Eagles in Congress backed every military venture proposed after 9/11: the invasions of Afghanistan and Iraq, drone assassinations in Pakistan, Somalia, and Yemen, Bush's "surge" of additional US and Iraqi troops in Iraq in 2007, and Obama's similar surge against the Afghanistan and Pakistani Talibans in 2009. The Soft Eagles opposed the Iraq War from the start and at every step of the way. A majority of Democrats in both Houses voted against the invasion and the surge and whittled Bush's proposed long-term basing agreement down to a short-term withdrawal agreement. On drone warfare and the wars in Afghanistan and Pakistan, though, Soft Eagles for five years balanced their criticism of Bush for starting the "wrong war" in Iraq by saying he had ignored the truly important war with the Talibans. As a result, when Obama took office most Democrats in Congress were willing to give him with a wide berth in addressing these conflicts.

Obama's initial surge in Afghanistan in the spring of 2009 from 38,000 to 60,800 troops made the Soft Eagles uncomfortable as many of their constituents were becoming increasingly vocal in their opposition to the war. However, as was the case with Bill Clin-

America's Growing Dependence on Imported Petroleum, Metropolitan Books, New York, 2004.

1 Robert Dreyfuss, *Devil's Game: How the United States Helped Unleash Fundamentalist Islam*, Metropolitan Books, New York, 2005, pp. 315-316.

ton, the concerted attacks on a Democratic president by the Hard Eagles and their media machine on domestic issues encouraged Soft Eagles to come to Obama's defense, and mute their criticisms of his foreign policy. During Obama's months of discussion with his advisers in the fall of 2009 on his commanders' request for an additional surge in Afghanistan, Soft Eagles mostly watched and waited. While some opposed escalation, few called for withdrawal. Virtually none challenged proposals to push and aid Pakistan to wage war with its own and Afghanistan's Talibans, groups that it had, in many senses, created itself. When Obama presented another troop increase to 100,000 as a way to begin a withdrawal in 18 months, Soft Eagles were disarmed.

Turkeys were aghast at the decision, and finally began pulling away from Obama. In stark contrast to both varieties of Eagles, they had been consistent opponents of both pillars of the long war — access to oil and support for Israel — and of the post-9/11 wars in Iraq, Afghanistan, and Pakistan. Eagles chant the mantra of "energy independence" from Middle Eastern suppliers, but then shy away from the expensive steps needed to achieve it. Turkeys, though, really believe in that cause, and did so even before they became convinced that planetary suicide was afoot through global warming. They have always seen the fossil-fuel economy as the source of many modern evils, despite the remarkable increase in life expectancy that has been driven by economic growth in the carbon era. Turkeys see no need to play nice with Middle Eastern potentates, and would consider a punitive disruption of the world oil market to be an environmental favor. On Israel, they see the oft-cited fear of Israel and its mighty armed forces being "driven into the sea" by its Arab neighbors as a fraudulent bit of propaganda and dispute Israel's need for nuclear weapons. Most promote a settlement that returns land taken from Arabs, at least during and since the 1967 war, and some go so far as to organize boycotts of Israeli goods and cultural events to protest the treatment of Palestinians in Israel and the occupied territories and Israeli military operations in Lebanon.

Some analysts, such as former Harvard President Larry Summers, have seen anti-Semitic roots in the fervor with which Turkeys have taken the Palestinian side.[1] Historian Walter Laqueur is certainly right to note that the size of the affected population is suspiciously small compared to others whose oppression receives little condemnation from the left.[2] Turkeys' fervor can also be explained by their devotion to international laws on weapons and force and international standards on human rights that Israel's supporters acknowledge it believes it must flout at times to maintain its security. Whatever the reason, Turkeys' lack of concern for Israeli security and for access to oil effectively remove them from the policy debate in Washington and from inclusion in the mainstream media's coverage of it. As a result, their commitment to US security was suspect even before they opposed the retaliatory attack on the Afghan Taliban in 2001 and the war to disarm Saddam Hussein of his alleged weapons of mass destruction in 2003.

During the Vietnam War, Turkeys could humorously turn aside Eagles' claims that American security was at stake by saying that when the Viet Cong paddled up the Po-

---

1 Paras Bhayani, "Summers says British Boycott of Israeli Academics is Intentionally 'Anti-Semitic'," *Harvard Crimson*, June 2, 2006.
2 *The Changing Face of Anti-Semitism*, Oxford University Press, New York, 2006, p. 8.

tomac and started lobbing shells at the Pentagon, maybe then it would be time to talk about security. When al-Qaeda actually did attack the Pentagon and the Taliban government in Afghanistan refused to seize its leaders and turn them over to the United States, Turkeys opposed military action on the grounds that it would devastate Afghanistan without providing meaningful security to the United States. They proposed instead international police and financial actions to isolate al-Qaeda. In hindsight, the Turkeys were largely right. Police and financial actions have weakened al-Qaeda, and the war in Afghanistan has been a wonderful recruiting tool for militant Islam that al-Qaeda has happily watched from other sanctuaries. However, by taking a stand against retaliation after 9/11, Turkeys were as out of step with mainstream opinion as Congresswoman Jeannette Rankin was when she cast the only vote against war with Japan after Pearl Harbor. Turkeys were unfortunately no longer part of the national security debate.

THE BUSH ERA: "THEY HATE OUR FREEDOMS," AND THE WAR OF CHOICE IN IRAQ

Treasury Secretary Paul O'Neill reported being mystified when the very first cabinet meeting of the Bush administration turned to the topic of invading Iraq. Had he been paying attention to foreign policy as much as finance, he would not have been. George Bush may have run on a platform of moderation and respect in foreign policy, but the neoconservative crowd he gathered around him, from Cheney to Wolfowitz, had been openly calling for this moment of unrestrained American and executive power since their defeat in Vietnam. They used the shock of 9/11 to gain congressional approval of the invasions of Afghanistan and Iraq and of sharply increased military procurement, mostly of weapons systems that had nothing to do with current conflicts, but rather would maintain US primacy well into the future. The enduring contribution of the Bush administration to American foreign policy was not, however, found in wars and spending, but rather in a hypothesis whose acceptance by mainstream opinion guaranteed decades more of the long war.

The hypothesis, as expressed by Bush when addressing Congress after the 9/11 attacks, was that al-Qaeda and its sympathizers are at war with the United States because they detest its way of life:

> Americans are asking, "Why do they hate us?" They hate what we see right here in this chamber — a democratically elected government. Their leaders are self-appointed. They hate our freedoms — our freedom of religion, our freedom of speech, our freedom to vote and assemble and disagree with each other.

The Members stood and roared their approval of this cultural explanation, in which the United States was an innocent bystander attacked by feudalistic Islamic madmen in a "clash of civilizations" that had been predicted in 1996 in Samuel Huntington's popular book. The United States was not about to give up its freedoms, so the hypothesis implied that the attacks would continue until the madmen were hunted down and killed.

Bush's hypothesis was convenient, self-congratulatory, obviously false, and dangerous. The alternative hypothesis, which was that Muslims were angered by US foreign policy because of the freedoms it took in dominating their countries in the long war for control of the Middle East, was inconvenient, embarrassing, and easily confirmed, as a series of hearings on international opinion polling and a resulting congressional study showed in

2008.[1] The study identified the policies that polling revealed were responsible for the dramatic decline in approval for US leadership from 2002, when 83 percent of countries had pluralities with a favorable opinion, to 2006, when only 23 percent of countries did: the invasion and occupation of Iraq, torture and rendition, a perceived lack of balance in the Israeli–Palestinian dispute, unilateral action, the hypocrisy of talking about democracy, human rights, and new nuclear threats while aiding dictators and repressive regimes and maintaining a nuclear arsenal, the historical memory of previous US interventions, a lack of contact, problems in getting a visa, and the perception of a war on Islam that was fueled by insulting comments by members and adherents of the Bush administration. While al-Qaeda and its violent tactics were broadly unpopular in the Muslim world, its role as standard-bearer against this perceived war on Islam was found by pollsters to reduce significantly the Islamic public's willingness to report its activities to the police. Implicit in the alternative hypothesis was the possibility of promoting America's security from terrorist attacks by changing the unpopular policies and disarming al-Qaeda's operational space and appeal.

There was really no need to wait for a study to see the flaws in Bush's claim that his "Global War on Terror" was a campaign for freedom. As the report pointed out: "The major *jihads* by members of al-Qaeda at the time of 9/11 had been directed against a wide variety of governments." The common characteristic of these governments was that they were dominating or intervening in Muslim regions and countries: "The dictatorial Soviet Union in the 1980s, for its invasion of Afghanistan in support of a secular regime; militaristic Serbia in the 1990s, for its treatment of Bosnian Muslims; nationalistic Russia, for its ongoing domination of Muslim Chechnya; and the democratic United States, for its military support of repressive regimes in Saudi Arabia and Egypt." If it had been a hatred for Western freedom that motivated al-Qaeda, it would have attacked Sweden, which had far more civil liberties than the United States; a hatred for Western licentiousness would have brought attacks on the Netherlands, whose legal sex trade makes Las Vegas look like a prayer meeting. Al-Qaeda's leaders certainly despise Western ways, but they only began to target the United States for its maintenance of the regimes it truly despises: secular authoritarians blocking Islamist rule in Egypt and Saudi Arabia.

Al-Qaeda's two founders are Osama bin Laden and Ayman al-Zawahiri. Bin Laden was a Saudi citizen from a prominent family headed by a construction magnate, but his family was more fundamentally Hadrami, the people of the Hadramaut region of Yemen, whose ancestors took to the Indian Ocean centuries ago as the traders, bankers, and diplomats who brought both Islam and a system of reliable trading credits to Asia.[2] Like the Wahabists who have controlled religious doctrine in Saudi Arabia under a 200-year alliance

---

1 "The Decline in America's Reputation: Why?", House Committee on Foreign Affairs, June 11, 2008, US Government Printing Office. The report was written by Subcommittee Chairman Bill Delahunt, with the assistance of the author.

2 The credit system allows al-Qaeda to move money quickly, without records, since debts are maintained by memory, and can be held, and paid, across centuries. Briefing by Harvard (and now Duke) anthropologist Engseng Ho, Social Science Research Council, Washington, DC, 2002. See also Professor Ho's *The Graves of Tarim: Genealogy and Mobility across the Indian Ocean*, University of California Press, Berkeley, 2006.

with the Saudi royal family, the Hadrami are part of the puritanical Salafist sect of Sunni Islam, which recognizes the validity of the *jihad* against both Muslims and non-Muslims to protect the faith.[1] After helping drive the Soviet Union from Afghanistan in the 1980s, bin Laden's next *jihad* was against the House of Saud for refusing his offer to raise troops to drive Iraq from Kuwait and instead agreeing to host US troops for that purpose. He only turned his attention to the United States when he became convinced that he could never drive the Saudis from the throne and establish an Islamic caliphate until he drove the Saudis' protector, the "far enemy," from the region.[2]

Ayman al-Zawahiri is an Egyptian doctor who allied himself with followers of Sayyid Qutb, also a Salafist, who as a strategist in the Muslim Brotherhood in Egypt in the 1950s and 1960s argued for *jihad* against Western-oriented regimes in the Islamic world. As a member of the Brotherhood, al-Zawahiri was imprisoned after the assassination of President Anwar Sadat, held for three years, and tortured. He served at a clinic in the war against the Soviets in Afghanistan in 1980, and again as a strategist there in the mid-1980s. After the Soviet withdrawal al-Zawahiri went home to Egypt to aid the Brotherhood's rebellion against Mubarak. In 1993 he became the leader of a splinter group, the Egyptian Islamic *Jihad*, and planned bombings while living in the Sudan, such as one that killed 17 people at the Egyptian embassy in Pakistan in 1995. In the mid-1990s al-Zawahiri became aware that Clinton's CIA was carrying our renditions of his colleagues who were hiding in Eastern Europe, bringing them to Egypt for torture, and he decided to extend the war to the United States. In 1998 he allied with bin Laden and they formed the International Islamic Front for *Jihad* on the Jews and Crusaders. The group's first attack on the United States, the African embassy bombings in 1998, were a direct retaliation for a recent CIA rendition to Egypt.[3]

Ignoring these complexities or even the existence of the long war, the Bush administration, in the memorable phrase used by White House chief of staff Andrew Card, "marketed" the wars in Afghanistan and Iraq as missions to protect the freedom of both Americans and foreign citizens to live as they wished. The word was everywhere: the National Football League saluted "freedom's heroes," a Marine Corps general told his troops with a straight face that the whumping of the blades of US helicopters was the "sound of freedom," Congressman Walter Jones Jr. got the House restaurant to rename French fries as Freedom fries as a criticism of France's opposition to the invasion of Iraq, and just as it did in Vietnam, the slogan on the cap of the Army's Green Berets read "to free the oppressed."[4] Scholars such as Michael Mandelbaum and Niall Ferguson joined in the orgy

---

1 Febe Armanios, "The Islamic Traditions of Wahhabism and Salafiyya," *Congressional Research Service*, Washington, DC, 2003, report RS21695.

2 Peter Bergen, "Profiles in Terror," Book Section, *Wall Street Journal*, August 11, 2006, which is a review of Lawrence Wright's *The Looming Tower*.

3 Andrew Higgins and Alan Cullison, "Saga of Dr. Zawahiri Sheds Light on Roots of al Qaeda terror," *Wall Street Journal*, p. A1, July 2, 2002.

4 A sign at Geno's, the home of the cheese-steak in the Italian market section of Philadelphia, creatively compared the role of teachers in reading to the role of the armed forces in preserving freedom: "If you can read this, thank a teacher. If you can read this is English, thank a Marine." Geno's has a history of controversial signage. A tribute to Daniel Faulkner, the policeman killed by Mumia Abu-Jamal, adorns the shop, and a sign reading "This is

of self-congratulation, identifying the United States in their books as the indispensable altruistic guarantor of political and economic freedom.[1] The acceptance of this mantra of freedom created a disconnection between American and world opinion that was nicely revealed when Bush addressed the Russian parliament in 2002. Referring to the Chechnyan campaign of terror bombings in Moscow, Bush tried to make common cause with Russia, saying that the Chechnyans hated Russia for the same reason that al-Qaeda hated the United States, "because of your freedoms." Instead of the cheering he had heard in Congress, Bush received a mystified silence from the Duma, whose members knew full well that Chechnyans were attacking Russia because it was refusing to give up its rule over these Muslim people that the czars had imposed in the 19th century.

Turkeys understood the long war, and they railed against Bush's hypocrisy of talking about freedom and democracy in the Middle East while refusing to demand the release of jailed democratic dissidents in Egypt and movement toward fair elections there and in the Gulf states. Coordinating their protests with groups in many other countries, they took to the streets in large numbers to protest the start and the continuation of the Iraq War. However, there was no room in the mainstream media for the Turkeys and their fundamental rejection of American domination of the Middle East. In 2002 the media focused on the technical questions of whether or not Saddam Hussein had weapons of mass destruction, and whether UN inspections could ensure that he could not develop them. From the Turkeys' perspective, countries with such weapons, including all the five permanent members of the UN Security Council, had no standing to block other nuclear states when for 30 years they had violated their commitment under the Nuclear Non-Proliferation Treaty to negotiate away all of their weapons.

A surprisingly large faction of the Turkeys claimed that the Bush administration permitted or even carried out the 9/11 attacks. Websites and local offices sprang up featuring photo and engineering analyses purporting to show how the commercial airplane crashes at the World Trade towers, the Pentagon, and in rural Pennsylvania were government hoaxes, with Air Force missiles and CIA explosives being the real culprits. At rallies sponsored by the World Workers Party's ANSWER coalition, as opposed to those sponsored by the more traditional United for Peace and Justice coalition, the organizers glommed the North Korean dictator and a Philadelphia cop-killer onto the list of victims of American imperialism, virtually guaranteeing that they would be excluded from the mainstream news cycle.[2]

Soft Eagles in Congress instinctively shied away from the anti-war movement because of its loony left, but also because they instinctively feared confronting Bush's apolitical characterization of the role of American troops overseas as protecting "freedom" against irrational terrorists who hated women, modernity, and the West. They could not only hear but see daily the results of the Pentagon-fueled clamor to "support our troops," as

---

America — when ordering, speak English" was the subject of a suit before the Philadelphia Commission on Human Relations.

1   Michael Mandelbaum, *The Case for Goliath: How the United States Acts as the World's Government in the 21st Century*, Public Affairs, New York, 2005; Niall Ferguson, *Colossus: The Price of America's Empire*, Allen Lane, London, 2004.

2   David Corn, "Behind the Placards," *LA Weekly*, November 7, 2002.

millions of magnetic stickers in the shape of yellow ribbons proclaimed on Americans' vehicles — sometimes matched with red, white and blue ribbons stating that "Freedom isn't Free." Turkeys happily sported buttons saying "Support our troops: Bring them home," but Soft Eagles believed that the Democratic Party would send itself to electoral purgatory for decades if it were cast as insufficiently supportive of troops in the field. Being "soft on terror" had replaced being "soft on Communism" as a charge that the Dixies, now called Blue Dogs, said could cost them their seats. If it did, their party would never regain the Congress it had lost in 1994.

In 2001 the entire Congress voted to overthrow the Taliban government of Afghanistan for hosting al-Qaeda. The only exception was Barbara Lee of Berkeley, California, perhaps the only true Turkey in Congress, and the only Member who refuses to nominate her quota of constituents to the military academies. The argument that the United States had brought the 9/11 attacks upon itself by maintaining the authoritarian governments that al-Qaeda sought to overthrow was a toxic one in mainstream politics. University of Colorado professor Wade Churchill, who received public attention for saying that "the chickens have come home to roost," lost his job, much as Malcolm X did after he made the same comment after the assassination of John Kennedy.[1] In 2002 most Soft Eagles voted against invading Iraq — the exceptions being Jewish Members under pressure from the American Israel Public Affairs Committee (AIPAC) and potential presidential candidates like John Kerry and Joe Biden — but they justified their vote by arguing not that the war was an immoral exercise of domination, but that there was little evidence of Bush and Cheney's claims of weapons of mass destruction and an Iraqi connection to the 9/11 attacks. By taking this tack of arguing on the facts rather than the assumptions, they implicitly affirmed the neo-conservative position that the United States was justified in attacking countries who were indeed developing nuclear weapons or who would not line up with America in the long war.

Once the war started, a small coterie of Soft Eagles in the House energetically fought a rear-guard action to discredit it. Lacking the ability to force the Republican majority to hold oversight hearings, they formed an Out of Iraq caucus that sponsored frequent floor speeches on tactical issues they hoped might attract converts from Hard Eagles. They publicized reports by journalists such as Seymour Hersh about torture at the Abu Ghraib, Guantanamo, and Bagram prisons, the administration's own revelations that there had been no weapons of mass destruction, field reports about how poorly the war was going, and dramatic but mistaken claims that the oil industry had divided up Iraq's fields under Cheney's guidance before the war.[2] The 80 members of the House Progressive Caucus put

---

1 Churchill's writings were investigated by an academic review panel, and he was fired for poor scholarship. Malcolm X's comment referred not, as often thought, to the assassination schemes of Kennedy's CIA, but to Kennedy's weak response to violence against civil rights activists in the United States. He was disciplined by Nation of Islam leader Elijah Muhammed, leading to his eventual schism with the Nation. Both the Nation of Islam and the University of Colorado were motivated in part by adverse media reaction to the claim.

2 The claim about oil fields originated in a book by Ron Suskind about Treasury Secretary Paul O'Neill, who recalled seeing a map of Iraq before the war with areas designated for American oil companies. The map in question actually displayed existing contracts for foreign firms. *The Price of Loyalty*, Simon & Schuster, New York, 2004.

up posters in front of their offices that publicized the cost of the war, and contrasted it with the domestic programs that could have been funded instead. This attempt to reach out to the deficit-hating Blue Dogs implied that the problem was not that the war was immoral but rather that it was delaying the building of day care centers. The argument was made explicit in a 2006 bill by Congressman Rahm Emanuel requiring that as much money be spent on social projects in America as was being spent on the war in Iraq.

Minority leader Nancy Pelosi, an ardent anti-war Member but a cautious caucus leader trying to help Kerry win the presidency, announced at the 2004 convention that the Democratic party "is the party of more body armor" for the troops in Iraq. Kerry had voted for the war in 2002, but then was hammered by the Republicans for allegedly opposing funding for body armor the next year when, in his own words, "I actually did vote for the $87 billion before I voted against it." Kerry was referring to debate on a supplemental military funding bill in which, shades of Rahm Emanuel and the Progressive Caucus, he unsuccessfully proposed an amendment to provide the funds so long as they came from new taxes on the wealthy, and then voted against the underlying bill when it simply added to the deficit. Kerry's behavior seemed illogical to both supporters and opponents of the war in the general public. Why would the way of funding a war determine whether or not you supported it? But in the congressional maw, where the goal is to build a temporary majority from diverse perspectives that can at least constrain, if not reverse, a policy, such illogical "bridges" toward the goal are the rule, not the exception.

When the Democrats took control of both Houses for the first time in 14 years in 2007, the Turkeys whose grassroots campaigning had helped with the victory believed that the war was about to end. House Speaker Pelosi and Senate Majority Leader Harry Reid were firm opponents of the war, as was Pelosi's choice for House majority leader, Jack Murtha. The hawkish former Marine and military appropriator was reprising his role as Dixie defector from the days of the Jesuit murders in El Salvador, speaking out forcefully against the war and its negative impact on the armed forces. While Murtha was defeated by Steny Hoyer, who was not as ardent a foe of the war, he was still the chairman of the defense appropriations subcommittee, serving under equally anti-war committee chairman David Obey. Their appropriating counterparts in the Senate, Daniel Inouye and Robert Byrd, were also opposed to the war. When President Bush in January announced a "surge" in US force levels to clamp down on inter-sect violence and allow the Maliki government to promote "reconciliation" between the deadlocked major parties in Parliament so that reconstruction programs could resume, Pelosi had the House pass a resolution stating its opposition to the surge, and Reid achieved a majority for a similar resolution in the Senate. All the Democrats had to do, thought the Turkeys, was to hold on party lines the 50 percent of members needed in the House and the 40 percent in the Senate to block consideration of bills funding the war.

The Turkeys had badly misread the situation. Bush had threatened to veto any bill that did not contain full funding for the surge of new troops, even if that meant shutting down the entire government. Pelosi realized that her 50 Blue Dogs would break with her during such a high stakes game of "chicken" and back the Republicans not just on Iraq but on many domestic issues. Determined not to repeat her predecessor Tip O'Neill's loss of control over the Democratic caucus in the early 1980s, she masterfully balanced the demands of the Blue Dogs and the Progressive Caucus by setting up a complex series of votes in which the majority of Democrats would go on record for voting against funding the war, but the funds would magically emerge intact.

Majority Leader Reid made the same calculation and the same decision. Carl Levin, the chair of the Senate's Armed Services Committee, even announced in advance of the request for funds for the surge that Congress would in the end "support the troops" if the administration included non-binding "benchmarks" for Maliki's progress on political reconciliation. He was correct, as the Democratic leadership arranged the enactment of a supplemental appropriation in May. Not one to let a moving train pass her by, Pelosi forced the president to swallow some long-denied Democratic domestic priorities in the supplemental bill, such as an increase in the minimum wage and funding for farmers, hurricane victims, and children's health care. Turkeys screamed betrayal and vilified Pelosi for her alleged hypocrisy for voting against a bill that she had skillfully set up to pass with Republican support, but the leaders knew how to count, and they believed that it was irresponsible to sacrifice their party's entire agenda for a vote they would eventually lose.

Four months later, in September 2007, General David Petraeus, the US commander in Iraq, came to Washington to make his case for the next year's regular appropriation in highly-publicized hearings. MoveOn.org, a group funded by pro-Clinton dot-com moguls that fell somewhere between Soft Eagles and Turkeys, published full-page newspaper ads calling him "General Betray-us" for the requisite positive gloss he put on Maliki's half-hearted attempt to reach the "benchmarks." The tactics backfired as Members fell all over themselves to denounce MoveOn.org and praise Petraeus. The Soft Eagles lost the heart to debate even the tactical question of whether the surge was working, let alone the core question of whether the United States had the right to try to make it work. The outcome of the fall debate, though, had never been in doubt, with or without MoveOn.org and Petraeus. Once the Democratic leadership blinked on the Supplemental in the Spring, all of Washington knew that Bush would receive every penny he asked for throughout the rest of his term.

Unable to curtail funding, anti-war Democrats in Congress had to return to their previous strategy of using tangential issues to discredit the war, such as the decline of the "coalition of the willing," corruption in Iraqi ministries, waste in US reconstruction programs, and Iraq's refusal to use its own cash reserves from oil sales to fund reconstruction. They took a similar approach in attacking the administration's "Global War on Terror." Now that they were the chairs of the committees, Democrats could hold hearings and schedule floor votes on the violations of human rights they had raised while in the minority. To reach out to the Blue Dogs, Soft Eagles eschewed arguments that the anti-terrorist strategy of killing or seizing members of al-Qaeda or the Talibans was itself immoral, or irrelevant so long as support for Middle Eastern autocrats in the long war continued to spur al-Qaeda's recruitment. Instead, they argued that the tactics of "soft power" and "smart power" such as milder rhetoric, multilateral initiatives, and more human treatment of prisoners were more likely to achieve success in the long war.

Congressional committees held a number of high-profile hearings on torture at Guantanamo and Abu Ghraib, on the CIA's secret prisons, and on the "rendition" program of kidnapping and torture in other countries that started under the Clinton administration and was greatly expanded under Bush. Many of the hearings focused on the negative impact of the publicity about these tough tactics on international approval of the United States and its policies, and made the case for handling prisoners according to international law and humanitarian standards. The pinnacle of this amoral appeal came in Senate hearings that brought in former investigators to testify that torture was an unreliable method to gain information. This was a classic Soft Eagle response to the Hard Eagles' claims — bolstered by television shows and movies — that torture had saved American lives by revealing plots. Rather than label torture as an immoral act that Americans simply would not countenance, the Soft Eagles tried to argue that it didn't even work. By making this case, they implicitly accepted the assumption that torture would be acceptable if it did work, and weakened their clear moral appeal against torture.

A number of Democrats focused on another fruitful area for tactical, rather than policy, dispute: the balance of presidential and congressional powers. They advanced the constitutional argument that the combat authority provided to Bush in the 2002 resolution was specifically limited to meeting the threat posed by the government of Saddam Hussein, and so it had expired, as it were, with him. They claimed that the war would therefore become illegal and require a new vote of authorization if another component of the 2002 resolution that permitted combat under a mandate of the United Nations Security Council were also to lapse. Bill Delahunt, the chair of a House Foreign Affairs subcommittee, and his colleague Rosa DeLauro, who had run an anti-Contra group in the 1980s, sponsored legislation to force such a vote on the administration's plan for a long-term troop and basing agreement with Iraqi Prime Minister Maliki that would replace the UN Mandate. The administration claimed that the agreement could be approved by the executive branch without congressional approval, and that the continuing congressional appropriations for the war and a broader reading of the 2002 resolution contradicted the Democrats' entire constitutional argument. Stung by Barack Obama becoming the candidate of choice for anti-war voters in the Democrat primaries, Hillary Clinton sponsored a similar bill in the Senate, which Obama quickly endorsed.

Starting in December 2007, Delahunt held a year-long series of nine hearings whose purpose was more to convince the Iraqi Parliament than the Congress of the unconstitutionality, in both countries, of any agreement that was not submitted to them for ratification.[1] Using the political connections and skills of Raed Jarrar, a 30-year-old Iraqi working for the Quakers' American Friends Service Committee whom he jokingly christened the "alternate foreign minister" for his contacts at the highest levels of the Parliament, Delahunt prodded the parliamentarians to assert their obligations under the recent and largely uninterpreted Iraqi constitution. He frequently appeared on Arabic news shows, and Iraqi parliamentarians would gather in Speaker Mahmoud Mashhadani's office to

---

1 Testimony and statements from the hearings on this complex and hotly disputed topic can be found at the website of the Subcommittee on International Organizations, Human Rights, and Oversight at http://foreignaffairs.house.gov.

watch him approvingly on BBC-Arabic and al-Jazeera as he emphatically explained why the proposed agreement would not enter into force if either the Bush or the Maliki administration refused to submit it for ratification. The parliamentarians had little idea that the spell-binding legislator with the impressive mane of white hair and the knowledgeable grasp of both constitutions was merely a subcommittee chairman in a party that had already resigned itself to giving Bush whatever he wanted.

Jarrar arranged for a number of opposition parliamentarians to fly to Washington and testify against any agreement that did not include a withdrawal deadline for US troops. As political pressure against the agreement grew across the Iraqi political spectrum, with every faction trying to portray itself as more opposed to foreign occupation than the others, the White House saw its July 2008 deadline slip away. In November the Bush administration finally caved in and signed an agreement that, far from establishing the originally-sought "long-term" presence of US forces, required a complete US withdrawal within three years. Ironically Delahunt and the dissident parliamentarians ended up supporting the agreement they had done so much to torpedo, although he noted that it still required congressional approval to be valid, particularly since it replaced the UN Mandate that he claimed provided the sole authority for US combat operations.

In a related assault on the administration's power, Delahunt and Republican dissident Walter Jones Jr. used the administration's provision of false information during the debate on invading Iraq to justify their push to replace the weakly-worded and oft-evaded War Powers resolution with a ban on funding for any combat mission not approved by Congress. Jones had come a long way since the days of "Freedom fries." A "born-again" Christian, he became convinced that he had a duty to God and the Marines at the base in his district to stop the war, and he began to speak out for Bush's impeachment and even criminal prosecution. The Republican party responded by stripping him of his seniority on the Armed Services committee and unsuccessfully trying to defeat him in his primary. The 1973 War Powers resolution, enacted over Nixon's veto, allows a president to use troops in combat for only 90 days without congressional approval. Its original sponsor, Senator Tom Eagleton of Missouri, voted against it for allowing any time before congressional approval, while presidents have challenged its constitutionality for imposing the 90-day limit. Delahunt held a series of hearings on the issue, but as he and Jones prepared to introduce their bill they were undercut by the endorsement by respected former Members Lee Hamilton and Abner Mikva of a presidentialist proposal by former secretaries of state James Baker and Warren Christopher that eliminated the 90-day limit on unauthorized deployments.[1]

While they attacked Bush on Iraq, many Soft Eagles tried to outdo him on Afghanistan and Iran. To argue that Iraq was the wrong war, for five years they cited Afghanistan as the right war, and criticized Bush for diverting attention, funding, and troops from the effort to build an effective anti-Taliban government. It became a mantra for Pelosi and Reid that

---

1 The Baker–Christopher plan is available from its sponsor, the Miller Center of Charlottesville, Virginia, at http://millercenter.org/policy/commissions/warpowers. It proposed replacing today's binding but disputed limits on presidential power with a consultative committee of executive and legislative leaders.

the real threat to national security was in Afghanistan.[1] AIPAC, the Washington Institute for Near East Policy, and other pro-Israel lobbies made their priority for 2008 the isolation of, and if possible a US attack on, Iran. The leading Democratic presidential candidates endorsed using military force as a last resort to stop Iran's completion of a nuclear weapon. Neo-conservative think-tanks and columnists openly called for military strikes on Iran's nuclear complex, and throughout the year rumors in Washington had the attacks only a few days away. Gary Ackerman, the chairman of the House Foreign Affairs subcommittee on the Middle East, pushed a resolution on AIPAC's behalf that called for an embargo on Iran's imports of refined petroleum. Opponents characterized it as a declaration of war, since enforcing such an embargo could, legally and practically, lead to hostilities. Ackerman energetically rounded up a majority for the bill, but committee chairman Howard Berman, also a strong ally of the pro-Israel groups, smoothly delayed its consideration until after the presidential election. In this matter, as in much of foreign policy, the Democrats from June on could smell the White House, and tried to delay, weaken, and discredit controversial Bush initiatives so that Obama would have maximum flexibility if he won the election.

THE OBAMA PROGRAM: NEW RESPECT, OLD ALLIANCES, AND WARS OF PERCEIVED NECESSITY AGAINST THE TALIBANS

Few issues separated Barack Obama from Hillary Clinton during the Democratic primaries of 2008, but one was the Iraq war. Obama was not in Congress in 2002, but he said at the time that he would not have voted to give President Bush the authority to launch the invasion, as Clinton did. It is impossible to isolate the reasons why Clinton lost her inevitability and Obama surged to the lead, but many primary voters made it clear that this difference on the war led them to choose him. Obama's position on Iraq, his apparent debt to anti-war voters, and his refusal to join the Clintons on the neo-imperialist Democratic Leadership Council led any number of Turkeys to hope that with his election a new day had dawned for US foreign policy. This hope was unreasonable and went unfulfilled. During the campaign Obama had never made any bones about being anything but a Soft Eagle with hard edges. He had refused to renounce the use of military force to disrupt Iran's nuclear program, and he proposed adding 100,000 troops to the Army and Marines. Since he also supported withdrawing most of the 140,000 US troops from Iraq, it was clear that he wanted to have a lot of deployable power ready to use, globally and in the long war for the Middle East. His policy might have been called "smart primacy."

Obama's first year as president was a study in soft power. He announced the closing of Guantanamo prison and the end of torture, and world opinion of the United State began to rebound. He listened respectfully to and promised to consult and cooperate with US allies and international institutions, and America's standing in those countries and bodies

---

1 As former Bush official Stephen Rademaker pointed out, this was the second time in recent years that Democrats in Congress had backed combat Afghanistan as a "good war" to offset the perception that they were soft on US security because they opposed another war, in this case in Iraq. The first time was in the 1980s, when Democrats were opposing war in Central America. See his op-ed, "Barack Obama as Charlie Wilson?", *Washington Post*, September 5, 2009, p. A21.

rose as well. He ended the use of the phrase "Global War on Terror" that the Bush administration had coined to cover virtually its entire military and covert budget. But there stopped the "change we can believe in." The military and covert budgets continued to rise, the long war continued without an official name, and a coterie of Soft Eagles with a record of projecting and using military force were brought in to run it.[1] Prominent among these were Clinton herself as secretary of state, Iran–Contra figure Robert Gates staying on as secretary of defense, former European commander General James Jones as national security adviser, and long-time Middle East mandarin Dennis Ross in his perpetual role.

The most telling appointment for the long war was that of Richard Holbrooke as director of policy in Afghanistan and Pakistan. A Democratic version of the Republican Party's Paul Wolfowitz, Holbrooke had been belligerent in personality and policy since his three years as a counter-insurgency operative in the Vietnam War. Serving on Kissinger's staff in 1970, he pointedly refused to resign with Anthony Lake over the invasion of Cambodia, and as Carter's assistant secretary of state for East Asia he coordinated the embargo on Vietnam and aggressively derailed the plans of Patt Derian, leader of the State Department's new bureau on Human Rights, to hold back military aid from the dictators in the Philippines, Indonesia, and South Korea.[2] As assistant secretary of state for Europe, Holbrooke was instrumental in Clinton's decision to intervene on the side of the Croats and the Bosnian and Kosovar Muslims against Serbia in the civil wars in the former Yugoslavia. Placing someone in charge of policy in Afghanistan who still thought that the Vietnam War could have, and should have, been won made it clear that withdrawal and non-intervention were not among the options on the table.

Obama's intent to combine soft talk and hard action in pursuit of American dominance was revealed in his much-noted trip to the Middle East in June 2009. The centerpiece of the trip was a speech in Cairo that adviser David Axelrod said was designed to "repair the breach" between the Islamic world and America, thereby "opening up avenues of understanding so that small groups of extremists can't exploit the mistrust."[3] In the speech Obama called for a "new beginning" based on American respect for Islam. Obscured in the positive emotional response to the speech in the Muslim world was the reality that his vision of the long war was simply a softer, internationalized version of Bush's paean to American freedom. Like Bush, Obama cautiously and obliquely called on the authoritarian regimes in the region to reflect the will of the people and offer them justice and the right to speak out, but he did not condition US relations on any particular electoral reform on their part. Like Bush, he dismissed any charges of policy being rooted in access

---

1 The base military budget of roughly $550 billion, in constant 2009 dollars, excludes supplemental appropriations for ongoing wars, as well as the cost of previous deployments, such as the Veterans Administration. See http://www.globalissues.org/article/75/world-military-spending#USMilitarySpending. Figures from the Center for Arms Control and Non-Proliferation. See also "Obama Raises Intelligence Budget," May 9, 2009, at http://www.darkgovernment.com/news/obama-raises-intelligence-budget.

2 Interview in 1983 for Caleb Rossiter, with Anne-Marie Smith, *Human Rights: The Carter Record, the Reagan Reaction*, International Policy Report, Center for International Policy, Washington, DC, September 1984.

3 "Before Obama Speech, Aide Cites 'Undeniable Breach' Between US and Islamic World," ABC news report by Karen Travers, June 2, 2009.

to in oil, saying that "America is not the crude stereotype of a self-interested empire," and described the motivations of militants who mysteriously killed people on 9/11 "who had done nothing to harm anybody" without a hint that they were attacking the United States for backing regimes they hoped to overthrow.

According to Bush, the 9/11 attacks flowed from an irrational hated of America's freedoms. According to Obama they flowed from the "sweeping change brought by modernity and globalization [that] that led many Muslims to view the West as hostile to the traditions of Islam." Since neither American freedom not modernity and globalization could be bargained away, there was no policy choice for either president but to offer the militants perpetual pursuit and death. Obama pledged to "relentlessly confront violent extremists who pose a grave threat to our security, [the] violent extremists in Afghanistan and Pakistan [who are] determined to kill as many Americans as they possibly can." Like Bush in Iraq, and indeed like Johnson with his offer of a Mekong Valley Authority to the Vietnamese and Reagan with his economic and "humanitarian" aid to Central America, Obama tried to portray economic assistance as apolitical in its purpose as well as its content: "We also know that military power alone is not going to solve the problems in Afghanistan and Pakistan. That is why we plan to invest $1.5 billion each year over the next five years to partner with Pakistanis to build schools and hospitals...and that is why we are providing more than $2.8 billion to help Afghans develop their economy and deliver services that people depend upon."

When it came to the Israeli–Palestinian conflict, a touchstone issue for Obama's listeners, he presented a fairy tale about non-violent liberation struggles in America and South Africa that could not withstand a whiff of historical scrutiny:

> Palestinians must abandon violence. Resistance through violence and killing is wrong and does not succeed. For centuries, black people in America suffered the lash of the whip as slaves and the humiliation of segregation. But it was not violence that won full and equal rights. It was a peaceful and determined insistence upon the ideals at the center of America's founding. This same story can be told by people from South Africa to South Asia; from Eastern Europe to Indonesia. It's a story with a simple truth: that violence is a dead end.

Obama did not similarly admonish Israel to cease using its armed forces to protect itself. Israelis would have quickly disabused him of the notion that survival of an oppressed people can be achieved without the threat or use of force. Obama calling violence a dead end while in the midst of a surge of troops to Afghanistan, drone attacks in Pakistan, arms sales to Middle Eastern dictators, and Special Forces assassinations in Somalia was as bizarre as President Clinton doing the same thing with gang members at American high schools after launching air strikes in Afghanistan, Somalia, Iraq, and Kosovo.

It was indeed violence, the Union effort in the Civil War and in the occupation of Reconstruction, that won African-Americans an end to the "lash of the whip." Segregation, too, was continuing to resist non-violent protests until confronted with the threat and the reality of violence in the 1950s and 1960s. Federal or federalized troops were sent to city after Southern city to enforce integration and voting orders, black citizens formed armed units to protect their non-violent protestors from police and Klan attacks, civil rights marches increasingly brought vandalism by angry young men, and the specter of black rioters in Northern cities scared Congress into enacting meaningful anti-discrimination and affirmative action laws.[1]

The South African liberation movement openly rejected its failed Gandhian half-century in the 1960s and instructed Nelson Mandela to form the "Spear of the Nation." This guerrilla army's early bombings sent him to prison and its attacks on economic and civilian targets played a role, along with violent unrest in the townships and international economic pressures, in the apartheid government's decision to release him and negotiate 26 years later.

If what Obama said in Cairo was short on reality, what he did before the speech was not. He traveled there through Saudi Arabia to show how he valued its "friendship and strategic relationship" and to praise the "wisdom and graciousness of His Majesty, and seek his counsel." Upon arriving in Cairo he met privately with Mubarak, whom he later described as "a counselor and a friend to the United States." Meeting with these two autocrats without a mention of their opposition to democracy sent a message to the region, and to his own policy-makers, that the twin goals of access to oil and security for Israel would continue to define US policy under Obama just as they had under Bush.

Nor did Obama make any significant changes in US policy in Africa, in which access to resources and logistical support for US military forces and covert operations had determined relations for decades. In Sudan he dropped his campaign pledge to take "immediate steps" to save Fur villages and continued the Bush policy of rewarding the Sudanese government for providing information on Islamist terrorists. In Ethiopia he continued military aid to Meles Zenawi, who stole the 2006 elections and arrested his opponents, in return for his cooperation with US attacks on Islamists in Somalia, some from a base in the dictatorship in Djibouti. The new US African Command expanded its involvement in counter-insurgency in Uganda, and the Navy held high-profile port visits with the armed forces of various unelected or fraudulently elected West African governments.

In Iraq, Obama could let policy run on, as the clock ticked toward the complete withdrawal of US forces required by the bilateral agreement of 2008. In Afghanistan, though, he needed to fashion a new policy, both because he didn't want to take over another president's deployment without understanding it, as Clinton had in Somalia, and because the assessments of his military officials were so dire. In March he acceded to the request of the commanding general he inherited from Bush to deploy a "surge" of 21,000 additional combat troops, which with adjustments to 30,000 raised the US total to 68,000 by the fall of 2009. Additional forces included 35,000 NATO troops, 74,000 Pentagon contractors, and an unknown number of CIA covert operatives.[2] Ironically, Obama cited the need to provide a secure environment for the upcoming presidential election, which was then brazenly stolen by President Hamid Karzai.

---

1 See Lance Hill, *The Deacons for Defense: Armed Resistance and the Civil Rights Movement*, University of North Carolina Press, Chapel Hill, 2004.

2 The figure for contractors comes from Moshe Schwartz, "Department of Defense Contractors in Iraq and Afghanistan: Background and Analysis," Congressional Research Service (R-40764), September 7, 2009. The US troop figures come from Pentagon data and the NATO figures from NATO's ISAF website.

The troop surge was to be matched with a State Department-led increase of civilian officials to manage local development projects, although it proved difficult to get foreign service officers to be like Holbrooke in Vietnam and agree to these dangerous postings. In addition, the Afghan security forces were to be tripled to a staggering 400,000 with US training, equipment, and funding.[1] The number of active Taliban fighters that all this power was to be deployed against was never estimated by military analysts at more than 15,000. The Taliban were almost exclusively members of Afghanistan's largest ethnic group, the Pashtun, whose 40 percent of the population is based in the south and east of the country. Non-Pashtun regional militias hostile to the Karzai government were also considered a threat to its authority, although negotiations rather than combat generally dominated their relationship with the government.

In May 2009, Obama chose his own commander, General Stanley McChrystal, who had led the Special Operations Command in its classified hunts for insurgent leaders in Iraq and Afghanistan. McChrystal reviewed the situation and found that the surge was insufficient to support his new strategy of "protecting the population" by a constant security presence in the territories occupied or penetrated by the Taliban.[2] It was soon leaked that he was going to request an additional surge of 40,000 troops for this new surge. McChrystal's decision to maintain a scattered troop presence with minimal air and artillery support rather than send larger cohorts out on heavily-supported combat missions from protected bases had been tried with some success in Iraq in 2007 at a time when violence was already on the wane because of payments to previously hostile Sunni militias. That strategy had led to a sharp initial rise in US forces killed and wounded as they took control of areas they had avoided, but soon contributed to a relatively stable security environment in which it was hoped that the feuding Iraqi parties would fashion an acceptable dispensation of power, employment, and oil revenues. Despite the failure of the Iraqis to address those political questions, McChrystal saw a similar surge in Afghanistan as his best option.

The request for an additional 40,000 troops led Obama into a lengthy and detailed review of US goals and prospects in Afghanistan that lasted throughout the fall of 2009. With a similar review, Obama had already brilliantly found a confusing and hence politically palatable solution to the problem of Bush's pledge to deploy anti-ballistic missiles in Poland, with guiding radar in the Czech Republic, to counter Iran's development of long-range missiles. He guided a complex Pentagon review that justified replacing the existing plan with a long-term proposal for interceptors designed to work only against the short-range missiles that Iran already had. Russia applauded the reduction of the threat to its strategic missiles, Poland's Russo-phobic leaders could claim that they were still as closely tied to US forces as possible, and the predictable neo-conservative fuming against Obama's betrayal of US interests and coddling of Russia and Iran was a one-day story.

---

1 Thom Shanker and John H. Cushman Jr., "US Reviews of Afghan Forces Raise Doubts on Training Goal," *New York Times*, November 6, 2009.

2 McChrystal's July 6, 2009, tactical directive on his new approach of protecting the population can be found at http://www.nato.int/isaf/docu/official_texts/Tactical_Directive_090706.pdf.

In his March speech announcing the first surge, Obama tried to limit the Afghan mission by reminding Americans that the goal of the war was, as it always had been, to deny a sanctuary to al-Qaeda from which to plan attacks on the United States. However, he also stated: "[I]f the Afghan government falls to the Taliban — or allows al-Qaeda to go unchallenged — that country will again be a base for terrorists who want to kill as many of our people as they possibly can." The mission therefore became defeating the Taliban and building an Afghan government and army that could prevent their resurgence. With this judgment, Obama ruled out any fundamental change in strategy. His response to McChrystal's proposal for another surge therefore became a matter of tactics. The message that was transmitted to the planners who were preparing options was that he had decided to "give it a go."[1] "It" was clearly a campaign to defeat or at least badly damage the Taliban while the Karzai government extended its control. The tentative nature of "give it a go," though, revealed Obama's uncertainty of the logic of his analysis. He was certainly aware that al-Qaeda, as an unconventional force, didn't need Afghanistan as a sanctuary. The 9/11 attacks were planned primarily in Germany and Florida, and al-Qaeda's leaders had dispersed to Pakistan, Yemen, and perhaps Somalia after the US invasion of Afghanistan. It was also possible that a combination of threats and covert operations by US forces would make the Taliban unwilling or unable to provide training bases or operational sites to al-Qaeda even if it joined a coalition government or, in a much less likely scenario, eventually took power itself.

During Obama's fall policy review vice president Joe Biden and in-house Afghan scholar Barnett Rubin were reported to be promoting a reduction in US forces to take away the Taliban's appeal, paired with targeted attacks on al-Qaeda, whether in Afghanistan or Pakistan. In contrast to Afghanistan, which had a population of 28 million and a disjointed, feudal structure of tribal regional leaders, Pakistan was a modern country of 180 million under a cohesive bureaucracy and military command. The exception was the FATA, or Federally Administered Tribal Areas, near the "Durand Line" that was cavalierly drawn through the Pashtun lands in 1893 to demark the extent of British influence and came to be the border with Afghanistan. While the tribes in the FATA had never been integrated into the state, they had generally sound relations with the central government and were simply ignored by most Pakistanis in and out of government. This isolation came to an end with the US invasion of Afghanistan, which drove the Afghan Taliban across the border and subjected the Pakistani side to US raids, bombing, and drone attacks.

The Bush administration threatened the Pakistani Army and its covert directorate for Inter-Service Intelligence, or ISI, with military action if they did not endorse the US attacks and themselves pressure the Taliban, who they had largely helped create and sustain as part of their anti-Indian foreign policy. In return for a billion dollars in US cash assistance, the Army made some desultory incursions into the FATA to root out the Afghan Taliban. The tribal leaders resisted forcefully, and formed a Pakistani Taliban that carried out terror attacks in Pakistani cities to force an end to US and government attacks. Obama's plans could not include a direct US combat role in Pakistan, which would have been so unpopular among the proud populace that it would have driven from power any

---

1 Interview, administration official, September 2009.

government that agreed to US troops. He simply continued the Bush administration's policy of paying the Army to continue its half-hearted military drives into the FATA and stepped up US drone attacks on suspected members of al-Qaeda and the two Talibans.

In its length and detail, Obama's review contrasted favorably with Lyndon Johnson's secret decision to send combat troops to Vietnam in 1965. It contrasted even more favorably with the public relations scare and rush to judgment of Bush's invasion of Iraq, leading to complaints by Cheney and neo-conservatives about Obama "dithering" while US troops died without adequate support. However, by being based on many of the same political and strategic assumptions that Johnson and Bush held, the review merely delayed the inevitability of a decision to fight on in some fashion. Obama assumed that withdrawal would damage the credibility of the United States and the political life of the Democratic Party, and the concept of reducing al-Qaeda's appeal by breaking the alliance with Saudi Arabia and Egypt was too alien even to include in the policy options, because of the belief that it would jeopardize access to oil and security for Israel.

Soft Eagles and a scattering of libertarian Republicans in the House reacted to Obama's March decision by promoting an amendment requiring the Pentagon to prepare an exit strategy, and to his fall review by sending a letter to Obama opposing any second surge. Both were sponsored by Jim McGovern, who had been a key House staffer 20 years before in the struggle to end wars in Central America.[1] The amendment barely won within the Democratic caucus and gained 138 votes in all, and letter had only 58 signatories. However, they represented the only significant stand by liberals against Obama's centrist foreign policy during his first year, and were intended to send a clear warning that unlike in his major domestic victories of 2009 he would have to fund any Afghan surge with the politically risky strategy of needing the support of nearly all Republicans. However, the warning lacked credibility, since 20 progressive House Democrats who had voted against a war funding bill that had passed in May with Republican support acceded to a request by Speaker Pelosi and provided the margin of victory for the bill in June when it returned from the Senate with a provision for funding the International Monetary Fund that led Republicans to oppose the overall bill.

Like similar appeals during the Vietnam and Central American wars, the McGovern letter took issue with the tactics and not the assumptions of the Afghan mission. It cited regional experts who believed that the presence of foreign forces spurred recruitment by the Taliban, and obliquely proposed "applying the lessons of the Cold War where we isolate and contain" threats to US security. This was a strange and unclear proposal, given that in the 1980s Soft Eagles had largely opposed the fundamental building blocks of Cold War containment, such as the deployment of US forces to Europe and the nuclear weapons that protected them, as well as the military alliances with dictators that pressed the Soviet Union globally. Finally the letter returned to the sort of economic argument used during the Iraq War, saying that the current economic crisis made a "quagmire" even less attractive. The letter was an attempt to put arguments in Obama's hands that he could use against the surge proposal, but it offered him nothing in a positive sense that could

---

1 Cindy Buhl, who had coordinated the lobby groups in that effort, was now McGovern's staffer on foreign policy issues.

address his concern that a Taliban victory would provide al-Qaeda with a staging ground to attack the United States.

Hard Eagle Democrats like House Armed Services chairman Ike Skelton counseled their Soft Eagle colleagues that failing to take a clear, hard line in favor of doing everything possible, including a surge, in Afghanistan, would be political suicide for their party. "Any attack and we are through," Skelton was reported to say, meaning that any terror attack in the United States, even if not planned in an Afghan or Pakistani sanctuary, would devastate the Democrats if they were perceived as obstructing the wars there. Senate Democrats generally seemed to believe this as well, as they were nearly completely quiet on Afghanistan during Obama's review, preferring to focus instead on providing even more aid to Pakistan to help it take control of the FATA. The reluctance of Soft Eagles to confront Obama was also due to the sense that he needed support from the left as he took a fierce shellacking from the right. The Republican Party, both in Congress and in a grass-roots animated by a coterie of talk show hosts, vituperated over Obama's "socialism" and excoriated his decisions. As they had done when Bill Clinton had been the subject of similar hatred, Soft Eagles felt the need to back him firmly and lacked fervor and commitment when criticizing his foreign policy. Their avowed need to pursue constitutional principles by forcing votes on the Iraq Agreement, the legality of combat in Iraq, and the strengthening of the entire War Powers legislation became less urgent with Bush out of office and a Democrat in power, and none of these initiatives was pursued.

Turkeys too were disarmed by their hopes for Obama, their joy at his defeat of John McCain, and their partnership in many aspects of his domestic agenda. Their leading think-tank, the Institute for Policy Studies (IPS), was a tiny, lonely anti-imperialist voice in a sea of dozens of far better-funded Washington bastions of primacy, including the Soft Eagles' Carnegie Endowment for International Peace, Council on Foreign Relations, Center for American Progress, Center for American Security, Stimson Center, and Brookings Institution, and the Hard Eagles' Heritage Foundation, Center for Strategic and International Studies, and American Enterprise Institute. Like the libertarian Cato Institute, the only other recognizably anti-imperialist think-tank in Washington, IPS might as well have been based in another city. Despite having a solid minority of citizens supporting their point of view, these institutions' foreign policy proposals were fundamentally at odds with the operating consensus in Washington, and received little press attention and even less consideration in Congress and the executive branch.

Cato was opposed on principle to regulation and foreign involvement, and legislation purporting to control the global climate. In contrast IPS was socialist in its approach to both domestic and international economics, and interested in the United States actively assisting rather than economically and militarily dominating developing countries. Founded in 1963 by Richard Barnet and Marcus Raskin, arms control analysts who left the Kennedy administration in opposition to the Vietnam War, IPS had been maintained by a thin but broad and loyal band of like-minded citizens through 45 years of media neglect, red-baiting, government harassment, and even the 1976 murder of two of its staff in a Washington car-bombing directed by the Chilean dictatorship. Obama's victory in some ways complicated IPS's work, because like the Soft Eagles, its supporters were loath to see

Obama attacked from the left when he was facing a right-wing assault. Long-time director John Cavanagh, an economist opposed to Western advantages in trade and aid rules and high-income advantages in domestic tax laws, had to balance IPS's euphoria over Obama's new language of international respect with its disappointment over his continuation of international dominance and the long war. In addition, Obama was a standard bearer for a progressive approach to IPS's agenda on the domestic economy, such as government-guaranteed health care and limits on executive pay, and like IPS a believer in a climate "catastrophe" that justifies controls on carbon emissions.

In 2009 IPS was part of a coalition chaired by the grass-roots leader Peace Action that opposed the surge, but was silent on both maintaining current levels of US and NATO troops and on the massive aid program intended to triple the Afghan security forces. The coalition probably did not support those tactics, but its members seemed to recognize that unlike in Vietnam, El Salvador, Iraq, and all the other wars they had spent a lifetime protesting, for once the security rationale for some sort of intervention, in this case to stabilize Afghanistan so that al-Qaeda could not return with the Taliban and plan its attacks, was legitimate. After years of disputing liberals who saw the Vietnam War and its many successors in developing countries as tactical "mistakes" instead of logical expressions of US imperial strategy, Turkeys finally found themselves in a situation where they had to make the same case. When a IPS team met with Obama's Afghanistan planners at the Pentagon — itself an unthinkable event during the Bush years — part of its appeal sounded much like Soft Eagles arguing against the war in Iraq on economic rather than moral grounds. Lyndon Johnson thought he had to send combat troops to Vietnam to save his "Great Society" agenda and protect the Democratic Party from charges of being soft on communism, IPS argued, but in fact the cost and the uproar destroyed his domestic hopes, and the Republicans attacked the Democrats' patriotism anyway, helping lead to Nixon's two presidential victories.

It might seem strange that IPS found itself portraying Afghanistan as Obama's Vietnam on domestic rather than international grounds, but it was consistent both with the unique reality of 9/11 and the hopes that the Turkeys held for Obama. Turkeys detested Obama's top choices for his national security team, were badly disappointed by his refusal to adopt an activist policy on Darfur, and were appalled by his military budget. Still, when he talked their language about eventually banning nuclear weapons, ending the use of the phrase "Global War on Terror," stopping torture, working with rather than attacking Iran, respecting other nations like China rather than using them as excuses for a military buildup, and joining rather than blocking a successor to the Kyoto treaty on heat-trapping emissions, their anger melted. Tone matters in framing the national debate about foreign policy, and Obama's reasoned tone reminded Turkeys every day how thankful they were that he was doing the framing, and not John McCain and Sarah Palin. Obama was their guy, a black progressive under vicious attack from their right-wing enemies, and they were willing to cut him some slack.

Obama's December 2009 decision to add 32,000 troops brilliantly undercut anti-war Democrats in Congress by incorporating a loose "exit date" in 18 months. The way he announced it undercut them even more. Obama seized control of the Republicans' patriotic mantle in a Reagan-esque speech at the military academy. He portrayed US foreign and military policy since World War II as a "noble struggle for freedom" in which "we have spilled American blood in many countries on multiple continents" so that "other people's children and grandchildren can live in freedom." Obama did not dwell on the spilling of other people's blood in these wars, although he allowed that "we have at times made mistakes" in fulfilling a "special burden in global affairs" that has "underwritten global security." He argued that, "unlike the great powers of old, we have not sought world domination...we do not seek to occupy other nations. We will not claim another nation's resources." Obama completed his happy myth by reprising the neo-conservative complaint that "we have not always been thanked for these efforts."

The Turkeys were having none of it. The combination of the decision and the rhetoric seemed finally to begin a process of alienation between Obama and his progressive supporters. The split could well reduce the excitement and turn-out that won him the 2008 election, and jeopardize his re-election. Emboldened by opinion polls showing that most Americans were against escalation, despairing of any meaningful action in Congress, and convinced that Obama's foreign policy was simply a better-packaged version of Bush's, Turkeys planned anti-war demonstrations they hoped would rival the protests over the Iraq War.

PART II. NOBLE DISTRACTIONS

CHAPTER 8. THE HUMAN RIGHTS TRAP

The Turkeys' greatest single accomplishment in foreign policy, not just for the United States but for all nations, was the introduction and then the incorporation of the concept of human rights. In roughly 20 years, from 1965 to 1985, a collection of citizens' groups led by Amnesty International and Human Rights Watch and their courageous non-governmental collaborators made previously sovereign issues of how governments and rebel groups treat civilians, enemy soldiers, and prisoners a factor in international relations. The great appeal of the human rights movement was that it was proudly and purposely apolitical. It took neither side in the Cold War and rejected the justification from both sides and their allies that rough tactics were only used to forestall the far greater human rights abuses that would result if their enemies prevailed. In impact if not intent, however, the human rights movement was necessarily political. Dictators of the right and left weren't seizing and torturing random citizens but activists who were calling for an open contest for political power. Demanding the release of dissidents was also effectively demanding that their fellow citizens hear them.

Given the growing power of the concept of human rights, it was only a matter of time before autocrats and the Eagles who backed them tried to game the debate to maintain US access to strategic resources and military and covert cooperation. In the two decades after the demise of the Warsaw Pact, the human rights movement often became a trap for the Turkeys who started it. Its informal, organic path became institutionalized and predictable. Repressive rulers learned to co-opt rather than confront foreign concern. They realized that they could retain international legitimacy by transparently and humanely jailing dissidents on trumped-up corruption charges rather than "disappearing" or torturing them. Then they discovered the beauty of stage-managed elections, which could fully legitimize their regime as "democratically-elected" with international aid donors, even though opposition figures, usually from competing ethnic groups, were denied a chance to win or to take true control of government and the armed forces. Finally, these rulers found that foreign objections to civil wars, which resulted from their monopoly on power and killed millions of civilians indirectly by triggering malnutrition and disease, could be assuaged by following the "laws of war" and not using tactics that brought violence directly to civilians, such as burning villages, impressing children, and laying anti-personnel landmines.

The impressive accomplishment of making the treatment of the innocent an important element in the calculations of the two super-powers and their allies led some in the human rights movement to hope for dramatic improvement after the Cold War. It was not to be. The movement was bewildered by the continuing reality of a world full of massive abuses and a death toll approaching ten million from the slaughters of ethnic civil wars in Rwanda in 1993, the former Yugoslavia and southern Sudan throughout the 1990s, the Fur region of Sudan in the 2000s, and the eastern Congo through both decades. Its reaction was again legalistic, reactive, and apolitical: the creation of individual United Nations tribunals and then an International Criminal Court to prosecute the authors of the attacks on civilians. These conflicts were uniformly complex, rooted in ethnic tensions imposed by artificial borders and colonial rule, and fed by weapons and support for compliant governments by Western countries, but the focus of the human rights movement was on identifying and punishing bad individuals as a warning to others. In their eagerness to achieve consensus on the Rome Treaty that set up the court, human rights advocates assured Hard Eagles that US officials, from the Henry Kissingers to the lowly privates, would not be hauled before the court in the event of a US war. It was a telling comment on the Hard Eagles that they wanted assurances that their country need not fear the consequences of an unjust or illegally prosecuted war, and on the Soft Eagles and Turkeys that they provided them.

During the Cold War Turkeys had often convinced Soft Eagles to join them in thinking that the United States was on the wrong side in its alliances — for example, with the Contras, the UNITA rebels in Angola, and the Salvadoran Army. In the 1990s Soft Eagles in turn convinced some Turkeys to call for the United States to fight for a supposed right side — as in Bosnia, Kosovo, and Rwanda. After 9/11, when the contours of the long war became transparent and torture became openly advocated by the Hard Eagles and quietly accepted by the Soft Eagles, most Turkeys realized with no small degree of despair that the United States was not just once again on the wrong side, but was itself the wrong side. Even under Obama, many of the Turkeys who had invented and sustained the human rights movement with demands for US diplomatic and economic intervention remained uncomfortable collaborating with a 21st century version of the British empire that similarly cited apolitical humanitarian impulses as it interfered in foreign governance to cement its global primacy and economic domination.

Given the progressive manipulation of the human rights paradigm, a new paradigm of political legitimacy will have to be developed to continue pursuing the original goal of a more free life for more people. Turkeys will have to stop focusing on kinder prisons, technical compliance with stacked electioneering rules, and the regulation of civil wars and become explicitly political, judging governments by whether they have established legitimacy with their citizens and created predictable, peaceful ways to transfer power. The paradigm will have to be explicitly political not just in developing countries, but internationally as well. The economic pressures that constrain even fully legitimized governments result from the developed nations' tariffs, subsidies, and controls on foreign investment as well as the developing countries' still-colonial trade patterns and terms of trade. Turkeys hoping to support such governments will have to attack these barriers in domestic legislatures and international bodies dominated by the West, such as the World Trade Organization and the International Monetary Fund. Human rights are fundamentally political, but the environment in which governments address them is fundamentally economic. If Turkeys want their government to play a role on human rights different from that of the European empires, they will have to confront America's protectionism as much as its military alliances with dictators.

POLITE DICTATORS

At a 1996 meeting with human rights advocates in his regally-appointed office, Assistant Secretary of State for East Asia Winston Lord listened to proposals to condition US military relations with countries such as Indonesia, China, and Thailand on their records on human rights. He responded that, because unlike the activists he was responsible for US interests broadly defined, and not just human rights, he would have to balance their proposals with those that promoted security and commercial interests. A member of the delegation remonstrated forcefully that the group would not have made any proposals that did not already take into account the US interest, and that affirming human rights as a prerequisite for closer military and economic relations with repressive regimes was precisely the way to aid the democratic transition and open economic environment that official US policy claimed were sources of long-term US security. Lord looked taken aback by this intervention, as if he had always thought of human rights groups as insensitive to US security.

This exchange illustrates the limitations of human rights advocacy. To be credible, it must be political and relevant to a particular situation, rather than merely principled and universal. Yet its founding principle and the bureaucratic structure that promotes it are artificially apolitical. When liberal Tom Harkin and conservative Jesse Helms collaborated in the 1970s to produce legislation barring US approval for development banks' loans to nations not engaging in "gross and consistent violations of internationally-recognized human rights," they did so against the efforts of the "responsible middle" of Soft and Hard Eagles. Harkin and Helms were united in their distaste for the World Bank's support for dictators, one for rightists, and the other for leftists. Carter's international adviser at the Treasury, Fred Bergsten, led the successful charge to insulate the International Monetary Fund from this requirement. However, the legislation was eventually extended to include military and bilateral economic assistance, except for direct aid to the poor.

Much like the War Powers resolution of the same era, the human rights laws were honored in the breach. While no nation was ever formally designated as a violator, even when the United States opposed or abstained on their loans at the development banks, concern over gross violations often forced administrations to insist on improvements before providing aid. Progress, though, was generally measured in the treatment of dissidents, not in the relaxation of the repressive rule they were protesting. The isolation of human rights from regional policy-making was enforced by the decision of Congress to mandate the creation of a new Human Rights bureau at the State Department and by Carter's selection of someone without foreign policy experience, Patt Derian, to be its assistant secretary. Regional assistant secretaries, like Lord's predecessors in East Asia Richard Holbrooke and Paul Wolfowitz, treated any proposal from the Human Rights bureau like a complaint from a nagging aunt, and Holbrooke went so far as to order his bureau to refuse to speak with the officer Derian chose to cover that region. Deputy Secretary Warren Christopher resolved this and the more general crisis by lowering the stakes. The inter-agency committee he established on human rights decisions reviewed only loans from the development banks, which the United States could not block on its own. Dictators might be embarrassed by having the United States abstain on a power project that was still approved by the World Bank, but the troops they relied on to preserve their rule could be, and were, fully US-armed and trained.[1]

As the Cold War heated up in the developing world in the 1980s, Soft Eagles seized on human rights as a bridge to engage Hard Eagles in ending the conflicts. In El Salvador, Angola, and Nicaragua, lethal misconduct by US-backed troops, rather than the lethality of the civil war itself, was used to discredit plans for additional aid. Similarly, wanton brutality in Indonesia, Argentina, Chile, the Philippines, and even South Africa eroded US support for authoritarian rule more than the fact of the rule itself. By the 1990s dictators and rebel groups alike were showing that they had learned the lessons and even the language of the human rights movement. They no longer "disappeared" their opponents, but rather placed them under house arrest. They shut down newspapers in court or by pressuring advertisers, not by ransacking the presses and shooting employees. In a word, they were more polite in preserving their illegitimate rule.

When Amnesty International, as described in Chapter 6, reworked the "no arms to dictators" Code of Conduct into a ban on exporting weapons that could be used for assaults on civilians or torture, it affirmed for dictators that how they ruled, not whether they ruled, determined their international standing. In some cases, such as the Philippines and much of Eastern Europe, the softer tactics backfired, as crowds that could finally gather without fear of slaughter toppled dictators, but in many others, particularly in Africa, softer repression reduced the international heat and allowed continued dictatorship. Like women's rights, carbon off-sets, transparency of mineral revenues, anti-malarial bednets, and other causes of the day, human rights had by the 2000s become another way for repressive regimes to engage with Western governments and gain legitimacy for taking symbolic steps.

The Pentagon too learned how to absorb the popular language of the human rights movement. Complaints about human rights abuses by US-trained troops in Latin America led to the addition of "human rights training" to the International Military Education and Training (IMET) program, which usually focused on command and control courses for

---

1   For a review of the history of legislation and executive branch activities in the 1970s and early 1980s, see Caleb Rossiter with Anne-Marie Smith, "Human Rights: The Carter Record, the Reagan Reaction," International Policy Report, Center for International Policy, September 1984.

officers and training for soldiers in technical military skills like shooting and patrolling. Tens of thousands of officers and troops were trained at the US Army School of the Americas, first at a US base in Panama in the 1960s and 1970s and then after the Canal Treaty at Ft. Benning, Georgia. When the human rights training began in the 1980s it focused very narrowly on the laws of war that barred attacks on civilians and prisoners. The School did not address the reality that the better-behaved troops would still be serving a dictator or, in countries like Brazil and El Salvador, would comprise an army holding virtually independent political power within a dubiously-elected government. In fact, among the pictures on the School's Wall of Fame in 1988 were not just alumni who had risen to flag-rank in dictatorships but were dictators themselves.

Trainers at Ft. Benning did not teach their students of their duty to report abuses up the chain of command. Nor did they challenge the morality of violating the laws of war. Both, they felt, would be a waste of teaching time. Supporters of the training in Congress and the media appeared often to be unaware of the different roles played in society by US armed forces and their Latin American counterparts, and to believe that the training would simply transfer the US role to the hemisphere. The trainers, often US Green Berets with regional experience or officers from Latin American armed forces, had no such illusions. They knew that reporting soldiers, let alone officers, involved in abuses would be suicidal in the Latin American armies of the day, and that the actions on both sides of the guerrilla wars in the region had long since buried any concerns about morality. Instead the trainers stressed that brutality and torture garnered negative international press attention and were harmful to the mission of pacification, since villagers would be more eager to cooperate and rebels to surrender if they knew they would be treated well.[1]

A congressional staffer inspecting Ft. Benning in 1988 witnessed a revealing example of how futile the human rights training was, a full year before the murder of the Jesuits in El Salvador by a US-trained brigade at the orders of the US-trained senior officers in the High Command confirmed it. The staffer had been under the strictest supervision of Dr. Spiro Manolis, a top IMET official. Having boarded a commercial aircraft in Washington he found that Manolis had somehow arranged with the airline to place him in the middle of a phalanx of officers. Not for an instant did the phalanx recede as the staffer observed instruction of hundreds of Salvadorans and other foreign officers, non-commissioned officers, and soldiers in command, combat, and human rights. Finally, in a hallway between classes, the staffer noticed that one of the lecturers was wearing the uniform of a different country, and asked him in Spanish where he was from. Peru, he proudly declared, and explained that there were other foreign officers working as instructors, including Chileans.

Manolis, who did not speak Spanish, blanched at the mention of Chile, which was barred from US military training because of the assassination in 1976 of ousted foreign minister Orlando Letelier and Ronni Moffit, his assistant at the Institute for Policy Studies in Washington, by Chilean agents. The US Army was engaging in a backdoor trick to maintain relations with the Chilean armed forces, and Manolis feared, correctly, that the staffer would report the evasion to Senator Ted Kennedy, the sponsor of the legislation banning military aid. But the worst was yet to come. The staffer asked the officer about

---

1 Extensive interviews with trainers, Fort Benning, 1988.

a recent massacre by the Peruvian Army in its highland war with the *Sendero Luminoso*, or Shining Path, rebels. "Well," said the Peruvian officer, "that was a *villa roja*." The officer made it clear that when "red villages" help the rebels, they have to be punished. One of the US officers in the protective phalanx interpreted this exchange for Manolis, and the Peruvian was hustled away.

The remark was included in a congressional report with the finding that having such an attitude in an instructor indicated that deeds would trump words — that the human rights message included in the training could not get through to Latin American officers as long as their actions, like murdering civilians, did not lead to a cut-off of aid.[1] The US Army's response was to fire the Peruvian and say publicly that one bad apple should not be seen as tainting the rest of a fine barrel. Concerns about IMET's ineffective human rights approach led Soft Eagles to propose a broader one in 1990. In an attempt to squeeze IMET's military training funds, Senator Patrick Leahy won enactment of a requirement that ten percent be spent on a program to promote civilian control of the armed forces. This "Expanded IMET" program was intended to instruct civilian officials how to oversee the military budget and bring civil society leaders together with military officials for free-ranging discussion of their roles in society. As with many progressive congressional mandates, without consistent oversight, the program slowly lost its original focus and devolved into management training for senior officers.[2] A decade of oversight in the 2000s from Congressman Jim McGovern and his staffer Cindy Buhl did gradually soften the mission of the School of the Americas, which was renamed the Western Hemisphere Institute for Security Cooperation, and began to reduce its combat training.

By 2000 all of Latin America, excluding Cuba but including Chile, was ruled by elected governments that were usually in control of their armed forces. The contradiction of "professionalizing" armed forces that would then more effectively entrench a dictator or undermine a democrat seems to have been resolved, although an old-fashioned coup in Honduras in 2009, the transfer to the Chilean armed forces of 10 percent of copper revenues, and the virtual independence of Brazil's armed forces show the fragile nature of civilian control. In Africa, though, the debate over human rights training erupted again after 9/11, when Defense Secretary Donald Rumsfeld approved a Pentagon plan to create an African Command, or in Pentagon parlance, AFRICOM. The new command would take over all of Africa except Egypt from the European and Central Commands and would focus on establishing "partnerships" with armed forces willing to cooperate in the Global War on Terror. The announcement in 2006 of a plan to base AFRICOM on the continent

---

1   Mark O. Hatfield, Mickey Leland, and Matthew F. McHugh, "Danger Point: The Developing World and US Security," Arms Control and Foreign Policy Caucus, August 1989.

2   In a humorous case of Senators trying to handle staff-level work, an aide to Senator Alan Cranston was having a hard time convincing Senator Leahy's foreign policy staffer Eric Newsom to make a particular modification in Expanded IMET, and so sent Cranston to talk to Leahy about it on the Senate floor. Leahy had never heard of Expanded IMET, but he listened politely and then told Cranston to have his staffer talk to Newsom...who of course was then even less amenable to the modification because of the breach in protocol.

was a shock to civil society groups in Africa and probably to a lot of African governments that had not listened too carefully during low-level discussions.[1]

Hastily back-pedaling, the Pentagon appointed a black general and announced that it was spurning the bid by the only interested country, Liberia, and keeping the command's offices at the European command's base in Stuttgart, Germany. The new commander, Kip Ward, beat his breast over the manner in which AFRICOM was "rolled out" by the can-do Army and cast the command as a social service agency assisting the Agency for International Development in implementing its projects. The reality of the anti-terrorist mission remained, however. Ward's forces continued to train the armed forces of nearly every African country willing to take part, regardless of the nature of the government and the abuses by those forces, and conducted combat missions in Somalia from a previously-established base in Djibouti. Training the armed forces of non-democratic or weakly-democratic African countries had already been taking place under the Clinton administration. The African Crisis Response Initiative (ACRI) was intended to prepare African armed forces for the peace-keeping, or more properly peace-making, missions for which Clinton would not use US forces after the 1993 debacle in Somalia.

Clan leaders there had used their militias to take control of districts after the civil war of the 1980s drove the US-backed dictator Siad Barré from the country. Attempts by UN forces in 1993 to establish their authority rather than just ensure the delivery of relief supplies as they had in Bush's 1992 intervention were repulsed by the militias. When US forces raided a house in the capital, Mogadishu, to capture clan leaders who had ordered an attack on Pakistani soldiers in the UN force, the resulting firefight and death of 18 US soldiers after two Black Hawk helicopters were shot down obscured the success of the raid and led to US withdrawal. When genocide erupted in Rwanda the next spring as Hutu militias slaughtered the Tutsi minority and its Hutu sympathizers, and then an invading Tutsi army slaughtered Hutus who had allegedly aided the militias, Assistant Secretary of State for Africa Susan Rice and others in the administration were unable to generate support for any meaningful UN action, let alone US action. As a result, they developed plans for the ACRI so that there would African troops available for future crises.

The Pentagon seized on the ACRI as a way to replicate the deep penetration of Latin American armed forces it had achieved through the School of the Americas. The Latin American training had served both a general intelligence-gathering function through the relationships that developed between the foreign and US officers and a strategic function through strengthening the foreign officers and their anti-leftist role in politics. As in Latin America the Pentagon tried to disarm critics with the claim that it was precisely the worst abusers who should be given US training, because they had the most to gain from exposure to American values. While Soft Eagles had learned how to counter this claim with disastrous examples of US-trained forces engaged in torture, murder, and coups in Latin America, they were confounded in Africa by the claim that the training would be primarily for peace-keeping. The Soft Eagles could see that many of the troops being trained came

---

1 For a detailed critique and history of AFRICOM by two august Africanists, Daniel Volman and William Minter, see "Making Peace or Fueling War in Africa," Foreign Policy in Focus, March 13, 2009, at http://www.fpif.org/fpiftxt/5960.

from dictatorships or repressive regimes that would generally benefit from the association with the US armed forces and would specifically be having their armed forces strengthened for use against internal dissent. However, they were also eager to have a capacity to prevent the sort of genocide they had witnesses in Rwanda.

Under Clinton the Pentagon also inaugurated the Africa Center for Strategic Studies as a Washington meeting ground for US officers and top defense officials and officers from the continent, again regardless of whether their regime was freely-elected or not, or had committed human rights abuses. Its original intent was to recreate the atmosphere of the Inter-American Defense College, where this sort of interaction and discussion of security issues had been taking place for decades, but after 9/11 it was retooled to "build awareness and support for the war on terrorism." With ACRI and the Africa Center having established the principle of training and legitimizing powerful armed forces in Africa, there was really nothing new about AFRICOM's support for armed forces in dictatorships like Ethiopia and Equatorial Guinea.

In Ethiopia Meles Zenawi used his US-trained forces to arrest the opposition when it won the 2005 election and to invade Somalia in 2006, at US request, to dislodge an informal Islamist government. In Equatorial Guinea, Teodoro Obiang presided over torture and looted the country's substantial oil revenues from American firms while US Navy ships from its Africa Partnership Station program paid port calls, trained the armed forces, and appeared in friendly soccer matches with them.[1] "Exposure to American values" in these cases meant that Africans saw that strategic and commercial considerations trump human rights in US policy. In some ways US policy in Africa was a few decades behind its approach to Latin American. In Africa in the 2000s, like Latin America in the 1960s, dictators who were really important to US interests did not even have to be polite.

A fitting coda shows the fundamentally apolitical impulse of the human rights movement. In 2008 the Washington Office of the Open Society Institute, a global fund for social activism bankrolled by currency-trader George Soros and directed by Aryeh Neier, the founding father of human rights, promoted legislation to relax the 1970s ban on aid to foreign police and prisons so that prison conditions could be improved in poor countries. Ethiopia and Equatorial Guinea could have qualified for the aid, and indeed had this proposal been turned into law in the 1980s, the South African apartheid government could have received US support to buy a new bed for prisoner Nelson Mandela. Human rights policy was never so starkly put: keep your dissidents alive, and we will help you keep them in prison.

PHONY ELECTIONS

Frequently thwarted by his parties and turned out of office by his electorates, British prime minister Winston Churchill loved to say that "democracy is the worst form of

---

1 For a review of US motivations and actions in these two countries, see "Is there a Human Rights Double Standard? US Policy Toward Equatorial Guinea and Ethiopia," House Committee on Foreign Affairs, Subcommittee on International Organizations, Human Rights, and Oversight, May 10, 2007. Available on-line at http://foreignaffairs.house.gov/hearing_notice.asp?id=821.

government — except all those other forms that have been tried from time to time." As an imperialist, Churchill did not deign to extend his advocacy of popular rule to the billion people living under British power during his tenure in various ministries. Still, his preference for the regular contesting of power through fair elections has become engrained in the former colonial world. Democracy is the stated goal of nearly every government on the globe, with even Cuba, China, and Vietnam claiming that their Communist Party elections, in which local assemblies promote candidates to national ruling bodies, are models of democracy. Just 220 years after the American constitution introduced classless voting, at least for white males, into a world of kings and emperors, only a few monarchs still claim a national status for their tribal role.[1]

Americans of all feathers seem to believe in promoting democracy abroad. Hard Eagles claim that democracies don't attack other countries, because electorates constrain their leaders' ambitions. Soft Eagles claim that democracies don't suffer from civil wars, because aggrieved parties know that power can be gained peacefully. Both agree that reducing conflicts of either type serves American economic and security interests by maintaining local and global growth that provides American firms with export and investment opportunities. While counter-examples abound — consider the United States attacking Iraq in 2002, or Angola's civil war resuming in 1992 after a rebel group lost a decently-run election and returned to combat — the overarching truth of these claims is clear.

Turkeys who recognize the need to move beyond apolitical human rights to the underlying question of governance want to support the growth of democracy abroad too, not for American self-interest but primarily on the moral grounds that people have a right to choose their government. In this they sound like President Reagan and his neo-conservative advisers, who claimed that democracy was the altruistic goal in the Central American wars of the 1980s, President Bush and the same neo-conservative advisers who claimed that goal for Middle East policy in the 2000s, and every president who ever stopped to outline the goals of US policy in Africa. Turkeys would argue that while they really mean it, Eagles like Reagan and Bush, and indeed Obama in his Cairo speech, are giving democracy a bad name by just talking about it to mask their economic and strategic interests.

Proof for the Turkeys was found in the hypocrisy of Eagles calling for democracy while arming anti-democratic allies. Reagan wanted to aid the Ovimbundu revolt against the Cuban-backed Angolan government, so Jonas Savimbi, the revolt's brutal Maoist leader, hilariously recast himself as a democratic capitalist and walked the halls of Congress in a suit rather than his usual fatigues to talk to Members about his plans for tax cuts and investment incentives. Savimbi revealed his own definition of democracy by resuming the civil war after he lost the well-run election of 1992. The armed embrace of Egypt and Saudi Arabia by both President Bushes was another good example, but the problem was bipartisan. The Democratic Party's National Democratic Institute guided foreign elections and trained political parties in the 1990s even as its congressional board members, like Dick

---

1 Most are tiny principalities like Monaco in Europe, Qatar and Bahrain in the Persian Gulf, Swaziland in Africa, and Brunei in Asia, although the large and powerful states of Saudi Arabia in the Persian Gulf and Morocco are a reminder of the norm of the past.

Gephardt of Missouri and Chris Dodd of Connecticut, pushed for the sale of weapons made in their states as part of Clinton's record arms transfers to authoritarian regimes.

The Eagles' version of democracy has certainly at times meant elections that exclude parties hostile to US policy, as in vote-happy Vietnam and El Salvador during their civil wars, or are hopelessly fraudulent, as in Afghanistan in 2009. As Henry Kissinger presided over a National Security Council meeting in 1970 on keeping Salvador Allende from winning the Chilean election, he allegedly said: "I don't see why we need to stand by and watch a country go communist due to the irresponsibility of its people. The issues are much too important for the Chilean voters to be left to decide for themselves." The CIA then funded and armed dissident officers who assassinated the Chilean general who was standing in the way of a coup, and the Nixon administration spurred and supported the seizure of power in 1973 by another general, Augusto Pinochet.[1] This view of democracy as useful only if your favored candidate wins continued to be reflected in US rigging of the Salvadoran election in 1984, acceptance of the Algerian military coup against the victorious Islamist party in 1991, and a cut-off of aid to the Palestinian Authority after the victory of the Hamas party in 2006.[2] Still, the real differences between Turkeys and Eagles on democracy arise from the difficulty of defining it.

Most democracies have a unique form of representation that is not a simple "rule of the people" that gives the majority the right to make decisions. The American Founders made this goal explicit, and in fact used the word "democracy" in a negative way, to describe the sort of untrammeled rule of a brief majority that characterized the ability of the mob in ancient Greece to turn on a minority. When Benjamin Franklin was asked what the convention had given to the American people, he responded, "a republic, if you can keep it." Constitutional guarantees of the minority and individual rights that are central to democratic republics are approved by one generation of voters or their representatives, but can be overturned only by another generation's super-majority. For example, constitutional amendments can be imposed in South Africa only by two-thirds of the parliament and six of the ten provincial governments, and in America by two-thirds of Congress and three-fourths of states. Even day-to-day governing is often undemocratic. For example, the Nigerian constitution fixes a percentage of oil revenues that must be returned to oil-producing states, and American states all have two votes in the Senate, regardless of the size of their population — and the latter is a protection that the Constitution states cannot be amended, even by a super-majority.

Democracy is always a tough business in practice. In the United States wealthy donors, corporate and union interests, personal wealth, payoffs, gerrymandering, exploitation of incumbency, bottom-feeding advertising, and scary rumors all conspire to mock the notion that elections reflect the people's will. Legislatures are run dictatorially by majorities who mindlessly obstruct executives of the other party and forget to conduct oversight on executives of their own. Campaign cash not just from corporations and unions,

---

1 Administration documents from the era have been assembled by Peter Kornbluh, director of the Chile Documentation Project at the National Security Archive, and are available online at http://www.gwu.edu/~nsarchiv/latin_america/chile.htm.
2 Jim Zanotti, "US Foreign Aid to the Palestinians," RS22967, Congressional Research Service, July 16, 2009, pp. 1-2.

but from the legislators' own political action committees changes hands as the fortunes of bills advance and decline. In the formerly colonized countries, however, all this would be considered harmless foreplay. Europe had gone through centuries of violence and forced exclusion to shake its ethnic groups into bordered countries, yet it imposed economic systems and borders in Africa, the Middle East, and the Asian subcontinent that destroyed long-standing ethnic nations and forced them into, or split them between, illogical countries. As a result, in much of Africa, and in other tribally-divided societies like Iraq, Afghanistan and Pakistan, the primary purpose of an election is not to take the public's true pulse, but to gain or hold power for your people's benefit and even survival. Clausewitz famously said that war is an extension of politics by other means, but the converse is also true: in post-colonial countries politics is an extension of war by other means.

Aside from Iran and Iraq, the Muslim countries of North Africa and the Middle East have not been subject to any significant expectation, let alone pressure, from the United States to embrace elected transitions of power. The reasons certainly include the desire for access to oil and for stability for Israel. However, US officials also endorse a largely unspoken, yet largely valid, belief that many of the countries constitute sound feudal systems in which governments have maintained legitimacy through consultation and the distribution of benefits. Similarly, US reluctance to sanction the governments of China, Vietnam, and Singapore for their refusal to test their popularity in open elections is based not just on economic relations, but on a sincere, if convenient, belief in an Asian tradition based on the Confucian teachings of 2500 years ago. Confucius stressed the need for average citizens to accept wise leaders and live a harmonious life, advice that is similar in important respects to the concepts developed by Plato and his pupils in the same period for government by philosopher-kings.

In Latin America, though, Turkeys were successful by the 1990s in forcing Eagles to insist on fair elections as the basis for US acceptance of legitimacy. This helped end the cycle of dictatorship and fraudulent elections that had been running in the region since independence in the 1800s. In large part this success came from the power of Latin America's well-developed civil society, the religious and non-governmental organizations that promote free speech, the rule of law, and labor and women's rights. It was also made possible by the marginalization — and in many cases the cultural and even physical elimination — of indigenous people over centuries by the powerful colonial immigrants. With little ethnic tension infusing electoral politics, class issues, even in ethnically-divided societies like Bolivia, Peru, and Guatemala, provided economic identities to political parties and made electoral defeat a threat to livelihoods but not lives. However, in parts of the world where personal affiliation is stronger with the tribal nation than with the country, even honest elections convey little legitimacy to the victors, and frequently spur just the sort of civil conflict that Soft Eagles claimed would be reduced by democracy.

In Sub-Saharan Africa the colonial powers sponsored superficially Western-style elections to establish governments as they fled in the late 1950s and early 1960s. The experiment failed and became known as "one man, one vote, one time." Military forces the Europeans had created to enforce colonialism took over in a series of coups that defined African politics for 30 years. With the end of the Cold War nearly every functioning state began to hold multi-party elections in the 1990s, as the United States had less need for embarrassing allies and the Soviet-backed model of one-party assemblies disappeared with its mentor. Only one leader left office as a result of losing an election in the 1980s, but 12 did so in the 1990s.[1] However, the elections generally were shows designed to win Western approval and continued foreign aid, rather than true open contests.

Freedom House found in 2009 that only 21 percent of sub-Saharan countries were politically "free," with another 48 percent "partially free" and the remaining 31 percent "not free." While these percentages were significantly better than the nine, 32, and 59 percent division in 1980, they had hit a plateau after the 1990s.[2] Elections in Africa often stimulate ethnic clashes during campaigning, and after the results are announced. "Partly-free" Ethiopia in 2005 and Nigeria and Kenya in 2006 saw their elections stolen by the ruling party, with predictable consequences of protest, riot, crackdown, death, and jail. Even the Democratic Republic of the Congo, which allowed the United Nations in 2006 to run as good an election as a sprawling, unconnected, dysfunctional country could ever see, found the event irrelevant to the continuing civil war waged by the losing parties and their ethnic allies in neighboring states.

The ill-fated attempt to jump-start Western democracy in Africa was promoted in large part by a public foundation called the National Endowment for Democracy, which passed congressional appropriations for foreign programs on to the National Democratic Institute and its Republican counterpart, as well as to American labor groups. Soft Eagles had been pushing for such a foundation for decades, and tapped into the Reagan administration's efforts to topple the Sandinista government in Nicaragua to get it approved. Unlike election-monitoring groups like the Carter Center or parliamentary observers, delegations and staff from the Endowment and their grantees roam the globe with a mandate to improve both the machinery of elections and the operations of parliaments and political and civic groups. There is a comical naiveté in their devoted efforts, given that they come from a country whose election system is, contrary to all the advice they give others, overseen by party officials at the county and state level, and so in close races (like Florida's presidential vote in 2000) politicized and often spectacularly dysfunctional. Similarly, the American system of governance focuses on trading cash and favors to extract local benefits from general funds, regularly lurches into a hysteria that obscures rather than enlightens the populace, and can grind to an embarrassing halt at the state and federal levels. Recommending either system to new democracies with different cultures and economic conditions is an exercise in hubris and futility.

In Malawi in 1994, during the first election campaign after the long-time dictator agreed to leave office with much of the economy in his personal possession, the American party institutes descended on the country with pollsters and political operatives who had never been in Africa. Shortly thereafter, one of the new Malawian parties began running slick radio commercials claiming that if another party won, it had a secret plan to circumcise all the men of the other tribes. This led one of the courageous ministers who had led

---

1 Christopher Clapham, Jeffrey Herbst, and Greg Mills, eds., *Big African States*, Wits University Press, Johannesburg, 2006, p. 260.
2 "Freedom in Sub-Saharan Africa," Freedom House, Washington, DC, 2009.

the pro-democracy movement to ask a meeting of the American experts, "and just what *have* you been teaching the parties?"[1] The National Democratic Institute's operatives were surprised and chagrined when their Malawian staff told them that campaigning on issues and personalities was irrelevant to voters because they, like the staff themselves, would all vote for the party of their own ethnic group.

The complaint of a Malawian subsistence farmer at that time explains why democracy cannot be defined by elections, even those that are fairly conducted, when a ruling party or the armed forces continue to operate without legal constraint. The farmer had gone to the government's district office to get the bag of fertilizer that a foreign donor had provided for each farmer, and had been asked for two chickens as a pay-off. "When those officials get punished for demanding my chickens," he said, "that is democracy." The reality for Africa today, as it was for Latin America in the 1980s, is that even after fair elections ruling parties and independent armed forces often operate without legal constraint and without criticism from media that have been cowed by advertising boycotts by government contractors or raw force. Ethnic divisions and poor performance mean that for many citizens the government lacks elemental legitimacy. Turkeys as well as Eagles are caught in the conundrum of promoting elections, which might eventually make the transfer of power more predictable and less violent than the alternative of civil conflict, when local activists are first demanding a spirit and mechanism of broad and open public consultation, or *concertation*, and a relaxation of the international economic pressures that can undermine even the most devoted governments.[2]

LANDMINE-FREE WARS

To understand why the campaign to ban landmines has proved to be a trap for Turkeys, one must understand the perspective of the campaign's founder and funder, Bobby Muller. When the gung-ho Marine lieutenant came back from Vietnam in 1969 paralyzed from the waist down, he was appalled at the poor medical treatment and support that he and other wounded veterans received. Being featured in a *Life* magazine story on the problem led to him becoming a prominent voice for the Vietnam Veterans Against the War. Muller's review of the decision-making that led to the Vietnam War made him a jaded Turkey, someone who had discovered a bit too late for his own health that nearly everything said by Washington policy makers about being motivated by a concern for the freedom and well-being of other peoples was "total [expletive] fantasies...absolute [expletive] [expletive]!"[3] After taking a law degree Muller worked for the Paralyzed Veterans of America and then in 1978 moved to Washington and founded the Vietnam Veterans

---

1 "Fighting Retreat: Military Political Power and Other Barriers to Africa's Democratic Transition," Demilitarization for Democracy, Washington, DC, July 1997, p. ii.

2 "Fighting Retreat: Military Political Power and Other Barriers to Africa's Democratic Transition," Demilitarization for Democracy, Washington, DC, July 1997, pp. i, 1-7.

3 Muller later found confirmation in a quote from a classified memorandum from 1948 in which George Kennan, often lionized for taking the liberal side of the foreign policy debate, reminded State Department planners that "to maintain this position of disparity" of wealth and power compared to the developing world was their only legitimate goal.

of America (VVA) to promote both better treatment for the casualties of that war and a foreign policy that would avoid the next one.

The congressionally-chartered VVA was a direct challenge to the power of the American Legion and the Veterans of Foreign Wars, which have traditionally been right-leaning and pro-intervention. When Muller began to speak out against Reagan's wars in Central America and then decided to start the process of reconciliation between the United States and Vietnam, he encountered resistance from those groups and some of his own membership. He decided to "neuter" the mission of the VVA by having it pared down to promoting benefits and services, and founded a new organization, the Vietnam Veterans of America Foundation (VVAF), to pursue his interest in "the causes, conduct, and consequences of war."[1] After Vietnam had deposed the Khmer Rouge, he made a trip to Cambodia, during which "the blood was still on the ground and the hair still on the devices" in the torture chambers he visited. This left Muller "connected emotionally with the horror" of a genocide that had killed a quarter of the country. When he and another wounded veteran met with an ostracized group of 80 Cambodians who had lost limbs or eyesight to explosives, ignoring them was not an option: "We couldn't not do something. We knew what it was to be knocked down, but we had gotten back in the game and lived a good life. These people were warehoused."

Muller's political awakening would not permit him to stop at aiding victims, which he eventually did in an impressive network of clinics in six countries. Cambodia convinced him that "war had become a slaughter of innocents," and the reality that "civilians were the targets and casualties" made modern wars war crimes in themselves. He dedicated his life to discrediting war as a viable policy option. Muller used VVAF to publicize the fact that wars had made a transition in the 20th century from having 90 percent military casualties to having 90 percent civilian casualties. Death rates increase dramatically in developing countries during a civil war. Millions of civilians can die from malnutrition and disease during wars in which only a few soldiers are killed in combat, because of the disruption of work, family, income, farming, and water supplies, and the subsequent migration to the squalor and hopelessness of refugee camps. Muller had seen the results of this sort of dislocation during his tour in Vietnam, and his own terrible injury in combat had attuned him to the suffering of all the victims of war, combatants and civilians alike.

As the VVAF began to treat victims, Muller discovered that many of them had been injured not during the fighting but well after it, as they tried to reclaim their fields and paths and stumbled upon dud munitions and, most frequently, abandoned landmines.[2] This led him in 1991 to ask the director of a German group that also provided international medical services to join him in founding the International Campaign to Ban Landmines, and then to enlist as its leading advocate Senate foreign aid appropriator Patrick Leahy and as its leading strategist Leahy aide Tim Rieser. Leahy and Rieser had established a War Victims Fund in 1989 after having been deeply moved during their trips overseas by the plight of

---

1 Unless otherwise noted, all quotations and attributions to Muller come from conversations with him from 1992 to 2002 and an interview on December 1, 2009.
2 Leon V. Sigal, *Negotiating Minefields: The Landmines Ban in American Politics*, Routledge, New York, 2006, p. 2.

wounded civilians, and VVAF had become of one its grantees. Muller told Leahy, "We need to go upstream" and stop the casualties before they occur. The ever-quotable Muller told the press the goal was "to put VVAF clinics out of the prosthetics business." This statement was a bit misleading, as people with artificial limbs require new ones through-out their lives as the underlying bone changes, but the meaning was clear: one could not in good conscience treat landmine victims without trying to stop the creation of even more such victims.

Muller's initiative became the non-governmental advocacy story of the decade. What he called his dual "wheel-chair legitimacy" as a wounded combat veteran and manager of prosthetics clinics helped get the campaign off the ground with a hefty dose of access to civilian and military officials and the media. He pumped at least $5 million into the campaign for staff, advertising, and consulting fees for lobbyists and strategists from the $40 million that his wife, a doctor who had inherited a fortune, gave to support VVAF's programs. Financier George Soros kicked in large amounts as well through the new Arms project of Human Rights Watch, which focused on violations of the laws of war. With this funding and smaller grants from a variety of foundations enabling many organizations to assign a few staff to work on the ban and travel to coalition meetings, the ICBL grew from six founding medical and human rights groups in 1992 to a coalition of hundreds of religious, human rights, and peace organizations around the world.[1] Under the constant prodding of Jody Williams, hired by Muller to coordinate the campaign, and using the new technology of the internet, they spurred each other into generating a tremendous amount of publicity as they hammered on governments to care for current victims, clear existing minefields, and adopt a treaty banning further use of landmines. Over 150 coun-tries eventually signed the 1997 Ottawa treaty banning the use of anti-personnel mines. However, the impact claimed for the treaty, and for its model of citizen involvement in national security decisions, by the ICBL and the committee that awarded the Nobel peace prize to the ICBL and Williams was vastly overstated.

The Ottawa ban did not resolve a key part of the concrete humanitarian problem that first attracted Muller's concern. It exempted the more powerful landmines that are de-signed to knock out vehicles, which are a significant source of civilian casualties. Many of these "anti-tank" mines have "anti-handling" features to guard them from enemy sappers, so they can be triggered by unwary civilians, just like anti-personnel mines.[2] In addition, the treaty was not signed by a number of countries that argued that their use of anti-personnel mines in border areas was a military necessity and posed little risk to civilians. These include prominent military powers such as Russia, China, Vietnam, Israel, Egypt, Pakistan, India, the Koreas, and the United States, as well as small but insecure coun-tries such as Cuba, Saudi Arabia, Finland, and Uzbekistan. Ban campaigners had hoped

---

1 The International Committee of the Red Cross, a quasi-governmental body in Geneva that monitors the conduct of war, was a crucial player in the campaign because of the credibility of its highly technical and legalistic reports, but was not a member of the ICBL.

2 "This allows antipersonnel mines...This treaty's junk," was the judgment of Rae McGrath, the director of a group that disabled abandoned mines, and so would have to contend with the anti-handling devices. Leon V. Sigal, *Negotiating Minefields: The Landmines Ban in American Politics*, Routledge, New York, 2006, p. 201.

that the adoption of a tough treaty banning anti-personnel mines, without the exceptions and transition periods sought by some of these countries, would create an international stigma that would force the non-signatories to bend to the new norm in practice, just as a limited ban on chemical weapons had done after World War I.[1] With the exception of exports of anti-personnel mines, which quickly stopped worldwide after Leahy passed a moratorium on US exports in 1992, in the 12 years after Ottawa it is not at all clear that this stigma had developed.[2]

Landmines continue to be used in combat operations in nine conflicts, largely by rebel groups, and remain as border barriers for many non-signatories.[3] It is also not clear that casualties have been reduced as a result of the treaty. Estimates of new victims of all explosive remnants of war (anti-personnel and anti-vehicle mines and dud munitions) have fallen since the 1990s from 26,000 per year to 7,000, but the initial estimate was shaky and the share of anti-personnel mines in all the figures is hard to identify.[4] Any decline in casualties could well be simply the result of the end of wars that saw their massive deployment, such as those in Angola, Cambodia, Ethiopia, and Mozambique, which stopped new laying of mines and permitted mine clearance. More importantly, the landmines campaign did not achieve Muller's underlying, "number one motivation" for it. He had hoped to open up a broader discussion of how wars inevitably harmed civilians, whichever weapons and tactics were used, but "we never succeeded in getting the changing nature of warfare understood." The paradox of Muller's work was that both the Ottawa Treaty and the rival Convention of Conventional Weapons (CCW), a UN agreement he also promoted under which nearly all significant military powers frequently update the rules for marking and monitoring minefields and other military tactics to reduce suffering by civilians, have the strange effect of making wars more acceptable if combatants use certain weapons and tactics.[5]

Where Muller wanted to use landmines as an example, many of the religious and peace groups that joined the landmines campaign wanted to use them as a first step in banning war, weapon by weapon. The Quakers' active Washington lobby office, the Friends Com-

---

1 "Commander in Chief; Contrasting Presidential Roles in the World Campaigns to Ban Chemical Weapons and Land Mines," International Policy Report, Center for International Policy, November 1990.

2 As of 2010 the United States, the country with the most highly developed alternative weapons and tactics, still had not signed the treaty.

3 International Campaign to Ban Landmines, *Landmine Monitor, 2009*, "Major Findings."

4 The State Department used the figure in its 1994 report, "Hidden Killers," citing the International Committee of the Red Cross. Both the State Department and *Landmine Monitor*, the ICBL's annual publication, continue to attempt to track reports of victims of post-combat explosions, but find it difficult to differentiate between those hurt by anti-personnel mines, anti-tank mines, and dud munitions.

5 The CCW operated by consensus, so no proposal to ban mines could be seriously entertained with China, the United States, and Russia as members. Many groups, including Human Rights Watch, had adopted a firm legal position that anti-personnel mines were already illegal under the Geneva Conventions' prohibition on indiscriminate weapons. This made them even more leery of using the CCW as a venue to address landmines, although they did support CCW protocols that might reduce casualties by, for example, requiring enough metal in mines so that clearance personnel could find them with detectors after a war.

---

mittee on National Legislation, sponsored briefings to describe the horror of the wounds inflicted by various weapons, and argued that they should be banned for that reason, as indeed "dum-dum" bullets and incendiary bombing of cities are under the CCW. At conferences and meetings Jody Williams talked dismissively about claims that mines could save the lives of US soldiers, saying "[expletive] yeah, we're gonna" take away all of the lethal "toys for the boys."[1] Her anti-military orientation contrasted sharply with that of Muller and VVAF as a whole, and created a bitter division within the campaign on both policy and in personalities that was almost immediately apparent.[2]

By 1995, Williams was ardently taking the side of Human Rights Watch's Steve Goose in negotiations over ICBL positions and the wording of joint statements. Goose would often argue that his organization could not sign on to any position that deviated from its carefully-crafted legal judgments. Muller wanted to avoid a breakdown of the group, so the ICBL he had founded for political reasons effectively came under the control of the apolitical Human Rights Watch. Muller considered firing Williams at this point, but after consulting with Rieser he decided that since "Jody didn't play" in Washington but with international partners, he could not justify disrupting the progress he saw on that front. He finally fired her in 1997 only after she refused to meet the press at the VVAF headquarters in Washington when she and the ICBL were awarded the Nobel peace prize.[3]

The goals of both VVAF and the Quakers represented a more fundamental challenge to the Pentagon than the question of banning landmines. Indeed, the very notion that non-governmental groups could influence a military decision for humanitarian reasons was at the core of the Pentagon's strenuous resistance to the ban. Early on in the campaign, when a curious VVAF staffer asked a Pentagon official why there was such resistance to the ban when so many former officers were telling VVAF that anti-personnel mines were

---

1 Williams considered VVAF discussions with retired officers to be "consorting with the enemy." Leon V. Sigal, *Negotiating Minefields: The Landmines Ban in American Politics*, Routledge, New York, 2006, p. 138. The one way she seemed to fit in with the culture of the veterans at the VVAF was in her purple language.

2 Muller's other key staff at the start of the campaign were John Terzano, a former Navy seaman, and Mark Perry, author of the first detailed book on the Joint Chiefs of Staff. Terzano's droll sense of humor was shown by his opening statement at a landmine meeting with administration officials in which he was introduced as Bobby Muller: "If this meeting were in Vienna, Austria, it would be Bobby. Since it's in Vienna, Virginia, you got me." Perry used his contacts with retired chiefs he had interviewed to establish VVAF's crucial coterie of military experts and supporters for a mine ban. He felt that VVAF's credibility was undercut by the publicity accorded to the high-profile stars like Emmy Lou Harris and Cheryl Crow who played at its concerts promoting a ban, and would grouse, "I'm sick of all this star-[expletive]!" Other important VVAF staff during the campaign were Marissa Vitagliano, who conducted much of the research and writing on military alternatives, and Mary Wareham, who staffed the American branch of the ICBL. The former was firmly in the Muller camp, the latter firmly in the Williams camp.

3 VVAF had invested heavily in Williams and the campaign, and felt it deserved the return of the positive publicity. Instead, the news was dominated by the nasty split in the campaign and a fight over her share of the prize money and the ICBL's. Kenneth Anderson, a lawyer who had been affiliated with Human Rights Watch, helped Goose maneuver the ICBL money away from Muller's control, and Williams took her share personally rather than through the ICBL, creating the ironic condition that it would be taxed and used in large part to support the Pentagon she so detested.

actually a hindrance to the modern, mobile tactics used by the US armed forces, the of-ficial pulled out of his desk a list of over 30 weapons that the Pentagon feared "would be next" on the advocacy groups' hit list for humanitarian or environmental reasons. If the groups succeeded in banning anti-personnel mines, he feared, they would smell weakness and come after anti-tank mines, cluster bombs, fuel-air explosives, and depleted uranium anti-tank weapons. It was the precedent, not the particular weapon, that was driving the intense opposition. Muller's opinion was that for the Pentagon, "it was never, never about the landmines," but rather all about staying off "the slippery slope" of permitting non-governmental groups and humanitarian arguments into discussions of weapons and war. Muller too was heavily motivated by the slippery slope, but from the opposite perspective of very much wanting to go down it.

Muller's take on the Pentagon was correct. When the Clinton administration asked the Joint Chiefs whether they could give up anti-personnel mines, the arguments that carried the day were about cost and the slippery slope, rather than combat missions. Leon Sigal's book on the ban campaign characterized the appeal of Army Chief of Staff to the other Joint Chiefs at a crucial meeting this way: "We have a good set of weapons that we've already paid for....Once the NGOs forced the Army to get rid of landmines, he won-dered aloud, which service would be the next to be disarmed?"[1] Sigal's informal recon-struction found a clear echo in an article by an Army colonel who feared "losing control of the national security agenda to NGOs." A general told Sigal: "Our capabilities sheet will look like Swiss cheese if we keep this up."[2] In public, though, the Pentagon threw up all sorts of mission-specific arguments in favor of anti-personnel mines, claiming that buried, long-lived anti-personnel mines were crucial in blocking North Korean infantry and slow-ing their sappers trying to disarm buried anti-vehicle mines, and that short-lived, self-de-structing anti-personnel mines that would be scattered from aircraft and artillery shells to keep sappers away from scattered anti-vehicle mines were needed to disrupt tank attacks in both Korea and the Persian Gulf.

Based on computer modeling, Secretary of Defense William Perry even claimed that Seoul could be "overrun" without anti-personnel mines, before persistent analysis by non-governmental groups forced a revised modeling claim that Seoul would be held, but with "tens of thousands" of additional allied casualties. Even this conclusion relied on "magic rain" that somehow reduced allied air superiority and warning of an invasion but didn't slow North Korean tanks.[3] A hilarious reversal of roles took place in which peace groups like VVAF and Demilitarization for Democracy issued studies that advised the armed forces in lurid detail about the many alternative ways to kill North Koreans and stop tanks without using anti-personnel mines, while the Pentagon claimed ignorance and helplessness about

---

1 Sigal's book is a valiant but, given the variety of actors and their mutual confusion about others' actions, necessarily hopeless attempt to recreate the thinking and actions of major military, civilian, and NGO actors throughout the campaign. His source for this characterization was VVAF analyst Edwin Deagle.

2 Leon V. Sigal, *Negotiating Minefields: The Landmines Ban in American Politics*, Routledge, New York, 2006, p. 117. The colonel was John Troxell, the general insisted on anonymity.

3 "Exploding the Landmine Myth in Korea," Demilitarization for Democracy, August 1997, pp.1-4.

how to operate without this suddenly indispensable weapon.[1] This furious back and forth was pure theater. The Pentagon rarely used anti-personnel mines, didn't even own the ones South Korea had in the ground, and knew very well how to deliver firepower onto enemy sappers of its anti-vehicle mines in the fantastically tough, prepared barriers along the few possible tank routes toward Seoul, which it could watch with its dominance in air power and real-time reconnaissance. In any event, South Korea maintained minefields mostly to discourage North Korea refugees in a crisis, and a North Korean attack would be "regime suicide." The well-publicized allied operations plan warned North Korea's leaders that US and South Korean forces would go north immediately to devastate and seize their capital, Pyongyang.

From Muller's perspective, one real tragedy of the campaign was that a Democratic president, a Vietnam war protestor, had failed to learn one of the central lesson of the Vietnam War: when it comes to civilian control over deciding what the armed forces should be doing in pursuit of national security, you don't ask, you just tell. The balancing of the military utility and the humanitarian consequences of using a weapon, or even of the short-term military advantage of using it and the long-term military advantages of banning it, Muller believed, was the job of the President, not the Pentagon. Clinton ducked this responsibility, apparently out of fear of antagonizing the Pentagon and enraging conservative members of Congress who backed it aggressively, and refused the pleas of the many administration officials who were imploring him to take command of a policy that concerned probably the least needed or wanted weapon in the US arsenal.[2] "Get the Joint Chiefs off my ass; I can't afford a breach with the Joint Chiefs," Clinton told Muller and retired generals David Jones and Robert Gard when Muller bought an $85,000 table at a fund-raising dinner in 1996 on the promise that they would be able to talk to Clinton about banning landmines. Over the next year Muller purchased a full-page advertisement in the *New York Times* in which 15 retired generals called for a ban, ran a $750,000 set of

---

1   "Making the World Unsafe for Landmines: A Timetable for Developing Military Alternatives and Implementing a Worldwide Ban on the Smallest Weapon of Mass Destruction," Project on Demilitarization and Democracy, June 1995; "Exploding the Landmine Myth in Korea," Demilitarization for Democracy, August 1997; Robert G. Gard Jr., "Alternatives to Antipersonnel Landmines," Vietnam Veterans of America Foundation, Spring 1999; "The Dupuy Institute's Research Study: Military Consequences of Landmine Restrictions," Vietnam Veterans of America Foundation, Spring 2000; Caleb Rossiter, "Winning in Korea without Landmines," Vietnam Veterans of America Foundation, Summer 2000; Edwin Deagle, "Creating a Landmine Free Military," briefing, Vietnam Veterans of America Foundation, February 2001.

2   Sigal identifies some of the officials hoping that Clinton would tell the Pentagon to find a solution that included a ban as Madeleine Albright and Lee Feinstein at the State Department, Nancy Soderberg and Bob Bell at the National Security Council, and Jan Lodal and Tim Connolly at the Defense department. Instead, Clinton asked the Pentagon to look at the implications of a ban, which of course led the Pentagon to reject it. Ironically the Arms Control and Disarmament Agency, a State Department office that had traditionally been the leading voice in government for reasonable constraints on US weapons in return for constraints on other nations, took the Pentagon's side. This was particularly galling for the American groups in the landmine campaign, and they wrote to and met with director John Holum, their usual ally, to complain about ACDA's advocacy of mines that could be scattered from aircraft and artillery shells and self-destructed after a set period, which its staff first called "safe mines" and then, when that brought hoots of disdain, "smart mines."

radio and TV spots just to "talk to the Clintons," and kept funding his army of lobbyists, campaigners, and military analysts — but he knew in his heart after that night that Clinton would never order the Pentagon to accept a ban.

Some ban campaigners faulted the NSC staff for not pushing hard enough on the Pentagon, claiming that their unfamiliarity with the Pentagon made them leery of pressuring military officers the way they would State Department officials. VVAF's John Terzano reported to NSC staff director Nancy Soderberg at a meeting at the White House in July 1997 that Army officers in munitions plants were simply ignoring Clinton's public pledges about searching for military alternatives. "They don't get it," a frustrated Terzano exclaimed. Soderberg replied: "I know — it's a cultural issue." In fact, it was an issue of leadership. The officers had never received direct orders because the NSC did not have the chance to clear Pentagon directives, and that was because Clinton treated the Pentagon with kid gloves. Some of his deference resulted from the way his promise to allow gays in the armed forces had blown up on him in 1993, followed by the debacle of retreat in Somalia. Most of the deference, though, was the result of Clinton's superb politics of "triangulation," in which he took care to stay close to his opponents' positions on a variety of issues so as to retain some control of the agenda. Like Lyndon Johnson on Vietnam, Clinton was simply too attuned to the electoral dangers of becoming perceived as anti-military ever to push the Pentagon on what would have been a quick, and easy change in military tactics. According to the campaign's sources in the administration, Vice President Gore was particularly forceful in counseling him not to irritate the Pentagon on landmines.

Leahy's foreign policy aide Tim Rieser "drove the strategy" of the ban campaign in the United States, Muller said: "We did nothing, nothing, without Tim's approval." Rieser was an unlikely power in a pompous Senate that was largely inert on foreign policy. A Vermont lawyer with a searing social conscience and an antipathy to decorum and modern comforts, he rushed around the stuffy corridors in blue jeans, and his version of cushy foreign junkets was traveling rough to humanitarian crises to see how US aid was being used.[1] As Leahy's foreign operations appropriation wended its annual way into law, Rieser would hold out for the best possible deal against overwhelming pressure from the administration and its aligned lobbyists, and he achieved literally hundreds of little victories that

---

1 Rieser first served as staff assistant to Leahy's subcommittee clerk, Eric Newsom, and became clerk when Newsom took a job in the Clinton administration. Muller was pleased with Newsom's move, and indeed weighed in with the administration to support it, since while Newsom was an effective advocate for Leahy's initiative, Muller had a better working relationship with Rieser. Ironically, the job that Newsom took at the State Department almost immediately made him the point person for the administration's advocacy for self-destructing mines. In one of his first meetings Newsom was subjected to the sort of tactics he had used himself while working for Leahy. Through a congressional office the VVAF had discovered that the administration was preparing a "US–UK control regime" that would sell self-destructing mines to countries that phased out long-lived mines. Tipped off by VVAF, the Project on Demilitarization and Democracy rushed around a signup letter against the regime and delivered it to Newsom with the signatures of 29 NGOs just as he began a briefing for the NGOs in which he planned to reveal the proposal and ask for their support. Newsom was also the chief US negotiator at the 1997 Oslo meeting, where he had to present demands that he warned others in the administration would be rejected. Muller found some humor in this role, since he recalled thinking that Newsom's move out of Leahy's office would improve the prospects of the ban movement.

improved a few lives in distant lands. After 25 years there are so many "Leahy amendments" that define the possible for so many issues in foreign policy that non-governmental groups had to reference them in detail.[1]

Rieser would ratchet up the pressure on landmines a bit each year with a new piece of legislation, using Leahy's chairmanship of the subcommittee that appropriated all foreign aid funds to gain supporters. In 1992 a one-year moratorium on exports of anti-personnel mines became law with little debate. In 1993 it was extended to a three-year moratorium on a 100–0 Senate vote. In 1994 Leahy introduced a moratorium on the production of mines and only held back on a vote in return for Clinton's pledge to order a policy review, push for a global export ban, and announce his support for the "eventual elimination" of anti-personnel mines.[2] In 1995 Leahy was no longer chair of the subcommittee because of Republican control of the Senate, but a remarkable 49 senators agreed to cosponsor a new bill requiring a one-year moratorium, to take effect in three years, on US use of anti-personnel mines except along international borders. VVAF's expensive lobbyists — dubbed by Williams "the sleaze team"[3] — traded in behind the scenes on the campaign contributors they coordinated, grassroots activists worked the media in home states, and the measure passed 67–27 with the support of Majority Leader, and wounded veteran, Bob Dole.

The Clinton administration was confident that Leahy's moratorium on mine use would not survive a conference committee meeting with the more conservative House, which had also passed to Republican control under Speaker Newt Gingrich. And it would not have, had it not been for a quirky connection to the murder of the Jesuit priests in El Salvador in 1989. As described in Chapter 5, Father Paul Tipton was the president of the association of Jesuit colleges who had prevailed upon Senator Hatfield to appropriate $10 million to pay off the building debt of the Jesuit university in San Salvador. A Hatfield staffer who had founded a non-governmental group that was working on the landmine ban remembered that Tipton was a former teacher and close friend of the House leader of the conference committee, foreign operations appropriations subcommittee chair Sonny Callahan. The staffer called in the $10 million chit, and Tipton, who joked he could always convince Callahan to do one thing each year, took it is a matter of honor to get Callahan to "recede" to the Senate position that Leahy had included. Bypassing Callahan's wary staff, Tipton tracked him down and stayed with him all day, even through a trip to the White House on another matter, before he wore him down and got his agreement.[4]

---

1 A bizarre testament to Rieser's importance to the landmine campaign was the circulation within the Pentagon of a memorandum by Army lawyer Hays Parks that appeared to be designed to discredit Rieser and weaken his effectiveness. The usually measured Parks recklessly accused Rieser and Tom O'Donnell, the landmines staffer for Leahy's House partner Lane Evans, of "treason" for discussing with the International Committee of the Red Cross the executive branch's concerns about a proposed treaty to ban blinding lasers. After letters from congressional offices and non-governmental groups brought the matter to the attention of Parks' superiors the memorandum was "recalled," so that it technically never existed.

2 Leon V. Sigal, *Negotiating Minefields: The Landmines Ban in American Politics*, Routledge, New York, 2006, pp. 43, 47.

3 James Bandler, "Laureate in a Minefield," *Boston Globe Magazine*, June 7, 1998.

4 In 1999 Leahy traded the use moratorium for a policy announcement by Clinton that set 2006 as the target date for deploying alternative weapons that would permit signing of

When the moratorium on use became law in February 1996, it "started a clock run-ning" at the Pentagon and added a sense of inevitability about a ban in both domestic and international politics.[1] The most important development of the year, though, came not from Rieser and Leahy, but from another forward-leaning staffer and his mainstream boss, in Canada. Former army officer and tank commander Bob Lawson was the staffer, and the mainstream boss was Lloyd Axworthy, the minister of foreign affairs. Axworthy had been exposed to dissent on national security questions and unconventional approaches to poli-tics as a graduate student at Princeton, where he took part in the 1963 Birmingham civil rights marches. These tendencies showed in 1996 when he saved the ban campaign from obscurity by first deciding in May at a disappointing review conference for the CCW in Geneva to call governments to come discuss a ban in Ottawa in October, and then decid-ing to announce at that meeting that Canada would host a signing meeting for a ban treaty a year later. Stunned US diplomats were enraged by both announcements, which under normal protocol between close allies would have been discussed and negotiated behind the scenes.

Many campaigners and administration officials believe that if Clinton had come fully on board the Ottawa process in 1996, the other nations would have given him much of what he wanted on Korea and scatterable mines. This dubious analysis misses the reality that the Pentagon's resistance was fundamentally about civil society imposing any restric-tions on any weapons, not particular ones on landmines. In addition, the ICBL would have opposed such a treaty, and Axworthy had showed his commitment to keeping the ICBL on board when he dropped the word "primarily" from the definition of an anti-personnel mine in early Ottawa drafts in response to the ICBL's bitter criticism that it would create a loophole for anti-vehicle weapons that could be also triggered by a person. In any event, by the time of the crucial Oslo meeting in September 1997 where the final Ottawa text was negotiated the train had left the station. The ICBL and the core countries preferred a treaty with no loopholes — other than the complex exception for anti-handling devices on anti-tank mines that had replaced the word "primarily" — without the United States than a treaty with phased-out exemptions with the United States.

A flurry of unsuccessful last-minute concessions and lobbying by the White House should not obscure the insurmountable difficulties to US agreement.[2] Perhaps because of his own sense of American exceptionalism and perhaps because of the exceptionalism imbedded in the Congress, Clinton had never accepted that the United States, like all the other nations in any international agreement, would have to give up some short-term freedom of action in return for long-term benefits. His entire approach was to demand that the Ottawa nations give him exemptions, rather than that his own Pentagon give him

the Ottawa treaty. Leon V. Sigal, *Negotiating Minefields: The Landmines Ban in American Politics*, Routledge, New York, 2006, p. 221. Callahan later gained an undeserved but humorous notoriety when Monica Lewinsky claimed that while she was engaging in oral sex with Clinton he was negotiating an issue on the phone with him. Members of the House would call out to Callahan on the floor: "Phone call, Sonny."

1 Quote from Pentagon official Jan Lodal, in *Negotiating Minefields: The Landmines Ban in American Politics*, Routledge, New York, 2006, p. 125.
2 Leon V. Sigal, *Negotiating Minefields: The Landmines Ban in American Politics*, Routledge, New York, 2006, pp. 213-215.

alternative weapons and tactics. The exception for Korea and the use of self-destructing scatterable mines were always non-negotiable, both between the White House and the Pentagon for the entire five years of policy reviews and between the administration and Axworthy during the year of preparation for Ottawa. The only hope for progress had come in June 1997 when Army General Wesley Clark was tasked to review landmines by the Joint Chiefs between his assignments to head the Southern and European Commands. At the request of the NSC's Soderberg he met with the ICBL groups that had studied military issues, and described a "crash search" he was starting to field alternative weapons and tactics. Referring to the operations directorate of the Joint Chiefs, he reminded the groups that the Pentagon "got rid of tactical nuclear weapons with a J-3 led process" and promised that "J-3 will lead again, with timetables and matrices for staff. If you don't hold people accountable at the action level, it's all rhetoric." Clark's initiative collapsed with his departure for Europe.

Late in the Clinton presidency, after the signing of the Ottawa treaty, Rieser engineered a desperate ploy to get the United States on board before Gore, who was thought to be even more pro-Pentagon on the substance and domestic politics of the mine ban, or Bush took office. Aware that the European powers were refusing to treat their anti-vehicle mines as banned under the treaty, despite having anti-handling devices that could be triggered by a person, Leahy and VVAF reversed their earlier castigation of the Clinton administration for arguing that the anti-personnel mines that were deployed alongside scatterable anti-vehicle mines met the Ottawa definition by being "linked to" those systems by their proximity. Now they tried to get Clinton to make that claim and Axworthy to accept it.[1] The reasoning was sound on moral grounds, since the long-lasting European anti-vehicle systems certainly posed more of a threat to civilians than the self-destructing American systems. However, in the opinion of the key State Department legal adviser, Mike Matheson, too much water had gone under the bridge in negotiating language and positions on what the actual words of the treaty meant for the United States to make that argument.

Others in the administration who had worked on heavily-fudged arms control treaties disagreed with Matheson.[2] A VVAF staffer reminded him that his predecessor Abraham Sofaer could easily have found an argument for the US mines complying with the Ottawa treaty, given the way he brazenly denied the need to comply with the judgment from the World Court on the mining of Nicaragua's harbors. Matheson responded: "I'm no Abe Sofaer." The initiative still might have succeeded, but the NSC staff never advised Clinton to raise the matter with Axworthy, who had been encouraged by Leahy to accept the US interpretation. According to a VVAF staffer who met with Axworthy during this period, without Lawson by his side he had such little grasp of the treaty itself that the significance of the new interpretation was lost on him. When the gambit failed, Leahy and VVAF went

---

1 Memo to Patricia Narry from Tim Rieser, January 6, 2000.

2 For example, State Department official Lee Feinstein had taken this position during the Oslo negotiations. Leon V. Sigal, *Negotiating Minefields: The Landmines Ban in American Politics,* Routledge, New York, 2006, p. 212.

back to their original, not necessarily contradictory position that the European weapons were banned.[1]

Muller tried one final time to move the United States onto the treaty during the Bush administration when he received a positive signal from the White House budget director for foreign policy, Robin Cleveland, who had been Rieser's Republican counterpart on Leahy's subcommittee. He added retired Army Major Edwin Deagle and General George Joulwan to his roster of military experts, and Deagle and retired Lt. General Robert Gard prepared a strong briefing that they delivered to a number of Pentagon audiences on military alternatives to landmines. Again, without White House guidance, nothing came of the initiative. Bush renounced Clinton's timetable for fielding alternatives and signing the treaty, and the Pentagon pointedly developed an alternative weapon that did not even comply with the Ottawa treaty. Under pressure from Leahy, the Pentagon finally relented after 11 years in 2008 and made it compliant.[2]

The campaign's failure to alter civil-military relations and convince the United States to join the treaty dispirited Muller, and America's rush to war in Afghanistan and Iraq convinced him further that nothing had come of his life's work of promoting the lessons of the Vietnam War: "It's like it never happened, and you do the same absurd things and [expletive] the troops." Muller began to drift away from active involvement in politics but provided a final gift to the landmines campaign. Ironically, it was a gift that was rejected by nearly every other group in the ICBL: his decision not to support a campaign to ban cluster bombs. Cluster bombs are small fragmentation weapons that are released by the hundreds from large canisters that are dropped from the air or fired by artillery. As they near the earth the small bombs appear to "cluster" around the target, and they devastate troops and light vehicles. US forces use cluster bombs to minimize the number of air sorties or artillery rounds needed to clear areas of enemy forces, particularly when there is no need to destroy buildings. It takes far fewer sorties and far shorter firing periods to deliver the needed firepower with cluster bombs than with normal, heavy bombs and shells, and that means fewer US casualties from counter-fire by the enemy.

Muller had his military experts Deagle and Gard analyze the Pentagon's claims, much as VVAF had done for landmines. To their surprise they found that everything the Pentagon had been claiming incorrectly for landmines was true for cluster bombs: they did have significant military utility, and they could be altered and used in such a way as to minimize civilian casualties.[3] By accepting a Pentagon argument when the facts seemed to agree with it, VVAF gained credibility for its earlier analysis of landmines. In contrast, the ICBL adopted the findings of Human Rights Watch's Goose and moved seamlessly from

---

1 For a careful legal analysis of that position, see "Arnold and Porter Legal Opinion Clarifies Landmine Treaty," International Policy Report, Center for International Policy, September 2000, Revised December 2000, and the Arnold and Porter memorandum dated September 7, 2000.

2 The "Spider" was an explosive that would be detonated not by contact with a victim, but by a "man in the loop" who would be watching the minefield for attackers. The Pentagon insisted on including a "battlefield override" in the Spider that during combat would turn the weapon into a...landmine.

3 "Proposed Protocol to Address Explosive Remnants of War," briefing by the Vietnam Veterans of America Foundation, Geneva meeting of the CCW, September 25, 2001.

arguing that mines had little military utility to arguing the same for cluster bombs, and said they should be banned because the roughly five percent that failed to function when used properly posed a threat to civilians as dud munitions. Leahy and some lobby groups, remarkably including the Quakers, supported VVAF's call for an international agreement to require back-up fuses on cluster bombs, which could well reduce their dud rate to a quarter of one percent. However, when that failed to be incorporated into a CCW agreement on cluster bombs, the ICBL as a whole backed the negotiation of a farcical imitation of the Ottawa treaty in Oslo in 2008 that banned cluster bombs. Again, many major military powers that actually possessed and used cluster bombs ignored the treaty.

The Pentagon responded to concerns about cluster bombs by developing non-explosive but equally horrific area-clearing weapons like packages of flechettes and by ordering the services to cease using their stockpile of cluster bombs, which had a failure rate of five percent, within ten years, and replace them with new cluster bombs that would use the backup fuse suggested by VVAF and Leahy to achieve a dud rate of less than one percent.[1] The ICBL dismissed the policy as insufficient, but if such an order had been issued for anti-personnel landmines at the time of the Ottawa treaty, the United States could have signed it in 2007. In the end, whether Deagle or Goose was right about the utility of cluster bombs or whether VVAF or the Pentagon was right on alternatives to landmines was irrelevant to Muller's original goal of discrediting war as a viable policy option. The campaign to ban anti-personnel landmines certainly saved some lives and limbs, but Muller's goal was no closer to fruition in 2010 than it was in 1991.

---

1 Memorandum for Secretaries of the Military Departments: DoD Policy on Cluster Munitions and Unintended Harm to Civilians, Secretary of Defense Robert Gates, June 19, 2008.

CHAPTER 9. MRS. JELLYBY AND LORD CHELMSFORD SAVE AFRICA: FOREIGN AID AND HUMANITARIAN INTERVENTION

Former World Bank President Paul Wolfowitz and rock star Paul "Bono" Hewson, Iraq invader Tony Blair and invasion opponents Kofi Annan and his economic adviser Jeffrey Sachs, actress Angelina Jolie and Christian Coalition founder Pat Robertson, super-capitalist Bill Gates and quasi-socialist relief groups Oxfam and Save the Children. What do these strange bedfellows have in common? They all back the popular campaign to "make poverty history," particularly in sub-Saharan Africa, through a quadrupling of foreign aid. The campaign is tinged with more than a shade of Charles Dickens' Mrs. Jellyby, the do-gooder in *Bleak House* who neglects her own children as she raises money and sends colonist–teachers to save the suffering children and child-like parents of the village of Borrioboola-Gha on the banks of the Niger. The very breadth of the backers affirms their apolitical claim that reducing poverty is a matter of funding. Poverty, though, is intensely political, and is affected by domestic and international power relations and struggles from dictatorship and civil war to the control of trade and investment rules by developed nations. Like Mrs. Jellyby, today's aidists hope to soften the effects of empire without abandoning it, but they will find that just as difficult under King Barack as it was under Queen Victoria.

The aid charade is a project of Soft and Hard Eagles, but it is given wider exposure by corporations hoping to give consumers another reason to buy their products, and by UN agencies and religious groups trading on pledges to "save the children" if you can't save the adults. In upscale parts of American cities it is hard to buy a cup of coffee, a bottle of water, or a shirt without being told that some of the proceeds are being used to save babies, farmers, and AIDS victims in Africa. Handing out candy on Hallowe'en means handing out cash as children "trick or treat for UNICEF" and its campaign to cut the death rate for children under five to zero. UNICEF's pretense that its programs can achieve this goal is symptomatic of the entire genre of anti-poverty claims. As of 2008, seven percent of children in developing countries were dying before their fifth birthday, down from 10 percent in 1990 (and 14 percent in Africa, down from 18 percent) versus less than one percent of children in developed countries. UNICEF carries out targeted projects, but the big drops in these rates come from both an end to conflicts and increases in a country's and particularly a family's income, which bring access to cleaner water, regular nutrition, and medical care. UNICEF points out that India, Nigeria, and the Democratic Republican of the Congo account for 40 percent of the developing world's child mortality.[1] The stubborn mortality rates in these resource-rich countries are largely due to domestic and international choices and constraints, such as ethnic competition, corruption, conflict, and dependence on and theft of revenues from unrefined exports, and cannot be significantly affected by foreign aid.

Foreign aid has received a free pass from Turkeys. While understanding that the primary purpose of aid is access and not altruism, and that of necessity it serves Western political and economic rather than African humanitarian interests, most Turkeys continue to call for significant transfers of wealth to the developing world in hopes that some good will come of it.[2] The record shows that these hopes are unreasonable. As economist Dambisa Moyo shows convincingly in *Dead Aid*, the bulk of the trillion dollars worth of cash, goods, and services the West has sent to Africa on concessional terms has been either wasted because the projects could not be sustained or was used to prop up the unrepresentative regimes who were creating much of the problem in the first place.[3] The legions of young Westerners who go off with good hearts to save Africa would have more impact if they stayed in their own countries to fight for structural changes in power relations between the West and the South.

Wide-spread poverty will remain an integral part of the world economy until the rich nations, and particularly the United States, stop propping up cooperative but repressive regimes who spur devastating civil wars and stop blocking the poorest countries' transition from producing raw materials to refining, packaging, and retailing. Even then, as the persistence of poverty in the growing economies of China, India, and South Africa warns us, making poverty history will be largely a matter for each country to address with its own choices about sharing opportunity with the poor during the painful transition from a traditional to a modern economy. It also involves choices by the poor themselves. In the post-colonial world, not everyone wants to leave the traditional life, not everyone wants to work and save, and not everyone who does want to has the ability to do so. To talk of reducing poverty is fine, but to talk of ending it in a time of empire is silly.

---

1   All figures from UNICEF's database, 2009.

2   As a "guidance" to aid administrators stated during the Reagan administration: "US foreign aid will be channeled primarily to countries that directly benefit US security interests." See "Objectives of US Foreign Assistance: Does Development Assistance Benefit the Poor?", Hearing before the Committee on Foreign Affairs, US House of Representatives, August 17, 1982, p. 89.

3   Moyo shoots the fish in that barrel easily enough, but the silver bullets she proposes as alternatives to aid, such as international bonds and microfinance, often miss the mark. She expects that these will make African governments more accountable to their people, but both the pressure to maintain imports and the struggle for ethnic power that constrain their choices will remain. Allen Lane, New York, 2009.

The Lords and Ladies of Poverty, the highly-paid overseers and functionaries of the government and private foreign aid industries, know that efforts to "end poverty" are just a small piece that must fit itself into a complex puzzle. Yet they play their part in the aid charade, appearing dutifully at concerts to declare that the World Bank exists to make the world "free of poverty," railing against recipients' sporadic rather than donors' systematic corruption, and holding weepy panels on "poverty reduction" at events like the annual Davos and International Monetary Fund meetings that are actually devoted to maximizing the economic returns and assuaging the consciences of wealthy countries and their wealthiest citizens. The sheer gall of the Lords and Ladies was captured in Wolfowitz's pledge to change Africa "from a place of despair to a place of hope."

African commentators were bemused by this pledge, since most Africans live in modest but functional fashion, and much of what despair does exist could be traced to Wolfowitz's then-current and previous employers. The World Bank, whose voting shares are controlled by a US and European majority, helps trap Africa in its low-growth role as exporter of raw materials, and the worst poverty is found in refugee camps created by civil wars against thugs who were armed in return for cooperating with US military, covert, and mineral operations: Savimbi in Angola, Mobutu in the Congo, Doe in Liberia, Barré in Somalia, and Nimeiry in the Sudan. US arms and training under the new African Command for regimes that cooperate with the "war on terror" lay the seeds for the civil wars of the future.

The lobbyists for the campaign are the concert-givers and goers, whose white wrist bands ask developed nations to quadruple aid and end domestic farm subsidies that gut production in poorer countries, pleas that can be technically met and practically evaded at the same time. Subsidies are just one of a bagful of techniques, from research to price floors, that developed countries use to maintain reliable domestic food production. Their export corporations will always have a comparative advantage over low-tech African producers unless the Africans are protected by tariff walls and their own subsidies, which developed nations have taken off the table in foreign aid policy. At the series of concerts in 2005 designed to prod the "Group of 8" industrial powers, the organizers applauded President Bush for roughly doubling economic aid, both globally and to Africa, during his tenure. However, the doublings did not come in long-term development accounts addressing poverty. Globally, the doubling came from the US occupation of Iraq and Afghanistan, paralleling the similar periods of charity when US development aid shot up to subsidize counter-insurgency campaigns in Vietnam in the 1960s and El Salvador in the 1980s. In Africa, the doubling came not in development programs, but from the cancellation of long-unpaid and unpayable debts and from emergency food aid from American surpluses to countries experiencing drought or overwhelmed by refugees from civil wars.

Even US "humanitarian assistance" like food aid during a famine is a double-edged sword. It too promotes US political and economic purposes, such as buying cooperation from governments and promoting US commercial food exports. The repressive regime that caused the famine — and as economist Amartya Sen has argued it is always such a regime, and not weather-based disaster, that is at the root of the problem — is strengthened by controlling the sales and distribution of food aid, and local farmers are undercut by cheap imports. In the few years following a "successful" distribution of relief food, many more can die because of continued conflict or lower prices for domestic crops. In his brutal but brilliant 1997 book, *The Road to Hell*, aid worker Michael Maren showed how US food aid helped destroy Somalia in the brief period from Carter's alliance with Siad Barré in 1980 to Clinton's withdrawal in 1994.[1] Even the boost in US funding for prevention and treatment of AIDS in Africa should not be seen as long-term aid that can end poverty, since success would simply take matters back to where they stood before the epidemic struck. More importantly, there is no evidence that truly adhering to every demand of the aidists would reduce poverty, let alone end it.

What economist William Easterly in *White Man's Burden* calls the aidists' Big Plan is described in the UN's Millennium Challenge Goals and *The End of Poverty*, a book by UN adviser Sachs.[2] The Big Plan is both ahistorical and apolitical. A strange mixture of Adam Smith and Chairman Mao, it would open the economies of poor countries to international competition while carrying out a massive "scaling up" of foreign aid projects. It treats poverty as a technical problem, and sidesteps the issue of power relations between and within countries. Poverty, though, is deeply political. In the last great foreign push for African development in the 1980s, both the IMF/World Bank "structural adjustment" of protected African economies and the Live Aid/We Are the World campaign for famine relief in Ethiopia probably did as much harm as good. The former implemented the "Washington consensus," a cookie-cutter dogma holding that cutting deficits, selling off public investments, and opening the economies of poorer countries to competition with powerful ones will promote economic growth. African economies, though, continued to contract. The latter put food aid and relief materials directly into the hands of the Mengistu regime, which had created the famine through civil war and forced relocation, and this helped the regime hold power for another six devastating years of civil war.

Another round of massive aid without fundamental changes in both the international political economy and domestic African politics is a fool's bet. More than $1 trillion in today's dollars in government foreign aid (and probably as much again in private donations) has been showered onto Africa over the past 50 years, mostly as high-priced goods and services, rather than untied cash, from the donor nations. Why should another $1 trillion over the next seven years, through the quadrupling of aid to the famed one percent of developed nations' GNP the campaign hopes to achieve, be any less likely to disappear with little effect? The aidists say that poor countries need debt relief from low-interest loans for previous projects, and then call for many more projects in the same political and economic environment. The World Bank's analysts had predicted that the old projects would generate not just repayment but solid growth, and they'll probably make the same claims for the new projects as well. The fine print of the "debt relief" package imposes classic "consensus" conditions and transfers poor governments' dollar debts into local currency that are to be used for even more projects.

---

1   *The Road to Hell*, The Free Press, New York, 1997.
2   William Easterly, *The White Man's Burden*, Penguin, New York, 2006; Jeffrey Sachs, *The End of Poverty*, Penguin, New York, 2006.

The Big Plan proposes credible solutions for none of the root causes of poverty and slow growth, such as:

- dictatorships and the provision of weapons and training to them by the West and China in return for military cooperation, minerals, and markets;

- the ethnic civil wars that result from undemocratic rule, and the massive migration from these conflicts and poorer regions in general toward pockets of growth;

- corruption in both donor and recipient governments, including the tying of aid to purchases from the donor's economy, such as development consultants and military hardware;

- the natural brain drain of talented and trained personnel from the low and inconsistently-paid civil service to higher-paying foreign aid projects such as AIDS clinics, to cities, and to the developed countries;

- the resistance by developed nations to refining, packaging, and retailing by poor countries, which keeps them in their colonial roles as producers of raw materials with deteriorating terms of trade, even unable to compete with subsidized Western agriculture;

- the inability of African governments, as a result, to generate foreign currencies for the small but crucial imports needed to sustain foreign aid projects, power stations, and irrigation systems, or to generate sufficient domestic growth to produce the tax revenues needed to keep colleges, schools, bureaucracies, and clinics staffed and open, rather than on strike or functioning minimally; and

- the unavoidable dislocation of entire generations during the transition from traditional rural production to a modern urban economy.

Each of these problems has derailed previous grand development plans, and each will lie in wait for this new one.

The Big Plan's proponents note how small America's foreign aid is relative to its military spending and claim that US security against terrorism would be enhanced with more foreign aid. This theory assumes that counter-insurgency and development are complementary rather than incompatible, and accepts the Bush and Obama administrations' stand that the answer to 9/11 should be perpetual war rather than an end to US domination of the Middle East. Secretaries of State from Colin Powell through Condoleezza Rice to Hillary Clinton have argued that foreign aid can reduce anti-Americanism by providing social services for the poor and employment for the young. This trivializes the thousand-year struggle for control of the Middle East, which started with the first Crusade, into a push for better jobs. Adherents of al-Qaeda, many of whom are already educated and wealthy, are no more likely to trade the *jihad* for economic progress than Ho Chi Minh was to trade South Vietnam for the Mekong Valley Authority that Lyndon Johnson offered in 1965.

The campaign to "make poverty history" could be called the London consensus, since it was part of the rehabilitation of British Prime Minister Tony Blair, who talked about saving Africa whenever faced with questions about the tens of thousands of unnecessary deaths caused by the invasion of Iraq. The London consensus merges a Hollywood consensus, which holds that if movie stars talk about and raise money for a problem, it can be solved, with the Washington consensus. In 1983 the resources for the Washington consensus were provided through the International Monetary Fund and the World Bank. The conventional wisdom in responsible foreign policy circles was that the consensus would be briefly painful but eventually successful in restarting growth. The only member of the House Banking Committee who was openly skeptical of the IMF's plans to increase its lending to Africa with the usual onerous conditions was freshman Marcy Kaptur, who had been promoting legislation to focus international lending on the basic human needs of the poor.

When the time came for the committee to approve new resources for the IMF, as part of a deal in which the administration agreed to support domestic low-income housing provisions favored by Democrats, she was the only person to vote no. The committee's chairman, the princely, oleaginous Freddy St. Germain, looked down the long dais at the most junior member at the very end, and condescendingly gave her a chance to get on board: "Ms. Kaptur, how is it that you alone are right, and not all the many witnesses we have heard testify in favor of this increase for the IMF?" Kaptur reddened but held her ground, and said that she thought the IMF had precisely the wrong approach to be engaging with developing countries. She politely did not mention that all the witnesses had been selected because they did support the IMF's approach. In retrospect, Kaptur was indeed the only one in the room who was right. The IMF's approach proved disastrous to African countries in the 1980s because their open economies could not compete with developed nations, their currencies quickly lost value, and their social services and public infrastructure declined. The brilliant chairman was defeated four years later after the Justice Department found "substantial evidence of serious and sustained misconduct" in his acceptance of gifts from lobbyists.[1]

In an effort to avoid scrutiny of their decisions, the IMF and World Bank for decades managed to maintain with a straight face that they were "apolitical" institutions by citing a provision in their charters that required decisions to be taken on economic grounds. The Reagan administration's intention to vote for a request by the apartheid government of South Africa to borrow from the IMF during a cash crunch in 1983 led Representative Howard Wolpe, the new chair of the House Africa subcommittee, to ask the Congressional Research Service to assess whether the argument about the charters was true in practice by reviewing US politicization of the international financial institutions. It was obvious what Wolpe was trying to do, which was to get a respected non-partisan organization to counter Reagan administration claims that it could not oppose the IMF loan to South Africa. The issue was sort of silly, since IMF and World Bank directors are appointed to represent their governments and can vote any way they want, and there is nothing more political than a decision about handing out money. Further, both the Carter and Reagan administrations had openly used the substantial US voting share to oppose or abstain on

1 See "The Race for Congress; St. Germain is Pursued by Rival and Questions," *New York Times*, November 2, 1988

loans on human rights grounds at the World Bank, because such positions were required for "gross and consistent violators" of human rights by US law.[1]

An analyst at the research service interviewed the bureaucrats who prepared the US position on votes at the international lending institutions, and asked them why they had opposed lending to communist or leftist governments, such as Vietnam, Cuba, Grenada, and Afghanistan, and had pushed so hard for lending to allied governments like El Salvador. The answer was obvious, although the candor was unexpected: political decisions from high up in the State Department about who was on the "financial hit list" were transformed into economic jargon by the bureaucrats. For example, Secretary of State Haig would publicly claim his opposition to "politicization" of the international lending institutions while privately telling a staffer, "not one penny for Grenada." When the explosive draft was toned down, the analyst left the research service and redid the report for the Center for International Policy. CIP's research director leaked the original draft to a *Wall Street Journal* reporter, who used it for a story titled "US Charged with bias in IMF votes."[2] Ironically, the new report was effectively censored as well, because CIP was busy helping Members of Congress argue that the IMF loan in fact violated a number of the IMF's own economic criteria, an argument that the new report dismissed as the same sort of game-playing engaged in by the administration when blocking loans to leftist governments. Publication of CIP's report was delayed until after the IMF denied the loan to South Africa.[3]

Economics is known as the dismal science, but the economists behind the Big Plan are modern Panglossians, incurable optimists who will just get in there and fix it with the certainty of a Ross Perot or Sarah Palin. They insist that despite the implosion of many of the African economies that had to follow the Washington consensus in the 1980s, now "we know what to do," and all that is missing is the will to provide sufficient aid. Cheerleader Hewson supplies white guilt to go with his certainty: if the poor were not black, he says loudly, we would never let them suffer this way. In fact, most of the poor are brown and yellow, living in the successful economies of India and China, yet nobody seems to put those destinations on their appeals or on their checks. Only the African remains the infant in need of protection, just as he was in Dickens' day.

In a more sophisticated version of Heritage Foundation studies that incorrectly interpret as causal the simple correlation of rich countries with open economies, Sachs conducts thoughtful statistical inquiries showing that open economies grow faster, even when a variety of intervening factors are controlled. However, he too then errs by engaging in predictions of the future from the attributions of the past, which of necessity had weak data, dubious definitions, and causal relationships that may not work the same way in a new time and set of conditions. Sachs argues that if the slow-growing African countries would just open their economies, they would grow too. He expends a lot of energy arguing

---

1 Carter, at the strenuous urging of Fred Bergsten, his assistant secretary of the Treasury for international affairs, has successfully kept Congress from applying this requirement to the IMF.

2 J. Kwitny, "US Charged with bias in IMF votes," *Wall Street Journal*, May 18, 1983, p. 39.

3 Caleb Rossiter, "The Financial Hit List," International Policy Report, Center for International Policy, 1984.

that the factors that led to Britain's industrial revolution 200 years ago should be applied to Africa. The impossibility of such a policy, since global conditions are so different today that similar actions would be unlikely to have the same effect, is affirmed in his slippery dismissal of the notion that colonialism, slavery, and naval domination played key roles in Britain's acquisition of wealth. If Sachs agreed that they had, he would logically have to propose those policies for African countries as well.

By generalizing from the successful to the unsuccessful, and from Asia and Europe to Africa, Sachs' conclusion ignores not just the many other factors of slow growth, such as conflict, ethnic rivalry, and the distorted internal and international trading systems that have survived independence. It also overlooks the simple fact that many small and weak economies would be overwhelmed and buried by the openness on which larger and stronger ones thrive. Even the IMF does not expect the poorest countries to allow the free flow of exchange rates and fixed capital, since private investors could then snap them up, hold them hostage, and destroy them before tea-time. The Big Plan includes dozens of intertwined technical strands, from education to foreign inputs, that are all said to be necessary, but it never makes clear if success is to be defined as economic growth or a reduction in the share of people living in poverty. These are very different things, and nobody knows how to create either one consistently in the best of circumstances. In fact, the Londoners don't even know how to measure them.

One favored variable is the percentage of people in a country that the World Bank says are living in "absolute poverty" on a dollar a day of local purchasing power. Updated from its 1985 beginnings, the measure is actually $2.05 in 2009 dollars, or $3,741 a year for a family of five, which actually can provide quite a stable life in many poor communities. This variable is hopelessly confounded by infrequent measurements that cannot be meaningfully compared across economic classes or countries. It ignores government services, making it look as though a South African in a cement house with free water, toilets, electricity, schools, and clinics is as poor as a Somali refugee in a Nairobi slum with none of those services. The other commonly-used variable, gross domestic product per capita in purchasing power parity, is confounded by income inequality and by currency conversions that reflect the life of the average, rather than the poor, citizen. It also ignores the informal economy in which most poor people find their purchasing power. Poverty is like pornography: you know it when you see it, but it's difficult to define, especially across cultures. Many students of poverty have concluded that these "money metrics" should be discarded in favor of physical, verifiable indicators, such as infant mortality or the percentage of people with healthy caloric intake and access to clean water.

Any way they are measured, though, economic growth and reductions in poverty in the post-colonial era have often come in places where main tenets of the Big Plan — unprotected competition with foreign businesses, and an externally-funded welfare-to-work state for the poor — have been firmly rejected as impractical. Aidists love to note that the Asian tigers had lower per-capita incomes after World War II than the African colonies. However, China, Korea, India, and Singapore had coherent economic and political systems and more favorable international opportunities, and in any event they used statist policies, the opposite of the Washington consensus, to protect local economies and build predatory export industries. Indeed, the success of statism in Asia should lead to caution about the likely success of the Big Plan, which eschews it.

Wealth cannot simply be transferred to an uncompetitive economy. If the foreign exchange is used for consumption, it quickly disappears; if it is used for investment, the foreign-based projects must be domestically sustainable. They generally are not in Africa, because the donor nations ignore its post-colonial weaknesses and block its drive for true competitiveness, which would displace some of their businesses. Foreign exchange can be flooded into an extractive economy, but it cannot create domestic productivity on its own. The African oil economies of Angola, Equatorial Guinea, Gabon, and Nigeria have been rightly criticized for failing to translate external revenue into poverty reduction, but even Saudi Arabia, with oil wealth far in excess per capita of those countries, saw income levels fall dramatically and slums develop over the past 20 years, as its debt has escalated to more than its GDP.

If actually implemented, the Big Plan would undoubtedly fail, littering Africa with more abandoned projects like the Canadian combines that stand rusting in the Tanzanian fields, their furrows too deep for the holding capacity of the soil. In one of Hewson's previous excellent African adventures, he traveled in 2002 with US Treasury secretary Paul O'Neill to villages where people asked for wells to be dug so that they could have clean water. Hewson and O'Neill immediately turned to the assembled international reporters to make a plea for an Africa-wide project to put wells in every village. Standing with them, shaking his head as if to say, "been there, done that," was then-World Bank president James Wolfensohn, whose agency had seen many such wells dug and then abandoned. The causes for the frequent deterioration of development projects are many and complex, and have to do with the social realities of ethnic identity, sense of ownership, and local economic interests. A constant problem putting pressure on the social realities, though, is that the villagers, and the government, cannot generate consistent domestic funding for the bureaucratic infrastructure and spare parts needed to maintain the projects.

Fortunately, the aidists' proposed scale of resources simply cannot be transferred from wealthy Northerners to impoverished Southerners. The purported success of their own Borrioboola-Gha, the model UN Millennium Village in Sauri, Kenya, shows why. In this village of 4,000, massive and immediate foreign inputs are provided by large numbers of highly-skilled foreign and Kenyan personnel whenever a hitch develops in the effort to demonstrate that poverty can indeed be ended. If a truck, a road, an agronomist, foreign fertilizer and mosquito-repellent pyrethroid, a clinic with doctors, a school with teachers, food for the students, or cash for a small business investment are needed, they are provided. Cabinet ministers and foreign celebrities traipse through constantly to see what more is needed, and then rush back to Nairobi to make sure it is provided by the government or the donors. The aidists cite Sauri's purported improvements as proof that the Big Plan can work. Sachs proudly admits to intervening personally to move up the villagers' planting date so that the results of the harvest could be publicized at the G-8 summit in 2005, encouraging a boost in aid so that the model can be replicated throughout Africa. But Kenya could never replicate this level of focus and support in another village, let alone in its tens of thousands of others. As is the case in the well-intentioned AIDS clinics being established in southern Africa by Bill Gates and other donors, the aidists would find that despite their high pay attracting trained domestic personnel, the planned expansion would grind to a halt by exhausting the meager supply that emigration of the educated has left behind.

Most African countries have far more conflict and far less industry and trained personnel than Kenya. There too any attempt to create hundreds of thousands of Sauris would stimulate a development meltdown. Uncountable numbers of trained local personnel would have to accompany the flood of foreign consultants, from agronomists to zoologists, disrupting the national development civil service in performing its prosaic but essential duties. The surge of foreign synthetic inputs like fertilizer and pyrethroid would destroy local investment and sales in natural but lower-quality domestic versions, just the way free foreign food aid destroys incentives for local farmers to plant the next year's crop. The Kenyan founder of the Development Medicine health network, Dr. Macharia Waruingi, summed up the problem with Sauri this way on a web forum, after an on-line debate with Sachs:

> Jeff is making a fundamental error here, by shifting the burden of rural development to himself or the international development community. The burden of development lies with the creative imagination of the people of Sauri and other villages. Foreign prescriptions, and imported fertilizers, only serve to disrupt the ecosystem. It is still not clear whom he is lifting out of poverty — the fertilizer manufacturer in Europe who sells fertilizer to him, or the local biomass entrepreneur who is trying to make a living on biomass.

The response of Congress to constituents' calls for helping Africa out of poverty illustrates the political difficulties of adopting a meaningful Big Plan, even in its own terms. Domestically, foreign aid is a jobs program, and the very heroes who appropriate billions of dollars to prevent and treat HIV infections fight to extract their pound of local benefit, reducing aid's purchasing power dramatically. A welter of laws and regulations require that much of US food aid and development assistance funds be spent on American goods and services or shipped by American crews, carriers, and companies. Cornell University agricultural economist Christopher Barrett, the co-author of the authoritative 2005 book *Food Aid After Fifty Years*, describes "tying" as "a classic example of policy incoherence...a clumsy attempt to limit commercial competition for domestic constituents (that) explicitly couples foreign assistance with protectionist behavior" and cites a figure of 57 percent for the share of all US aid that is tied.[1] Even as the European nations untied their food aid in the 2000s, Congress thwarted the Bush administration's efforts to permit the use of up to 25 percent of food aid funding to purchase local foods, and save on both commodity and shipping costs.[2] According to a 2007 Government Accountability Office study, the

---

1 *The Status of and Pathways Towards Coherence in United States Foreign Assistance Policy*, background paper prepared for the August 15-16, 2008, meeting of the Foundations Working Group on US Policy for Poverty and Hunger Reduction, held in Detroit, Michigan, p. 2.

2 Agriculture, Rural Development, Food and Drug Administration, and Related Agencies Appropriations for 2008, Part 10, Subcommittee on Agriculture, Rural Development, Food and Drug Administration, and Related Agencies, House Committee on Appropriations, 2007, pp. 20, 206, 217, 267, 270, 277, 301.

requirement that 75 percent of food aid be shipped on US-flag carriers increased costs by $134 million per year.[1]

Barrett estimates that "buy and ship American" laws cut the value of US food aid in half.[2] He notes that, ironically, the protectionist goals of the shipping requirements are not being met, since foreign companies, such as Denmark's Maersk lines, often win the contracts through the use of US subsidiaries.[3] Estimates of the reduction in purchasing power from tying all forms of US aid range from 15 to 30 percent.[4] A 2009 study of aid-tying by Oxfam American includes this quote from a Ugandan: "USAID is notorious for using US inputs, especially consultants. 'All the money goes home' is a popular saying with USAID." Individual providers of American goods and services, such as contractors, universities, farmers, and shippers, benefit from these "buy and ship American" measures. However, their overall benefit to the American economy is probably quite low, because untied spending overseas rebounds to the American economy as a whole through the "additionality" factor — any increase in international income leads to additional demand for American goods and services. Still, Soft Eagles in Congress fight hard to keep the food, the shipping, the consultants, and the university research coming from their districts, even as they sign on to "make poverty history."

The Soft Eagles in Congress also reveal their understanding and support for the strategic rather than the humanitarian mission of foreign aid in the way they propose to organize its planning and delivery. In 2008 Chairman Howard Berman of the House Foreign Affairs committee, the congressional leader of the effort to "reform" a foreign economic aid program that had grown to a tangle of 26 federal agencies since its formalization in 1961, rejected a proposal that a coalition of Soft and Hard Eagles in the non-governmental community insisted was necessary to make a significant dent in international poverty. The United Kingdom, Canada, and a number of other aid donors have made poverty reduction the purpose of an independent, cabinet-rank department with its own budget, and give that department control over their vote at international financial institutions. The United States frequently proclaims that poverty reduction is a core element of its foreign policy, yet administrations have kept the Agency for International Development and its foreign economic aid programs under the control of the State Department, so that the aid can be used to promote strategic objectives, and the vote at the international institutions under the Treasury department, so that it can be bargained for economic goals.

---

1 Agriculture, Rural Development, Food and Drug Administration, and Related Agencies Appropriations for 2008, Part 10, Subcommittee on Agriculture, Rural Development, Food and Drug Administration, and Related Agencies, House Committee on Appropriations, 2007, p. 141.

2 "US Food Aid: Time to Get it Right," Institute for Agriculture and Trade Policy, Minneapolis, July 2005, p. 1; Christopher B. Barrett and Daniel G. Maxwell, Food Aid After 50 Years, Routledge, New York, 2005, p. 167. The methodology of the claim — which systematically contrasts open markets costs with the costs required by the "tying" rules for US food aid — is described on pages 165-170.

3 Phone interview, November 3, 2008.

4 "The Tied Aid Roundtrip," January 2009, http://www.oxfamamerica.org/whatwedo/campaigns/aid_reform/news_publications/Tied-Aid-AidNow-FactSheet.pdf, footnote 4.

The Modernizing Foreign Assistance Network concluded that leaving development policy and aid under the State Department "would undoubtedly subordinate development to diplomacy (and) risk allocating larger amounts of funding to meet short-term political and diplomatic objectives at the expense of longer-term development objectives." It called for cabinet rank for the development function so that its secretary would have "the budgetary authority and mandate to lead policy formulation."[1] Berman's bipartisan proposal for reform rejected this proposal and also avoided addressing farm subsidies, aid tying, and the earmarks and global mandates that both the executive branch and Congress have made a practice of inserting into the foreign aid program. These mandates, such as increasing the share of projects going to promote women's development, disrupt the flexibility that AID field managers and programmers need to respond to the opportunities they identify as they work with host-country officials, civil society, and other donors. Under such a "reform" foreign aid will remain, as it has since its inception, a strategic tool to promote US dominance and counter-insurgency operations, an economic tool to benefit the United States, a political tool to benefit Members of Congress and their districts, and a set of demonstration projects that can only hint at how to address long-term poverty.

Although the Londoners incorrectly characterize the entire African continent as living in despair, they are correct that there is a lot of suffering and life-shortening disease there, as in Asia and Latin America, especially in refugee camps, urban shanty towns, and make-shift AIDS clinics. Although they are wrong to assume that foreign aid can end poverty and spur growth, they are right to want to ameliorate the effects of disease and of the raw poverty that often accompanies the disintegration of the traditional economy. What should the truly benevolent in the North, the Turkeys, as opposed to the imperial civil servants among the Soft Eagles, do to support the poor in the South?

Above all, the aidists should do no harm, which means taking on the tougher task of cleaning up their own houses and tossing out the predatory, self-interested military and economic policies that their governments pursue. The five permanent members of the UN Security Council dominate the arms trade to developing countries, with the United States well in the lead of the other four. Even in the best cases, where the recipient is democratic and not fomenting a future civil war, this trade can devastate development. South Africa could hold on to its invaluable cadre of elite black school teachers and professors, rather than lose them to business, foreign-funded projects, and emigration, if it paid them just a fraction of the $10 billion it is wasting on arms deals aggressively promoted by those paragons of aid to education, Britain, Germany, and Sweden. Instead of singing, "we are the world," aidists should be asking, "why do we arm the world?"

Where arms trading and military training aren't sufficient to gain cooperation and market access in poor countries, the United States, France, and Britain threaten to inter-

---

1 "New Day, New Way: A proposal from the Modernizing Foreign Assistance Network," June 1, 2008, p. 6. *http://modernizingforeignassistance.net/documents/newdaynewway.pdf*. The recommendation states that placing AID under the State Department "would undoubtedly subordinate development to diplomacy, risk allocating larger amounts of funding to meet short-term political and diplomatic objectives at the expense of longer-term development objectives, and place responsibility for development policy in a department with only limited expertise in development."

vene directly, and often do so. The "war on terror" has replaced the "Soviet threat" as the latest justification for the half-trillion dollar Pentagon budget, but it is US domination of the Islamic world from Senegal to Indonesia that the budget supports that itself spurs the sporadic armed protests by Islamists. The armed forces of the United States, France, and Britain function as the collection agencies for their corporations, and their covert operatives are the paymasters of corruption. This armed diplomacy is incompatible with "making poverty history," because it sustains the very conflicts and regimes that hamper development. Northern citizens hoping to create a system capable of reducing poverty in the South must remove the halter their military forces have placed on the South. They should burn into the public consciousness a vision of minimal military budgets that would decommission much of the fleets and air forces of the United States, France, and Britain, bring home their soldiers and covert operators, and end support for cooperative regimes.

There is another northern barrier to southern growth and the opportunities it can provide for the poor that northern citizens must dismantle. This is the complex of subsidies, protections, and institutions that block poorer countries not only from producing and exporting raw materials, but more importantly from engaging in refining and light manufacturing at home and retailing in richer nations. These are so deeply embedded that only a national discussion and commitment, rather than the sort of porous, grudging changes sought by the Londoners, can do the job. Even a truly level trading field will often not be enough. Given the systematic weakness of their extractive economies after 500 years of underdevelopment by Europe, African countries in particular need domestic and international subsidies and protections so that they can build capacity in selected areas of domestic commerce and international competition.

A healthy supply of untied foreign exchange could certainly help with such a strategy, just as it could help a government that is serious about reducing suffering not just by solid growth, but also by maintaining basic health, sanitation, and educational services, which need small-scale but timely imports. There is no need to raise fresh cash from new taxes and government spending to subsidize the foreign aid industry, as the proposed "Tobin tax" on currency transactions, the EU airline ticket tax, Tony Blair's poverty bonds, or American deficits do. Instead, the foreign exchange for penetration of northern markets and attacking pockets of poverty can be generated by closing down the very institutions that the North created to guide the South.

The World Bank has long outlived its founding role as a big-item, big-picture lender to post-war Europe. Its hard-loan operations can be easily absorbed by commercial lenders, and its soft-loan operations in the poorest countries consistently perform far below projected returns. The Bank should simply forgive its debtors and shut down, apportioning among the governments of the poorest countries with the weakest exports, by population, whatever convertible currency remains after it pays off its bonds. Similarly, the IMF should terminate its bizarre anti-poverty role, revert to its original mission as a currency adviser and short-term adjuster, and distribute much of its reserves of gold or its own currency, the convertible Special Drawing Right, to poor countries.

Some pretty rotten governments would gain purchasing power from these payouts, and there is no guarantee that even the honest ones would choose their imports wisely.

Distribution to all, though, is morally preferable in practice to having the donors pick winners and losers. In fact, the donors already appear to recognize this. While the new US Millennium Challenge Corporation, the recent World Bank "anti-corruption" drive, and the fine print of the Londoners' plan all claim to rule out aid to countries with poor records on "governance," they don't really mean that any more than they do when they say that aid should be denied to countries whose governments abuse human rights. In the end, some and usually most of planned aid does flow, regardless of a government's behavior. This is for two reasons, one strategic and one humanitarian.

At the strategic level, as a US official said at the dawn of the human rights era under President Carter, conditions are for the little countries and countries that don't matter, not for big countries or countries that do. China's domestic record on human and political rights is one of the worst in the world, ranking with America's international record of invasion, torture, and support for repression. Yet the World Bank begs China to accept billions of dollars in loans every year that it could well borrow commercially, since the Bank needs to move its money. Indonesia was famously corrupt under Suharto, with its armed forces controlling entire sectors of the economy, yet the United States and the Bank provided large-scale loans to a valued ally.

Even when human rights conditions affect the important countries, they are counter-balanced by other aid. President Carter had the United States vote against South Korea's loans in the World Bank because of human rights violations, even while he was funding its army. Today the United States withholds bits of aid to Egypt over its rigged elections, even as it pours another $2 billion in annually in military and economic aid and works with Egypt's covert services. Similarly, President George H. W. Bush held up a smidgen of Israel's housing aid so as not to support permanent occupation of the West Bank, but didn't touch the $3 billion in annual aid used for US weapons. It should be noted that he paid a stiff political price for even this symbolic gesture, and that because of Israel's special treatment under foreign aid laws, the American arms-dealers would have been paid from US tax revenues if orders were cancelled.

At the humanitarian level cutting aid to the dictator of a poor country has the effect of making poor people suffer twice for their governments' sins. The popular alternatives of directing funds through non-governmental bodies or controlling the government's budget are largely window-dressing. The case of Zimbabwe in the late 2000s shows how funding non-governmental efforts effectively subsidizes and sustains the regime in power, and frees up its budget for more military spending. Foreign control of the recipient's budget, as the IMF learned in the 1970s when it insisted on taking over every possible level of government finance in Zaire for Mobutu, and as the World Bank learned in the 2000s when it tried to direct Chad's new oil revenues to poverty programs, is problematic as well. Any government that requires outside policing is not going to conduct a coherent anti-poverty program in any event. Any government that is determined to steal aid is always able to do so, either at the international front end with the foreign exchange or at the domestic back end with favoritism and payoffs on the projects.

As northern activists work on getting their own citizenry to demand an end to support for repressive strategic partners and predatory economics, there is certainly a humanitarian argument for rich nations to continue research, exchanges, and small pilot projects in poor countries in the areas of agriculture, education, and the prevention and treatment of disease. However, there should be no disruptive "scaling up" to countrywide efforts before an infrastructure of personnel, plant, and culture has been created by long-term growth. A fundamental change in poverty will come only with a fundamental change in North-South power relations. What is needed is not a Big Plan, but a fair deal. The aid-ists might respond that the North will never renounce dominance, and that the London consensus is the best way to address poverty in a time of empire. Then they shouldn't talk about making poverty history, because empire keeps making more of it.

LORD CHELMSFORD'S DESCENDANTS: HUMANITARIAN INTERVENTION

Another apolitical fantasy in the West that is related to the aid charade is the call by both Hard and Soft Eagles, and in this case echoed by some Turkeys, to "save" Darfur, Somalia, Rwanda, Zimbabwe, or the Congo, or any number of failing states by sending in US, UN, or foreign military forces under a "responsibility to protect." Civil war is indeed the bane of African development, but by the time a long-simmering African ethnic conflict erupts, armed intervention is most likely only going to exacerbate it. US military aid that strengthens African dictators and forces their opponents to turn to revolt is a factor in such conflicts. Americans calling for intervention in hopes of reducing the toll of African civil wars would do better to focus on ending US support for regimes that cooperate with its mineral, military, and covert policies, so as to help prevent future conflicts.

The expectation of the interventionists is that foreign forces can sweep aside geno-cidal thugs as easily as they defeated African armies in the colonial era and establish gov-ernments that will promote human rights and stability. The advocates of humanitarian intervention need to become familiar with its history in colonial wars, such as the British invasion of Zululand in 1879, in which Lord Chelmsford's British machine gunners devas-tated King Cetshwayo's spear-carrying impis. Sir Bartle Frere, the British governor of the Cape Colony, had been looking for an excuse to confront Zulu power and found it in Vic-torian England's concern for women's rights. The Zulu nation required all its men to serve as warriors until they were in their 30s and to complete their military service before they married. A couple who defied this edict were executed, horrifying the British public and building support for the removal of such a brutal form of government. It is worth noting that this first "humanitarian intervention" was not an easy victory, did nothing to improve the status of women in Zululand, and resulted in Zulu strife and created problems of gov-ernance that linger even today.

At the start of the invasion a detachment of 1,200 British soldiers was wiped out at the battle of Isandlwana, a pyrrhic victory for the Zulus, who lost thousands of men as they overran the British position. Chelmsford reinforced his army and later that year defeated Cetshwayo at Ulundi, the capital. Frere then anointed 13 princes to run separate sections of Zululand, but chaos followed after Cetshwayo was released from the Robben Island prison to go to London and meet Queen Victoria. His visit to Britain became a triumphant pageant, and Victoria became his advocate. He returned to Zululand to claim his rightful place, only to find that the 13 princes had no intention of relinquishing their power to him.[1] The tensions between the followers of the king and those of the princes were visible in intra-Zulu violence in the dying days of apartheid and continue today between traditionalists who follow the descendant of Cetshwayo, King Zwelithini, and his hereditary counselor, Inkhata party leader Mangostho Buthelezi, and modernists who reject the king's authority and tend to support the African National Congress. As will be discussed below, modern humanitarian interventions in Africa have been no more successful than Chelmsford's.

News of the Zulu victory at Isandlwana swept through Africa, emboldening other nationalists. Just six years later a garrison of 7,000 Egyptian soldiers under General Charles "Chinese" Gordon was similarly slaughtered during the fall of Khartoum to the army of the Mahdi. British officials demonized the Islamist Mahdi as a brutal feudalist who was disrupting the stability and development the colonial powers were bringing to East Africa. In 1896 they sent Herbert Kitchener to the Sudan, where he avenged Gordon by dispatching the Mahdi's army to take Khartoum in 1898 and secure his elevation from general to lord. As in Zululand, the victory only delayed the resolution of long-standing conflicts. Ironically the humanitarian disasters in the Sudan that motivate today's Kitcheners' calls for intervention flow directly from the victory over the Mahdi and Britain's administrative division of the Sudan during its 60 years of nation building and exploitation.

The notion that Kitchener's expedition to the Sudan was a humanitarian intervention was widely accepted in Britain. Indeed, the purpose of the entire imperial enterprise was, according to a young officer in India named Winston Churchill in 1896, "to give peace to warring tribes, to administer justice where all was violence, to strike the chains off the slave, to plant the seeds of commerce and learning." For the future prime minister the empire was a duty and a joy: "What more beautiful idea can inspire human effort?"[2] A remarkably similar chord is struck in the incessant refrain today by the leaders of the US African Command, or AFRICOM, who claim that "engagement" with African armed forces will bring the "stability" needed to permit economic growth and the institutionalization of democracy. As noted in Chapter 8, only 21 percent of Africa's governments are "fully free," 46 percent are "partly free" because of dubious elections, and a full third are outright dictatorships. As a result, on much of the continent the armed forces serve and preserve non-democratic governments, and even in many of the democratic countries the armed forces overpower civilian institutions and test civilian authority. Still, AFRICOM labors ahead, sending US forces to publicize support for the dictators in Equatorial Guinea and Ethiopia, repeating the disastrous example of Latin America, where US military aid and training strengthened dictators for decades and led to horrific civil wars.[3]

Turkeys have rightly claimed that AFRICOM's aid to repressive "partners" among Africa's armed forces shows that the United States remains more interested in access to

---

1 A fine history of the war and its aftermath is Donald Morris, *The Washing of the Spears: The Rise and Fall of the Zulu Nation*, Simon & Schuster, New York, 1965.
2 Fareed Zakaria, "The Previous Superpower," *New York Times*, July 27, 2003, a review of Simon Schama's *A History of Britain: The Fate of Empire, 1776-2000*.
3 Letter from House Foreign Affairs subcommittee chairs Bill Delahunt and Donald Payne to Secretary of Defense Robert Gates, September 16, 2008.

strategic resources and military bases than support for representative government.[1] Yet in 2010 Turkeys affiliated with the Enough project and Human Rights Watch helped Soft Eagles Congressman Jim McGovern and Senator Russ Feingold enact a call for AFRI-COM's intervention in the Ugandan civil war on behalf of 25-year dictator Yoweri Museveni, even after a US-backed debacle in December 2008 left 900 civilians dead. AFRICOM had provided logistic and intelligence support for a Ugandan raid on rear area base in the Congo of an Acholi resistance group, the Lord's Resistance Army, but the fleeing fighters overwhelmed the trap set for them and leveled villages that stood in their way.[2] Sporadic foreign intervention like Uganda's with small combat forces in the economically fragile and ethnically volatile African environment has generally increased rather than reduced conflict. Examples include US and UN forces in Somalia and Nigerian "peace-keepers" in West Africa in the 1990s, OAU forces in Darfur and UN forces in the Congo in the 2000s.

Intervention with sufficient forces to lock down an African conflict has not been attempted since the flurry of UN interventions to reverse Katangan secession and stem the chaos in the Congo in the early 1960s.[3] The imposition of such a heavy footprint today would be just as disruptive and eventually futile as that UN intervention. Millions would be driven or drawn to refugee camps and the intervention and the imposition of an external authority would only prolong the resolution of problems of political legitimacy that stem from the vacuum of authority brought to Africa by colonialism. In some cases the international community could logically support a redrawing of illogical borders, as it is trying to do in the southern Sudan. However, as continual conflict between Ethiopia and Eritrea show, without a resolution of ethnic tensions, new borders will only substitute international wars for civil wars. Foreign military intervention in Africa remains as chimerical a hope for stability today as it was in 1879. The case of Darfur under the Obama administration shows that even its advocates are starting to recognize this reality.

Susan Rice was a 30-year-old NSC staffer in April 1994 when the Rwandan government's Hutu army and related militias seized on the assassination of the Hutu president to begin a two-month slaughter of at least half a million Tutsis and other suspected opponents. As she continued in her career, first as assistant secretary of state for Africa in 1997 and then as a non-governmental analyst and finally as Obama's ambassador to the United Nations, she would often declare that not pushing hard enough to get the United States to act to stop the genocide was her greatest regret and motivation. However, as Rice's NSC colleague Nancy Soderberg has pointed out, there was never "serious consideration" given by the Clinton administration to using US troops or funding a sufficient foreign force to stop the genocide in Rwanda. Clinton had just finished quietly withdrawing all US troops from Somalia, where the death of 18 US soldiers the previous fall had generated a tremendous backlash in Congress and the public against peacekeeping missions. If he

---

1 See the website of the NGO coalition, ResistAFRICOM, which is led by Emira Woods of the Institute for Policy Studies.

2 Jeff Gettleman and Eric Schmitt, "US Aided a Failed Plan to Rout Ugandan Rebels," *New York Times*, February 6, 2009.

3 Cuba intervened with tens of thousands of combat troops in Angola in 1975 and 1988 and Ethiopia in 1977, but these were wars to defeat invasions from, respectively, South Africa and Somalia, not attempts to end civil wars with negotiations.

had decided to make humanitarian intervention a core function for US armed forces, there were plenty of other conflicts to choose from, from Bosnia to Rwanda's neighbor Burundi, where Tutsi and Hutu forces had each slaughtered tens of thousands of civilians the previous year.[1]

During April 1994 Hutu forces roamed Rwanda in small bands, wantonly killing Tutsis and politically-suspect Hutus and ignoring the protests of the 2,500-man UN force that had been deployed to supervise a cease-fire and political settlement agreed to the previous fall between the Hutu government and a Ugandan-based Tutsi rebel army. Following the Hutu army's murder of ten Belgian soldiers guarding a Hutu politician who had been dismissed as prime minister for opposing the regime, Belgium withdrew its contingent and the UN Security Council then withdrew the entire force because of fears that it would be slaughtered. Perhaps half a million people were murdered before the end of April, when a Tutsi army raised in Uganda had fought its way to the capital, Kigali. Over the next two months the Tutsi army drove the Hutu army into the Congo as large-scale killings of civilians took place on both sides of the ethnic divide and raised the total toll towards a million. In mid-May the UN Security Council, with US support, approved a new 5,500-man force to protect pockets of civilians within UN perimeters, but it took months for African nations to contribute enough forces to make it functional.

Human Rights Watch has popularized the claim by Romeo Dallaire, the outspoken Canadian general who commanded the initial UN force, that a rapid infusion of "5,000 experienced forces could have ended the genocide." It argues that "because the operation of the genocide was highly centralized, stopping the killing in Kigali would have quickly quelled violence elsewhere in the country." Adopting a comically colonial vision of the importance of foreign opinion to African enemies engaged in a fight to the death, Human Rights Watch presents the following scenario: "Any serious challenge from foreign troops would have signaled that the interim government was illegitimate in the eyes of the international community and unlikely to receive the support it would need to survive, far less prosper. This would have discouraged Rwandans from joining the killing campaign and might even have stimulated some opponents of the genocide to come together to oppose it."[2]

This fantasy overlooks the reality of both the situation on the ground and the way foreign armies would have had to fight. By the time any foreign troops could have been deployed, much of the original slaughter would have been accomplished and the Tutsi army would have brought on its general engagement with the Hutu army and started attacking Hutu civilians. To lock just the capital down would have required tens of thousands of troops to separate the rival armies, and if they had resisted, the foreign forces could easily have been drawn into full-scale combat that would have devastated the city. The genocide was continuing all over the country, though, so additional tens of thousands of foreign troops would have been needed to save lives. The military lesson that the Pentagon took from Somalia, where many more Pakistani peacekeepers had been killed than American,

1 *The Superpower Myth: The Use and Misuse of American Might*, John Wiley and Sons, Hoboken, New Jersey, 2005, pp. 282-284.
2 *Leave None to Tell the Story*, Human Rights Watch, March 1999.

was that peacekeepers in volatile situations need full logistical and protective support, including tanks, artillery, and aircraft, to back up their supposed moral authority as international arbiters. No foreign force other than the United States could have moved quickly enough and with enough resolve to shut down the killing in Rwanda. Romantic notions of parachuting in a few thousand troops from the 82nd Airborne Division would have found no support among the Joint Chiefs of Staff. It would have taken an American occupation and reconstruction of Rwanda to save even a few thousand of the nearly one million civilians who died, and the American way of war, with its premium on force protection, would have killed far more civilians than it could have saved.

Rice's mentor, Madeleine Albright, was the strongest advocate in Clinton's cabinet of using US troops to protect civilians. As UN ambassador in 1993 she advocated intervention in Bosnia by famously asking Joint Chiefs chairman Colin Powell, "What's the point of you saving this superb military force you're always talking about if we can't use it?" Powell, as he humorously described it, almost had an aneurysm at this outburst. Albright not only failed to achieve intervention in Bosnia, but in 1994 was put in the uncomfortable position of having to argue the administration's minimalist case at the UN during the Rwandan genocide. Some of Powell's dismissal of Albright's views could be attributed to her reputation for being not a strategic thinker, but rather a mere fund-raiser who, like Clinton's ambassador to France, Pamela Harriman, had parlayed her husband's inherited fortune into prominence within the Democratic Party. More fundamentally, though, Powell and his peers in the Pentagon had rebuilt the armed forces from the debacle in Vietnam and had developed a doctrine that held that US forces were only to be deployed massively, to meet a fundamental challenge to US national security, with public support, and with a clear strategy for departure. The war to drive Iraq from Kuwait had validated their doctrine, and the mess in Somalia had in some ways validated it even more. Powell's doctrine lived on for at least the first few years of the Clinton administration, until interventions in Haiti, Bosnia, and Kosovo that arguably left those states no better off in the long term.

During this period Turkeys struggled with the concept of humanitarian intervention. While few were as supportive as Human Rights Watch, which under its director Ken Roth consistently advocated military action to force settlements to the spiraling conflicts in the former Yugoslavia, many anti-imperialist thinkers found themselves in the position of recasting the US armed forces as benevolent peace-makers rather than the guardians of imperial privilege. In May 2000 Kai Bird, an editor at the *Nation* magazine, published a special issue on humanitarian intervention in which he made an argument that was a Turkey's version of Soft Eagle Albright's position: the empire's forces are paid for and deployed, so they might as well do some local good even as they promote a globally-damaging mission. Bird's position was not as crude as that of Senate staffer and future US ambassador to Croatia Peter Galbraith, who appealed to the Arms Transfer Working Group to support intervention in Bosnia because "these are Muslims, but they are white" (even though there were black staff at the meeting of the NGO coalition) but it did contain more than a hint of colonial ideology.[1]

---

1 Oral report to director, staff assistant at the Project on Demilitarization and Democracy, 1993.

Neo-conservatives traded on Soft Eagles' and Turkeys' humanitarian horror at Saddam Hussein's abuses both when first calling for "regime change" in Iraq in the 1990s and then before the 2002 vote to implement that call with a US invasion. Similarly, in a reprise of the justification for Chelmsford's invasion of Zululand, Turkeys were confounded during the Obama administration by arguments that leaving Afghanistan would sacrifice the women there to medieval oppression under the Taliban. The myth that US forces are deployed to protect foreign civilians, rather than achieve US strategic objectives, is one that has been promoted since World War II, including by Obama in his 2009 speech justifying his decision to increase US forces to 100,000 in Afghanistan. It is the Achilles heel of the peace movement.

Rice and her fellow former NSC staffer John Prendergast and his Enough project lambasted George W. Bush throughout his administration for not stopping Sudan's killing and displacing of civilians in its efforts to quell the secessionist Fur rebellion. Rice cited Rwanda as an example of what would happen without intervention, although the death toll in Darfur was largely due not to individual murders, but to disease and malnutrition as hundreds of thousands of refugees fled to UN camps in Chad, the same causes of the far bigger death toll in the nearby Democratic Republic of the Congo. Advocates of intervention raised sufficient funds to sponsor a national advertising campaign calling for the United States to "take action" to stop the genocide. Student activists on campuses across the country took up the call to "Save Darfur." However, when Rice became Obama's UN ambassador, she suddenly seemed to become aware of the practicalities and limitations of armed intervention, and approved a policy of watching and talking with Sudan that was indistinguishable from Bush's. Prendergast's Enough project endorsed Obama's policy as well.

CHAPTER 10. CLIMATE CATASTROPHE: CONVENIENT FIBS AND DANGEROUS PRESCRIPTIONS

Statistical tests and mathematical models are important tools of social and physical science. They are at the core of the constant barrage of claims about causality that analysts and advocates make with charts, numbers, and correlations between variables. Which economic policies have led to the greatest reduction in poverty rates in African countries? Which anti-retroviral drug regimen best prolonged the lives of AIDS patients? What military forces and tactics are best designed to achieve victory in an engagement? The answers are rarely self-evident, and since controlled experiments in which just one variable of interest is changed are hard to arrange in human and natural systems, only complex multivariate modeling can isolate the contribution of each variable.

If the researcher is brutally skeptical about all assumptions and so can test them impartially, if the variables are clear and measurable, and if the data are fantastically accurate, one just might be able to identify which combination of characteristics tends to correlate with what type of result, and how sure one can be of these tendencies. Then the evidence of correlation in these models can be used to sneak up on causation, always mindful that one is describing statistical averages and not certainties that are always replicated. For example, many smokers go their whole lives without a trace of lung cancer, but the difference in cancer rates between large populations of smokers and non-smokers after statistically controlling for confounding influences such as income, ethnicity, and exercise, proves to a high degree of certainty that smoking causes lung cancer. The inability of the average citizen to understand statistical studies and the inherent self-interest of their authors have caused many on the political left to be highly skeptical of studies that contradict their instincts, such as those purporting to show that setting a minimum wage costs jobs or that DDT does not cause health problems for humans. The popular bumper sticker

"Question Authority" is the left's answer to the mainstream "experts" who translate such studies into society's conventional wisdom.[1]

Due both to the complexity of the system and the potential impact on people of the policies being proposed, no topic in international affairs is more in need of statistical analysis than the effect of industrial emissions and other human activities on the global climate. Unfortunately, the analyses and even the underlying data have been politicized and misused to the point that they are a hindrance, rather than a help, in determining the truth. Leaders of the world's governments and of the UN's Intergovernmental Panel on Climate Change (IPCC) brush aside the towering uncertainties involved in attributing past changes in the chaotic and cyclic climate system to human activities such as emitting heat-trapping gasses, let alone in predicting devastating changes for the future. They have transformed the well-hedged suggestions of the IPCC's scientists, statisticians, modelers into a firm belief, as expressed by both President Obama and UN Secretary-General Ban Ki-Moon at the 2009 Copenhagen summit, that human-induced "global warming" has brought on "climate change" that will expand into a climate "catastrophe" that threatens human existence.

In Copenhagen the leaders bandied about policies to head off that catastrophe by raising the price of carbon-based fuel, which would be merely costly and inconvenient for people in developed nations but deadly for people in developing nations by reversing the growth-led trend toward longer life expectancy.[2] Thanks to China's refusal to contemplate such a reversal, these policies were blocked at Copenhagen, but ripple effects of the governmental consensus were already being felt by Africa from reduced exports due to European taxes on the carbon-content of their journey there and from the resistance of foreign aid agencies to building any coal-fired plants, even the clean-coal plants that could spare Africans the illnesses brought on by the residue of "unscrubbed" sulfur dioxide.[3] The

---

1 The slogan is somewhat illogical, since it says nothing about what happens after the question is satisfactorily answered. It seems to imply that the questioner should then agree with the authority, but also that the questioning should continue indefinitely. It is certainly more logical than another favored leftist bumper sticker, "Well-behaved Women Rarely Make History," a phrase coined by Harvard professor Laurel Thatcher Ulrich. Women and men alike rarely make history, so their behavior is irrelevant to that task unless someone were to argue that well-behaved women perform more poorly in that regard than poorly-behaved ones. In addition, the slogan implies that women should be impolite in their daily lives, when making history is a matter for the public arena.

2 Low-cost energy production is a crucial component of economic growth, particularly in countries that are only now industrializing. In those countries one can observe a clear, causal connection between wealth and life expectancy. Increased wealth for poor people and countries permits cleaner water, consistent energy, better education, and better nutrition, all of which combine to reduce mortality rates, especially for infants. Economic growth doesn't necessarily have this effect; it can be stolen or hoarded by dictators and a tiny upper class. However, without economic growth, there will be lower life expectancy. There is a precautionary principle that says the world should reduce the use of fossil fuel on the chance that global warming threatens a climate catastrophe. However, the impact of such a reduction on life expectancy reveals another precautionary principle, which demands that solutions to the problem of emissions retard economic growth as little as possible.

3 A World Bank loan for such a plant in South Africa was finally approved in April 2010, with the United States abstaining on the vote.

demand of African leaders in Copenhagen, acting as a bloc led by the dictators of Sudan and Ethiopia, for $67 billion annually from developed countries to relieve the purported damage from purported warming in Africa was a measure more of their addiction to foreign aid than of their concern for the well-being of their citizens.[1]

The left's skepticism seems to have deserted it on climate change. Far from questioning authority, Turkeys are among the leaders in proclaiming climate catastrophe, based on a reverential reference to the IPCC and "the scientists" who spin off far more alarming scenarios. Turkeys have abandoned their stock in trade, the diligent digging into research claims on, say, military strategy in Afghanistan or export-led growth in Africa, to uncover self-serving misrepresentations and unlikely simplifications. Why is this the case? Why are the Turkeys happily hopping into bed with Al Gore, a Dixie whom they have fought on foreign and military policy from the MX missile to aid to the Salvadoran army to landmines? Why do they ostracize as firmly as the Democratic Party any contrary conclusions, or even questions that might lead to them?

The answer is that for the Turkeys global warming is the perfect storm, a rare chance to find common cause with the American mainstream on policies that will achieve long-sought goals. The consensus about the dangers of climate change is a welcome license to dismember the carbon-driven capitalism that many Turkeys see as the source of numerous political and social ills, from poverty to dictatorship in developing countries, and from the income gap to ostentatious consumption in the developed world. In addition, the leftist wing of the "green" movement that began in the 1970s in Europe and the United States has always had an apocalyptic streak, a fear that population, consumption, and development are unsustainable and tending toward disaster. As John Feffer of the Institute for Policy Studies has written: "Cutting back on consumption, reducing fossil-fuel use, bringing the developing world into the post-industrial age in a sustainable manner: Even if the mercury weren't rising, these are critical goals. The climate crisis is precisely the giant lever with which we can, following Archimedes, move the world in a greener, more equitable direction."[2]

Leftists hoped that the green movement would provide a fundamental challenge to capitalism, but in fact, starting with Earth Day in 1970, at the height of protests against the

---

1   The claim by African leaders that recent droughts are due to warming from industrial emissions by developed countries is a close second in fantasy to the claim that rising seas are threatening their existence of island nations. Dramatic under-water cabinet meetings notwithstanding, neither Tuvalu and the Maldives have experienced a meaningful rise in sea level, which is itself affected by numerous variables unrelated to changes in global seas, including the actual rising of land and overuse of sea shore. The existence of lengthy regional droughts in Africa over thousands of years makes it particularly difficult to attribute any recent one to greenhouse gasses. The IPCC records a two degree rise in mean temperature for Africa that matches the rises recorded for the northern hemisphere's land masses, but this rise is probably the least credible of the IPCC's measurements. Warming has been observed primarily in the northern hemisphere, mostly on land and ice, and particularly in the higher latitudes where heat, and snow-melting black soot, is transported from warmer regions. Only about half of the African continent is even covered by a station that measures temperature, and satellite data for Africa usually show lower temperatures than those estimated by the IPCC from the land stations.

2   John Feffer, "Crapshoot in Copenhagen," World Beat, *Foreign Policy in Focus*, Institute for Policy Studies, Washington, DC, December 8, 2009.

Vietnam war, it has been a self-interested, mainstream distraction that siphons energy and activists away from a fundamental challenge to imperialism. Organizing on the principle of "not in my backyard" has kept Turkeys in the United States and Europe from focusing on what is being done by their governments in other peoples' front yards. American skies and waters are a lot healthier today than they were in 1970 because the environmental movement forced elected politicians to cater to their beliefs, but acceptance of America's global role of domination remains as fixed in mainstream politics as ever. Turkeys are trying to use global warming as a "giant lever" to link the two concerns, but they are expending resources on what is certainly a non-solution to what is most likely a non-problem, and providing legitimacy to the Soft Eagles who control the climate change debate, and who have no intention of fulfilling Feffer's program.

Economist Robert Samuelson wrote presciently in 1997 that a heightened consensus among the public and political leaders that human-based emissions could lead to climate dangers would have only one consequence. It would not be reductions in heat-trapping gasses, because cost-effective alternatives to their use for power simply do not exist, and the necessary heavy tax on the gasses to reduce consumption of them would "impose pain on voters for no obvious gain to solve a hypothetical problem." Instead, all that would be produced would be a "a gushing source of national hypocrisy."[1] His prediction came true in the 2000s, but the hypocrisy was not just American. Everybody, from China to the United States, from NASCAR to American universities, from Shell and other carbon fuel producers to the IPCC and its carbon-heavy conferences, found a way to claim that they were "green" by reducing their "carbon footprint" of "global warming pollution" — even as they continued on with their carbon-based lifestyles just as they had before they feared for the survival of the human race. The limitations on developed nations in the iconic Kyoto treaty were evaded by the creative use of starting points, targets, "credits" from the collapse of the Warsaw Pact economy, and dubious "offsets" from funding hydro-power or cooking stoves in developing countries.[2] The net result of the global warming scare, thankfully, has simply been more creative advertising. The Turkeys have wasted monumental amounts of time and energy on a chimera.

---

1 "Dancing Around a Dilemma: Global warming promises to become a large and gushing source of national hypocrisy," *Washington Post*, July 9, 1997.

2 Emission studies found no reductions caused by the Kyoto protocol by 2012, despite a pledged 5.2 percent target. Any reductions were "due largely to the collapse of former communist economies, including East Germany, and the restructuring of the energy sector in Great Britain. There had been little deliberately accepted pain in the name of climate change policy." See "Impact of the Kyoto Protocol on Stabilization of Carbon Dioxide Concentration," Niklas Höhne, ECOFYS energy & environment, Cologne, Germany, 2005, available on: http://www.stabilisation2005.com/posters/Hohne_Niklas.pdf. For the way countries created their targets, see *International Environmental Policy: Interests and the Failure of the Kyoto Process*, Sonja Boehmer-Christiansen and Aynsley John Kellow, Edward Elgar Publishing, 2002, p. 56, available on: http://archives.cnn.com/2001/WORLD/europe/italy/03/29/environment.kyoto/ and Chapter 6, "The Kyoto Process," pp. 53-84, generally. Even leading Kyoto advocate Eileen Claussen, president of the Pew Center on Global Climate Change, acknowledged that "the greatest value is symbolic." See "Kyoto Treaty Takes Effect Today: Impact on Global Warming May Be Largely Symbolic," by Shankar Vedantam, *Washington Post*, Wednesday, February 16, 2005, Page A4.

AL GORE'S MOVIE: APOCALYPSE SOON

The interchangeable terms "global warming" and "climate change" have come to refer to a four-part belief:

First, that the roughly one degree Fahrenheit rise in surface temperature over the past 150 years has been caused primarily by human activities, rather than by variations and chaotic interactions outside of human control;

Second, that this one degree rise, rather than other natural variations and interactions, is itself the primary cause of many of the recent changes claimed for other climate variables, such as decreased ice cover, hotter and higher seas, and more intense and more frequent storms, rains, and droughts, and even of changes in such non-climate variables as the number of earthquakes, the rate of species loss and the speed of the migration of diseases;

Third, that much more dramatic increases in temperature, perhaps from three to eight degrees, will occur in the next century if industrial emissions are not severely limited; and

Fourth, that these dramatically increased temperatures will in turn cause changes in the other climate and non-climate variables that would be catastrophic for human culture.

It should be noted that there is no inherent reason that someone who believes one of the parts of this quartet need believe any of the others, since the four beliefs comprise separate sets of research questions, all of whose answers are not yet clear, that hinge on different physical facts. For example, there is no reason why the one-degree rise could not be largely natural and the changes in variables still due to it. Or, the rise could be caused by human activity, but the changes in variables could in fact be minor, or have come mostly from sources other than the increased heat. Similarly, the first two beliefs could be true, but the effects of increased emissions on temperature, or of increased temperature on the other variables, from this point on could less potent than in the past, as "saturation" levels are reached. What is known of the complexity of both the theory and practice of climate physics and the unpredictable dampening, expanding, and interactive effects of both emissions and heat make it extremely unlikely, *prima facie*, that for all important response variables this quartet of beliefs is either wholly right or wholly wrong.

Be that is it may, it seems that most people who focus on the issue either believe the entire quartet or none of it. Perhaps as a result, Americans' beliefs break down along the lines of political parties, even though, again, there is no logical reason for there to be Democratic and Republican approaches to the complex science and statistics involved. According to the Pew Research Center, in 2006 more than two times as many Democrats as Republicans (54% to 24%) believed there was solid evidence that the Earth was warming and that this was mostly due to human activity rather than natural patterns. By 2009 politicization was even more intense, with Harris Interactive finding that half of Republicans but only eight percent of Democrats do not believe that industrial gasses lead to warming.

Nothing brought more public attention to global warming in the United States than "An Inconvenient Truth," a film featuring former Vice President Al Gore's brief for the quartet. This jeremiad makes a blizzard of claims about the causes, effects, and policy responses to recent warming that violate so many basic rules of logic and misuse and exaggerate so many studies that thoughtful viewers may react by rejecting his accurate portrayal of the underlying reality that human-generated carbon dioxide, methane, and nitrous oxide are indeed important heat-trapping gasses, and by dismissing the imprecise but improving attempts to model the impact of these gasses. In a nutshell, his convenient fibs discredit an underlying truth and valiant attempts to discern its impact. Gore emulates the two most misguided practices of environmental lobbyists. He attacks opponents over who funds them and he generates hysteria about isolated events — Hurricane Katrina, chunks of ice "calving" (dropping off into the sea), ice cover melting on Greenland, Antarctica, and Mount Kilimanjaro, droughts, and the spread of diseases and invasive species — whose causes are complex and often not mostly related to global or even local temperature.

Such violations of the rules of logic (the *ad hominem* attack, that focuses on who makes a claim rather than what evidence is provided for it, and the *post hoc ergo propter hoc* fallacy of confusing correlation with causation just because one thing happened after another) are found not just on the "green" side. Some of the think-tanks and Members of Congress on the other side of the great global warming debate consistently characterize their opponents as being bought by research grants, and cite isolated places where temperature is dropping, calm is prevailing, and ice is building, as if that too were proof of some overall trend. Just as having intense hurricanes during a period of increased temperature does not mean that carbon-based warming is to blame, the existence of similar hurricanes throughout the ages does not establish that the current intensity is unaffected by human activities. The fact that the recorded rise in global mean temperature from 1910 to 1940 came at a time of minimal industrial emissions and the plateau in temperature from 1940 to 1980 came during a time of far larger emissions does not mean that the similar rise in temperature from 1980 to 2000 was not driven by emissions, just as the plateau from 2000 to 2010 was proof for neither camp. Science needs to establish a model that convincingly predicts expectation levels from both the powerful chaos and inexplicable patterns in climate before we can analyze the causes of deviations from these levels.

Consider one of the film's most dramatic images — people suffering in the water-filled streets of New Orleans. There have been a few interesting statistical explorations of hurricane cycles that suggest that hurricane intensity has increased recently in response to warmer waters in some regions of the world, such as the Caribbean, but these very tentative findings represent much more the beginning than the end of that inquiry. With a series of measurements for a variable, a change from one period to another is meaningless until the standard deviation, or the typical variation, in the data is calculated, and until changes in other powerful causes of the variable's movement are factored in, but Gore ignores these fundamental statistical concepts. In addition, the suggestive studies have not been well-replicated, and are largely balanced out by studies of other regions, which suggests in turn that natural causes, latent cycles, and random variation rather than global mean temperature are at play.

In any event, Katrina was not a powerful storm at landfall in the context of 20th century hurricanes or even the most powerful in the year in which it occurred, and to the extent that intensity and frequency have been accurately measured over the years, Atlantic hurricanes experienced a similar spate in the early 20th century. The cause of the suffering in New Orleans had little to do with the recently-increased warmth of water in the Caribbean, even if one attributes all of that to human-created emissions, which is probably not the case, given the huge variations and cycles in sea-warming caused by various ocean currents like the Gulf Stream and by air streams from lengthy African droughts from long before there were factories, cars and emissions. Katrina was devastating because the lakes and rivers of southern Louisiana were full and New Orleans is built below sea level.

Similar conclusions arise when analyzing Gore's treatment of ice-calving (a natural process of formation that may be related to both increases and decreases in ice cover), and Kilimanjaro's glacial recession (a century-long trend, probably largely related to non-industrial changes in tree cover and rainfall, and not temperature). When he shows what would happen if Greenland's ice-sheet were to melt away, with the world's coastal areas submerging under 20 feet of water, he is discussing changes that could take thousands of years at current rates. His presentation contradicts the mainstream of the modeling collected by his usually-favored IPCC, which predicts about a one-foot rise in the next century. Again, the degree of melting appears to be a long-term phenomenon rather than a recent response to increased temperature, and is dominated by natural changes and decades-long oscillations in currents and ocean temperatures.

Gore's film confirms his reputation, much magnified by Republican attacks and reporters' investigations during the 2000 presidential election, as someone who can't resist making a good point better. Bush strategist Karl Rove, quite a black pot himself for his promotion of the fraudulent war in Iraq, labeled Gore a "serial exaggerator" for such policy claims as having helped create the internet and started the examination of toxic waste sites like Love Canal, and such personal claims as being the model for the hero in Love Story and having his mother sing "Look for the Union Label" to him as a lullaby...when the song wasn't written until he was 27 years old. Gore's defenders have parsed each of the many claims in search of excuses, but even they acknowledge his tendency to stretch it at times.

Gore starts the film with just a little demagoguery, just a little fib. He wants to show that scientific consensus can be wrong, a point that ironically cuts against his silly and insistent chant throughout the film that such a consensus supports him on his certainty about the quartet of beliefs about the effects of carbon-based fuels. He claims that Tommy, one of his sixth-grade classmates in 1959 at the elite St. Albans private school in Washington, was laughed down by the geography teacher for pointing out that the continents look as if they used to "fit together." This is almost certainly a tall tale of the "Union Label" type, and Gore implies as much by continuing with the remark that the teacher became the science adviser to the Bush administration. Gore includes this yarn to make the point that "the trouble is what we know for sure that just ain't so." Never could truer words be spoken — about the certainty he holds for the quartet of beliefs.

In fact, the thought that the continents had drifted apart was one of Benjamin Franklin's favorite theories, and it became widely accepted in European science shortly after Alfred Wegener published his compendium of identical, widely-flung plants, fossils, rock-types, and coal deposits in 1912. American geologists resisted it strongly for another 20 years because no mechanism for the drift had been posited, but by the time Gore was in sixth grade, even before the causal mechanism of plate tectonics had been widely validated, most recognized the possibility, if not the certainty, of drift. For a geography teacher at St. Albans to have laughed off "Tommy's" suggestion would probably have meant that she was ignoring the discussion of it in her textbook. Did Gore go back and check the textbooks and talk to the surviving teachers and students and see if she really said it and meant it the way he remembered it from childhood? Of course not: it's just a political tall tale, indeed one that may have modified from an incident in the childhood of novelist and prominent climate skeptic Michael Crichton.[1] Still, this yarn sets the tone for the movie and for the way Gore continues to present what he calls his "story" on climate change: pick an incident or finding, take it from context, drop the possible uncertainties, present a correlation as a certain cause, and stigmatize anyone who disagrees.

Gore chuckles as he dismisses anyone who disputes his story, which he has called a "scientific consensus unmatched since Newton's second law of motion." This particular joke is on him, however. Since the publication of Einstein's Theory of Special Relativity in 1905, every physicist has known that Newton's Second Law, in which the Force needed to accelerate an object is equal to the Mass of the object multiplied by the Acceleration one wishes to produce, is wrong. Einstein, with his heartfelt cry of "forgive me, Newton," showed that the Second Law requires a new term in the denominator, the "Einstein" factor that boosts the force needed to accelerate an object exponentially, and infinitely, as the speed of the mass increases toward the speed of light, and, strangely, time slows down to a crawl. In fact, it is this modification of Newton's law that led directly to Einstein's calculation of that most famous relationship in science, which was confirmed over Hiroshima in 1945: a stationary object has a latent Energy equal to its Mass times the square of the Speed of Light.

Gore's error about Newton's consensus ironically plays a crucial role in perhaps the most misleading scene in the film, one that he words so carefully that it is hard to escape the conclusion that he is being disingenuous. He displays a gigantic chart showing how concentration levels of carbon dioxide coincide with temperature as it travels up and down 10 degrees every 100,000 years for the past 650,000 years. These rough changes in global mean temperature are very credible, as opposed to the far finer claims about changes from 1,000 years ago, which are based on regional inferences and then global extrapolation from a few northern tree rings. There is a surreal quality to the intense debate about the disappearance from IPCC's charts over time of a "medieval warming period" that was similar to our century's rise in heat, and the substitution for it of the dramatic "hockey stick" that shows a flat rather than oscillating line for the 900 years preceding a now unprecedented jump in the last century. As even the error bands on the IPCC's hockey stick show, accurate measurement of global mean temperature at this level of detail was impossible prior to the 20th century and still difficult until the advent of satellite sensing in the 1980s.[2]

Gore does everything he can to imply that carbon dioxide is causing the 100,000-year cycle of temperature. He is careful to state that the causes of changes in global mean tem-

---

1 Personal communication with the author.
2 F.W. Taylor, *Elementary Climate Physics*, Oxford University Press, New York, 2005, chapter nine. This text by the Halley professor is a superb and balanced presentation of the science and statistics of climate change.

perature are "complicated," but then immediately says that "nothing is more powerful than CO_2." He invokes poor Tommy again by asking, "don't they fit together?" Most dramatically, Gore chooses a scale for representing carbon dioxide that forces him to rise up in a lineman's bucket over the chart to track the jump in expected levels for the next century, and then makes it clear that we should conclude that the temperature will continue to follow the carbon dioxide up, even though his chart shows that we happen to be at the top of the temperature cycle and are clearly about to come down. ("About" is a relative term here, since it takes about 85,000 years for temperature to drop to its low before the usual 15,000-year rebound to the peak.)

A defender of Gore on the website realclimate.org argues that he never actually uses the word "causality," but that is quibbling with the entire intent of the scene. Gore points out that the current 15,000-year, 10-degree rise in temperature coincides with a 100 parts per million, or 36 percent rise in concentrations of CO2, and asks whether the projected rise in the next 100 years of another 100 parts per million, or 27 percent, would not have much the same, 10-degree effect on temperature. The answer to this question is obviously intended to be "yes," and the reason is obviously intended to be that carbon dioxide drives temperature. This is intellectually unconscionable. What Gore clearly knows, but doesn't say, is that temperature on these scales is almost certainly driven by the 100,000-year Milankovich Cycle, a gradual oscillation in the shape of the Earth's elliptical orbit around the Sun, with contributions from shorter cycles of the tilt and tip of the Earth. One must say "almost certainly" because as the seemingly omniscient Oxford physics professor Fred Taylor points out, "all is not rosy for the Milankovich model." Differences in the radiation delivered to Earth due to the orbital changes are not large enough to account for the incredible power it would take to reverse the rise or fall of temperature.[1] This implies that feedback mechanisms are at work that science has not yet uncovered, which is precisely the sort of problem that bedevils attempts to model the current climate. There are mechanisms that currently can only be guessed at that provide various levels of equilibrium.

The oscillating ellipse that accords with Milankovich's temperature cycle is correctly predicted by Einstein's theories of special and general relativity, the latter of which was first confirmed in 1915 by modeling accurately a variation in the ellipse of Mercury that violated Newton's Second Law, and Gore's consensus about it. The point Gore obscures in his dramatic elevation is while carbon dioxide is part of the positive feedback mechanism during the rise and fall of temperature, at the important turning points its level is clearly being caused by, rather than causing, temperature change. This is true both at the low end, as when the increase in carbon dioxide followed rather than preceded the turnaround in temperature 15,000 years ago, and at the high end where we are now. During the climb, temperature drives carbon dioxide levels by releasing land and sea-stores of it, and then carbon dioxide in turn helps drive temperature by the "green-house effect." However, when temperature comes back down every 100,000 years, which is precisely the period that Gore is focusing on while riding in his bucket, it is obviously from causes other than carbon dioxide, since its high levels always follow temperature down rather than keep it up.

---

1 F.W. Taylor, *Elementary Climate Physics*, Oxford University Press, New York, 2005. p. 164.

It is on the topic of "scientific consensus," Newtonian or otherwise, that Gore shows his most troubling side, a robust and aggressive anti-intellectualism that ill befits his role as author of a book called *The Assault on Reason*. It is silly to list scientists who support or don't support the view that human activities can affect temperature, because there is no scientist who thinks they can't. That odd-numbered molecules oscillate and create energy-absorbing spectral lines, and that carbon dioxide's lines happen to be strong at a frequency at which infrared radiation leaves the earth, is not in doubt. That is physics, and can be confirmed in a laboratory. What is in doubt is how this reality interacts with various parts of climate out in the real world of changing pressure, wind, humidity, solar fluctuation, cloud cover, and ocean absorption. On long timescales, it is clear that heat-trapping molecules — mostly water vapor, but with about one-third of the effect due to naturally-occurring carbon dioxide — do raise temperature. If they didn't, the Earth would still be at an average of zero degrees, rather than today's 59 degrees. On timescales of centuries, though, the question is awash in uncertainty, both in observations and in mathematical modeling of those observations. These inquiries, as even Gore has said when pressed on why his claims of possible sea-rise are wildly greater than even the outside range of most modelers, are always continuing, properly subjecting findings to questions about assumptions, measurements, interactions, and logic.

The contextual omissions and exaggerations in Gore's presentation seem to have built up year by year. He himself says in the film that when he finds a "barrier" to convincing people of his "story," he works hard to figure out how to "demolish it." Here we see starkly the difference between science and lawyering. Scientists are glad to hear new ideas and dissonant evidence, because investigating them may broaden their understanding of a phenomenon. Lawyers try to "demolish" rather than test a new perspective. As a senator Gore infamously bullied MIT atmospheric physicist Richard Lindzen in hearings, badgering him and claiming for the cameras that he had trapped him into retracting his finding of two years' before that human influence may not be the dominant cause of recent mean warming. In fact, it was obvious to observers that all Lindzen was doing was updating data and findings on feedback mechanisms in clouds. Even more grotesquely, Gore's Senate office portrayed his claimed mentor on human-driven increases in atmospheric carbon dioxide, Harvard professor Roger Revelle, as senile and manipulated when Revelle disputed Gore's dire predictions of carbon dioxide's ability to drive up temperature. Revelle's co-author, physicist Fred Singer, sued the Harvard professor who assisted Gore's office in this portrayal, and won a full vindication.[1]

In the film Gore says that Revelle "saw where the story was going," and implies that Revelle's story is the same as his own. He further bemoans the fact that Revelle's appearance at Gore's first hearing in the 1980s did not result in the conversion of the Congress, and the country, to Gore's belief in the quartet. However, Revelle's appearance could not conceivably have led to anybody's conversion because, as noted above, he studied the effect of human-created carbon dioxide on global levels of the gas, and not its linkage with

---

1   Singer and Lindzen continue to be harassed by environmental lobbyists who have joined the State of California in asking a federal court to require the surrender of any communications between these scientists and auto companies who are challenging the state's emission controls.

temperature. Indeed, it was his published judgment that there was not enough evidence of a causal link between the two variables to justify dramatic policy action on emissions that led to the attempt by Gore's office to smear him.

Gore portrays himself and scientists who are warning about the dangers of emissions as Churchills sounding a warning of something as dangerous as Nazism. By analogy, those citizens, legislators, and scientists who do not rally to his banner are dismissed as complacent ostriches, cowardly collaborators, or paid liars. All this has echoes of the deplorable term the most extreme environmental lobbyists use to describe people who don't promote the quartet: "denialists", a word that had previously been reserved for the kooks who dispute the reality of the Nazi slaughter of millions of civilians from Jewish, Polish Catholic, and other non-Teutonic ethnic groups. Gore pointedly quotes Upton Sinclair — "It is difficult to get a man to understand something when his salary depends upon his not understanding it" — and clearly identifies the "skeptics" of the quartet of beliefs as heirs to the researchers for tobacco companies who produced studies questioning the link between smoking and cancer.[1]

Gore's caustic dismissal of uncertainty about the quartet of beliefs recalls one of his old nemeses, Richard Perle, a Pentagon official in the Reagan era who emerged as a leader of Bush administration officials who showed no uncertainty in claiming that intelligence information showed that Iraq was involved in the 9/11 attacks and possessed weapons of mass destruction. Back in the 1980s Perle defended his similarly incendiary, and in hindsight similarly incorrect, portrayal of Soviet capabilities and intentions by saying that, "democracies will not sacrifice to protect their security in the absence of a sense of danger." With his musings on how disappointed he is that American democracy has not responded to his warnings, Gore seems to be revealing that he too thinks that Americans will not sacrifice to guard against the possibility of environmental damage in the absence of a sense of certain disaster.

Very much like Michael Moore in another documentary, "Fahrenheit 9/11," that mixed bathos, bombast, and balderdash, Gore has erred and exaggerated when he need not. It is not the possibility of human-driven climate change that is false, but the certainty. There is more than enough that is inconveniently true about energy policy to justify dramatic research and subsidy programs for developing alternative fuels and ways to capture the waste from current fuels, but Gore's misleading claims and his pre-judged policy recommendations of taxing or capping power production to reduce emissions — which, despite his assurances, could severely cramp global economic growth and its powerful live-saving

---

1 This is all very tricky ground for Gore. He wants to hold the tobacco scientists responsible for his sister's death from cancer, but his family farmed tobacco, and he voted for tax breaks and price supports for tobacco even after her death. He wants to blame global warming skeptics for some unspecified but clearly harmful changes he claims to see happening "quickly" on the river near his home in Tennessee after what he says, incorrectly, has been ten thousand years of stability, but for 30 years he leased a zinc mine next to that river in a deal made in 1973 with famed energy mogul Armand Hammer, creating flow-off pollution that at times exceeded permitted levels. Neither supporting constituents who are tobacco farmers nor making trade-offs in mineral extraction between profit levels and pollution controls is evil, but bitterly attacking others for the same sorts of actions is a bit strange, particularly given the weaker fit of theory with reality in the realm of climate change.

effects in lower-income countries — discredit more sensible policy responses.[1] The Bush administration promoted research on novel ideas for energy production and the sequestration of emissions, and while Obama will continue this research, he is also pushing for constraints on emissions in a variety of direct and indirect ways. The end-game is clearly on the side of the research, because big changes in power production will be required within a century, whether or not human activity increases temperature significantly and dangerously, as fossil fuels became more expensive to extract. Starting the search for economically-viable power sources now is a wise investment, just as finding ways to keep emissions out of the heat cycle is the next logical step in American industry's generally good record of reducing emissions per unit of production.

THE COMPUTER MODELS THAT CAPTURED THE WORLD

In its 2007 report the IPCC announced that it was 90 percent confident that "most of the observed increase in globally-averaged temperatures since the mid-20th century" has been caused by human activities rather than natural variation, latent cycles, or chaos. How did it arrive at this modest conclusion, which has itself been exaggerated into claims of climate catastrophe? The use of language about "confidence levels" implies to anyone versed in statistics and science that a calculation has been performed on the variability of the data, and that the chances that the rise in temperature is simply random variation is less than 10 percent. In fact, the IPCC is not using "confidence level" in this traditional statistical sense. The claim of 90 percent certainty is just an informal summary of "expert judgment," and the sole basis cited for this judgment in the 2007 report is the following: "No climate model using natural forcings alone has reproduced the observed global warming trend in the second half of the 20th century."[2] There you have it. The consensus that drives the world's leaders to contemplate dramatic restrictions on the global economy is based on computer models that purport to have isolated a powerful effect for "radiative forcings" from industrial gasses. So, what are these models, and how do they work?[3]

First, it should be noted that the IPCC's sentence is not technically true. Using just a handful of the assumptions, averaged observations, estimated correlations, and mathematical "tuning" techniques that allow it to force a good but by no means perfect fit between modeled and observed temperatures over the past 150 years, the IPCC could easily

---

1 Gore tries to downplay this concern, jumping *non sequitur* to a discussion of how American manufacturers of cleaner technology could prosper from increased demand. They certainly won't be prospering if they can't get any energy to do all that manufacturing.

2 This particular quote is from the section of the 2007 report of the IPCC's Working Group on Physical Science Basis that the IPCC's summaries refer readers to for evidence. This section also states, more broadly: "The fact that climate models are only able to reproduce observed global mean temperature changes over the 20th century when they include anthropogenic forcings, and that they fail to do so when they exclude anthropogenic forcings, is evidence for the influence of humans on global climate."

3 F.W. Taylor provides a general description of the models in his *Elementary Climate Physics*, Oxford University Press, New York, 2005. For their detailed operations, see A. Henderson-Sellers and K. McGuffie, *A Climate Modelling Primer*, John Wiley and Sons, New York, 1987, and for the history of the models, see David Randall, editor, *General Circulation Model Development*, Academic Press, New York, 2000, and Spencer Weart, *The Discovery of Global Warming*, Harvard University Press, Cambridge, MA, 2003.

find as good a fit using baseball statistics, presidents' heights, or solar variations. Complex correlation models can recreate beautifully the rise and fall of the stock market, but they soon lead to disaster if one buys stocks based on their predictions about tomorrow, let alone the 100 years typically reported for climate models, either because the correlations were not causations, or because new factors modify their future impact. What the IPCC is really saying is that it cannot find a theoretical reason to manipulate natural forcings, such as solar variations, long-term oscillations like the North Atlantic and the Pacific Decadal, or complex feedback mechanisms from minor natural changes, into accounting for the movement of global mean temperature. MIT's Lindzen has caustically labeled the IPCC's logic "proof by lassitude."

Given the fact that the huge changes in temperature that accompany the Milankovich cycles are currently inexplicable, the IPCC's claim that it understands the causes of tiny changes in modern temperatures is dubious. The claim is even more questionable because it has been made consistently by advocates of global warming theory for 40 years, regardless of the credibility of the models being used. In 1979 advocate Jule Charney issued a report for the National Academy of Sciences based on crude one-dimensional models that has both guided and been repeated by complex three-dimensional models ever since. Charney endorsed a "climate sensitivity" of six degrees for a doubling of carbon dioxide levels and argued that that there were no "overlooked or underestimated physical affects that could reduce (the sensitivity) to negligible proportions."[1] The models were poor representations of reality then, and are poor representations of it now, despite the 40 years of new "physical affects" that have been incorporated into them. Oxford's Taylor politely reminds readers that the models are in their "infancy," but given the complexity and randomness of climate responses, it is possible that they will never grow up.

Climate models are mathematical representations of the inter-workings of all the potential influences on the climate. They were originally developed for the Defense Department after World War II by Janos (John) von Neumann, a famed Budapest and then Princeton mathematician, computer developer, and game theorist. The goal was to create a "general circulation model" (GCM) of the movement of air, heat, clouds, and rain by simultaneously solving fundamental differential equations for the conservation of mass, momentum, and energy in a particular box of air, and then solving them again and again in subsequent time period as the boxes interacted. A successful model would have allowed the government to understand the climate over the Soviet Union so it could be disrupted to undermine communist rule. The project was a failure. It proved impossible to predict the conditions that formed clouds or caused rain, so controlling them to create droughts or floods was out of the question. However, when paired with judgments from weather experts, the models allowed improved local forecasting for a few days, and began to be incorporated by television stations.

A small band of modelers continued to add complexity to the models as computing power increased in the 1950s and 1960s, and used them to contemplate, again without

---

1   David Randall, editor, *General Circulation Model Development*, Academic Press, New York, 2000, p. 136. See also Spencer Weart, *The Discovery of Global Warming*, Harvard University Press, Cambridge, MA, 2003.

much success, the causes of the remarkable changes and patterns in temperature visible in the ice core and terrain records from the "paleo-climate" of the past million and even the past hundreds of millions of years. The models were also used by opponents of Reagan's missile plans to promote fears of a "nuclear winter" that might result from the dust generated by a massive nuclear war. A consensus that the models were worth using as predictors of future climate only developed with repetition of the claim, particularly during the hot summer in Washington, DC, of 1988 by NASA official James Hansen, who testified before Gore's committee.[1] GCM now stands for global climate model, a change that recognizes both the advances in providing a global rather than local forecast and adding approximations of numerous physical processes in the oceans, ice, and land, as well as the failure of the models to predict local conditions. GCMs now accept that their predictions for any particular spot for any particular time are incorrect, and are rather intended to provide average estimates for the distant future. Tellingly, the IPCC's modelers refuse to use the word "prediction," and instead say that they are providing "scenarios" for the possible outcomes of "story lines" of different levels of population, economic growth, emissions, land clearance, and other human activities, which are themselves difficult to predict.

Today's modelers divide the oceans, land, and skies into boxes and then mathematically solve rate of flow equations that estimate what would happen in that box, on average and based on previous measurements, in a period of 30 minutes to such variables as temperature, pressure, humidity, wind speed, energy, and mass when natural and man-made elements enter it. The smaller the box, the more boxes there must be to represent the globe, and the greater the computing time required to run a model into the past, or the future. Boxes in the air are usually 70 miles in length and width, and the atmosphere is divided vertically into perhaps 20 levels of varying heights. The sea, the land, and the ice are divided into roughly similar boxes. Given these box sizes, obviously these are not models of what happens to individual carbon dioxide molecules after they absorb energy, but rather are models of average responses. After the changes are estimated for all the variables in all the boxes for one time period, the boxes themselves provide new inputs to their neighbors for the next time period, and then all the boxes are calculated again. This process is repeated for the desired period, usually the past or future hundred years.

The IPCC persistently claims that these models are more valid as representations of the past and predictors of the future than social science models, because they are based on equations of physics rather than on theorized correlations. This claim is simply nonsense, as is made clear in the technical annexes that accompany the IPCC reports. The dream of modelers of both short-term weather and long-term climate is to make sound predictions just from equations representing the laws of physics, such as the speed with which heat moves in a vacuum at various levels of pressure. This is a fleeting dream because the probabilities of both normal distributions and quantum physics preclude certainty in any physical response at the atomic level, even before one factors in the many interactive combinations of the thousands of important variables that determine temperature, humidity, wind

---

1 Spencer Weart, *The Discovery of Global Warming*, Harvard University Press, Cambridge, MA, 2003. The dean of the modeling efforts was Akio Arakawa of UCLA.

speed, or energy for an atmospheric or ocean box of any size.[1] Also, the raw equations of physics do not produce reliable interactions, so modelers must observe in the real world, and then replicate in the model, how much impact variables have on each other on average in various combinations, and then factor these results into the mathematics of the model.

Such a result is called a parameter, and it is directly analogous to a coefficient of correlation from social science modeling. None of this is dishonest — it is indeed how physical and social scientists alike model complex phenomena — but it is misrepresented, not by the modelers, who are all too aware of and actively discuss the limitations they are trying to address, but by the IPCC and the leaders of the global warming camp. Proposing parameters is just one of the many "tuning" techniques used by the modelers, first so that the model will not run away to rapid boiling or freezing and second to tune their output until it reproduces a nice match with previous temperatures. The models initially predicted far too much heating from human activity, so much so that they were obviously incomplete and even wrong in their physics. The modelers returned to the fray, identifying more and more variables to include, but this only increased the number of parameters and interactions. As a result, the models are now so complex as to be what Taylor, again politely, calls "opaque." Modeling has become a fascinating exercise in theory and curve-fitting, constantly informed by scientists' new thoughts about factors in creating climate, but it is not "science" the way that word is commonly understood, and there is no "consensus" about its track record for recreating the past and little certainty about its strength for predicting the future.[2]

---

1 Gore of all people should be sensitive to the role of chance, whether in creating weather in the short-term and then climate in the long term, or in politics. The famous truism that a butterfly flapping its wings in one part of the world can lead to a hurricane elsewhere appears to have found its political expression in the decision by Palm Beach County in the 2000 presidential election to use a "butterfly" ballot, which places in the middle of the page all the punch choices for two separate columns. This decision was not extended to the absentee ballot. The fact that election-day voters in Palm Beach supported Buchanan, whose punch hole appeared quite close to Gore's, at four times the rate of absentee voters, an aberration not even remotely approached in other counties once their size is accounted for, offers strong support for the hypothesis that the butterfly siphoned off about 2,000 Gore voters to Buchanan and gave Florida and the White House to Bush. The hurricane from this butterfly has since been felt in Iraq, since it is unlikely that Gore's response to the Al Qaeda attacks on American soil in 2001 would have been to invade a country with no hand in the attacks. Of course, an even stranger case of chance kept Gore out of the presidency as well: the person counting the votes in the contested state was his opponent's brother!

2 The politicization of the scientific component of the climate debate adds another layer of weakness to the modeling effort. The complex calculation of the actual global mean temperatures that the models try to replicate is conducted by the very IPCC characters who run the models and make and advocate for policy prescriptions. If another difficult but important variable, the consumer price index, was calculated each year by the modelers in Congress and the administration who try to predict it into the future to make their proposed budgets meet artificial deficit targets there would be an understandable outcry from the millions of retirees whose income is determined by the calculation. Instead, to preserve credibility, the Labor department isolates away from all political pressures an economic unit of career employees that manages the methodology and calculates this particular rate of inflation.

The various IPCC "story lines" produce "scenarios" of increases in temperature of three to eight degrees over the next century. By now, though, such predictions are almost definitional: they follow from the "sensitivity" included in the model, which is based on hypothesized "radiative forcing" formulas for greenhouse gasses that themselves have been generated by tuned models. Carbon dioxide's current saturation levels in the atmosphere make temperature's response to it not linear, or steady, but by the square root. This means that increased carbon dioxide has less and less of an effect on temperature, because its heat-trapping effect has already captured most of the escaping energy at its particular frequency. How will this relationship change at higher concentrations? How much more carbon dioxide can the massive and crucial sink of the oceans absorb than its current 50 percent of emissions? How quickly will the winds take the excess heat from equator to poles, as they go through the three major "Hadley cells" of circulation to get there? Will hotter air lead to a feedback of cooling, as more clouds result from more humidity, and increase the albedo, the 30 percent of solar radiation that is reflected before entering the earth's energy balance? Or will hotter air create enough water vapor to trap more heat than is being reduced by the increased albedo from more clouds? The possible variety in answers to all of these questions dwarfs the modeled impact of increased industrial gasses. Recent suggestions about the possibly major role in Arctic and glacial heating of black soot from cooking fires in poor countries poses yet another fundamental challenge to the models, which include little effect for this non-industrial emission. If a model is validated by a past fit without a major factor, how can a future "scenario" be based on such an incorrect model?

Lindzen has been pointing out for 20 years that the models assume a positive feedback at a two-to-one ratio, meaning that they find human-generated gasses directly account for only one-third of the one-degree rise in global mean temperature since 1860, and then attribute the other two-thirds of a degree to warming caused by increased water vapor that itself resulted from the initial warming. He has published studies finding that increased cloudiness and increased rates of escaping radiation have created a negative, rather than a positive, feedback to increased temperatures.[1] Such suggestive work is no reason to discard the models; in fact it is all the more reason to work on them. But it is also reason to be cautious with the ranges of response they indicate. According to the IPCC, model "sensitivity," or the range of temperature response used by most modelers to represent the effect of a doubling of carbon dioxide, has remained at Charney's initial rough estimate of six degrees, with an error range of from three to eight degrees, for the past 30 years. When the range for a crucial input is roughly equal to the size of its mean prediction, one should be cautious about the using the prediction as the basis for public policy.

As noted previously, the best estimates for the path of global mean temperature over the past 150 years show how tricky looking for causality between carbon dioxide and temperature can be. The one-degree rise in temperature emerges from a complex and perhaps chaotic history, with half of it coming during a sharp rise from 1910 until 1940, before

---

1 Richard Lindzen, "Resisting Climate Hysteria," *Quadrant Online*, July 26, 2009; Lindzen, Yong-Sang Choi, "On the Determination of Climate Feedbacks from ERBE Data," *Geophysical Research Letters*, Vol. 36, August 26, 2009.

there was enough of an increase in carbon dioxide to make even a theoretical difference in temperature, followed by a cooling trend for 40 years, despite the massively increased carbon dioxide from the unprecedented industrialization after World War II, and finally a resurgence from 1980 to 2000 that brought the other half of the total rise before reaching a plateau in the most recent decade. The modelers attribute the first half of the rise to unusually high solar activity and the second half to human-generated gasses, but are somewhat perplexed by the two pauses.

In the stolen emails from the "climate-gate" affair of 2009, the IPCC's lead author on physical science, Kevin Trenberth, apparently admitted as much to his colleagues in discussing the pause in measured warming from 1999 to 2009, which flatly contradicted the models' predictions of a significant rise of about half a degree: "The fact is that we can't account for the lack of warming at the moment and it is a travesty that we can't." Since the core of the IPCC's "90 percent confidence" is the ability of its models to recreate the past climate, his admission should have been troubling for catastrophists. Of course, it was not, since the division of people's opinions about the importance of the leaked emails perfectly correlated with their previous position on climate change. The IPCC and its apologists dismissed the plateau by saying that the past decade was the hottest in the past 1,000 years, but this claim, even if measurements were good enough before 1850 to assess it, is meaningless as proof of human impact. Of course at the top of a cycle there is maximum heat, and global means do not change more than a bit of a degree in any year, so once there is a high period, there are a lot of high years. It certainly could be that the swings in the last 150 years represents some complex process of equilibrium that absorbs an increase, rests, and starts up again. Still, a rise or fall of one degree in 150 years is not at all extraordinary during the current, 15,000-year climb of 10 degrees that, as noted, will "soon" turn into the next swing down. None of us will be around long enough to see whether the "scenarios" come true, and even then there will be no way of telling if the scenario was the result of natural variation or human-based emissions. It would have been nice if von Neumann's idea had worked out — except for people living in the Soviet Union, of course — but it didn't.

PART III. REFORMS AND REVOLUTIONS

CHAPTER 11. ELECTORAL REFORMS: SHACKLING THE EAGLE, FREEING THE TURKEY

If human rights, foreign aid, and "global warming" are distractions, then what is the right way to address the real issue in foreign policy, and change the intent of US foreign policy from domination to cooperation, and its impact from repression to liberation? What should Turkeys be promoting to bring about such a change? The answer is two-fold: structural changes in an electoral system that favors the Eagles and a cultural assault on the attitudes and myths that promote American domination. This chapter presents three electoral reforms that would stunt the neo-imperial project, the next rejects campaign finance reform and proposes instead an effort to disband the union and deprive it of its power to dominate others, and the final three outline plans for changing attitudes, a far more important task, whatever the structure and electoral rules of the United States. The three electoral reforms are:

- a change in the House to proportional representation, which would allow the anti-imperial minority to be represented by a third party in Congress, and as a result in the national debate;
- a reduction of the powers of the undemocratic Senate, which by having two votes for each state, regardless of population, gives 35 percent more power to white, imperial voters who live disproportionately in small states at the expense of black, less interventionist ones, who live disproportionately in large ones; and
- an end to the system of presidential electors, whose undemocratic weighting of states' votes to include one for each senator provided Bush with his margin of victory in the 2000 election, despite receiving a lower popular vote than Gore. Even its House-based votes are undemocratic, because their distribution can be up to 10 years behind the census on which it is based.

Achieving proportional representation would require only changes in law, at both the federal and state level, although a constitutional amendment could also set the rules for

House elections. The other reforms would almost certainly require constitutional amendment. A tall order — except when compared to trying to end US domination without such structural changes. If the same effort by Turkeys went into pushing these changes as goes into the never-ending fights against individual wars and weapons, let alone against ephemeral "climate change," success on some of them might well be possible in the next decade. Even having a discussion about the reason why the evil of empire requires such changes would elevate Turkeys' concerns in the mainstream political arena.

CHOOSE THE HOUSE THROUGH PROPORTIONAL REPRESENTATION

A poll in 2009 found that 16 percent of Americans identified themselves as progressive, as opposed to liberal, moderate, conservative, or libertarian.[1] Support for the proposition that the United States "mind its own business" rose from 18 percent in 1964 to 41 percent by the end of the Vietnam War, then slid down to 30 percent in 2002 before rebounding to 49 percent in 2009.[2] The public is evenly split on whether the United States has a right to use force to stop another country from acquiring nuclear weapons.[3] These polls affirm something that is apparent from the abundance of coffee houses, book stores, websites, and organizations promoting an anti-imperialist point of view: the United States contains a fair number of Turkeys. However, the House of Representatives consists almost entirely of Hard and Soft Eagles. In recent years there have been only a few true anti-interventionists, such as Republicans Ron Paul and Walter Jones Jr. and Democrats Dennis Kucinich and Barbara Lee. They are kept at the absolute fringe of power by their party leaders. Indeed, Jones was disciplined with the loss of his committee seniority when his disgust at being duped about Saddam Hussein's weapons of mass destruction led him to come out against the war in Iraq. How did this lack of representation come to pass, and what can be done to correct it?

Members of the US House are chosen at the state level in single-member districts under a "winner-take-all" rule. To Americans who have known nothing else, this seems like the only way to choose a national legislature. However, there are many other ways of doing so, and in fact the United States is among the very few countries where winner-take-all, single-member seats are used rather than proportional representation through at-large or multiple-member seats.[4] Of the 36 countries with more than two million people that were judged by Freedom House to be fully free in 1998, 30 used proportional representation.[5] Canada, Great Britain, and France join the United States among the holdouts. The election methods for proportional representation include counting single or multiple votes by each voter for multiple-member districts or at-large seats as well as preference

1 "State of American Political Ideology," Center for American Progress, March 2009.
2 See Survey Report, Pew Research Center, December 3, 2009.
3 Project on International Policy Attitudes, 2003.
4 Douglas Amy, "A Brief History of Proportional Representation in the United States," available at http://www.mtholyoke.edu/acad/polit/damy/articles/Brief%20History%20 of%20PR.htm, based on "The Forgotten History of the Single Transferable Vote in the United States," in *Representation* v. 34, no. 1, Winter 1996/7.
5 Robert Richie and Steven Hill, "The Case for Proportional Representation," *Boston Review*, February/March 1998; available on the Fairvote website.

voting (also known as single transferable balloting or instant runoff voting), in which a voter ranks the candidates and lower-ranked candidate receive votes if a higher-ranked one has either passed a threshold to election or failed to cross a threshold staving off defeat.

In seeking the majority needed to win each seat, the Democratic and Republican parties naturally gravitate toward independent voters who "swing" between the two. The parties' foreign policies reflect the mood, rather than some articulated philosophy, at this center point of the electorate. The stranglehold of the two-party system in America was not at all expected by the Founders, who generally abhorred parties and feared their populist appeals, and it certainly was not pre-ordained. By the mid-19th century, though, parties were so popular and powerful that even the disintegration of the Whigs over their refusal to oppose the expansion of slavery simply led to the creation of a new party, the Republicans. Since those days of Lincoln the two main parties have been institutionalized at the local, state, and national levels, and their control of the political process has become a self-fulfilling machine. The essential tool they use to maintain control is the single member congressional district — something that is not enshrined or even considered in the Constitution. The effect of single-member districts is to exclude from government advocates of minority viewpoints, including the minority of Americans who hold firmly non-interventionist and anti-imperial beliefs. Indeed, it was a fear of blacks and communists being represented by small parties that led the two major parties to eliminate proportional representation in the early 20th century, when it was widely used in the United States, including in House elections.

Massachusetts governor and later US vice president Elbridge Gerry has his name enshrined in political history because after his party redrew district lines to their advantage in 1812, one of the districts was credibly portrayed by a cartoonist as having the shape of a salamander.[1] However, he was neither the first nor the last politician to understand the importance of drawing the lines. Today Gerrymandering (and please say that with a hard G) is a computerized art form and politico-legal war that every ten years, after the national census shows where the bodies reside, offers a delicious opportunity for state legislators to favor their parties' incumbents as they navigate a variety of complex, conflicting, and much argued laws and court decisions that require roughly equal populations in districts and a fair chance for minority ethnic groups to elect representatives in proportion to their share of their state's population.

The mischief the parties do in this pursuit is legendary, and its variations are legion. National parties pour money into the state parties to win majorities in the states' legislative bodies, and then federal candidates pour in money and favors for state legislators to win support for having their boundaries packed with a majority of their supporters. The result is that most House seats are "safe" for a particular party, so that election to the House effectively takes place in the primaries, and not the general election. The parties have one goal: to capture a House majority, so that they can control the floor and the committees and set the agenda. They eschew candidates whose foreign policy views are

---

1 Gerry lost a re-election bid in part because of the controversy about his over-reaching on the redistricting plan. Similar power grabs by the Democratic Party in California in the 1980s and the Republican Party in Texas in the 1990s also eventually led to public reaction and defeat.

unpopular with the majority, and candidates themselves trim their sails to increase their chance of victory. Once in office, the electoral imperative only grows. The parties and their Members of the House promote a foreign policy profile that tends toward the middle, both of their district and the nation, to preserve their seats and their chance for a majority.

Breaking the strangle-hold of the parties and their imperial orientation requires the end of single-member districts in favor of a proportional system that allows smaller parties to win their share of seats. This would require no change in either the federal character of the United States or the Constitution, which leaves election rules to the states. There are many methods of conducting proportional elections for the states to choose from, but in general to win 20 percent of the seats, which in a state with five seats means one seat, a party would have to win 20 percent of the vote. Assuming the general accuracy of the poll showing that 16 percent of Americans identify themselves as progressive, this means that in the 24 states with from one to five members of the House, proportional representation would not guarantee an anti-imperial party any seats. However, these 24 states have only 64 members in all. Assuming that progressives are spread smoothly around the country, a 16 percent share of the other 371 House seats would result in 59 representatives of an anti-imperialist party holding office, or 14 percent of all the seats.

Proponents of single-member districts will protest that the system provides an advocate within the government for the particular needs of local officials and citizens. Indeed, many Americans have come to rely on their House member to seek federal support for regional rather than statewide projects, and to intervene with the federal bureaucracy on missing social security checks and the immigration status of their relatives. However, in practice, such "constituent service" adds little real value to what citizens could achieve by contacting federal departments or their senators. It also further distracts legislators, who already spend their best intellectual energies raising money for their and their party's electioneering. Staff time devoted to sending home flags, nudging along federal grants, and giving tours of the Capitol is more an investment in re-election than a fundamental purpose of government. However, if constituents feel they must have a House advocate, rather than or in addition to a Senate one, they might actually fare better by picking an advocate from a broader range of at-large legislators, by choosing one whose party and political preferences predispose them to be of assistance.

In any case, even at-large systems can still provide a direct connection with a single local representative. In South Africa, the parliament is apportioned by party percentages at the province and federal levels, but the parties agree informally, based on local returns, to appoint members to represent certain areas. In Germany, half of the seats are based on winner-take-all and so provide a constituent connection, but the number and distribution of at-large seats is adjusted to make up for the exclusion of minority parties in the constituent seats, so that the overall representation is proportional to the national vote. Given that the House's 435-seat limit was set in 1911 and American's population in the states has increased more than three times over in the past 100 years, there are strong grounds for emulating the German model, and expanding the House to 1,380 members as if the population of the average district had been held constant. Today's 435 members would be elected in districts, and the remainder would be apportioned to achieve proportional representation at the state level. However, a less cumbersome approach would be simply to retain the current number of representatives under an at-large system, and use House rules to award additional voting power for Members on the floor and in committee based on their party's proportion of the national vote.

The one problem that will bedevil schemes for proportional representation in the House is what W. E. B. Dubois clairvoyantly called in 1903 "the problem of the 20th century...the problem of the color line." At-large districts are currently prohibited by a federal law passed in 1967 because of concerns by both proponents and opponents of black representation in Congress. After enactment of the Voting Rights Act in 1965 southern Members of the House feared that courts would rule, accurately, that the current seats had been Gerrymandered to give whites a majority in each one, and order at-large elections. Conversely, proponents of black representation were fearful that white-dominated legislatures would then set voting rules with which white voters would still be able to win all the seats.[1] For example, a requirement in a five-member state with a 60 percent white majority that voters cast five votes, for different candidates, could be used to elect an all-white slate if all white voters voted for the same five. In contrast, permitting voters to give all their five votes to one or two candidates would virtually assure that the 40 percent black minority would win their two seats.

The 1967 law, like so much of national law and court precedent on federalism since the founding, is of questionable constitutionality, although in the end constitutionality is less an abstract concept than a matter of whatever has been decided by the latest Supreme Court.[2] The Voting Rights Act has been successful in forcing white-dominated legislatures to draw black-majority districts, and in giving African-Americans their fair ten percent share of House seats. Representative Mel Watt's bill that would end the ban on at-large districts recognizes this by requiring that the Justice department ensure that at-large plans protect these gains from the era of segregation. Overseeing the integration of the twin goals of proportional representation and the protection of ethnic minorities' voting power will require the development of careful schemes that could well have to vary in each situation.

As with any policy recognizing the reality of ethnic power struggles in an America whose white majority likes to think of itself as color-blind, these schemes would generate controversy. Many have already been developed in the writings of former NAACP lawyer and Harvard Law professor Lani Guinier, whose nomination to the Justice department in 1993 was withdrawn by President Clinton after he chose not to contest right-wing misportrayals of her as a "quota queen" who wanted to guarantee a certain number of seats for black politicians. Ironically, some of her most caustic critics, like Lally Weymouth, the daughter of the publishers of the *Washington Post*, had called for such guarantees for the

---

1 See William V. Flores' chapter on the Baker law in his historical review at Fairvote's website, http://archive.fairvote.org/library/history/flores/district.htm.

2 The 1967 law itself appears to contradict a 1941 law on what should occur if a state legislature fails to agree on a redistricting plan. See David C. Huckabee, "Congressional Redistricting: Is At-Large Representation Permitted in the House of Representatives?," Congressional Research Service, CRS RS21585, August 7, 2003.

white minority in South Africa during its transition to democracy, a call that was firmly rejected by Nelson Mandela and the African National Congress.[1]

The voting behavior of the 40-member Black Caucus, and the 80-member Progressive Caucus to which most belong, shows why anti-imperialists should form a new party to take advantage of a change to at-large elections, rather than continue to back progressive candidates within the Democratic Party. African-Americans are historically the most anti-interventionist of America's ethnic groups. Their most prominent public intellectuals — including Martin Luther King Jr., Stokely Carmichael, Marcus Garvey, Malcolm X, and Julian Bond — have been anti-imperialist by instinct, from mistrust of white claims of devotion to others' freedom, and by their analysis of the capitalist underpinnings of US collusion with local elites in the drive for domination. Only 29 percent of African-Americans percent favored invading Iraq, as opposed to 78 percent of whites. Starting in 1960, after candidate Kennedy's simple expression of concern over the jailing of Martin Luther King Jr., and continuing through the increasing identification of the party with civil rights and social programs, blacks have become reliable voters for the Democratic party, ironically the former party of "states rights" and segregation, at a rate of over 90 percent.[2] Yet even in heavily black districts, anti-imperialists are unlikely to form a majority, so single-member districting brings Soft Eagles, not Turkeys, to Washington. The Black Caucus can be counted on to join its progressive white mates from big cities and college towns in opposing most US military interventions, but when such a stance endangers the Democratic Party as a whole and its domestic agenda, both groups invariably fold.

After four years of voting against Bush's "supplemental" requests for funding the wars in Iraq and Afghanistan while the Republican majority and conservative Democrats easily passed them, after the Democrats took the House in 2007 opponents of the war suddenly found themselves in a position of apparent power. Speaker Nancy Pelosi, herself one of them, needed their votes to pass all manner of legislation on the war and rules allowing the consideration of that legislation, because of solid Republican opposition to the minimal restrictions she had placed in the bills. In theory, the anti-war liberals, and indeed the Black Caucus alone, could have blocked funding for a "surge" in the Iraq war by denying a majority to both the Democratic and Republican plans. As noted in Chapter 7, Pelosi's superb political nose told her that if the liberals blocked funding for the surge in an initial vote, in the end, even though it might take months, she would lose not just the vote on the funding, but perhaps also effective control of the House. Bush would veto any Pentagon funding bill that blocked his "surge," and when the money began to run out, conservative and centrist Democrats would feel the heat and join Republicans in backing Bush's original request. With a defeat like that, Pelosi might have lost control of her ability to control the House, ceding it on both domestic and foreign policy to the sort of Republican-Dixie coalition that took control away from Speaker Tip O'Neill in 1981.

---

1 See Guinier's response to Weymouth, in her piece "Challenge to the Press." http://www.fair.org/extra/best-of-extra/guinier-queen.html.

2 The story of the 1960 conversion is told in detail in Chapter 9 of Taylor Branch's masterful history, *Parting the Waters: America in the King Years, 1954-1963*, Simon & Schuster, New York, 1988.

House member Bill Delahunt of Massachusetts, an early and leading opponent of the war in Iraq, explained why liberals like him felt compelled to back Pelosi's judgment: "Pragmatism set in. There would be sufficient funding in the pipeline" for Bush's plans for Iraq thanks to creative Pentagon budgeting, so "nothing was going to change until we had a new president." As far as being accused of voting for the Iraq war by supporting Pelosi's ploys, he and other opponents could point to their vote against the 2002 authorization. Given the size and breadth of the Pentagon's programs, "there is never a 'war funding' bill," but only bills that also include "items essential to progressive policies" and district needs, so that liberals can credibly say "I felt compelled to vote for a bill like this." In any event, Delahunt noted, "we knew we couldn't win a get-out vote, even with the declining enthusiasm because of US casualties," so why "take a political hit" for not supporting the troops, let alone for shutting down the Pentagon, if it would have no impact on the ground? Indeed, Carl Levin, a war opponent and chair of the Senate Armed Services committee, had publicly acknowledged even before Bush made his "surge" request that in the end, Congress would give Bush his money.

The "political hit" Delahunt wanted to avoid was not one he would feel in his safe district. If anything, he had been hit from the left, not the right, on the war, by protestors who occupied his office to protest him not doing more to end the war. His concern was for losing majority control of the House in the coming election: "Any vote, it goes beyond the issue at hand. There are repercussions for health care, civil liberties, the environment. In the majority, you set the agenda, you influence the debate." As an example, Delahunt pointed out that his Republican predecessor as chair of a Foreign Affairs oversight subcommittee "held zero hearings on Iraq" or torture and rendition, while he himself held dozens, including the ones so damaging to Bush's plans for a long-term US presence in Iraq, as recounted in Chapter 7.[1] Delahunt's perspective was shared by the Black and Progressive Caucuses, and in vote after vote they helped Pelosi pass rules for floor debate that allowed them to register their opposition to her slightly-modified versions of Bush's war requests without actually blocking their passage. Controlling the House was deemed more important than challenging the war with all available means. Soft Eagle George Miller is fond of saying, "Before you can save the world, you have to save your seat," and this necessary belief in one's importance is magnified by the majority imperative into, "before you can save the world, you have to save your majority."

When Obama took office and asked for funds to conduct his own surges in Afghanistan, the anti-war Democrats found themselves in an even more dangerous game of chicken with a president of their own party, and they had to blink even more dramatically. In June 2009, 20 of them who had voted against a supplemental war appropriation when it had passed in May with Republican support provided the margin of victory for the bill when it returned from the Senate with the addition of funding for the IMF, which had led Republicans to oppose it. Similarly, in December 2009, Senator Russ Feingold reversed his opposition to the consideration of an "irresponsible and misguided" military appropriation in one of the rare circumstances in which his opposition could have, at least temporarily, stopped such a bill. Republicans had decided to filibuster the military bill as

---

1 Interview, January 13, 2010.

a way of delaying consideration of health care reform until after Christmas. Feingold was roundly cheered by even the most anti-war senators when he announced in the Democratic caucus that he would vote to consider the defense bill so as to block the Republican ploy.

Would members from a third party, with an anti-imperialist platform, have been as willing as anti-war Democrats to facilitate continued funding for the wars? It is impossible to say until the politics of the third party are tested in an at-large system. Certainly the anti-imperialists would understand the logic of the anti-war Democrats who swallowed the war rules and votes because of the importance of blocking Republican control of the House and passing important domestic reforms and programs. If they did accede to the wars, though, they couldn't count on re-election, unlike Delahunt and his Democratic colleagues, because they would be depending on the support of the minority in their state who cared most deeply about stopping foreign wars. The electoral imperative would weigh more heavily on their minds to the extent that they were unable to convince their narrow electoral base, as opposed to Democrats' broader base, that the deal was worth making.

While proportional representation in the House could be achieved without a constitutional amendment, it would fundamentally alter the way Americans conduct elections. It is therefore probably advisable to package at-large districting into an amendment that clears up confusion and defuses possible court challenges. Significant changes in governance have occurred outside the Constitution both through practice and constitutionally questionable laws and court decisions. The American people, through conventions or their legislatures as provided by the Constitution, deserve to have the opportunity to hear and decide on the case for at-large districts. The other reforms described below would certainly require amendments, so the changes proposed for the House could be packaged into them in a single amendment designed to redefine democracy as appropriate for today's circumstances, and not those of 1787.

MAKE THE SENATE CEREMONIAL, LIKE THE HOUSE OF LORDS

In general, non-white ethnic groups are more liberal and anti-war than whites, and as the percentage of non-white Americans increases from one third in 2010 to one half in 2040 (after being only one-tenth in 1960), the House will tend to become more anti-imperial with or without a shift to at-large elections. In the Senate, though, a great train wreck is coming, because it will get less, rather than more, representative of the country in both members and voting pattern as an unintended result of the Great Compromise of 1787. The original "Virginia plan" brought to the constitutional convention by James Madison featured both a House and Senate in which each state had at least one member, but larger states had more, in proportion to their population. The small states of the day — such as New Jersey, Connecticut, Maryland, and Delaware — refused to accept union on that basis, given that under the Articles of Confederation each state had the same voting power. This standoff led to the compromise in which the House is a democratic body while the Senate provides the states with equal power, regardless of population. The compromise unintentionally favors white voters and an imperial foreign policy because less imperial non-white voters, for a variety of historical reasons largely related to discrimination in land ownership and capital, tend to be congregated in states with larger cities and hence larger populations.

A measure of the impact of this unintended distortion is a calculation, using census data from 2000, of "power for the average black" and "power for the average white." This is obtained by first calculating the power of each resident of a state, which is two senators divided by the number of residents who share them. A resident of Wyoming has a "power" score 69 times that of a resident of California, because there are 69 times as many people in California to share the same two senators. Then the power score for each state is multiplied by the number of white residents in those states, to provide a power total for whites in the state, and the sum of those power totals is divided by the total number of white people in the 50 states, to provide a figure showing "power for the average white." Similarly, the state power score is multiplied by the number of black people in a state, and the sum of these 50 state totals is divided by the total number of black people in the 50 states, to provide a measure of "power for the average black."

The ratio of the white and black power scores is 1.35, meaning that the 194 million white people have, on average, 35 percent more power than the 34 million black people on the Senate floor.[1] The figure is almost identical for the 10 million Asians, at 36 percent, and for the largest non-white group, the 35 million Hispanics, the disparity is even worse: the average white has 76 percent more power. For the 15 million people identifying themselves as "some other race," the figure is 80 percent. These imbalances will only get more pronounced with time, since minorities are growing much faster than whites, and there is no indication that they will stop concentrating in large states. In fact, the concentration is likely to get stronger. In 2040 an America that is 50 percent non-white will likely be faced with a Senate that is virtually all white and almost as disproportionately inclined toward white policy preferences, like domination.

The obvious constitutional fix for this problem, a return to the Virginia plan, would, strangely, itself be unconstitutional. An amendment to make the Senate democratic would require ratification not by the usual three-fourths of state legislatures, but, effectively, all of them. As part of the Great Compromise, the drafters put in a poison pill to protect the large states from reneging once the Constitution was in operation: "No state shall be deprived of its equal representation in the Senate without its consent." This is the only such barrier to amendment in the Constitution, although Congress was also prohibited from passing any laws constraining the slave trade until 1808. It is conceivable that all the state legislatures would comply under a credible threat of something worse. In 1911 British Prime Minister Herbert Asquith, with the concurrence of cabinet member Winston Churchill, was frustrated by the resistance of the hereditary, thoroughly antique, and undemocratic House of Lords to legislation promoting social welfare. He convinced the Lords that if they did not voluntarily relinquish their equal power with the democratic House of Commons, he would have King George appoint hundreds of additional Lords,

---

1 Including the predominantly non-white residents of the territories (Puerto Rico, the District of Columbia, the Virgin Islands, Samoa, and Guam) would make the figure even higher, but they have no vote in the Senate in any event. All data drawn from the 2000 census, at http://www.census.gov/population/www/cen2000/briefs/phc-t6/index.html.

from the commonest and most radical of backgrounds. This did the trick, and the Lords agreed to vote themselves into the largely ceremonial body they are today.[1] An American example is President Franklin Roosevelt's 1937 threat to "pack" the Supreme Court with an additional justice for every one of the six who had reached the age of 70 and refused to retire. This proposal came after the court found some of his depression-era economic laws unconstitutional. The proposal was defeated in the Senate, but in a number of important cases the court began to back off its harsh stance against new federal programs and powers.

The threat in this case should be a constitutional amendment to turn the Senate into a sort of House of Lords, with severely limited policy powers. As part of a compromise to win the support of 33 state delegations and achieve the two-thirds of the Senate needed to pass an amendment, the Senate could be offered a few of its current privileges, such as consenting to nominations, and be allowed to hold up non-spending bills for a few months. Faced with a devil's choice between two amendments, one for democratic representation and one for an emasculated Senate, perhaps all the legislatures of the small states will provide their consent. The eventual surrender of every member of the European Union to its Lisbon Treaty, completed by the signature of recalcitrant president Vaclav Klaus of the Czech Republic in 2009 in return for an "opt-out" clause on its human rights provisions, implies that such a development is not impossible. However, if one small state balks, then three-fourths of the legislatures could adopt the other amendment providing for a ceremonial Senate. In either case, control over policy would be returned to the majority, which by 2040 will mean a non-white, less imperial majority.

The winnowing of the Senate's power by constitutional amendment is itself a sneaky way of evading the clear spirit of the Constitution. It should still be done. What is "constitutional" is both simple and complex. A 5-4 majority of the Supreme Court is the simple answer, while the complex answer is anything that is necessary to deliver on the often-contradictory promises of the Constitution and the "penumbra" of natural rights and federal necessities that courts have found implicit in its omissions. In addition, Lincoln's perspective during the trauma of the Civil War and the transition from slavery to freedom has incorporated into considerations of constitutionality both the purposes of the Declaration of Independence as well as the oath of office of the president to "preserve, protect, and defend" the Constitution. Hard cases make bad law, as Supreme Court Justice Oliver Wendell Holmes said, and as implied by the Supreme Court's instructions to other courts not to glean any precedents from its decision to stop the Florida courts from directing a recount in the 2000 presidential election.

The United States operates with a separation of power more than a separation of powers. All three branches struggle to establish their power over every area of policy, and so constitutionality is also a political question of what the traffic will bear on a particular issue at any particular time. As the following section on the constitutionally-dubious practices used to elect a president indicates, stranger things have happened than an amendment to evade a prohibition on amending the Great Compromise. In this case, with

---

1 http://www.publications.parliament.uk/pa/ld199798/ldbrief/ldreform.htm provides the Parliament's official history of the reform.

the goal of equal protection for minorities in direct conflict with the goal of equal protection for the states, the need for a fundamental change is so great as to justify the sleight of hand. In contrast, a similar evasion of the Constitution, a proposal to enact a law providing representation in Congress for the residents of the District of Columbia, does not rise to a similarly sufficient level of importance. That proposal seeks to achieve by law what advocates of representation failed to do by a constitutional amendment, which was defeated when not enough states ratified its passage by Congress in 1978. Fortunately, an easy solution to the District's lack of representation exists. All land other than a small section around the mall containing federal buildings could be ceded back to Maryland, just as the Virginia portion of the original District was in 1846.

JETTISON THE ELECTORS

The Founders had a devil of a time getting the selection of a president right, and in fact they got their complicated system of using "electors" rather than the popular vote so wrong that its unintended consequences forced a complete revision within 15 years. The revision itself left in one glaring flaw, a slightly disproportionate weighting of electoral votes in favor of small states by allocating them not just for the number of House members but for the two senators as well. This undemocratic vestige of the Great Compromise periodically plunges the nation into crisis and results in the election of a president who has been defeated in the popular vote. In 1876 the inclusion of the two Senate votes per state resulted in a disputed election being thrown into the House despite a solid margin of popular votes for Democrat Samuel Tilden. The crucial barrier to a Democratic victory was Republican control of the counting of ballots in the disputed election in Florida. Democrats eventually agreed to promote Republican Rutherford Hayes to the presidency in return for the withdrawal of federal troops from the former Confederacy, which ended Reconstruction and ushered in 100 years of segregation. In 2000, strangely again in an election where Republican control of Florida played the pivotal role, George W. Bush won 30 smaller states and their 60 Senate-based votes while Al Gore, the popular vote winner by half a million, only won 20 larger states and the District of Columbia and their 42 Senate-based votes. The 18-vote spread provided Bush with his four-electoral vote margin of victory. A drafting quirk in 1787 caused a war in Iraq that killed over 100,000 people.

How did all this come to pass? It is one of the strangest tales in American history, and it includes state coups that continue to overthrow the Constitution every four years. Fearful of the leveling and passions of a popular vote for a king-like figure, the Founders gravitated in Philadelphia toward the concept of electors, based in part on the princes and archbishops who chose an emperor in the Austro-Hungarian Holy Roman Empire, but without the tinge of royalty or religion. A president would be a respected, non-partisan figure, chosen not by the people, but by other wise men, the electors. And who would these electors be? Proposals at the convention included the governors, people chosen by them or the state legislatures, and either Congress or a selection, by lottery, of its members. Another proposal was for the people of each state to select their "best citizen," and have Congress elect one of them to the presidency. Unable to choose in this hailstorm of ideas, the convention appointed a small committee that only made matters worse. The committee's proposal, which made its way directly into the Constitution, reversed a tentative earlier decision to have Congress elect the president for a single seven-year term, with one vote given to each House and Senate member. The new proposal permitted perpetual election of a "natural born" president by electors chosen at the state level, in the number of the state's House and Senate members and in any fashion the state legislature chose.

After their selection, the electors would meet as what is informally called the electoral college, and each would vote for two different presidential candidates, of whom only one could be from their state. The candidate receiving a majority of the votes would be president, while the candidate with the second most would be vice president. A tie or a multi-candidate race resulting in no candidate receiving a majority would be resolved in the House, where each state's delegation would have one vote, and a majority again would be needed for election.[1] By 1800 the system had produced a disaster. With the unexpected development of political parties, a patently unconstitutional shift had quickly taken place. State legislatures mandated the election not of prominent wise men who would choose a president, which was what had motivated the complex constitutional scheme in the first place, but rather of a slate of electors pledged to vote for the candidates backed by a party. A pair of allied candidates would run for president, and their partisans would vote for electors who pledged to use their two votes for them. This way a winning party would control the presidency even if the president died in office, and in any event would control the vice president's role as presiding officer and tiebreaker in the Senate.

In 1800 most states chose to have their legislatures select the electors, although the use of a state's popular vote for this purpose would soon become universal. It was understood within the Democratic-Republican Party that, as in 1796, Thomas Jefferson was the presidential candidate and Aaron Burr the vice presidential one. However, when the party's victory left him, predictably, tied with Jefferson in electoral votes, the bad boy of the Founders' generation refused to stand down. Burr tried to win the necessary nine votes of the 16 state House delegations with the help of Federalists, but one powerful Federalist, his hated New York rival Alexander Hamilton, "an host unto himself," according to Jefferson, stood against him. Jefferson finally gained the ninth state after 36 ballots, and Burr, hating Hamilton all the more, killed him in a duel three years later.

The constitutional amendment of 1804 that attempted to fix this mess removed the uncertainty about which candidate was standing for which office, but did not confront the obvious subversion of the intent of the Founders by the states as they turned the electors from wise men into ciphers for the popular plurality. As a result, all states today provide voters with a "beauty contest" or "short" ballot that lists the presidential candidates, a few deign to note the fact that "a vote for the candidates will actually be a vote for their electors," and only a handful actually list the electors who have pledged to vote for the candidates. More than half of the states require by law that electors vote as they have pledged, and a few threaten legal penalties for "faithless" electors — actually, those who keep faith with the Founders and the Constitution by voting for the candidate they personally be-

---

1 See Clinton Rossiter, *1787: The Grand Convention*, Macmillan, New York, 1966, pp. 198-200, 218-221, which draws heavily on James Madison's *Notes of Debates in the Federal Convention of 1787*.

lieve will make the best president. The candidate with the plurality of the popular vote in the state receives all of its electoral votes, except in Maine and Nebraska, which follow this rule for their two Senate-based votes but award the House-based votes by plurality in individual congressional districts.

None of this — the substitution of the judgment of the people for that of the electors, the pledging or binding to candidates of "their" electors, the awarding of all electoral votes by state or district to the candidate with the popular plurality — is envisioned in the Constitution, although it can be argued, and courts have held, that it is all implied by the failure of the 1804 amendment to correct the practice of party pledges that was already in evidence.[1] The ease with which the nation accepted the results of Gore's loss in the 2000 election despite his winning the popular vote indicates that this hodge-podge, counter-constitutional system is deeply ingrained and accepted in America's political consciousness. This is unfortunate from the perspective of both democracy and, given that interventionists are disproportionately represented in small states that benefit from the distortion of the Senate-based electoral votes, anti-imperialism.

There is any number of solutions to the problem of the undemocratic impact of Senate-based votes. The most logical is a constitutional amendment establishing a straightforward national voting system based on the popular vote plurality. The Founders' fear of the mood of the populace was quickly discredited with the populace itself, and it is high time to recognize that officially. If the nation is going to go to the trouble of establishing an amendment to use the popular vote as its standard, it should also take the opportunity to substitute a national election commission for the embarrassing mixture of state and county party-based decisions that create a hodge-podge of partisan standards for registering voters and counting votes. When US-funded electoral experts are sent to nations emerging from dictatorship and conflict, they invariable propose the use of a respected, non-partisan national election body to determine eligibility and ensure fair balloting and counting. This sound advice should be applied at home, and end the spectacle of party officials effectively denying the Constitution's guarantee of equal protection by tossing out voters and votes at the state and county level to their partisan benefit. Representative Jesse Jackson Jr., the sponsor a national Right to Vote amendment, makes a strong case that ham-handed efforts by Republican-controlled states to root out former convicts from their voting rolls threw the 2000 election to Bush, because black Americans have criminal records at dramatically higher rates than white Americans.

The National Popular Vote plan offers a way to make the candidate with the plurality the president, without recourse to a constitutional amendment. As of 2010 five states with 61 electoral votes had agreed to cast their electoral votes for the winner of the national plurality if states representing 270, or a majority of the electoral votes, also agree. Although the numbers will vary slightly after the 2010 census, if only the eight largest states also signed up, these 13 states could institute the compact without the agreement of the 37 smaller states and the District of Columbia. As an organizing tool, the plan is brilliant; as a

---

1 See "Faithless Electors: A Wild Card," a December 2000 review of the issue by Professor William G. Ross of Stamford University Law School at *http://jurist.law.pitt.edu/election/electionross4.htm.*

compact it create a social and legal crisis. With or without the approval of Congress under its duty to authorize interstate compacts under Article 1, Section 10, of the Constitution, the compact would immediately be challenged in court by the disagreeing states, and the legitimacy of an elected president would for the first time be widely disputed.[1]

There are two schemes to fix the presidential selection that do not require a constitutional amendment, and would be unlikely to generate a meaningful court challenge or popular rejection. However, they only lessen rather than eliminate the undemocratic danger, and indeed they point out another fundamental flaw in the system of electors, its reliance on dated and so also undemocratic population figures. The first proposal is for states to change their laws to award their electoral votes by proportion, rounding up or down each candidate's share. A candidate winning by a slim margin in a state with, say, 12 electoral votes, would receive seven, and the losing candidate would receive five. While this scheme still provides two additional votes for each state, regardless of population, it would surely reduce the chances of the popular vote winner not taking the majority of electors. However, it would also create chaos unintentionally by throwing most elections with a significant third party into the House for the undemocratic state-by-state vote for president, since the Constitution only allows the winner of a majority, not a plurality of electoral votes to take office. For example, if Gore had surpassed Bush in an electoral vote based on proportions, as is likely, given his popular vote margin, the three votes that Nader's three percent share of the vote would have given him in California and New York would still have kept Gore from the necessary majority, and resulted in Bush's election by the small states in a House run-off.

The other scheme is simply to increase the size of the House by law, as proposed above in the discussion of proportional representation. This would dilute the impact of the two extra votes per state. As noted, if the House today had the same ratio of Members to constituents as in 1911, it would have 1,380 members rather than 435. This would reduce the importance of the 100 Senate-based votes. Applied to the 2000 election, it would have given Gore a lead of about 44 electoral votes rather than the 14 that were then overcome by Bush's 18-vote lead in the Senate-based votes. However, to say that both schemes would have improved the democratic character of the election is to forget that the so-called democratic distribution of House seats and hence electoral votes in 2000 was based not on the relative populations of the states at that time, but in 1990, when the previous census had been taken.

In fact, a dramatic movement of population toward Republican states in the South and West during the 1990s meant that the Democrats received a strong, undemocratic boost in 2000. When the census results from 2000 are applied retroactively, the states won by Bush receive so many more House seats and electoral votes at the expense of states won by Gore that Bush would have eliminated Gore's 14-vote lead in House votes. The electoral race would have ended in a virtual dead heat before the addition of Bush's lead in Senate-based votes. Add in the bizarre fact that with a 120,000 more votes in Ohio John

---

1 Briefs in support of the plan are available at Fairvote's website. The contrary view is well expressed in John Samples, "A Critique of the National Popular Vote Plan for Electing the President," Policy Analysis 622, Cato Institution, Washington, DC October 13, 2008.

Kerry would have won the electoral vote in 2004 even with the 2000 reapportionment providing these additional electoral votes to Republican-held states, and even after he lost the popular vote by three million, and it seems obvious that the only way to hold a democratic presidential election in America is through a national popular vote, achieved through a constitutional amendment.

CHAPTER 12. A MODEST PROPOSAL FOR DISUNION

The reader will note that among the fairly dramatic reforms proposed in the previous chapter, the most common one in widespread debate, limitations on campaign finance, was not included. This chapter first dispenses with the belief that reforming campaign finance is possible or even desirable, but then, to compensate, offers a proposal that would even more fundamentally alter the American way of politics — disunion.

The laws governing campaigns and their financing are inevitably written by the two main parties in such a way that their lawyers can evade their intent in practice. Even if they were not, they would harm, not help, the ability of Turkeys to challenge domination. Reforms such public financing of campaigns, restrictions on spending, or free television advertising paradoxically would have the unintended consequence of restricting the speech of minorities such as anti-imperialists, while cementing the Eagles' two-party monopoly on debate and power.

In January 2010 the Supreme Court reversed 20 years of rulings that had limited corporate advocacy during political campaigns. While the matters decided were, as is often the case, arcane and apparently limited in scope, the Court's general intent was to reaffirm its landmark principle from 1976 that laws constraining spending on political campaigns and issues are fundamentally trumped by the First Amendment's guarantee of freedom of speech. The angry reaction of the political classes to the decision made it seem as if just about everybody in America except five justices and the American Civil Liberties Union supports restrictions on how much money people can give or spend to influence elections. Turkeys and Soft Eagles in particular are united in their support for the "clean elections" movement, which promotes the public financing of candidates who agree to hold their individual contributions and total spending below specified limits.[1] This concept has been incorporated into laws governing local and state elections, and even the presidential, but

---

1 See, for example, Steve Coble, "From the Democracy Thieves who Illegitimately Selected George Bush...," *Huffington Post*, January 25, 2010.

not congressional, elections. Turkeys should reverse their position. They need less, rather than more, restrictions on campaign fund-raising and political advertising, because they need more, rather than less, speech to reach American ears.

Money has been the mother's milk of politics in the United States since the development of parties at the start of the 19th century. The record since the beginning of campaign reform in the 1970s is clear: restrictions on spending are unworkable and easily evaded. The truly draconian changes needed to stop the evasions would require a constitutional amendment that would shred the right to free speech, could only be enforced by a police-like bureaucracy, and would probably limit the expression of minority rather than majority viewpoints. Turkeys need to get Americans to rethink a global philosophy of domination, and the time Americans think the most about political issues is during election campaigns. Turkeys must deliver a message not so much about candidates as about the root cause of domination, and not obscure it by focusing on its symptoms, or the undeniable but fundamentally irrelevant fact that Soft Eagles are the lesser of two evils. Breaking through will require traditional advertising as well as creative, cost-effective approaches based on old-fashioned personal contact and modern electronic communication. Both are expensive, and both require that Turkeys raise and spend money, just like the Eagles do. Anti-imperialists should stop whining that the Eagles spend billions to sway public opinion and start spending and swaying themselves. To build on the dictum of 20th century Justice Louis Brandeis, the Turkeys' answer to evil or banal speech should not be to limit it, but to compete with it by broadcasting more, and more insightful and inciting, speech. A more recent example would be director Spike Lee's response to critics of his portrayal of Malcolm X: "Make your own damn movie."

The typical member of the House or Senate has to raise about a million dollars a year for a re-election campaign, and probably another million in addition for the party, other candidates, and a personal "leadership" political action committee (PAC) to fund other candidates or broadly-defined political activities.[1] In addition, members encourage donations to a variety of "non-coordinated" entities that run their own campaigns to support candidates and promote related issues. That means that the first thing on Members' minds when they get up and a constant pressure on their minds throughout the day is the need to raise some money. A president or presidential candidate must raise far more, up to a billion dollars for a race, and so thinks about it all the more. Much of the money comes in increments of $5,000 from political action committees, or PACs, formed by members of corporations, unions, and every conceivable interest group, from national military contractors to local sheet-metal contractors, from nurses to hospitals, and from friends of Israel to friends of India. Far larger chunks are given to various party organizations, from the county to the national level, and to friendly, technically independent committees. All of

---

1 "Corporate Democracy," Common Cause press release, October 29, 2009, reports $3 billion in political and issue advertising alone in 2008. Total congressional spending was $1.4 billion. The FEC reported that presidential spending was $1.7 billion. Winning House candidates spent $1.4 million on average, and Senate winners $8.5 million. Corporate PACs gave $270 million to congressional candidates, four times as much as labor PACs' $66 million. Candidates can use their campaign and PAC funds in retirement to promote political causes, and so can effectively support their own activities.

these funds are easily routed by lawyers through the complexities and intentional weaknesses of campaign laws into election campaigns. The "watch-dog" that indeed watches this all happen is the bipartisan Federal Election Commission, which is usually frozen by tie votes along party lines as its staff try to levy ridiculously puny fines.

The primary purpose of the uncountable but certainly over $4 billion raised in each electoral cycle is to run, or simply to be in a position to threaten to run, television commercials in a close race.[1] Only about a fifth of House and about half of Senate or presidential campaign spending goes for commercials, and that is diluted further by the sweetheart practice in which the campaign consultant who books the time takes a cut of the "buy." However, like the CIA's covert operations, which account for only a small part of its budget, the final activity is the goal of all the rest, and is enabled by it. As commercial advertisers learned long ago, there are many ways to reach Americans and convince them to buy what you want to sell, but none is as effective as a wave of gripping visual images and memorable tag-lines washing over the viewing populace. The overriding complaint about the pursuit of the funds needed to run these commercials is that it corrupts politicians and parties, changing policy in return for donations. This charge is simplistic, and almost meaningless, given the contours of the interests and the parties that bring Members and presidents to Washington. We often hear that we have the best Congress money can buy. This phrase badly misstates what Congress is like. It would be better to say that we have the best Congress money can rent for a few minutes. That is the amount of time larger contributors can count on having with a Member to make their case on a legislative initiative. They may spend a lot of time explaining their position to the Member's staff, but staff talk to anybody who works hard to see them and sends them coherent memos.

The main outlines of Members' or parties' positions are well known and long-standing. Members attract donors who are happy with their orientation, rather than change their orientation to satisfy donors. Soft Eagles, from Dick Gephardt (fighters) and John Glenn (tanks) in the '90s to Maurice Hinchey (presidential helicopters) and David Scott (fighters) in the '00s, are going to push for foreign sales or Pentagon purchases of weapons that are built by their constituents, whether or not the unions and the corporate PACs fund their campaigns. Members are going to think of how a foreign policy vote will play back home, whether or not the lobbyist who arranges a visit from a foreign minister has "bundled" hundreds of thousands of dollars for them in the past, or can line up a high-paying job for them after they leave Congress. The Democrats aggressively pursued contributions from military contractors under House Whip Tony Coelho in the '80s and Bill Clinton in the '90s. However, the record level of arms sales to dictators under Clinton was not so much a payoff as a measure of the party's desire to look strong on defense and supportive on jobs.

A Member might decide a close call on a foreign policy question in favor of a colleague who has just pumped a few thousand dollars into his or her campaign from a leadership PAC, and an arms export might get a quicker review in the State Department because a

---

1 The total political media buy in 2008 was expected to be $4.5 billion, of which $3 billion would go to advertising, of which $2.3 billion would go to television ads. Louis Hau, "Political Ad Spending Set to Climb Sharply," Forbes.com, December 7, 2007.

long-standing party donor runs the corporation, but with the thousands of conflicting loyalties upon which a politician relies, there is no single piper for whom to dance. House member Marty Russo, a rakish Chicago machine politician, was right in the '80s when he would roar happily, "If you can't take their money, drink their whiskey, [expletive] their women, and then vote against them, you don't belong here." Russo's realism allowed him to hop happily to the other side of the fence at the conclusion of his congressional career. He was caught in a media sting in 1990 when he went with other members of the tax-writing committee to Barbados on a fact-finding mission that ABC news immortalized on videotape, including scenes of jet-skiing with lobbyists and golfing with the US embassy picking up the green fees.[1] Russo easily won his safe Chicago seat a week later, but 1992's redistricting pitted him against another sitting Democrat, and he was defeated. He became the head of the powerful Cassidy lobbying firm, using not just the usual technique of bundling and directing campaign contributions from his clients, but also his status as a former Member to maintain his direct access to Members in the House gym and on the floor. Ironically, Russo sees public financing of campaigns as a benefit to his profession, saying it is the only way "we will ever shed the 'pay to play' perception" of the public.[2]

Corporations spend $5 billion per year on their lobbying operations, far more than their PACs contribute to campaigns.[3] No conceivable reform can stop them from promoting their message, or politicians from hearing it, with or without campaign contributions. Their goal is to be ever-present in discussions that affect their profits, and they achieve that with a broad range of lobbying and publicity tactics. Rank corruption, such as the selling of a vote or a reversal of a policy in return for a contribution, is rare, because the system is already corrupted without it, in the fundamental sense that donors use money to solidify their connection to politicians who already support their goals. With re-election and majority status the obvious goals of the politicians and access and consideration the obvious reward for the donors, only the unintelligent ever need utter an indictable word. The one possible exception to the rule that campaign contributions don't determine policy is Israel.

Academics famously argue over the extent of the influence of Israel and its American supporters in making US foreign policy, but Members of Congress don't bother, because they live the reality daily. The proof that the lobby is even more powerful than the National Rifle Association is that it need not even designate votes for published ratings of Members, as the NRA does. The NRA has tremendous grassroots backing, with millions of citizens committed to vote for the candidate with the higher rating. With Israeli policy, there are rarely any floor votes, and there are few Jewish voters in any event to swing many elections. The American Israel Public Affairs Committee (AIPAC) is not even a political action committee, and so is ineligible to make campaign contributions. It gets its power from the funding it informally directs by simply letting it be known who it thinks is a reliable friend of Israel and who is not.[4] It tests this dichotomy a few times a year by asking

---

1 "Congressmen on Candid Camera in Barbados" (AP Story), *Reading Eagle*, October 26, 1990.
2 See his opinion piece in *The Hill*, October 17, 2007.
3 "Corporate Democracy," Common Cause press release, October 29, 2009.
4 As early as the 1980s AIPAC's network included 51 major organizations it could encourage to contribute to candidates. John Fialka, "Linked Donations?", *Wall Street Journal*, June 24,

Members of Congress to sign on a letter immediately about some complex aspect of US or Israeli policy. Those who move quickly are friends, and those who hesitate even briefly to ponder the matter become suspect.[1]

Every candidate knows some variant of the Chuck Percy story...or the Cynthia McKinney, Earl Hilliard, James Abdnor, or Roger Jepsen story. All were sitting Members of Congress who ran afoul of AIPAC and other Jewish groups and individuals devoted to maximum US support and assistance for Israel. All became ex-Members of Congress, very arguably as a result. Each story has unique explanations for the vulnerability of the Member to a challenger, but all faced such a pile of pro-Israel funding from outside the district that today's Members understand the moral of the story just fine. John Mearsheimer and Stephen Walt's careful review of congressional campaigns that were influenced by what they call the Israel Lobby notes that AIPAC's head himself claimed that Percy's defeat by Paul Simon in 1984 set the tone for the decades that followed: "All the Jews in America, from coast to coast, gathered to oust Percy. And the American politicians — those in office now and those who aspire — got the message." In 2002 the editor of a leading Jewish newspaper made the same point: "There is this image in Congress that you don't cross these people or they take you down." Mearsheimer and Walt were criticized by many for overstating their case, but for anyone who has worked in Congress or national politics, their revelations were actually banal and far too tame.[2]

Illinois senator Percy was targeted for defeat by pro-Israel groups for his support of Reagan's sale of battle-directing aircraft to Saudi Arabia and his mild expressions of support for Palestinian rights and for Yasser Arafat as a "moderate" negotiating partner. In his autobiography Simon recounted how promises from pro-Israel donors convinced him to make the run. In addition to seemingly unlimited contributions to his campaign that allowed him to outspend Percy, he was the wary beneficiary of an early example of an independent campaign by a pro-Israel California businessman, who spent a million dollars on advertising attacking Percy.[3] The businessman was eventually jailed for hiding the source of his backing for a far-right candidate who successfully siphoned votes from a Republican challenger to pro-Israel Senator Alan Cranston in 1986.[4] Wary or not, Simon defeated Percy in a close race. AIPAC and its interlocking host of related groups have continued to

---

1987, p.1. Mearsheimer and Walt bring the charade up to date in their 2007 book, *The Israel Lobby and US Foreign Policy*, Farrar, Straus and Giroux, New York, 2007.

1 AIPAC's friends are also expected to speak up and defend Israel in any discussion of its policies on human rights, combat, negotiations, or nuclear weapons. Congressman Henry Hyde would drive his Democratic colleague Steve Solarz wild in the 1980s by substituting "Israel" for "El Salvador" while reading aloud Solarz amendments that conditioned US aid on El Salvador's compliance with international agreements and congressional instructions on negotiations and human rights. Hyde was a strong supporter of Israel's legislative agenda; he was using the hypocrisy to weaken the appeal of Solarz's outrage over US funding for a government in El Salvador that didn't comply with its agreements with the United States.

2 John Mearsheimer and Stephen Walt, *The Israel Lobby and US Foreign Policy*, Farrar, Straus and Giroux, New York, 2007, pp. 152-162.

3 P.S.: The Autobiography of Paul Simon, Bonus Books, Chicago, 1999.

4 Kenneth Reich, "Goland Gets Jail Term for Illegal Campaign Gift," *Los Angeles Times*, July 17, 1990,

sponsor aggressive test votes and sign-on letters and then reward the cooperative and target the uncooperative. Even the arrest of top AIPAC officials in 2005 on charges of passing classified information to Israel has not tempered their drive.[1]

Arab opinion sees Israel as a strategic outpost of the West, and assumes that the United States has enough leverage from its aid programs and its unwritten but fundamental guarantee of Israel's existence to convince Israel to adopt certain policies on war, peace, military conduct, and human rights. Ironically, US policy-makers — both the many who line up with Israel's decisions and the few who openly dispute its claim to unique rights because of its unique threat — believe from bitter experience that this has not been the case. Israel's leaders are in nobody's pocket, from their perspective for good reason. While Truman's recognition of and aid to Israel were important to its formal creation, Jewish militias needed decades of violence, including terror tactics against Britain, to get to that point. From Eisenhower's termination of Israel's seizure of the Suez Canal with Britain and France in 1956 to US support for an immediate cease-fire after the Soviet Union threatened a dramatic, perhaps nuclear intervention to thwart Israel's impending destruction of Egypt's army in 1973 in the Yom Kippur War, Israel and US interests have often diverged. Israel takes the support America provides, but never relies on the latest representative of the *goyim*, the American president, who must balance this support with the perceived need to maintain close relations with Arab states. Israel makes its own military decisions, maintains an effective military force and nuclear weapons, and uses its supporters in Congress to constrain any administration's ability to pressure it.

It is, of course, impossible to say how US policy in the Middle East would be different if American Jews had not raised money so ferociously to shape Congress and the presidency. Once Truman overrode Secretary of State Marshall to recognize and aid Israel, US backing for Israel's long-term survival was assured. By playing an anti-Soviet role during the Cold War and an anti-terrorist role after 9/11, Israel has maximized its chances of US support. However, there is no doubt that American politicians have backed, or at least not opposed, such policies as building settlements in the West Bank, attacks on Lebanon and Gaza, US aid to Egypt and Jordan for making peace with and recognizing Israel, blocking US talks with various Palestinian and Middle Eastern organizations, US isolation of Iran and Libya, and the invasion of Iraq because of the instinctive fear of "crossing" AIPAC and its allies. Turkeys will make little headway in challenging America's exceptional right to dominate if they can't challenge Israel's. The solution, again, is not to ban such potent advocacy, but to match it.

What the money chase really brings to politics is not corruption, but distraction. A frequent response to a new idea in Washington is that "there's just no time" to think things through properly, in large part because everybody is putting their best energy into fundraising rather than policy-making. Bill Clinton spent most of his second term distracted from his Dixiecratic foreign policy by what few people realize was fundamentally a fund-raising scandal: the naming of an aimless, unqualified young woman named Monica Lewinsky as a prestigious White House intern. Lewinsky was taken in as a favor to

---

1 The case was dismissed in 2009 on a variety of technical grounds, but the official who passed the information first to the AIPAC officials was convicted and jailed.

Walter Kaye, a retired insurance executive and friend of her mother's who gave $300,000 to the Democratic National Committee. The diligent wooing of Kaye by Hillary Clinton in 1993, which included a front-row seat at the president's Middle East peace agreement, made her, to use another metaphor from Hamlet, woodcock to her own springe.[1] Distraction, though, is probably a good thing for anti-imperialists, since pursuing and thanking donors and then hearing their pleas keeps the Eagles busy, giving them less tie to make more mischief abroad.

Advocates of reforming campaign finance often point to other countries with less expensive races. Invariably, though, these countries provide a small amount of free airtime to parties on national television and then effectively limit additional broadcast advertising. They also provide financing for other electioneering activities based on a party's popularity in recent elections, in return for the party agreeing to limits on overall fundraising and spending.[2] These are not viable or desirable options in the United States. In any event, foreign elections are coming more and more to resemble American ones, with waves of paid advertising and shallow accusations. This is due in part to the role that Americans play in foreign elections as consultants or funders. Both the American left and right have funded successful presidential campaigns in Latin America.

Spending or advertising limits established by constitutional amendment could never be enforced short of a massive bureaucracy to police and punish every activity of a candidate and indirectly related individuals. The National Collegiate Athletics Association (NCAA) with its nit-picking rules about recruiting athletes and its favored penalty of barring teams from taking part in championships, is the best example both of what would be required, and of its fundamental futility. The nature of big-time college sports as a professional endeavor, like the nature of politics as a money-driven contest for power, has been changed not one iota by all the rules, investigations, and sanctions. When the goal is winning and the reward is in the billions of dollars and job security for all involved, both coaches and candidates will find a way to get it done. Bush in 2000 and Obama in 2008 revealed as much when they refused public financing and its limitations because they could spend more money by raising it themselves, and exploited every loophole in party and "independent" fund-raising to ensure their success.

Wealthy individuals such as New York mayor Michael Bloomberg and a raft of senators also fund their own campaigns without limitation. The Federal Communications Commission could include a requirement for free air time for their opponents in its "public interest" requirements for the renewal of licenses, which now only extend to a bit of discussion of local issues, or justify it by reviving the "fairness" doctrine that it repealed in 1987.[3] However, there would obviously have to be a limit on the free time, and rich or

---

1 David Finkel, "How It Came to This," *Washington Post Magazine*, December 13, 1998.

2 See "Campaign Finance: An Overview," by the Law Library of Congress, http://www.loc.gov/law/help/campaign-finance/, on the combination of mandated and voluntary advertising limits in place in Europe.

3 The FCC has an appropriately minimalist approach to regulation of content. It fines for obscenity, limits profanity, requires some educational children's television time, and ask for an undefined "significant treatment of community issues." It bars the broadcasting of intentionally false information about crime, catastrophe, or other news, but has real means to enforce this edict, other than a murky "public interest" clause when stations come for

better-funded candidates would immediately be bidding for additional commercial time. If time were limited by constitutional amendment and a NCAA-style police force, candidates and parties would simply swamp the internet, cable channels, and other new forms of electronic communication, and wink to supporters to run independent campaigns that walked up as close as possible from advocacy of issues to advocacy or opposition for the candidate who is identified with the issues. Eventually, the federal police force would have to monitor every citizen or group to judge intent and impact of their advocacy. The impact of the effort would fall heavily on minority opinion and unpopular causes, like anti-imperialism.

Mainstream television networks have a financial interest in blocking advertisements for unpopular or controversial causes, because they may drive away viewers. Moveon.org was denied the ability to air an anti-war commercial during the 2004 Super Bowl, and an anti-abortion group got the same treatment for the 2009 game.[1] Again, the answer is more speech, not less. Turkeys benefit from a heated public debate that becomes evident to less politically-active viewers. Fox News is effectively a 24-hour platform for a right-wing agenda. Radio Pacifica, its left-wing counterpart, should be plotting to launch its own television channel, even as it complains about Fox's distortions. There are many examples of criticism of corporate media being effective, from critics of the *New York Times'* shallow coverage of Vietnam in the early 1960s taking out successful fund-raising advertisements to make their case to Mobil buying a box on the editorial page to make its case. The White House weighs in to protest news stories; black leaders and white fundamentalist Christian groups call for boycotts of various media; climate alarmists and skeptics alike call for editors and reporters to be disciplined. It is all part of a game that should be entered, not ended.

DISUNION, TO DISRUPT EMPIRE

A desperate but quite logical way for Turkeys to disrupt US domination is to advocate splitting America into a number of nations, whether 50 or five, so as to deprive it of the means and perhaps some of the motive of imperialism. The case for disunion is, ironically, found in the very documents that created union, the Declaration of Independence and the Constitution. The Founders were beginning a worthy experiment to promote self-government and economic freedom for themselves, but the experiment now threatens the same for others. It was a great achievement for the Founders to have created a world power from a trembling coalition, but America has become what they hated, the new British empire. Ronald Reagan was being redundant when he called the Soviet Union an "evil empire." Empire is inherently evil. Untrammeled power backed by an unbreakable ideology

---

renewal every eight years. Candidates can buy time on an equal basis with each other and commercial advertisers, and any prosecution of "speech intended to incite or produce imminent lawless action" and likely to do so is left to "local authorities." The networks voluntarily support V-chip ratings so parents can block violent programs. See http://www.fcc.gov/mb/audio/decdoc/public_and_broadcasting.pdf

1 The anti-abortion commercial showed a fetus on a sonogram, and described how the child was abandoned by its father, raised by a single mother, and endured to become the first African-American president.

of superiority and benevolence cannot be a force for good, no matter how many times one hears the word freedom in an inaugural address or a military funeral.

The Declaration inaugurated a new sort of union, a federated republic delineated in the Constitution 11 years later that was to be a grand experiment in self-government. The United States was the first nation to apply to an entire people (absent the alien others, of course: Africans, Indians, and women) the principle that had been developed for elected government by a landed or moneyed elite, as in ancient Rome and Greece, 16th century Venice, 17th century Poland, or 18th century England. Quickly, though, an empire developed from the republic. Noam Chomsky has said that because empire was at the core of the project, with the Founders motivated to rebellion by a desire to take over Indian lands west of the Alleghenies, Canada, and Cuba, "talking about American imperialism is rather like talking about triangular triangles."[1] Whether or not it was inevitable, it is a reality that domination is now woven into the fabric of American life and politics. Disunion is necessary to realize the promise of union, whose purposes in 1787 were defined as being to "establish Justice, insure domestic Tranquility, provide for the common defence, promote the general Welfare, and secure the Blessings of Liberty to ourselves and our Posterity." For each clause, add the phrase "for others," and it will be easy to see that disunion is "more perfect" in the 21st century than union.

The future is impossible to predict, except to say that unpredictable events would follow disunion. There are terrible risks in a political change of this magnitude. The signers of the Declaration were aware of this, too. They came to union as unwillingly as Turkeys must come to disunion: "Prudence, indeed, will dictate that Governments long established should not be changed for light and transient causes; and accordingly all experience hath shewn, that mankind are more disposed to suffer, while evils are sufferable, than to right themselves by abolishing the forms to which they are accustomed." They were correct that it is far wiser, and more natural, to try to fix than to destroy and create anew, but also correct that at a certain point, the evil done by a current system requires the leap of faith to try a new one.

In the Declaration the representatives of the 13 colonies agreed that "a decent respect for the opinions of mankind" required them to explain why they had pledged "our Lives, our Fortunes, and our sacred Honor" to breaking the bonds that held them to King George and the British Empire. And then they went at it with a vengeance. Most of the Declaration details the "long train of abuses and usurpations, pursuing invariably the same Object" by the British. The claim that the evil being done by the American empire requires dis union is so shocking to Americans that it requires a similarly specific indictment. It should be noted that others are not so shocked: after Bush's re-election 53 percent of Europeans had come to consider the United States a threat to world peace, roughly the same percentage that identified Iran and North Korea as threats, and South Africa treated the United States like an international outlaw in an ironic reversal of roles from the 1980s,

---

1 http://chomsky.info/talks/20080424.htm (A talk at Boston University, April 24, 2008.)

with a democratic South Africa sanctioning a rogue America by barring visits by US warships on their way home from Iraq.[1]

The decline in America's reputation was certainly driven by a personal distaste for and fear of George Bush and his particular policies of invasion and torture, but he was no more guilty of this indictment than any other president since World War II. The problem of empire is not personal, but rather systemic, arising from the accretion of global power by the American empire and of domestic political power by its advocates. As noted in Chapter 3, Mr. Human Rights himself, Jimmy Carter, felt constrained to show his commitment to America's interests by arming and financing some of the nastiest dictatorships in Africa in return for their provision of military bases, intelligence facilities, and other elements of strategic cooperation. As a result, millions have died in Somalia, the Democratic Republic of the Congo, Liberia, and the Sudan in civil wars, some of which still rage, 30 years later. As noted in Chapter 7, Barack Obama has maintained the empire's core policies of military primacy, alliance with cooperative dictators, and domination, and justified the escalation of the war in Afghanistan and Pakistan by claiming that America's military adventures and foreign policies since World War II have "underwritten global security" so that "other people's children and grandchildren can live in freedom."

Here, in far less purple prose than the original Declaration's listing of King George's sins is a bill of indictment of American presidents for systematically disrupting the security and freedom Obama claims they were promoting abroad:

- By secretly paying members of other governments who assist in intelligence-gathering, and by promoting foreign sales by arms-makers who pay these foreign officials "consulting fees" to close arms deals, the United States has promoted corruption and treason, rather than transparency and modernization of government.

- By conspiring with dictators to let them steal the revenues from their people's resources or pledge them for dozens of years to buy new generations of unnecessary US weapons, the United States has bled countries' resources from economic growth, domestic infrastructure, and social services, condemning new generations of children to a life, and an early death, in poverty.

- By arming and training these dictators' armed forces and police, the United States has entrenched resistance to demands for popular government, and fomented civil wars that devastate the fragile support systems of people living in poverty, leading to millions of non-combatant children and the elderly dying of disease and malnutrition.

- By using the international financial and trading institutions to protect its corporations and workers, the United States has forced poor countries out of their logical points of advantage, binding them to their colonial role as suppliers of raw materials at declining terms of trade, and rendering their governments less able to provide employment, nutrition, health, education, and longevity, life itself, to their people.

---

1 Poll cited in Subcommittee on International Organizations, Human Rights, and Oversight, "The Decline America's Reputation: Why?," Committee Print, House Committee on Foreign Affairs, US Congress, June 11, 2008, p. 10.

- The United States is prone by its political system to contemplating and then committing the war crime of invasion, as in Vietnam and Iraq, in which it has killed millions of people for inessential policy goals. As shown by the fiasco of the widespread belief in Iraq's "weapons of mass destruction," the analytic functions of its executive branch agencies and the oversight function of its legislative branch cannot withstand politicization in pursuit of American domination.

- The United States has made preventive invasion a national policy, rendering international law moot, by claiming exemption for an exceptional status. This policy violates US law and the Constitution, since under the US-ratified United Nations Charter it is illegal, and a state must formally withdraw from a treaty in order to violate it.

- The United States made torture an official part of US foreign policy, not just as a case of a few "rogues" at Abu Ghraib, Bagram, and Guantanamo prisons, but by deciding not to protect captured combatants and suspects under the Geneva Conventions, which are also part of US law by ratification and by customary international law.

The power amassed by the American empire may be too much for any nation to bear altruistically. The re-election of George W. Bush in 2004 was a ratification and an absolution by the electorate and the media of US dominance of the Middle East — from alliances with compliant dictators in Egypt and Saudi Arabia to the fraudulent invasion of Iraq — and of the use of torture to sustain this dominance. It showed that such power is certainly too much for America to bear. In particular, the approval by the majority of a candidate endorsing torture took America across a Rubicon from which there is no retreat. When asked what they would do if captured American soldiers were abused until they broke and talked, as prisoners were in Iraq, Afghanistan, and Guantanamo by US forces, by being hooded for days, denied food and water, kept naked in cold cells, deprived of sleep, and beaten, and then "rendered" to known torturers like Egypt and Syria if even that level of abuse failed to move them past name, rank, and serial number, these voters replied, in essence, "but they're not Americans, so it's all right." At that moment, America ceased to exist as an ideal, and became just another thug in the long line of empires from Caesar's to Tojo's.

What is it about the United States that has led to the evil of empire? Lenin's hypothesis that empire is simply the highest stage of capitalism is easily rejected. Yes, America's military dominance protects the far-flung economic interests of its ruling tier, but all sorts of socio-economic systems, including Leninism, can lead to empire, and most capitalists are happy to trade with, rather than waste money physically dominating, their markets. The "war for oil" refinement of this hypothesis is similarly flawed. There was nothing but rice in Vietnam, and nothing but coffee in El Salvador, yet the United States devastated both countries rather than let uncooperative regimes take power. Furthermore, natural resources can't be eaten, and so are sold, rather than hoarded, by the cash-hungry kleptocrats of the Middle East and Africa.

Cultural factors are always popular as explanations for imperialism. It is true almost by definition that some combination of personalities creates a national direction, but the trail toward the core of causality is hopelessly twisted. In any event, motive is nothing without means. While it is fair to say that deluded exceptionalism, superficially proud (but truly embarrassed) anti-intellectualism, and the expansive belligerence that results from both are frequent and culturally celebrated parts of the American personality, one must have still have power in order to act on them. There have been empires driven primarily by economics, like the Dutch empire of the 17th century, and primarily by culture, like the Zulu empire of the 19th century, but the primary cause of today's American empire may well be size, finally unconstrained by competition.

Every country's instinct in its relations with another is to benefit itself. This is human, natural, and usually benign because it is rare that a single country combines tremendous power, tremendous need, and a self-congratulatory ideology holding that it brings good to the world as it dominates it. Portugal, Spain, the Netherlands, Britain, and France played that role from 1450 to 1950 in the devastating Western experiment of colonialism. The United States played that role in its own continent, then in bits of Asia and much of Latin America from the start of the 20th century until World War II, and then throughout the formerly colonized world since the start of the Cold War, and on into today's war for control of the Middle East. The motives are clear: the ability to project military and covert power and the desire to gain resources at predictable prices and trade and invest at will. The means are expensive: overwhelmingly superior military forces, covert operations, and economic inducements. What creates the motives and funds the means is, fundamentally, the size of the American polity, which provides its power. The former colonial powers no longer have the means to dominate, because they have become comfortable letting the United States carry the ball. This hand-off from colonialism to neo-colonialism was only made possible by America's size and economic success.

From 1945 to 1990, the United States and its rival multinational, continental power the Soviet Union were like two hot gasses with the same charge, trying to expand to cover the same area but constantly repelling each other at their meeting points. Suddenly, one gas went inert, and the other was allowed to expand unimpeded over the whole area. Only local spots of other repellent gasses, meaning nuclear-armed countries like France, China, North Korea, India, and Pakistan, or countries with conventional armed forces capable of delivering a sharp blow on the way down, such as Cuba, are safe from invasion or military punishment. This explains the recently-discovered interest in arms control by the court sycophants and military mandarins of the American empire, who disparaged it during the Cold War as irrelevant. Now a fear of the proliferation of "weapons of mass destruction" provides both a frequent *casus belli* and a convenient *casus imperii*.

Size was ironically the very factor that James Madison claimed in the Federalist Papers would lead to success for the United States. Like the Founders as a whole, Madison was no dreamy idealist. He held the classically conservative view that while people, and particularly "the people," *hoi poloi*, may have an altruistic side, their primary loyalty is to self-interest. He demonstrated that reality himself by profiting from insider land speculation when making the deal with Hamilton and Jefferson to establish the District of Columbia as the new nation's capital. In the tenth of the op-ed pieces designed to bolster support in New York State for ratifying the federalist Constitution Madison argued that a single large nation was far preferable to a number of small ones because its multitude of self-interested "factions" would be more likely to balance each other. This balancing would keep any one faction from seizing control of the government and engaging in actions that a minority strongly opposed, and so might lead to turmoil and alienation from the union. Federalist Number 10 has become a national touchstone, praised by political philosophers both liberal and conservative for its world-weary caution about the human propensity for the delusion that self-interest can be recognized, let alone contained, by the self. Madison's Americans are not the noble souls mawkishly portrayed saving Vietnamese by Lyndon Johnson, Iraqis by George W. Bush, and Afghan women by Barack Obama. They are inherently rascals, looking out for themselves, and can only be deterred from running off with the store by the size and complexity of the American polity.

Read dispassionately, Federalist 10 is a weak brick on which to build a nation, being largely based on historical examples and logical turns that could just as easily be argued to the contrary. However, it was not meant to be read dispassionately, but rather as a love song to the driving force of the political life of Madison and his colleagues: union. While they all identified themselves primarily as members of a particular colony, rather than as members of a general colonial entity, the Founders discovered that to free their states from British rule they had to rely on other states. The lesson they learned was that only union could check foreign influence in other states that could eventually harm their own. Emotional identification with the states persevered more strongly in the South, where whites sensed a threat to slavery from the North's disdain. Even today Southern whites are moved to tears or cheers when hearing strains of Old Virginia, Maryland my Maryland, Sweet Home Alabama, and the Yellow Rose of Texas. Being from New York, Massachusetts, Ohio, or Pennsylvania is more a matter of address.

As identification with the state gained importance in the slave-holding South, so did identification with the union grow in the North. When young white men from Wisconsin and Vermont, few of whom had seen a Negro in their lives, rushed off to volunteer after the attack on Fort Sumter in 1861, they did so to preserve a thing called Union. For them, and for Americans in the main today, Union became an end in itself, a religious identity with its own relics and rituals, and a tribal nation with its own peculiar chauvinism. As the United States expanded its power, first across the continent after the Civil War, then across the Pacific in the Spanish–American War, Latin America in the early 20th century, and Europe and Asia in World War II, and finally to all corners of the globe in the 45 years of competition with the Soviet Union and the 15 years of searching for competition afterwards, the loyalty to union that had grown from loyalty to state was transformed into loyalty to the unspoken empire. To question the imperial project, whether in seizing Colorado from the Indians, occupying Cam Rahn Bay against the Vietnamese, or taking Baghdad from the Iraqis, became akin to treason. To be part of the respectable debate, to take part in the governing of the country in any formal manner, required an acceptance of the imperial project that had sprung from the acts of union in 1776 and 1787.

Madison's prediction that size would work to Americans' benefit by balancing powerful interests has been largely confirmed by the economic success and political stability of the United States. Corporations and unions, petro-cowboys and Indians, groups for and against gun control or legal abortion, and any number of industrial, social, religious and regional interests pour fantastic sums into the political process, yet largely fight each other to a standstill as they contest in Congress, in the administrative bureaucracy, in the courts, and in the media the other's every advance. The self-interested factions make America a giant ocean liner, extremely slow to turn even when the controls are in the hands, as has too often been the case, of a truly demented captain and a devoted crew.

America's wealth, technological innovation, and power have increased inexorably under Madison's political system and, to be fair, Hamilton's economic system. Our problem today is not that Madison was wrong about size allowing the blunting of competing factions' influences, but that he was right. America succeeded, and then turned its burgeoning power toward an arena that Madison forgot to address, because he could not imagine that his struggling colonial enclave would amass sufficient power and interest, foreign and military policy. In this arena, where usually competing American economic interests collude on policy against foreign targets, the imperial faction has indeed run off with the American store, right from the beginning, allowing the capture of the nation's power by brazen advocates of world-wide military reach and economic empire. A small part of the price for Madison's omission is paid by Americans, who receive the benefits of global economic domination but must sustain the armed forces that preserve it. The larger part is paid by the dominated countries, former colonies that were left economically and militarily dependent and socially distorted at independence by the European empires, and largely remain so today. Representing the interests of its citizens, albeit the wealthy somewhat more than the middle and lower economic classes, successive governments of the American republic have amassed power and influence that threatens the life, liberty, and pursuit of happiness of most of the people in the former colonial territories.

The primary justification for pursuing disunion, as opposed to trying to reform the fundamentally repressive relationship of the American empire to the former colonial world, is that the reformers simply cannot win in the foreseeable future. It is morally unacceptable to sit back and wait for the inevitable "two, three, many Vietnams" (or Iraqs, or Afghanistans) that Che Guevara gleefully predicted would drain the empire of troops, domestic political will, economic power, and international alliances. A majority of the nation and nearly two thirds of non-Jewish white males, the subgroup that dominates the political economy, showed in the 2004 election that it has grown comfortable with its leaders' determination to dominate the world militarily under the messianic guise of carrying an undefined "freedom" to it, and to exploit it economically under the benevolent guise of promoting an undefined "development" of it. More troubling is that the minority was required in 2004, as it has been in every election since World War II except 1972, to vote for a Democratic candidate who also believed in empire, albeit a smarter and more enlightened one: John Kerry had voted for the invasion of Iraq, and was at pains to present himself as a combat veteran, and not an anti-war activist.

Worst of all, Soft Eagles continue to draw the vast majority of Turkeys' votes, as in the case of the openly imperial Obama, because the Turkeys fear an even more aggressive outcome if the Hard Eagle wins. Senator Richard Russell, chairman of the Armed Services Committee and an arch-segregationist and imperialist whose name was soon to adorn a nuclear submarine, said in the 1960s in a rare moment of caution: "If we can go anywhere and do anything we will always be going somewhere and doing something." Since presidents always appear to be able to convince the public to go somewhere and do something, it is only by breaking up the power to do so that the empire can be stopped. Union was an act of states, ratified in each state by special conventions elected by the people. Disunion can also only be an act of states. State by state, opponents of empire should prepare and promote local calls for disunion, and then state legislation and a referendum withdrawing from the Union. California, or perhaps just its central third, New York, Massachusetts, and Vermont would be good candidates for the first campaigns. The legality of such a dramatic action under the Constitution is secondary, and perhaps unknowable, as President Jackson showed in challenging Chief Justice Marshall to enforce his ruling about Indian lands and as President Lincoln showed in suppressing Southern secession. It would be nice to have symmetry between the end of the republic and its beginning by having Congress call for a convention and have a majority of states ratify its decision. But disunion is a political rather than a legal question, to be decided by the will of the states and the mood of the people.

It will certainly be difficult to convince Americans to vote to break apart an empire that is working for them, but inflicting violence and poverty on the world. It would be unnatural for many to rally to a cause that does not affect them materially, particularly when their culture promotes the convenient belief that the empire is in truth an act of charity and grace. Indeed, three times a choice between union and the rights of others has been offered to white Americans, and three times, like Peter with Jesus, it was denied in a terrible trial. First, the Northern delegations at the constitutional convention, while vividly aware of and publicly opposed to slavery, had to accept it in the Southern states as the price of union. All the North could extract from the South was a chance to end the importation of slaves, but not the internal trade, in 20 years. Four score years less seven years later, anti-slavery activists had captured Northern opinion, and Southern states threatened to secede if they were not permitted to extend slavery to the Western territories. In this second denial the Republican Party, ostensibly the new anti-slavery party, made clear through its presidential candidate, Abraham Lincoln, that the South could keep its slaves if it stayed in the union and kept them out of the new territories. In the third and final denial the Republicans then sold out black rights to maintain national power in the election deal of 1876, which ended the federal occupation to protect black rights, known as Reconstruction.

For almost another century northern Democrats, strong proponents of human rights, continued to accept the legal segregation of southern blacks as the price of union and power. Martin Luther King Jr. rightly despaired at the passivity of the good whites in his "Letter from the Birmingham Jail" to southern religious leaders who counseled delay and caution. Only courageous agitation and the resulting embarrassment abroad and violent reaction in northern cities at home forced the Kennedy brothers and then Lyndon Johnson to enact the civil rights protections and make the threats to enforce them with federal troops that led to the collapse of segregation. Fittingly, as soon as possible after legal integration white America declared the centuries of discrimination complete despite the wildly disproportionate share of wealth and income held by whites, and gutted affirmative action programs that were designed to equalize opportunity. If white America's conscience cannot be roused to sacrifice union for the rights of black Americans, it is unlikely it would do so for the rights of foreign citizens.

The task is indeed daunting, but anti-imperialist Americans would not have to go it alone. Just as those creating union needed outside assistance throughout the war from European officers and at the conclusive battle of Yorktown from the French army led by Rochambeau and the French fleet led by DeGrasse, so today those promoting disunion should look abroad for help. This time help won't come from governments, few of which can last long in open opposition to America, but from the non-governmental advocacy groups that have sprouted as the state in underdeveloped countries has withered in its weakness. The anti-globalization movement and to a lesser extent the campaign against landmines show how allying with the victims of empire in dominated countries can bring a message of protest to the attention of international and American public opinion. In addition, Turkeys would have to ally with fringe groups of the left and right who have very different reasons for promoting disunion. It would appear obvious that, at first, votes on disunion would lose, and so reinforce, rather than reject, union. However, the mere act of holding referenda at the state level may build momentum, and create unexpected new allegiances. After all, George Washington and Robert E. Lee, both traitors to their oaths, are worshipped in American culture for the supposed purity of their motives. Both risked all, and switched sides only reluctantly, when they could see no other way of achieving a sacred goal. Even if disunion is never achieved, agitation for it would, like an impending hanging, concentrate the minds of Americans on the evil of empire in a way that debate within the framework of today's union has not.

The Vietnam generation's mission has always been to seek justice. At home it did so through the actions of the national government, first by extending by law and force the protections of the Constitution to African-Americans who lived in states that were denying them, and then by funding federal programs to promote opportunity not just for the wealthy minority, but also for the middle- and low-income majority, consisting of the white working class and most of the descendants of slaves, Hispanic and Asian immigrants, and displaced Indian nations. Abroad, the Vietnam generation opposed its own government, and supported militarily-dominated Vietnamese, Salvadorans, and Angolans, and economically-enslaved Africans and Latin Americans, and the many others feeling the pain of America's empire. The generational mission has always been anti-imperialist, but it should be clear by now that it can only be achieved by being anti-American, meaning being opposed to the idea of a nation called America. However, even if there were some successes and a few states split away, unless there was a significant change in consciousness about international affairs to go with the change of identity, the new nations might well be polities with foreign policies like today's nation. They would, being American nations, still be dominated by America's ideology and Madison's powerful factions, and so would have the propensity to collaborate with other new American nations to promote the formation of compacts for military and economic domination of other nations. That is why, this Swiftian fantasy of disunion aside, the essential elements of anti-imperialism are intellectual and moral, and not structural. A solid core of Americans must come to understand and hate empire and the type of nationalism that permits invasion and torture, with or without disunion.

CHAPTER 13. THE CULTURAL PUMP OF EXCEPTIONALISM

To defeat an empire, one must identify and undermine the sources of its power. What is the source of America's domination? Any drive for domination, of course, has genetic roots. Violent territorialism has developed in many species. For example, in a platoon of baboons the newly dominant male will try to kill all the infants whose father he has just overthrown, so that the platoon will eventually replicate him alone. Baboons are such close genetic relatives of human beings that the task of constraining violence and channeling competition appears all the more daunting. But why does America, and no other nation in the 21st century, respond to human genetics by striving for global rather than local control? In the analysis toward the end of *War and Peace* to which he was driven by recounting the tale and grasping the scale of the inexplicable Napoleonic cataclysm, Tolstoy claimed that an unknown force moves nations. This force, he wrote, impels people in droves to leave the security and happiness of their homes and jobs and subject themselves to privations, dangers, and death far from everything they hold dear, all to dominate people who have never threatened them. This force is obviously not a separate physical entity, so it must be an agglomeration of the traits and attitudes that individuals develop in response to their environment.

What then are the traits and attitudes that made America into a "warrior nation," as Marcus Raskin has argued, one that celebrates the warrior and his global reach? A burgeoning population and the geography of wide, sparsely-inhabited spaces certainly provides a convincing explanation for the continental expansion of American power, especially when the people were inculcated with the British ideology of superiority and the British practice of empire. However, there must be more to the American imperial character than that, since there are many countries in which these factors led to a similar expansion in contiguous territories but not internationally. British immigrants also seized the land from poorly-armed nations in Canada, South and East Africa, and Australia, but did not replace the mother country as a regional and then global enforcer. Similarly, China, India,

Indonesia, and Brazil also have large populations and resulting economic might, but did not develop a national consciousness that accepts, and even demands, global hegemony.

Like all other empires — from the Egyptian, Chinese, and Roman expansions in the BC's to the Mongol, Malian, and Aztec in the first half of the 1000s AD, on through the modern European enterprises of the Spanish, Dutch, British, Russians, Nazis, and Soviets' in the second half — the United States can pursue domination only because a critical mass of its citizens accepts the premise that they have the right to determine the destiny of other countries and peoples. As heir to the European empires, the United States also comes from the tradition of the Enlightenment and Reformation, in which it has never been enough for might to make right. Might must also be right, but that is only possible if it is used to bring the right to others. The advocates of the American empire appeal to their citizens in the language of altruism, because a naked grab for domination and economic advantage violates the fundamental self-perception of a European people. They do not shy away from justifying alliances with despots on the grounds that reliable access to natural resources and trade relationships aid America's economy, but they also insist that these arrangements will eventually improve life for the despots' citizens, as part of an American-led drive for an undefined freedom.

For European imperialists, it was not immoral to dominate; indeed they argued it would have been immoral not to bring from a superior culture to the benighted natives the benefits of education, health, economic growth, security, women's rights, democracy, and, in most cases, salvation. Each of these benefits was an explicit justification they offered to their citizens in seeking support for occupation, alliance if possible with local authorities, and war if necessary. Each is an implicit justification for American domination today. Then it was a mission to "civilize" backward people; today it is a mission to liberate them from oppressive conditions. Ideas matter, as Ronald Reagan famously said, and the idea that matters for America is that it brings good to those under its protective mantle, and so has a right and indeed a duty to dominate. At the core of this idea is exceptionalism, a belief in America's special character and global destiny. American domination is maintained by elected officials who fund it. The officials' election is permitted by citizens who endorse it. The citizens' attitudes are forged by media who accept it. The media reflect a culture that celebrates it. And the culture is rooted in a self-perception of American exceptionalism. The Eagles are ascendant and the Turkeys marginalized primarily because of this self-perception. Electoral reforms such as proportional representation in the House, the emasculation of the Senate, and direct election of the president, and even the structural reform of disbanding the union can weaken the imperial drive, but only a change in the public's self-perception of exceptionalism can defeat it.

Exceptionalism is deeply rooted in American history. It can be traced back to 1630 and Puritan imagery of "a city upon a hill" with a messianic charter to lead the rest of the world. Wealthy landowner John Winthrop was on his way to America as governor of the prospective Massachusetts Bay Colony when he gave the sermon that first voiced America's belief in its exceptionalism. Winthrop is a problematic figure for historians charting the development of democratic institutions in the colonies, because his theocratic, intolerant colony was at best "a stage in the development of American democracy rather than democracy itself." He made no bones about his preference for aristocracy and his disdain for democracy, the "meanest and worst" form of government and one of "least continuance and fullest of troubles."[1] Indeed, Winthrop was governor not by anything resembling a democratic election by the free men of the expedition, but by the decision of the "proprietors" of a land grant from King Charles I, himself a noted opponent of democracy who frequently dismissed Parliament and tried to rule without it. His sermon on the ship *Arabella* (or prayerful) celebrated and demanded a religiously-sanctioned government for the colony. At its conclusion, Winthrop made reference to the passage of Jesus' "sermon on the mount" that tells his followers: "You are the light of the world. A city that is set on a hill cannot be hid. Nor do men light a lamp and put it under a bushel, but on a stand, and it gives light to all in the house. Let your light so shine before men." Winthrop's words were:

> We shall find that the God of Israel is among us, when ten of us shall be able to resist a thousand of our enemies, when he shall make us a praise and glory, that men shall say of succeeding plantations: the Lord make it like that of New England: for we must consider that we shall be as a city upon a hill, the eyes of all people are upon us.

He cautioned that failure to live as Christians and in communal support of the leadership would cause God to "withdraw his present help" and "special commission" and rupture the "covenant with Him for this work." This would lead not just to disaster for the colony, but would discredit Christianity itself. Given this holy mission, it is not surprising that Winthrop saw the hand of god in the extermination of the local Indian population by smallpox. In a letter home after the colony was established he cited Psalms 2:8 for this belief: "Ask of me, and I shall give thee, the heathen for thine inheritance, and the uttermost parts of the earth for thy possession." In Winthrop's view of the natives, "God hath so pursued them, as for 300 miles space the greatest part of them are swept away by smallpox which still continues among them. So as God hath thereby cleared our title to this place, those who remain in these parts, being in all not 50, have put themselves under our protection."

The "city upon a hill" has been cited and celebrated by politicians from Thomas Jefferson to John Kennedy as the image of America, pure and promising, in contrast to the self-interested corruption first of the European kings and then of the Soviet Union and its allies in the former colonies. Abraham Lincoln called America "the last best hope of earth," and Ronald Reagan transformed it into a "shining city upon a hill." Generations of US military trainers explained to an affirming Congress that American values would rub off on the repressive officers and soldiers they were training in dictatorships, from Haiti in the 1930s to Zaire in the 1970s to Saudi Arabia in the 1990s to Uzbekistan in the 2000s. The homage is bipartisan. Reagan made Jeanne Kirkpatrick UN ambassador because she had developed a moral framework in which right-wing US-backed "authoritarians" could be guided to democracy, while left-wing "totalitarians" could not be. Secretary of State Madeleine Albright provided explicit moral justification not just for misalliance, but also for military action: "If we have to use force, it is because we are America. We are the

---

1 Clinton Rossiter, *Seedtime of the Republic: The Origin of the American Tradition of Political Liberty*, Harcourt, Brace, New York, 1953, pp. 13, 53.

indispensable nation. We stand tall. We see further into the future."[1] George W. Bush used variations of the words freedom and liberty a mind-numbing 46 times in his second inaugural address, nearly all concerning America's role in providing them to other people. President Obama told his armed forces in 2009 that the country they were serving is "unlike the great powers of old" because of it has "underwritten global security." Military domination has been transformed into a humanitarian mission. Might is deployed only for right.

No single sermon, no matter how many times cited, could have created the powerful exceptionalism, embraced by America's public figures and sustained by its citizens, that led it across the continent and into global supremacy. What, then, are the American traits and attitudes that combined to form something of a national character that embraced exceptionalism? When House Democrat Bill Delahunt held a hearing in 2008 on the decline in America's global reputation after the invasion of Iraq, he quoted Ulysses S. Grant, when he was still a general: "The Nation united will have the strength to dictate to all others: conform to justice and right." Delahunt noted that Grant cautioned, though, that "[t]he moment conscience leaves, physical strength will avail nothing in the long run." This Soft Eagle was not bemoaning America's ability and mission to dictate, but rather the Bush administration's squandering of the moral authority to do so effectively. A scholar of exceptionalism, John Tirman, challenged Delahunt's orientation in his testimony by linking exceptionalism to acceptance of the convenient "myth" of a frontier held by savages:

> The fundamental self-perception of our mission and actions in the world, one we have carried for centuries, is that of the frontier — an exceptionally sturdy image for American politics, the backdrop for our national character and sense of purpose. For nearly 300 years, settling, cultivating, and "taming" the frontier drove the Europeans who came to this continent. When the frontier closed — when the last of the indigenous tribes was subdued and the land taken — it created a sense of crisis in American politics. Teddy Roosevelt in particular responded to this by looking outward, across oceans, to imagine frontiers abroad. Much of the ensuing century has involved America in such global frontiers....The myth of the frontier is an architecture of American politics and how we frame our role in the world....These ideas, so redolent in TR's time, remain powerful: one can see the war on terrorism, especially in Iraq, in terms virtually identical to our continental expansion, the suppression of Filipinos in Roosevelt's presidency, or the US war in Vietnam....These references not only assume that the whole world is our rightful domain of action, but that an innate, moral superiority guides and justifies this mission.

Committee member Greg Meeks, in questioning Tirman, said that his analysis was so far outside the boundaries of congressional debate that it was akin to the appearance of W.E.B. Dubois before that Committee in 1949 in opposition to a military aid bill. Meeks quoted Dubois' testimony:

> The idea seems to be that we can conquer the world and make it do our bidding because we are rich....Even if this were true, it begs the question of the right

---

1 Albright gets her geography confused when she celebrates American power. She has said: "I was a little girl in World War II and I'm used to being freed by Americans." Her family fled from Prague to London. The former was liberated by the Soviet Union; the latter was never occupied.

and justice of our role. Why in God's name do we want to control the earth? Is it because our success in ruling man? At this time, do we want to rule Russia when we cannot rule Alabama?...To teach the world democracy we chose at the time Secretary of State Byrnes, trained in the democracy of South Carolina....Also, our media and education perpetuate dangerous myths: how can we guide the world without exact and careful knowledge?

After supporting the insights of both Dubois and Tirman, Meeks, who represents a largely black district in New York and has little fear of seeing his re-election chances damaged by being painted as an anti-imperialist, still felt constrained to maintain his place in the mainstream debate with a little exceptionalism of his own: "I say all of that believing that we are living in the greatest country on the planet."[1]

Along with the myth of the frontier came the reality of enforcing it and a number of other frontiers, between white and red, white and black, and rich and poor. This led to a belligerent attitude that civil rights historian Taylor Branch calls deeply American. The "tough Jew" defensiveness that characterizes the neo-conservative movement is but a modern variant of the upper class bluster and lower class combativeness that were present at the creation of the republic, and have aided continental and global expansion. Franklin himself celebrated the belligerence, looking with favor on the rattlesnake as a national symbol long before his flirtation with the turkey. The rattlesnake adorned a revolutionary banner with the warning, "Don't Tread on Me," which follows closely the motto of the Scottish regiments impressed into service to the British empire, *nemo me impune lacessit* (Nobody harasses me with impunity), or its broad Scots version, *Wha daur meddle wi' me?* (Who dares meddle with me?).[2]

There are probably two main wellsprings of this belligerence, England's domination of its neighbors and the Atlantic slave trade. The Scottish and Irish settlers who dominated the Appalachian frontier had been inculcated with belligerence by a history of centuries of struggle against an overwhelming English enemy and, ironically, of crucial military service for its empire. Then, for their first 150 years on the American continent, they faced the Indian nations without the protection of government, since their encroachments were generally disavowed and discouraged by Britain, which hoped to retain Indian support in the struggle with France. While the new American government was more sympathetic to the settlers and used military force to push Indians to the West, most of the day-to-day violence of the 100 years of expansion that followed independence involved the settlers, who learned to live armed and ready, and to be unyielding in their demands for land. Criticism by what they perceived as urban elites of their rough ways and their grasping for a share of the American dream led to an alienation from and an anger at not the wealthy, to whose station they could, in classless America, at least aspire, but at the urban moralizers who asked them to limit their appetites, and intruded in their rural castles. Thus began the great divide in America that shows up in every presidential election between "blue"

---

1   US House of Representatives, Committee on Foreign Affairs, Hearing before the Subcommittee on International Organizations, Human Rights, and Oversight: Release of the Subcommittee Report, The Decline in America's Reputation: Why?, June 11, 2008, available from the Government Printing Office and on the Subcommittee's website.

2   This query occurs in a number of traditional ballads, notably "Kinmont Willie" and "Little Jock Elliot."

and "red" states, and indeed between urban and rural parts of states, a divide within the white population between gun-controlling French film-lovers and opera-goers of the cities and well-armed rural NASCAR and country-western fans, whose "Grand Old Opry" was pointedly named to reject the classical opera.

The slave trade left the Southern states with millions of individual tragedies and one structural one. Domination, not compromise, was the only way to run a plantation. Slaveholders and slaves alike, women and children as well as men, lived with violence and the undercurrent of its constant threat in their daily relations for 350 years, from the importation of the first slaves to Jamestown in 1619 until the consistent federal enforcement of voting rights in the 1970s resulted in the election of officials with an interest in unbiased police forces. Pockets of violence and alienation from authority in European cities had never been for the faint of heart, but because of the placement of Scots-Irish on the frontier and Africans in the rural South, America developed a more widespread belligerence. It sparked and then fueled the Civil War, and has led to rates of imprisonment that are among the highest in the world, dwarfing those of similarly wealthy nations.[1] General William Tecumseh Sherman, ironically named for the noted Shawnee patriot when he would lead the seizure of the Indian lands of the Great Plains after the Civil War, thought he saw a solution to at least the Southern belligerence that had led to the Civil War. After fighting his way into Mississippi in 1863, he told his commanding general in Washington that there were Southerners who could not be absorbed into the body politic, but rather had to be extirpated, root and branch:

> The young bloods of the South: sons of planters, lawyers about town, good billiard players and sportsmen, men who never did work and never will. War suits them, and the rascals are brave, fine riders, bold to rashness, and dangerous subjects in every sense. They care not a *sou* for niggers, land, or any thing. They hate Yankees per se, and don't bother their brains about the past, present, or future....This is a larger class of people than most men suppose, and they are the most dangerous set of men that this war has turned loose upon the world.... These men must all be killed or employed by us before we can hope for peace."[2]

While Sherman softened his approach in hopes of an easy reintegration in 1865, so much so that new President Andrew Johnson renounced the terms he offered to Confederate forces, Johnson was under no illusion that the war had broken the back of these Southern cavaliers. The Union eventually put their belligerence to work for it, as he suggested, and the US armed forces in the 20th century developed a decidedly Southern patina. The large number of officers from the network of Southern military colleges and of soldiers from the former Confederacy brought the élan of Sherman's "young bloods" to the stars and stripes, which has acquired as great a reverence in the South as the old stars and bars. The racism developed to protect slavery, like that needed to drive off the Indians, remained. Lincoln's "last best hope" was clearly a "great white hope," as novelist Jack London called the challenger needed to take black heavyweight boxing champion Jack

---

1 The *World Prison Population List*, King's College of London, International Centre for Prison Studies, sixth edition cites seven per thousand for the United States, versus one per thousand for Canada.

2 William Tecumseh Sherman, *Memoirs*, Library of America, New York, 1990, p. 363.

Johnson down a peg. John Kennedy's inaugural pledge to "bear any burden" in defense of others' liberty clearly concerned a "white man's burden," as Rudyard Kipling called the colonizing mission.

Another American trait that sustains domination is anti-intellectualism, arising first from the rough-hewn background of so many immigrants and then from the anger of white Southerners at high-flowing Abolitionist rhetoric. Criticism of foreign policy is seen as intellectual treason if domestic or intellectual ingratitude if foreign, and in either case a misuse of the benefits of education to bite rather than lick the hand that made the education possible. The mildest criticism of foreign policy from the left is willfully interpreted by individuals on the right, who are often far harsher in their criticism of domestic policy, as a personal insult to soldiers, their families, and their ancestors. Country singer Merle Haggard captured the sentiment brilliantly in the "warning" of violence he issued in "The Fightin' Side of Me" in 1970 to "squirrelly" intellectuals who were "harpin' on the wars we fight, "gripin' 'bout the ways things oughta be," and "runnin' down my country...runnin' down the way of life our fightin' men have fought and died to keep." France's refusal to take part in US wars is portrayed as reneging on a debt incurred in the World Wars, with no thought given to America's similar debt to France from the War of Indepence.

For intellectual leadership many Americans turn not to professors but to a state-oriented religiosity that places a veneer of sanctity, by its revelatory nature illogical and so unassailable, on imperial policy. Manifest destiny, the catchall justification for expansion across the continent, was routinely hailed as the equivalent of God's mission for the Israelites. America and its flag became conflated with Christianity and its cross. Military chaplains and generals alike invoked God's approval as they prepared American soldiers for battle or burial. New York's Cardinal Spellman called for the "holy crusaders" to win "Christ's war" in Vietnam, as he blessed with holy water the aircraft being prepared for bombing runs, and Baptist televangelists such as Jerry Falwell and Pat Robertson preached for what they portrayed as a Biblically-predicted and sanctioned Holy War against Islam and for Israel.[1] According to a Pew poll, 60 percent of Americans report that religion is "very important" to them, a rate that is from two to six times as high as in other developed countries, although it is lower than in most formerly colonized countries.[2] Nearly all Americans have some connection to an organized religion during their upbringing, and a majority of adults reports a belief that the Bible is literally true, with four out of five believing in the virgin birth of Jesus Christ as the son of god.[3] Even accounting for the exaggeration found by studies checking actual versus claimed religious practices, it is clear that most Americans finds reasonable the inherently irrational arguments of religious justification for state policy.[4]

---

1 See John Cooney, *The American Pope: The Life and Times of Francis Cardinal Spellman*, Times Books, New York, 1984, pp. 299, 306. Quotations by Falwell and Robertson are catalogued on mediamatters.org.

2 Pew Global Attitudes Project, December 19, 2002.

3 *Newsweek* poll, reported December 10, 1984. See http://www.msnbc.msn.com/id/6650997/site/newsweek/

4 See, for example, C. Kirk Hardaway and P.L. Marler, "Did You Really Go to Church This Week? Behind the Poll Data," in *The Christian Century*, May 6, 1998, pp. 472-475, which found church attendance to be half of what respondents claimed.

Americans who are atheists are trapped by good manners and the ethos of tolerance into respecting the expression of religiously-based opinions in policy discussions. It seems normal, perhaps required, for candidates to talk about how their faith informs their decisions. Presidents echo bumper stickers by ending speeches with "God bless America," whereas if they called on the equally proven Great Pumpkin it would elicit howls for impeachment or institutionalization. Religiosity adds an emotionalism to political deliberations, making other appeals to deep, irrational feelings more legitimate. People who are comfortable following religious inspiration in public policy have already left Plato's grove of Academus, where adherence to the rules of logic in inquiry was required. Given the imprimatur of religious sanctity and humanitarianism, it is not surprising that Americans display a maudlin self-perception of unappreciated benevolence that itself fuels their support for foreign wars and alliances. At the gathering of world leaders and opinion-makers at Davos, Switzerland, in January 2003, after a speech in which he tried out the "facts" about Iraq's alleged weapons of mass destruction that he presented to such effect at the United Nations a week later, Secretary of State Colin Powell struck another false chord, reprising Wilson's myth that America's surge to global dominance in the 20th century constituted disinterested sacrifice: "We have gone forth from our shores repeatedly over the last hundred years...and put wonderful young men and women at risk....and we have asked for nothing except enough ground to bury them in, and otherwise we have returned home... to live our lives in peace."[1]

So, we have some answers, and perhaps some targets. The exceptionalism that drives domination has its roots in a frontier ideology, a racially-tinged and class-driven cultural belligerence, the sanction of religion, reflexive patriotism, and an anger at not being appreciated for the good works all these attitudes convince us we are doing for others. However, America has a diverse and constantly changing population, with surprisingly little governmental control of its media and activities. How are these traits and the resulting belief in exceptionalism remade and sustained in succeeding generations?

HOW THEY DO IT

In 1969, the self-appointed vanguard of the Turkeys, the Students for a Democratic Society, published a call to arms in *New Left Notes* titled with a line from Bob Dylan's Subterranean Homesick Blues: "You don't need a weatherman to know which way the wind blows." The phrase was intended both to encourage young people to reject any authority figure who contradicted their untutored experience, and to take a "countercultural dig" at the Progressive Labor Party, which was trying to infiltrate SDS.[2] The Progressive Labor cadres cited Stalin, Lenin, and Marx in support of their argument that SDS should spend its time organizing workers against the capitalist class, rather than supporting "nation-

---

1 See http://www.state.gov/secretary/former/powell/remarks/2003/16869.htm for Powell's speech and http://www.state.gov/secretary/former/powell/remarks/2003/19747.htm for his remarks, which were made in response to a question. The context is discussed in http://www.truthorfiction.com/rumors/p/powell-empires.htm.
2 Mark Rudd, *Underground: My Life with SDS and the Weathermen*, William Morrow/HarperCollins, New York, 2009, p. 146.

alist" Vietnamese and black liberation movements. The "weatherman" being castigated was as much Lenin as Channel 7's suit and tie man. The Weatherman statement called for students and young white workers to support those struggling against imperialism, and heralded a transition from protest and disruption to outright war and bombing like that chosen by Fidel Castro in 1953 and Nelson Mandela in 1961. In the short-term both of those choices failed to ignite wider rebellion and led to defeat and imprisonment, and the Weathermen's revolution also failed.

Hidden in the manifesto, however, was another line from the same song that held then and holds today the promise of success: "The pump don't work 'cause the vandals took the handles." SDS took the pump to mean the physical infrastructure of bridges, power lines, and commerce that moves society along each day. Berkeley's Vietnam Day Committee trying to block troop trains and disrupt the draft board in Oakland, the Berrigan brothers burning draft records in Catonsville, and Sam Melville blowing up power plants, were the inspiration for SDS as it bombed dozens of imperial targets, like Harvard's Center for International Studies, the Bank of America, and the home of the judge who had sentenced Black Panthers. The "armed protests" were deliciously symbolic to the left, but to the average citizen, who was not steeped in dialectical debate, they were incomprehensible and counter-productive. Their primary effect was to turn the Weathermen into a Weather Underground that spent all its time evading the FBI. The pump that the Weathermen should have been vandalizing was not physical but cultural. The stream on which the entire imperial enterprise floats comes out of a cultural pump that constantly regenerates exceptionalism and celebrates the machinery of domination, if not domination itself. "Taking its handles" requires challenging and discrediting it with mainstream America, not blowing up the pump-house and killing the mechanics.

The cultural pump is seemingly everywhere in American life. While at times it disgorges coordinated propaganda by the federal government, corporations that benefit from empire, and neo-conservative cheerleaders, its primary flow consists of voluntary effusions by individuals with no vested interest in or ideological commitment to domination. This localized, informal participation makes domination seem normal and inevitable, so "day to day." The output of the pump is predicated upon two themes borrowed from European rulers: the *noblesse oblige*, or obligations of the privileged 18th century French nobility, and the 20th century German experiment in *Blutdenken*, or thinking with the blood, meaning an appeal to fear, pathos, and patriotic and protective emotions rather than to logic.

American *noblesse oblige*, an obligation to provide service not to the domestic masses but to the world, which conveniently means domination of it for its own good, has been handed down over generations in east coast preparatory schools and elite colleges. Biographer Kai Bird captured the transmission in his treatments of the paragons of the mid-20th century "Establishment," John J. McCloy and the Bundy brothers, McGeorge and William.[1] McCloy, the informal chairman of the establishment, was a War department planner, the first World Bank president, and the chairman of the Chase Manhattan bank. As the wis-

---

1 *The Chairman: John J. McCloy, The Making of the American Establishment*, Simon & Schuster, New York, 1992; *The Color of Truth: McGeorge Bundy and William Bundy, Brothers in Arms*, Simon & Schuster, New York, 1998.

est of the "wise men" he counseled Johnson that world order required that America keep its commitment to victory in Vietnam, and counseled Carter to admit the Shah of Iran for the same reason. The Bundy brothers were "the best and the brightest" of the government functionaries who were captured in David Halberstam's exposé of that name lying about motives and progress in Vietnam, again on the grounds that world order required that America maintain its reputation of being able to impose its will.

McCloy, the Bundys, and their imperial peers imbibed their devotion to serving the world's interests through America's at schools like Groton, Exeter, and Peddie and at colleges like Yale, Amherst, and Harvard. August headmasters and presidents hammered home the message that it was the responsibility of those privileged enough to attend these institutions to use their talents to rule benevolently but firmly. McCloy himself cited imperial Rome as a model for America's global responsibilities when he counseled the graduates at Haverford College in 1965 to defer to and then grow to emulate the *gravitas*, or sound judgment, of the current guardians of America and the world.[1] Throughout the rise of America to domination during the 20th century, this message of the duty to dominate was delivered in an atmosphere at once religious and patriotic, often in sermons in chapels adorned with American flags.

After the students at the elite campuses rose against the Vietnam War, the message at these institutions became subtler but no less demanding. They still imbue respect for diplomatic and military service as a gift to the fortunes of the developing countries, but also promote a doctrine of charity as foreign policy that obscures the way the unfortunates' misfortune is linked to American domination. Students spend their spring breaks and semesters abroad being flown at their parents' huge expense to impoverished communities to participate in construction projects. Speeches by and recruitment for the State Department and CIA are common in the School of International Service at American University, implying that their service is humanitarian rather than imperial. Many universities, including American, accept contracts from imperial interventions and have conferences on counter-insurgency and military supremacy. These activities are less directly war-related than, for example, American's hosting of the Army's chemical weapons program during World War I, which still offers up shells and poisons on its athletic fields, or Harvard and Cornell's counter-insurgency contracts during the Vietnam War. However, they spread the same educational message: US foreign policy brings order and good to others.

Blutdenken, or "thinking with the blood," is promoted more in the media than on campuses. To cement public debate firmly in acceptance of empire as the norm, its supporters have consistently devoted their intellect to propaganda rather than analysis. The scriptwriters in the White House, Pentagon, and State Department and the politicians and think-tank commentators, funded directly or indirectly by military contractors and global corporations, who discharge imperial propaganda have adopted the tactic that the Nazi Party refined in its rise to power: serve up fear and pathos, so that people will "think with the blood," rather than with the mind. The obvious effectiveness of this method over the past 60 years gives no reason to think that the grip of the appeal to the blood, happily and

---

1 Kai Bird, *The Chairman: John J. McCloy, The Making of the American Establishment*, Simon & Schuster, New York, 1992, pp. 574-575.

profitably broadcast through the quasi-statal media giants and a plethora of independent actors, will be loosened in the coming decades.

Two examples from the invasion and occupation of Iraq in the 2000s of the government and the think-tanks collaborating to support war and domination were the claims of "weapons of mass destruction" and the yellow ribbon campaign to "support our troops." As Woody Allen's lawyer said of his client's bizarre divorce proceedings, the fraud over weapons of mass destruction perpetrated by the Bush administration in the run-up to the invasion of Iraq was remarkable only because it was publicized, not because it was atypical. It does represent perhaps the fastest successful "marketing" campaign, to use the White House chief of staff's phrase, in American imperial history. Persistent demands from Bush officials for musings from intelligence analysts on the possibility of Iraq having functional chemical, biological, and nuclear capabilities overwhelmed the bureaucracy, which caved in and provided them. President Bush and national security advisor Condoleezza Rice were able to speak of a possible "mushroom cloud" over Cincinnati as the "smoking gun" of proof critics were demanding because they could point to intelligence reports on Iraq's possible intentions, even though the intelligence community knew, from its "sniffing" of the isotopes around Iraq, that no enrichment of uranium had occurred after Iraq's primitive capability was destroyed in the 1991 war.

Secretary of State Powell forced CIA analysts to approve every line in his speech at the United Nations in 2003 justifying invasion, and had CIA director George Tenet sit behind him to affirm that point. Yet virtually every claim in the speech, from mobile biological weapons labs to bomb-carrying drone aircraft to sites of stored weapons of mass destruction to the use of special metals for nuclear enrichment rather than artillery shells, proved to be false. Much of the false information about weapons and sites had been generated by US covert operatives such as Iraqi politician Ahmad Chalabi, and been leaked to and dramatized by the media, notably by Judith Miller of the *New York Times*. Similarly, SISMI, the Italian intelligence agency, passed to the CIA in 2001 and directly to the White House in 2002 a forged agreement for Niger to supply Iraq with uranium for enrichment. The agreement was cited by top officials in Britain and the United States, including President Bush in the State of the Union speech before the invasion of Iraq, and was reported widely by the world's press until a cursory review by the International Atomic Energy Agency revealed it to be fraudulent. Former US intelligence officials eventually identified neo-conservative writer, Iran-Contra conspirator, and Chalabi ally Michael Ledeen as a party in the forgery.[1] Simply by reporting the claims and counter-claims about weapons of mass destruction, even the most diligent media were making the national debate about whether Iraq had certain weapons, not about whether the United States had the right to enforce its own version of arms control even if Iraq did. Claims of Iraq's links to al-Qaeda, pushed so hard by Cheney and his Pentagon policy office under Douglas Feith, were similarly debated in the press as if their accuracy would justify an invasion, rather than a discussion of the roots of the 9/11 attack in the long war for control of the Middle East.

---

1   Ledeen denied the charge, although he acknowledged working for the same Italian magazine that received and distributed the forged documents. Ledeen had collaborated with SISMI and its shadowy offshoot *Propaganda-Due*, or P-2, during the 1980 elections to publicize claims about Libya's financial dealings with President Carter's brother.

Fear was the emotion purposely triggered by the fraud over weapons of mass destruction. Love of country and its young people was the emotion purposely triggered by the campaign to "support our troops." The slogan first appeared on a yellow magnetic ribbon on the back of a car in 2001, and quickly was replicated in millions of such ribbons, some in red, white, and blue with the subscript "Freedom isn't free," implying that military service equated with protecting freedom. There had been a similar campaign during the first Gulf War, in reference to a pop song from the 1970s in which a yellow ribbon was tied around an old oak tree to tell a returning prisoner, perhaps from Vietnam, that he was still his lover's choice. Indeed, the anti-war message of the Woodstock Nation was badly bruised when a yellow ribbon appeared on the cover of its trusted magazine, *Rolling Stone*, in 1991. For this second Gulf War, Wal-Mart, among other businesses, distributed the ribbons with no apparent coordination with the Pentagon, but the Pentagon jumped on the concept, and appropriated the words, "support our troops," for everything from carefully-screened marches to requests for funds to Congress. Those three words echoed through the political spectrum, even though their meaning was obscure in terms of policy. "The troops," in many ways, became the policy. In a reversal of roles, the purpose of the nation appeared to be to improve the lives of the guardians, rather than the purpose of the guardians being to improve the lives of the people of the nation. People calling for a US attack on Iran, like Barbara Ledeen, wife to Michael and a neo-conservative advocate in her own right, justified the move as a way to reduce the danger to US forces in Iraq, who included some of her children.

Liberal comedian, and future senator, Al Franken toured Iraq with *Blutdenken* country star Toby Keith to entertain the troops, and even Turkeys began to use the troops as the basis for their anti-war rallies by publicizing military families who had turned against the war and by sporting buttons and banners saying: "Support the troops: bring them home." That message softened the anti-war movement into a social service agency that wanted to end the war because US troops were dying needlessly, not because Iraqis were dying needlessly. For five years "the troops" were presented as an apolitical cause, feted by left, right, and center. Americans could disagree on the war, was the implication, but all should agree on supporting our troops. But what did that mean? Providing them with medical care when they came back broken and with jobs when they came back whole? Voting to fund their equipment and weapons, as Democrats implied when they became, in minority leader Nancy Pelosi's words, "the party of more body armor?" The Pentagon's investment paid off in 2007, when anti-war Democrats regained control of Congress but were unable to build a firm majority against funding the war. In the end, "Congress will support the troops" and pass the administration's funding bill, said Senate Armed Services chair Carl Levin, before the first penny was requested, and he was right. Too many Dixies and even Soft Eagles among Democrats were scared of being accused of cutting off troops in the field, when they knew that the only way to get the troops out of the field was to do exactly that. The drumbeat of reverence for "the troops, the troops" had had its intended effect.

Broadcasting appeals to emotions about "our troops" and bullying government analysts and the media into entertaining absurd conjectures about Iraq's weapons of mass destruction represented just another day at the office for the imperial advertising industry that has been operating since World War II. Indeed, it is the well-established and primary purpose of the industry to create a fearful and dutiful public from alarmist interpretations of phony "intelligence" findings, government "white papers" and think-tank reports. The technocratic, pseudo-analytic "white papers" that reveal dramatic facts and trends gleaned by experts and intelligence operatives are a particularly American contribution to the art of propaganda, and can be found in most foreign policy debates after World War II. In her book on President Reagan's battle with the nuclear freeze movement, *Way Out There in the Blue*, Frances Fitzgerald reported that Assistant Secretary of Defense Richard Perle, whose track record of wild exaggerations based on "studies" of such unknowable matters as progress in Soviet anti-satellite weapons drove liberal Members of Congress to the extreme of covering their ears in disgust when he talked to them, had as a credo: "Democracies will not sacrifice to defend their security in the absence of a sense of danger."[1] Perle's comment reveals the essence of the imperial advertising industry's approach, which is to define all military projects as vital to people's "security" and then create a sense of "danger" for them if the projects are not undertaken.

Perle is an appropriate person to cite, since he bridges the generational divide between the fear-mongers of the 1950s and those of the 2000s. He was brought into security studies by Albert Wohlstetter, the Pentagon consultant on nuclear war-fighting who was parodied by Peter Sellers in the film "Dr. Strangelove, or How I Learned to Stop Worrying and Love the Bomb." Wohlstetter provided intellectual support to Paul Nitze and his Committee on the Present Danger, which from its founding in 1951 broadcast claims of Soviet advances in weaponry, such as the supposed bomber and missile gaps, that were repeatedly proven false, yet stayed, by their very repetition, prominent in the public mind. Among Wohlstetter's graduate students was Paul Wolfowitz, who helped design the Iraqi fraud as deputy secretary of defense. Perle and Wolfowitz supported the US invasion and occupation of Vietnam while studying and then while working in Washington staff positions, and they were worried that losing the war would curb Americans' appetite for deploying power internationally. Even though the nonsensically optimistic claims of progress in Vietnam by the government and allied groups under Johnson and Nixon provided much of the reason for the eventual demise in public support for the war, the apologists decided to go back to that well, and continue manufacturing helpful intelligence.

The problem was that the CIA, burned by its errors of analysis in Vietnam, was wary of providing new false fuel for their fires of fear. Enter "Team B." The story of the Team B exercise is complex, and well told by Anne Cahn in her 1998 book, *Killing Détente*. At its core Team B was an attack on the CIA's judgment that Soviet military power was mediocre and that Soviet military intentions were parochial rather than global. President Ford permitted a review of this assessment by Wolfowitz and other Wohlstetter heirs, many of whom then helped revive the alarmist Committee on the Present Danger in the Carter years and maintain its drumbeat for military spending and imperial action. Predictably, one of the subgroups of the review team found that the Soviet Union, far from being weak and cautious, was engaged in a massive buildup and challenge to US security. The Com-

---

1 Simon & Schuster, New York, 2000, p. 179.

mittee on the Present Danger sent many of its members into the Reagan administration, where they largely had their way with both budget and policy.

Under President Reagan, the Pentagon spent as much as could be absorbed on expanding US power at sea, on land, in the air, and even in space, and the State Department and CIA funded a series of civil wars in Central America, Asia, and Africa. The administration cited the Soviet military threat to Europe and the supposedly Soviet-fomented wars of liberation and revolt, from South Africa to El Salvador. The claims were always dubious, often hysterical and frequently just fraudulent.[1] These fires that were used to heat the public's blood were fed by tax-funded offices for "public diplomacy" in the White House and State Department and by close coordination with semi-private entities, such as Freedom House, the Heritage Foundation, and neo-conservative activist Penn Kemble's PRODEMCA. During the Clinton administration the apologists for dominance continued their fulminations against Saddam Hussein, China, Colombian rebels, and anyone else who was handy in a largely benign period. They found some resonance in the Dixiecratic foreign policy of Bill Clinton and Al Gore, which accorded respectability to their Committee for the Liberation of Iraq and its call for "regime change."

Then the advocates of domination struck gold with the September 11 attacks, which they successfully exploited by turning a single counter-attack on the Afghan sanctuary into a full-scale and permanent war against "terrorism" and anyone they claimed was supporting terrorism or even might one day do so. To this they added President Bush's campaign for "democracy," and when that word failed to ignite public support, the simpler and even more ill-defined "freedom" for Americans, Arabs, and particularly Afghan women. A new generation of think-tanks backed by military corporations and right-wing foundations churned out both appeals to the blood and analyses justifying US military interventions. A third incarnation of the Committee on the Present Danger and the Center for Security Policy run by Frank Gaffney, a former aide to Perle at the Pentagon, identified the new enemy as "Islamo-fascism" both at home and abroad, and various sons and daughters-in-law of angry classicist Donald Kagan called for combat in more and more countries.

None of these activities would have been effective without the breathless eagerness of private media to outdo each other in "scoops" and participation in a raging, if misleading debate. By rote the media accord special status to government claims, leaks, and studies, particularly those featured in speeches by top officials, publishing them as news. The media do not formally endorse the claims by reporting them, and they assuage their conscience for balance by often including a contrary claim by an elected official or mainstream expert, rather than a critique of the imperial project itself. This constant drone of "balanced" features effectively enshrines invasion as a viable policy option, occupation as reasonable, and even torture as an unfortunate, tough choice to make in carrying out those decisions. Leading newspapers reinforce the sense of legitimacy by proudly announcing

---

1 Chapter 4 described how State Department lawyer Jim Michel simply ignored House staffer Cynthia Arnson's contradiction of his claims about a Salvadoran massacre. Chapter 5 described the case of Nicaraguan defector Roger Miranda, whose claims that Nicaragua was expanding its army to take over all of Central America were displayed prominently by major newspapers just days before a vote on aid to the Contras.

that they have withheld stories, sometimes for lengthy periods, because the administra-tion argued that publishing them would compromise an operation.

The big story, the imperial decision to dominate, is not a minute-by-minute action story, and so receives no airtime, but a decision to attack in one way versus another re-ceives hours of excited review by former officers, who by financial connections are some-times not so former. The South African constitution does not include in protected free speech the right to speak in favor of invading or threatening another country; if that were the rule in the United States there would be little left on the editorial pages. Actual war reports are rated PG: nobody dies and no village burns as they did in Vietnam before the Pentagon clamped down on access and the media became leery of becoming the "story" because of attacks on their "bias" by the White House and its mouthpieces in Congress. A favored photograph of the media after the invasion of Iraq was of a burly Marine cradling an Iraqi infant and sheltering it from the chaos around, as if the Marines had nothing to do with the creation of the chaos. In both national and local media, Americans are treated to a barrage of stories and photo features about their "fallen" combat heroes, while the foreign victims of US invasion or support for a brutal regime are ignored.

The military academies and services and the officer training courses the Pentagon happily funds and aggressively places in colleges, high schools, and even middle schools, spread the dual appeals of *noblesse oblige* and *Blutdenken* through a combined message that military domination is both a tool to preserve American freedom and a humanitarian mis-sion for the dominated. From lectures on campuses by current and former counter-insur-gency commanders to the crossed swords that a girls' soccer team enters the field under on senior day, from a Marine general calling the swoop of helicopters "the sound of freedom" to catchy advertisements in movie theaters showing soldiers rescuing flood victims and brandishing shiny guns and swords, service in the three-million strong active and reserve forces through which perhaps a third of American men pass is sold and resold thousands of times a day as a normal, necessary, and moral rite of passage. "Free the oppressed" is emblazoned on the Army special forces' berets, although they still favor "Kill them all, let God sort them out" t-shirts.

Marine Expeditionary Forces sound like they are on a scientific adventure, perhaps distributing their "Toys for Tots" on a Mercy ship. AFRICOM's port calls in which body-guards of dictators are trained produce pictures of kids in hospitals and bore-holes being dug, so much so that after hearing an AFRICOM briefing a South African scholar remarked that he had no idea that the US armed forces were a social service agency. President Obama accepted the Nobel peace prize with the same message: America must use deadly force to keep the world peaceful, and those who provide the force are on a humanitarian mission for others. Both in the armed forces and in the civilian offices of government the unquestioned assumption has become that in every country, in every contest for power, there are good guys and bad guys, and our troops are always on the side of the good guys, even though the good guys might recently have been bad guys until they switched their allegiance to us. Whatever happens, as President Bush said in 2007, "our cause is just."

This government-led message is amplified many times over by private actors who re-ceive no particular instructions. No political commissar in Soviet history, with credible threats of violence and economic punishment for the recalcitrant, could have ordered up a more pleasing stew than this one, voluntarily delivered. Sporting events start with the national anthem, replete with images of soldiers fighting for freedom even as they feed those displaced by the fighting, and active duty and wounded soldiers are introduced on the giant replay screens to standing ovations of thanks for defending freedom. The National Football League and the big state colleges are only too happy to accept the thrill of a fighter jet swooping over the field before kick-off. When the audience is large enough to justify the expense, as at the Super Bowl, they receive a number of jets in the "missing man" formation, to honor heart-warming loyalty and sacrifice. Film star Michael Douglas, liberal light and avowed proponent of stemming arms sales worldwide, took the field during the pre-game show in the 2005 Super Bowl and led a tribute to America's troops in their holy stand against terrorism and for freedom. The kickoff event for the 2002 NFL season, the first after 9/11, was so over the top in its accolades for troops protecting freedom that it was tough to top, but Douglas did it.

Corporations trying to read America's mood outdo each other in their generosity and thanks for troops. In millions of store windows, "thanks to our troops" is proclaimed, and troops get special lines and discounts on Amtrak and at private bus companies. Car dealerships duel with ever-growing American flags hovering over their lots. Fund-raising events for active-duty and wounded troops and their families fill the airwaves and the internet. Sears' "grant a wish" program lets customers "give thanks and fulfill wishes of military heroes and their families for the sacrifices they make" by buying them presents, and soldiersangels.com raises money to do the same. Caribou Coffee wants its customers to send coffee to the troops in Iraq, and Borders Books wants the coffee sent to the troops at the Walter Reed Army rehabilitation hospital.

Highways and bridges are constantly being named after veterans and their units. New York State renamed Route 38 the "Highway of valor" in 2009 to honor Vietnam veterans, and the road was inaugurated with a motorcycle ride organized by veterans. The leader was portrayed in the local newspaper as someone who, "[l]ike other Vietnam veterans, weathered the rage of his countrymen" when he returned from combat. He ritually included in his interview the mythical claim of being spat upon by anti-war protestors.[1] Every year a massive motorcycle rally of perhaps half a million bikes propagates another hoary myth, the claim that there were prisoners of war held by Vietnam after the war, which started as a political ploy by the Nixon administration and spun so far out of control that most government offices today fly the black POW/MIA flag.[2] All over the country one finds meetings halls that double as taverns for the American Legion, the Veterans of Foreign Wars, and the Marine Corps League, which serve as a constant advertisement for the normality of foreign intervention.

With no federal bidding, cities and towns organize parades and ceremonies to send off and then to thank their returning soldiers, alive or dead. With the demise of the draft, the

---

1 Raymond Drumsta, Highway Dedicated to Vietnam Vets, *Ithaca (NY) Journal*, October 10, 2009, p. 1A.

2 See the discussion of the POW and spitting myths in Caleb S. Rossiter, *The Chimes of Freedom Flashing: A Personal History of the Vietnam Anti-War Movement and the 1960s*, TCA Press, Washington, DC, 1996, pp. 289-292.

send-offs have less of the evil banality they did during the Vietnam War which turned into reality Shirley Jackson's 1948 short story, "The Lottery," about a pleasant town that ends its annual picnic by stoning to death a randomly-selected family. Still, the unquestioned assumption that going off to fight for the country shows goodness remains. The result is highly altruistic young people signing up for military service and the military academies. NFL star Pat Tillman, like so many people in his generation, reacted to the 9/11 attacks by joining the Army, as if it were obvious that further attacks could only be stopped by military action, rather than by rethinking the US role in the world, and all the Sunday afternoon commentary on his decision assumed it was an act of heroism and humanitarianism for Americans and Middle Easterners alike. The free publicity for exceptionalism and empire from Tillman's one act alone dwarfed every mention of anti-war activities in the mainstream media over the course of the entire decade after 9/11.

Americans are fed a constant diet of self-congratulation by scholars like Michael Mandelbaum in his 2005 book *The Case for Goliath: How America Acts as the World's Government in the 21st Century*, and by raving cheerleaders on Fox News like Bill O'Reilly and on Clear Channel radio like Rush Limbaugh. News and sports commentators alike seem to have an informal rule that requires them to wear American flag pins in their lapel, as if they feared being identified as Canadians. Emails circulate in the millions that tell the tale of foreigners either grateful or ungrateful for the American boys buried in their lands who gave them freedom. Even a disaster can be rehabilitated, as when a Vietnam War veteran explains to a former protestor that "you were right for the wrong reason, and I was wrong for the right reason" — meaning that the war was well-intentioned, but so poorly-managed that it should not have been prosecuted. All of this adds up, drip by drip, to make voters in the middle of the political spectrum comfortable with an aggressive, unilateral global role, even if they are uncomfortable analyzing it. A middle school principal cancelled an assignment for students to take the Taliban's perspective in a debate over Afghanistan, because of "the pain that touched many of our families and neighbors due to terrorist attacks" by the Taliban's ally, al-Qaeda, and "the sensitive nature of the conflict in Afghanistan involving many of our dedicated members of the US armed forces."[1]

Country radio does its best to celebrate exceptionalism and the US interventions it spawns. Odes to the goodness of the common man, his flag, and his military service include Merle Haggard's 1969 "Okie from Muskogee," who waves Old Glory down by the Court House, Toby Keith's 2001 "Angry American," whose bombs are delivered "courtesy of the red, white, and blue" against enemies who "sucker-punched" America while it was minding its own business, and tear-jerking tunes about soldiers who don't come back but leave behind cars, letters, children, and girlfriends for others to enjoy. From Vietnam to Afghanistan, whispering Bill Anderson has praised America's mission and troops in hushed and hallowed tones, in his first career as a performer and his later one as an XM radio host. Clear Channel, which owns 900 radio stations, orchestrated an angry reaction to the one country act that spoke out against President Bush and his invasion of Iraq, the Dixie Chicks. As one station described it: "Out of respect for our troops, our city and

---

1 Michael Alison Chandler, "School cancels Taliban debate," *Washington Post*, p. B1, December 15, 2009.

our listeners, (we) have taken the Dixie Chicks off our play lists." Despite a scattering of boycotts, the band held firm and easily maintained its commercial prominence. Ironically, the iconoclastic Haggard criticized the attacks on the band as an insult to the efforts of American soldiers, presumably because they fight to defend the freedom of speech.

While conservatives criticize Hollywood for displaying anti-American bias in its gritty portrayal of current US wars, overall the movies have been replete with approving images of state-sanctioned violence, domination, and refusal to compromise, from John Wayne's dozens of Western lawmen (Rio Bravo) and American warriors (Sands of Iwo Jima, The Green Berets) to Samuel Jackson's mayhem-heavy urban cops (Shaft, S.W.A.T.) and Muslim-strafing Marine colonel (Rules of Engagement). Television audiences as well can't seem to get enough of tough cops and noble spies, from the Untouchables, the F.B.I., and Mission Impossible in the 1960s to the proliferation of detective, crime investigation, and CIA dramas in the 2000s, culminating in series about the Navy's lawyers and Jack Bauer, a loveable covert rogue who saves America from bombings ever 24 hours. Belligerence is celebrated in the uniquely American and beautifully brutal sport of football, whose combination of armored combat and constant self-celebration hearken back to gladiators in a Roman coliseum, and in the scripted morality plays of professional "wrestling," in which a favored theme is that of the honest American being flummoxed, and then flattened, by the devious foreigner. Closing the loop on the propaganda, pro wrestling then takes its dramas to war zones, on tours that are a "tribute to the troops."

As a result of all these and many more urgings and soothings, a vast majority of Americans, whether saluting the colors at the start of high school football games, entering the voting booth to choose between Soft and Hard Eagles, or writing a check to the USO so that soldiers will have a friendly place to stop and chat in the airport as they go to or return from their missions, would agree with the great myth of exceptionalism. The World Wars, the Marshall Plan, Vietnam, and Afghanistan, and the hundreds of other interventions and military alliances in Latin America, Asia, the Middle East, and Africa since 1900 are seen as humanitarian rather than strategic acts. The ROTC cadets carrying the colors would agree as well, generally because this portrayal comports with the history they hear in school and in the community, but particularly because membership in the armed forces is consistently couched not just as a "service" that protects unspecified freedoms for Americans, but also as a gift that brings these freedoms to others. Whether generated by honest emotions or cynical politics, there now exists a powerful national memory, an uninformed and unspecific version of history, in which American armies are always heroically doing good while everybody else's in history were merely defending or extending their nation's power. Turkeys have as their primary task the confronting of this memory with reality, so as to break the grip of exceptionalism that provides the Eagles with their foundation for domination.

CHAPTER 14. THE ROLE OF MORALITY IN DOMINATION AND ITS REJECTION

Tolstoy has his Marshall Kutuzov say, as he muses about how to drive Napoleon's army from Russia, that while it is not hard to storm a fortress, winning a campaign requires patience and time. To plan a campaign to turn America from domination to cooperation, one must take the time to identify the target, the source of domination's strength, and then have the patience to stay focused on it, rather than skitter around and fritter away one's resources on storming the many attractive fortresses that abound in the foreign policy debate. This book has identified the target as the transmission of exceptionalism to each new generation.

It was exceptionalism that allowed the United States to justify taking up Kipling's "white man's burden" of managing the colonial world, first in the Philippines in 1898 and then more broadly after World War II. It is exceptionalism that today makes credible, rather than laughable, the constant celebration of the machinery of domination, the diplomatic, military, and covert US bureaucracies that sustain America's repressive partners and attack its purported enemies. It is exceptionalism that makes it logical that the US response to the development of its enemies' capabilities is to destroy these capabilities, rather than to ask why they are enemies. The long war for control of the Middle East is only the latest example of exceptionalism requiring US involvement rather than disengagement. Al-Qaeda's attacks led not to a rethinking of the reasons for the war, but an expansion of it.

Exceptionalism is America's belief in a moral, almost divine mission, sustained by a portrayal of an altruistic, heroic history: if America does it, it is good, and the proof is that America alone has sacrificed its own interests and borne the burden to bring good to the world. Eagles tell the American people that they are special and good and promote stability, and would do even more for the world if only their innate goodness and optimism didn't allow them to be tricked by someone — foreigners, liberal professors, and the liberal media, say Hard Eagles, and the right-wing media and corporate-fed hysterical militarists, say Soft Eagles. Both types have a final moral redoubt against retreating from American domination, Hard Eagles bristling and eager to bring American values to the world, and Soft Eagles wistful at the need to do so to pre-empt the amoral Chinese.

Hard Eagles are, of course, not shy about arguing baldly for American self-interest. As described in Chapter 13, they manufacture fear by promoting Richard Perle's "sense of danger" and the Committee on the Present Danger's constantly-shifting threat, which as of 2010 justifies forward-deployed forces and alliances with repressive regimes as a way to defeat "Islamo-fascists" and provide access to resources at favorable prices so that the economy can recover. Hard Eagles, however, clearly understand that appealing only to self-interest may fall short if the actions violate Americans' perceptions of their values. While most agreed with John Kennedy that ballistic missiles in Cuba posed an unacceptable threat, and some with Ronald Reagan that Mi-G fighters on the Central American mainland were unacceptable (although for some reason Cuba's much closer Mi-Gs were ignored), very few seemed to agree with Dick Cheney's law of probability — which held that if there is a tiny chance that torturing a captive or destroying a country will someday block an attack on the United States, then it must be done. Americans also have an aversion to alliances with cartoonish thugs like Kazakhstan's oil-boiling dictator and Equatorial Guinea's kleptocratic torturer, even though these thugs help protect Americans with information and support for covert and military operations, and pump sweet crude oil to American refineries. So, the Hard Eagles, in nearly every foreign policy debate, also appeal to Americans' better angels, their instincts to protect others, by draping self-interest in humanitarian garb.

The Sandinista Government in Nicaragua was portrayed in 1984 not only as a threat to invade Texas and place Soviet and Cuban military bases in Central America, but as a brutal dictatorship discriminating against Indians and Jews. The Hussein regime in Iraq was portrayed in 2002 not just as a threat to American shores, with its mythical ship-launched drone aircraft carrying their mythical weapons of mass destruction, but as a slaughterer of Kurds and Shiites. Ending the occupation of Iraq was portrayed in 2007 not just as threatening American access to Middle Eastern oil, but also as precipitating a "blood bath" for the innocents of Iraq. The Taliban are portrayed in 2010 not only as hosts to 9/11 plotters, but as abusers of women, just as America's imperial predecessor Great Britain justified the invasion of Zululand in 1879 by portraying King Cetshwayo as not just a threat to British commerce, but also as a violator of women's rights, for punishing by death those who married before the end of a husband's military service.

A powerful variation of the Hard Eagles' humanitarian argument is the claim that America plays the role of global policeman, providing both a general stability by deterring conflict and the leadership needed to promote human development. Fulfilling that role then requires that America retain its reputation for success. US wars in Vietnam, Angola, and Afghanistan were justified by Johnson, Kissinger, and Obama because losing would damage America's reputation as a reliable actor, leading to dangerous military and economic challenges in other parts of the world to, as Nixon put it, the resolve of the "pitiful giant." Like pure self-interest, this argument is problematic for the Hard Eagles, because a threat to reputation may not be concrete enough to galvanize public opinion. However, it continues to be trotted out, reinforcing the belief that America must be strongly armed and aggressively deployed to deter conflict and promote economic growth and democracy on behalf of a world that ought to be grateful.

Hard Eagles try to convince Americans that if they are not on the side of the good guys, they are at least on the side of the better guys. They paste the argument about the benefits of stability onto America's partners in various regions, from Iran under the Shah and Zaire under Mobutu to Egypt under Mubarak and Saudi Arabia under the House of Saud, clairvoyantly claiming that potential successors would be less socially progressive and more regionally subversive. The propensity to declare US allies good regardless of their particular evils can lead to hilarious cases of hypocrisy, as when Secretary of State Hillary Clinton in 2010 lectured Iran on its lack of democracy while sitting with the Saudi king, and called it unacceptable for Iran to do what the United States and Israel do: build nuclear weapons to deter foreign attacks.

Soft Eagles are also constrained to operate within the pleasing assumption of excep-tionalism, which is that America is engaged in an altruistic, even heroic, mission to bring freedom to others. Once bound by this assumption, they cede the moral high ground to the Hard Eagles, because if the cause is just, then anything less than success is a betrayal of humanitarian principles, and failure to try, just because of a fear of some collateral damage along the way, is an act of cowardice. Even in sharp disputes with Hard Eagles, Soft Eagles play into their hands by arguing within the framework of exceptionalism rather than por-traying the United States as its own rogue state. For example, when criticizing the Bush administration for torturing prisoners, Soft Eagles argued that torture violated American values, and that it would lead to the torture of US armed forces. The first adopts the myth of American goodness, the second the reality of worldwide US deployment. Soft Eagles' efforts to ban landmines and control cluster bombs treat the symptoms, rather than the causes, of America's imperial conflicts, and ironically affirm the basis for the International Committee for the Red Cross, which is that wars can be fought humanely.

While Soft Eagles rely on exceptionalism and morality to justify America's role as global policeman, they are almost apologetic about the short-term consequences of the long-term good America brings. World-weary but resolute, they explain that America simply must provide stability, keep the oil flowing so that the world economy can keep moving, and chase terrorists through military power and misalliance. In any event, they say, it is far better that America play that essential role than some other power with less willingness to raise the issues of human rights and good governance. This argument was used first with the colonial powers cast as the less worthy policeman, then with the Soviet Union, and today with that last refuge of soft power arguments for domination, China.

Soft Eagles agreed not only with the Bush administration's misleadingly apolitical hy-pothesis that "authoritarian governments and largely unreformed economies create the conditions of repression and poverty that could well become breeding grounds for further terrorism," but with its claim that improved human rights "will be a byproduct of our alliance with them."[1] Holding the former belief obscures the reality that the United States attracts attacks because of its central role in the long war; holding the latter accepts the Pentagon's assumption, unverified for 60 years in Latin America and now Africa, that military training will transfer American values of tolerance and respect for democracy to the armed forces of repressive regimes. The hubris of the exceptionalism in this claim can be found in the musings of a Pentagon official that perhaps the transfer won't last long, because "we can't change where these people come from," as if American people embodied superior values.[2]

Soft Eagles often oppose a decision to intervene, but then stress the humanitarian dangers to the people of the occupied country of an end to that intervention. This leads to the common refrain in debates over US or US-backed wars, from Vietnam through El Salvador to Iraq: how we got involved here is an academic exercise in irrelevant history; the pragmatic question now is how to manage the situation responsibly. In the mid-1960s the political cartoonist Herblock nicely captured his fellow liberals' confusion over withdrawing from a country they never wanted to invade. He portrayed handsome, wholesome American soldiers swinging sticks at Viet Cong fish swimming in a stream while well-intentioned US diplomats lectured South Vietnamese officials about caring for their people, with the two sources of US power worriedly asking each other, "how's it going?"

The problem was cast as a race between counter-insurgency and political reform, not as US intervention in a civil war to maintain a friendly regime. How to win with the least damage to the people, not whether there was any US right to intervene, was at the core of liberal concerns. This led to the famed distinction that liberals saw the war as a "mistake" in both strategy and tactics, while anti-war radicals saw it as "no mistake," but rather inevitable within the framework of accepting the European role of controlling Asia. Even famously disaffected liberal journalists David Halberstam and Neil Sheehan, who had no illusions about the South Vietnamese governments' implacable corruption and exploitation of the rural poor, endorsed muddling along rather than withdrawing. The cartoon could be re-run in 2010 simply by substituting the Taliban and the Karzai government for the Vietnamese actors. The journalists' roles too are recreated by many of this generation's jaded war reporters.

The moral argument that an end to US domination would be dangerous to others is also applied more broadly by both types of Eagles to the global deployment of US forces. It is a significant victory for proponents of domination that "what do we do?" is the constant topic of debate in the media, not "why are we there?" Eagles claim that ending domination would be initially destabilizing, and could perhaps even stimulate conflict for three American wards — South Korea, Taiwan, and Israel. This is a legitimate concern. While South Korea has developed more than sufficient means to defeat a North Korean attack on its own, the presence of a small US deterrent force on the peninsula has also served to constrain South Korea from itself attacking the North. While Taiwan could bloody China's

---

1   The first quote is from deputy assistant secretary of State Lynn Pascoe, *Washington Post*, July 12, 2008, p. A20 (editorial), and is consistent with the National Security Strategy prepared by national security adviser Condoleezza Rice. The second is from Peter Slevin, "Some War Allies Show Poor Rights Records," *Washington Post*, March 5, 2002, p. A13.
2   Esther Schrader, "US Boosting Allies' Military Aid," *Los Angeles Times*, March 5, 2002.

nose if it were invaded, just as Cuba's heavy investment in military power could take a toll on US forces for a few weeks, China could regain the lost province if the US fleet were not interposed. In addition, both South Korea and Taiwan gave up plans to build nuclear weapons because of US guarantees of defense, and would build them fairly quickly in response to the end of that guarantee. Finally, while Israel clings to Europe's relic from the Crusades through its own military might and nuclear weapons, an end to the symbolic $3 billion annual US foreign aid check and to the concrete guarantee of mutual defense could encourage some of its neighbors to try once more to rid the region of this troublesome historical anomaly.

It has never been a matter of US national security whether the Koreas reunite under either government, or China absorbs Taiwan, or if the experiment started by President Truman in 1948 of a Jewish, rather than Herzel's Jewish-friendly, state is ended. In each case, a strange brew of Cold War politics, imperial ambitions, and quirky local actors and actions led to 60-year American protectorates from which retreat is now problematic. Indeed, these three cases are examples of the larger problem of unpredictable responses to the end of US military domination. The problem should not derail the anti-imperial effort, but at times it certainly will require cautious implementation. As with the end of colonialism, the end of domination can be well managed or chaotic. Portugal is rightly criticized not just for brutal colonial rule in its African colonies, but for the rapid termination of it in 1975, which led to devastating civil wars. Eagles could focus on how to disengage responsibly, but instead they choose to cite the reasons why disengagement is too dangerous to try. After all, why would you want to disrupt the goodness of Pax Americana?

TURKEYS AND THE MORAL ARGUMENT

Turkeys also often play within the boundaries set by exceptionalism, because they find it hard to resist attacking the low-hanging fruit of US policies that are illogical, even in their own terms. The violence and repression in many wars or cases of support for dictators become so blatant that it appears more productive for Turkeys in the short-term to show the American public the impact of a policy on the foreign victims than to pick a contentious fight over whether the policy was morally-motivated. The benefits of domination are so often confined to a few corporations that it appears more productive to show how the average person contributes taxes and even troops and gets little in return, rather than to focus on the violence done to others, let alone the overall scheme and justification for domination. The capture of the military budget by the infamous iron triangle of financially interested corporations, the ever-growing Pentagon, and Members of Congress seeking federal spending in their districts produces such bizarre weapons systems that it appears more productive to attack those that don't work or are not needed for any current task than to attack those that do work for serving domination.

For example, Women's Action for New Directions opposes expensive new battleships because they are "more attuned to open-ocean warfare against a superpower than support of operations ashore in crowded, dangerous, close-in coastal areas."[1] The anti-imperial In-

---

1   WAND, "Making Sense of the Military Budget," p. 5, http://www.wand.org/csba/militarybudg.pdf.

stitute for Policy Studies collaborates with "cheap hawk" Larry Korb to propose an annual Unified Security Budget that would transfers funding for unneeded weapons from the Pentagon to the State Department, as if they were not two fingers of the same fist — and indeed this budget anoints State Department funding as being "preventive" of conflict.[1] In the 1990s Demilitarization for Democracy "Code of Conduct" argued for a ban on arming dictators by pointing out that the result of military rule in Africa had been civil wars that turned it into a continent of Somalias that required US aid and troops rather than democratic Botswanas that bought American exports. Peace Action and Code Pink leaders opposed Obama's escalation in Afghanistan by arguing that the US combat presence created more Taliban, rather than attacking the premise of the need to fight al-Qaeda over control of the Middle East. [2] Thomas Powers plausibly argued that Iran was driven to explore building a bomb by others having it and threatening it, and would not use the bomb first, if history is a guide, but didn't challenge the right of the United States to block Iran's progress, by military or economic means.[3]

Critics of the Bush administration's claims about Iraq's purported weapons of mass destruction picked them apart masterfully, rather than argue that even if they were true, the United States had no right to invade. American human rights activists ask their government to protect the human rights of particular people and groups abroad, while by backing the regimes those people and groups live under, the US government helps deny the rights of entire societies. Peace activists have promoted bans on various "inhumane" weapons, from nuclear and chemical bombs to defoliants, napalm, landmines, and cattle prods, implicitly permitting the provision of cash and "humane" weapons to repressive regimes that rule with less dramatic flair. Even the slogans calling for the United States to get out of various places are about a symptom of empire, and not its root cause, because they call for a withdrawal from overtly-dominated countries, while the empire's deeper evil is covert domination of countries through control of the global political economy. It is certainly important to know whether 100,000 or 600,000 Iraqis were killed as a result of the US invasion, as studies by the United Nations and a team of John Hopkins University epidemiologists, respectively, estimated in 2006, but the answer is not central to whether the invasion was justified. Human rights, democracy, arms control, transparency, and properly-oriented development aid should not be Turkeys' demands, because Eagles have shown that they can easily subsume and corrupt these demands. Reform within empire is still empire.

Of course, Turkeys also present critiques of domination. In his first speech against the Vietnam War, at Riverside Church in 1967, Martin Luther King Jr. painted a devastating picture of American militarism, racism, and unrestrained corporate power as its cause. The Institute for Policy Studies' "Just Security" proposal makes it clear that US global domination is wrong, for both the average American and the subjects of the global policeman, who have certainly not "called 911." Why, though, is it wrong? Fundamentally,

---

1 IPS, Report of the Task Force on a Unified Security Budget, FY2010, http://www.ips-dc.org/reports/usbfy2010.

2 http://www.cnn.com/2009/OPINION/12/02/wright.martin.afghanistan.against.more.troops/

3 "Iran: The Threat," *New York Review of Books*, July 17, 2008, p. 9.

Turkeys are trapped into arguing that empire is expensive and counter-productive, rather than immoral. This is probably true as an historical concept, but it obscures the real issue. Arguing against domination on its own merits — that it is costly to maintain an empire, that our troops and taxpayers pay a price for the benefit of a very few, that conflict is a source of depression when we need growth for our markets, that particular weapons and military projects are wasteful and irrelevant even in their own terms — is seductive, because so many of the arguments are right so much of the time. However, this method also implies that empire would be all right if it worked, and it lets people off the hook for supporting it if they disagree with the merits of particular arguments.

In the same speech in which he blasted America's values, King railed against the war for draining resources from the war on poverty. Turkeys modernize King's argument by saying that the cost of empire is greater than the benefit to the American economy. They argue that the claim that military force is needed to gain access to fuel, which is used to justify the maintenance of large armed forces and of alliances with cooperative regimes, is largely false. Nobody can eat oil, natural gas, platinum, or cobalt, they say, so these minerals must eventually wend their way to the world market, where anyone can buy them at prices that, historically, do not even keep up with inflation. Even in the unlikely event that enough of the disparate producers of a natural resource were able to form a cartel that controlled enough of the supply to boost prices artificially, they argue that paying those prices would be far less costly than the maintenance of the imperial forces that are arrayed to guarantee access.

The problem with all these claims is that they duck the moral question of whether empire would be justified if they were false. Like a politician running for office, the Turkeys are appealing to Americans' self-interest rather than their conscience. Americans can sense that not all the claims could possibly all be true, all the time, in all versions of the future. Even in the present, they need not socialize with military officers or diplomatic mandarins to know someone who benefits from such imperial results or policies as cheap oil, military spending, arms exports, the tying of foreign aid, protectionism, and the weakness of the manufacturing base in Africa. This makes them leery of a major shift in policy for a promised benefit, when the current benefit is tangible. In any event, empire is typically popular with citizens who clearly lack a direct economic benefit from it. Roman, British, Fulani, Zulu, French, and Russian, and almost any other imperial expansion that one can conjure up from the depths of history enlisted not just the elites, who hoped to profit handsomely by it, but also the masses, who could not hope for more than temporary plunder. As Democratic politicians have learned to their chagrin, being even slightly skeptical about dominating foreign lands makes an American politician look soft on national security and even slightly treasonous, and much harder to elect in any district not dominated by minorities, whose history makes them inherently anti-imperialist.

Americans need a reason to change policy, and that reason cannot be theoretical economic argumentation about self-interest. To take a chance, they need a better reason. Turkeys try to provide that reason with a vision of a post-imperial world based on cooperation. There is no shortage of thoughtful scenarios in which dramatic reductions in all nations' military spending fuel essential services at home and abroad, dictators are isolated instead of sustained, and poor countries get a fair economic shake from well-controlled international corporations and trading regimes. The vision is, however, tinged with a lingering resistance to capitalism, an unhealthy suspicion of consumption and growth, and an almost religious belief in both the threat of global warming and the ease of the transition to renewable energy. Americans are capitalists, and they believe, largely correctly, that all things being equal, economic growth and power production are strong drivers of life expectancy in poor countries. Turkeys lean to the socialist side, because of both fear of corporate political power and moral objections to greed and over-consumption. A vocal minority even perpetuate Lenin's claim that "imperialism is the highest stage of capitalism," seemingly in ignorance of the empire built by his Czarist predecessors and communist successors, and Nkrumah's variation that "neo-colonialism is last stage of imperialism," seemingly in ignorance of the bizarre cronyism that was as responsible as post-colonial trade relations for dragging Ghana down during his rule.

Turkeys support the global warmists' desire, expressed each year in a global "lights out" event, to have America look like Africa at night, dark and calm, rather than have Africa look like America, where non-stop economic activity is lit, warmed, and fed by clean coal power from plants that invest in scrubbers to reduce poisonous emissions. Turkeys have long been faulty harbingers of doom about over-population, the extinction of resources, conspicuous consumption, and the pursuit of profit even before global warming gave them an overriding moral argument against growth. This pessimism properly plays poorly with most Americans, who may not be rich but would like to be, and who certainly don't want to be told how many children to have and how many vacations to take. Unlike Soft Eagles, Turkeys have the courage of their global warming convictions, and respond to concerns about high gas prices and heating bills by saying that raising the price of energy is precisely what is needed to shock America into pursuing alternative energy sources. Ironically, they have become victims of their own their own warming alarmism, as the nuclear power they long opposed is making a comeback as a renewable source of energy and the Air Force is lauded as socially responsible for using "green" fuels in its jet fighters.

Even if it were modified to conform with America's capitalist, pro-growth, free action orientation, the Turkeys' vision would still be unable to take hold with the mainstream, just as their appeals to self-interest in campaigns against components of domination have rarely been able to block a weapon or wind down a war. Americans can never be convinced to accept dramatic change without a moral reason. Turkeys should take a pointer from Eagles, and focus on turning the foreign policy debate into a fight over America's moral right to dominate. They must acknowledge that once in a while the average person benefits from domination, but ask why he or she has the right to do so. The appeal to morality is perceived by advocates of domination to be important because they correctly sense that through all the other national traits and attitudes runs a stream of goodness, a desire to help others and respect their rights. The campaign to promote solidarity as a reigning paradigm must make a concerted effort to tap this stream as well, by encouraging Americans to ask themselves whether their country has the right to dominate others.

Citizen action based on morality has a solid track record of unexpected success in American history. Most notably, the church-based African-American revolt for civil rights in the 1950s and 1960s forced a fundamental national reconsideration of how things "have to be." A number of other remarkable campaigns that changed attitudes and policy were also primarily moral, including opposition to slavery and its expansion, the women's vote, the temperance movement, the anti-apartheid act, and, unfortunately, global warming. The anti-slavery movement was spurred by religious activists and one great book, *Uncle Tom's Cabin*, and galvanized four-score years of simmering northern disgust with perpetual plantation servitude for blacks, as opposed to the temporary servitude to which many white Americans came ashore. The movement did not, of course, make the North ready to fight for blacks' freedom, since as noted in Chapter 12, when war came, it was fought for the Union, and not for black rights. However, the anti-slavery movement broke the fence-sitting Whigs and created a pure new party, the Republicans, making it impossible for Congress to wriggle out of the way of conflict with yet another murky compromise, as it had done a few times before.

The temperance crusade of the 1920s piggy-backed on the success of the drive for women's voting rights, and in just a few years overwhelmed lobbying by business interests and achieved a constitutional amendment barring the sale of alcohol. Its tactics included dramatic marches and rallies, images of broken homes and abandoned children, and placing pressure on religious leaders to lend their names, if not always their pulpits, to the cause. The anti-apartheid movement in the 1980s similarly overwhelmed the business community and their reasonable claims that trade and investment helped black South Africans to a better life and forced a Republican Senate to override President Reagan's veto of stiff financial sanctions. The global warming movement burst out of its left-leaning cocoon in the 2000s with its own *Uncle Tom's Cabin*, the film *An Inconvenient Truth*, featuring vice president Gore's nonsensical attribution of nasty weather to human-based warming. By the end of the decade the world's governments had signed on to a consensus about the certainty of arcane climate models that could be manipulated to support Gore's contentions, although they made sure not to do anything about the supposed planetary catastrophe that might limit their citizens' access to cheap power.

Certainly all of these social movement featured arguments based on policy and logic, but at their core they were moral appeals to do the right thing, even if it hurt one's self-interests. In a direct analogy to today's US domination, the 19th century movement in Britain to ban the slave trade violated the *realpolitik* imperative of protecting the economy, but prevailed by arguing that no country had the right to hold the well-being of others hostage to the well-being of its own by extracting resources by captive labor. The anti-slavery movement did not challenge the empire or its use of hut taxes to force Africans to work in the cash economy, and it was manipulated into British control of East Africa, ostensibly to stamp out the Arab slave trade, but it did succeed in its overall purpose of the global stigmatization of slavery. It grew in a matter of decades from a few strident evangelicals haranguing their flocks on Sundays to a moral whirlwind to which all British politicians had to pretend obeisance. Through constant agitation and demands on Parliament the movement overcame the profits of the slave traders, which were distributed throughout the financial class, and the conventional wisdom of scientists and sociologists who had proven the genetic and social inferiority of Africans.

A freshman at American University once demonstrated the power of elemental moral argument in foreign policy. After other students had argued back and forth vociferously about the various methods by which the United States might deter Iran from developing nuclear weapons, she said simply, "What right do we have to tell Iran not to build what we already have?" The room fell silent, as students tried to think through the implications of a question that had never been asked on the floor of the House or Senate, just a few miles away. It is the sort of question all Americans need to answer. A student in an upper-class course, having spent half of a semester reading about 60 years of US leaders giving speeches about democracy and development while aiding European colonial powers and the African dictators who succeeded them in return for collaboration with military and covert deployments and access to minerals from the Cold War to the war on terror, blurted out: "The hypocrisy is staggering." Another student responded that the US government is responsible only to its citizens, and they want the cheap oil and information on al-Qaeda. Both made strong points; it was up to each student in the class to choose a side, in a way that few Americans ever do, because choice has been so obscured by a debate that focuses on "what to do now."

Politics is as much about ideology as it is about competence, contrary to what Michael Dukakis claimed when presenting himself to the nation as a candidate for the presidency in 1988, and that is also true for foreign policy. A choice must be presented not between ways of managing the neo-imperial project, but between the morality of domination and the morality of solidarity. Eagles know and fear the power of morality in the American people. That is why they include so much moralization in their rhetoric. That is why they are eager to find agreement on the bromide that, "we agree in our goals; we just disagree in out methods." By arguing about the short-term impact of various policies, Turkeys are signing on to the bromide. Turkeys need to explain why they disagree on goals with the Turkeys. They need to say it is because empire is evil, by definition, making President Reagan's claim the Soviet Union was an evil empire redundant.

An American University graduate student, appropriately enough a State Department official, once informed his fellow students that Britain was justified in ruling India because it left behind a solid infrastructure of railroads, presumably bringing India into the modern trading system, thereby raising growth and life expectancy.[1] An Indian student in the class politely "begged to differ" with this heir of the imperial civil service that the benefits of foreign rule can ever justify it for those who are ruled. Turkeys must be forthright in arguing that domination by violence against even the few would be immoral, even if there were tangible benefits to the many. They need to say to Americans, "even if it were all to your advantage, and much to the short-term advantage of others, would you have the moral right?" Until Americans can accept morality as the key choice in foreign relations, US domination will remain the norm, even at its increasing cost to the public. And they can't accept an argument if they never hear it.

---

1 The argument is also made in Niall Ferguson's recent apology, *Empire: How Britain Made the Modern World*, which holds that empire can be benevolent if it brings specific improvements to the oppressed in health or economics.

Turkeys need to make Americans see the great conflict between their stated values and their government's self-interested support for those who deny these values for their citizens, and reject the Eagles' argument that the values and the support are magically compatible. They need to tell Americans that even if they become a bit poorer or colder if the United State steps out of the long war to control the Middle East, they should push for that anyway. Right now, however, such discussions, like the Turkeys' appeals to self-interest, their broader critique of empire, and their vision of the future, largely fall on deaf ears, because exceptionalism holds such sway. It is simply not credible to most Americans that their leaders' motivations and hence their soldiers' and diplomats' actions could be amoral, and purely self-interested. Only after the handles have been taken from the pump of exceptionalism, and Americans start to see the global policeman not as the cop on the beat but as an enforcer for the mafia, will appeals to morality be able to have an impact. Then Americans will be fundamentally uneasy when confronted with the question of whether they have the right to dominate and devastate others to defend their need for cheap resources, open trade and investment, and military and covert collaboration. A plan to discredit exceptionalism and then pose such tough moral questions, through a combination of advertising, activism, and eventually a new party, is presented in the final chapter.

CHAPTER 15. TAKING THE HANDLES: DEBATING HISTORY AND MORALITY

Moving from domination to cooperation requires the discrediting of exceptionalism and the popularization of morality as the basis for US foreign policy. To accomplish this, Turkeys must undertake a media campaign to paint American history as fundamentally amoral and current policy as largely immoral, and then engage in activism to challenge the local generators of exceptionalism. Eventually this combination could lead to the formation of an anti-imperial political party with enough power in government to replace domination with cooperation as the core of US foreign policy. This final chapter outlines such a plan and suggests some tactics to use in pursuing it. The actual details would have to be determined by media experts and thousands of local actors as they plan and guide the process. To paraphrase the presidential counselor in the film, "The American President," who is asked by the president if they could have won a campaign featuring a "character debate," anti-imperialists don't know if they'll win a debate about history and morality, but they would like that debate very much. The neo-imperial portrayal of American domination as necessary and benevolent, and as a result virtually demanded by both security and morality, has never been contested on the playing field of mainstream opinion. Domination is now the norm; cooperation cannot be the norm until domination is seen as bizarre.

A robust campaign that discredits celebratory history and current misalliances and interventions would certainly handicap Eagles when they next trot out the next Saddam Hussein, a supposed enemy whose rule they propose to constrain or end by US pressure. Wary public opinion would be more likely to demur, having seen that the sliver in that tyrant's eye contrasts favorably with the timber in its own. Similarly, success in broadcasting moral challenges to the use of military and financial power to sustain cooperative and unseat uncooperative governments would certainly blunt the neo-imperialists' appeals for public support for the burgeoning Pentagon, CIA, and State Department budgets that make domination and intervention possible. However, the focus on the campaign must not be on present policy debates, but on reaching the generation that will succeed the current one. It takes a long time to turn an aircraft carrier around. Turkeys must start now to succeed in 20 years.

A MEDIA OFFENSIVE: ZINN ON STEROIDS, IN 3-D WITH GRAPHICS AND MUSIC

Whether it's television or web ads, sound-trucks or YouTube, snail mail or e-mail, billboards or pop-ups, or anything else geared to catch our attention, advertising works — that is proven daily in consumers' decisions and yearly in voters'. What would effective advertising entail for an attack on exceptionalism? There is no shortage of well-prepared analyses by anti-imperialists, as a quick perusal of the web and radical bookstores will attest. Those analyses critique every imaginable aspect of American history, attitudes, foreign policy, and morality. The material is there, reflecting the surprisingly rich undercurrent of anti-imperialism that exists at the margin of the foreign policy debate, but there has been a dearth of success in popularizing it throughout the array of venues where opinions are formed and legitimated. Historian Howard Zinn, who died in 2010, spent a lifetime writing books that attacked the pleasing history that underpins exceptionalism. His approach was pure revisionism: if the conventional history glorified America, his scholarship found the shit on its shoes. Every incident, from the founding to the latest war, was placed in the context of an amoral pursuit of power by the privileged and their satraps, apologists, and soldiers. Unfortunately, his powerful exposition was limited to those who sought it out, and was excluded from the mainstream's construction of America's glorious history and present noble calling.

Zinn's intellectual battle to discredit the empire actually reached its peak in his last years. The brazenness of Bush's policies of invasion and torture, the mindlessness of his incantations about freedom, and the absurdity of the neo-conservatives' 30-year, corporate-backed strategy of promoting fear through fraud did more recruiting for his perspective than Zinn ever could. Obama was the immediate beneficiary, as Turkeys no less than Soft Eagles were seized with the urgency of rejecting McCain, so as not to endorse Bush's legacy. Within a year of Obama taking office, though, it dawned on most Turkeys that he hadn't been just talking like an Eagle to win election, but really was one. This personalization of the struggle, though, first through anger with Bush and then disappointment with Obama, obscures the underlying assumption of domination.

What is needed to defeat domination is a concerted, creative, thoroughly modern media campaign that spurs dissonance and dissent against the assumptions, traits, and attitudes that sustain it. The campaign would discredit exceptionalism by exposing the majority of Americans to Zinn-like revisionism, an alternative interpretation of American history and morality, and then pose the stark moral questions about today's examples of domination: Do you want your government to support this? Is this what your security, your economy is worth? Do you have the right to do this? For every argument Zinn would have had with the past and present of US foreign policy, the campaign would dramatize it with memorable images of the people it has harmed, and demand a moral choice for today. The campaign must be both deep and broad, deep meaning explicit in its rejection of domination, maudlin self-perception, anger at criticism, anti-intellectualism, belligerence, and state religiosity, and broad meaning taking place at both the local and national levels, in all the media that reach both opinion leaders and the usually unengaged public. Its goal would be to discredit, cast doubt, and regain the high ground on morality and history by placing America's history and current policy on the low ground with everybody else's. If America becomes just another country, then it will have no more reason to dominate than any other large state, say, Brazil.

Like most peoples, Americans generally either have little awareness of their history or have gravitated to the self-congratulatory version promoted by their mainstream institutions, which allows them to criticize others rather than themselves. American University pontificates about academic freedom, the rule of law, and transparency as goals for developing nations, while refusing to divulge the contents of contracts it won support the US occupation of Iraq. The National Democratic Institute uses tax dollars to promote democracy in underdeveloped countries, while its board members include Members of Congress who promote arms sales from their districts to dictators. Human beings also have a propensity to go along with a repressive system, as long as they are not on the receiving end. In both apartheid South Africa and segregationist America, almost all white and even most non-white citizens went on with their lives as best they could, perhaps acknowledging the horrors, but lacking the imagination to see, and act on, the possibility of fundamental change until publicity and agitation made the change inevitable. Among the millions of white, wealthy, well-schooled Afrikaners during four hundred of years of race rule, there were only a handful like Bram Fischer, a corporate lawyer and the grandson of an Afrikaner prime minister, who became Nelson Mandela's lawyer and then a Communist Party revolutionary and was jailed for life.[1]

The failure of Americans to confront their history is the primary barrier to dismantling domination and adopting cooperation as the purpose of US foreign policy. Teaching or even talking about history as a collection of varied perspectives can be subversive and potent, which explains why revisionism — history that revises pleasing portrayals by peeling back the protective covering of manly heroism and saintly altruism and exposing the inevitable complex of human banality, chance, folly, and selfishness within — is attacked so bitterly when it manages to gain a foothold. Revisionism will alienate the next generation from exceptionalism, and make them receptive to the belief that the United States is just another powerful country going about the business of extending its power, and cloaking that crass reality, as such countries always do, with balderdash and bathos, using the grim terms of national security and the flowery language of global benevolence.

A media offensive to tar exceptionalism and feather domination should be managed like a sale, or an election, and not like a logical search for common ground. Policy papers in Washington are for reform within the framework of domination. Advertising in Peoria

---

1 Mandela often remarked wonderingly on Fischer's altruism, which he doubted he could have sustained himself. Fischer's beliefs and actions were unfathomable to his closest white friends and, as a nasty dispute over an honor at Stellenbosch University 30 years after his death showed, he continued to be ostracized in the Afrikaner community as a traitor even after his vindication by the transition to democracy. Even Fischer claimed that he was opposing apartheid in large part because of the evil it was doing to his own people, and the disaster it would eventually bring to them.

would be for the destruction of the framework. All's fair in love, war, and the making of public opinion. As Republican media master Lee Atwater said when confronted during George H. W. Bush's campaign in 1988 with yet another unfounded rumor he had parlayed into news, "everybody sees the story" on page one, and nobody sees the correction days later, on an inside page. "Perception is reality" was his favorite saying.[1] In 1992 Atwater's Democratic counterpart Sidney Blumenthal urged candidate Bill Clinton to pledge a middle class tax cut that he had no intention of pursuing, because it was "important to show concern" for the middle class. Al Gore's weepy collection of sloppy inferences, *ad hominem* appeals, wild predictions, and nonsensical claim that costly changes would somehow help the economy not only won him a Nobel peace prize, but galvanized support for "global warming" legislation.

The standard of truth is low for political advertising, since it is not regulated for accuracy like commercial advertising. Truly outrageous assertions and character assassination generate their own free replays. The two most famous and discussed advertisements in American politics — Lyndon Johnson's child playing with a daisy, which implied that his opponent, Barry Goldwater, might let loose a nuclear war, and Atwater's Willie Horton, which turned law-and-order Governor Michael Dukakis into someone who helped black parolees rape white women — had only the briefest of runs as paid advertising. The ads for the Turkeys' offensive should search for the same sort of impact, and be planned by specialists in marketing, using the same effective tools as the neo-imperialists and the private sector, such as focus groups and simple, repetitive, heart-rending, and chest-thumping text and images. *Blutdenken* for the troops and *noblesse oblige* to dominate others can be converted into thinking with the heart for others, and an obligation to do no harm to US troops.

There would be no lies, no exaggerations, but rather a fair but alternative interpretation, dramatically rendered. Lying would simply continue to debase the national debate, and in any event, just giving the other side of the story is sufficient. It is not important that the public accept a particular revisionist interpretation of an historical incident, be it Washington crossing the Delaware, Lincoln balancing slavery and union, Truman bombing Hiroshima, or Nixon's "Christmas" bombing of Hanoi, or any of America's hundreds of alliances with repressive governments. What is important is that the next generation of the public come to accept the implications of revisionism itself, which rejects the notion that history reveals an underlying goodness of intent and impact on the part of one's country. A history lesson is not a polemic, but a set of facts accompanied by possible interpretations and perspectives. Anti-imperialists need not bend the facts or strain their interpretations. They need only place the incidents before the usually uninterested public, and note how the traits and attitudes that sustain the mindset of domination might have factored into their occurrence and their subsequent portrayal.

Arguing over history is itself explosive, as shown by the national controversy generated in 1994 by the simple act of trying to write wall panels at the Smithsonian Museum

---

1 Another famed observation from this master race-baiter was: "You can't say 'nigger'—that hurts you. Backfires. So you say stuff like 'forced busing.'" Nearing death, Atwater repented and despaired for "the country, caught up in its ruthless ambitions and moral decay."

to accompany the airplane that bombed Hiroshima. Emotions ran high over text that cast just the slightest doubt on the morality and the military impact of the bombing. Not just the families of airmen and their backers in veterans' organizations but also mainstream politicians understood the potency of revisionism, and fought it vigorously. This is exactly the sort of fight that Turkeys should want on every television and radio station and on every computer and Blackberry screen in America, every day, about every element in the national narrative. The debate itself would undercut the supporting myths in the structure of domination. For Americans to be aware that there is even a debate about exceptionalism would be a victory for the campaign. The campaign needs first to attack the glorious portrayal of American history by painting it as a litany of amoral land grabs, and then to pose fundamental moral questions about today's domination and intervention. All of the advertising should incorporate repetitive tag lines, so that by the end of an aggressive year, it will have hammered into America's consciousness and political vocabulary provocative catch phrases such as: America: We're Special...'Specially Dangerous; If God Blesses America, Who Blesses the People We Kill?; Patriotism: the Last Refuge of a Scoundrel; Empire is Evil; Empire: No!; Cooperation, not Domination; Yankee Come Home; America: Cop on the Beat or Mafia Enforcer?; America: a History of Domination and Repression...It Stops with Us; or Free the World: Come Home, America.

This would not be a campaign to elect somebody, but rather to fashion the context in which elected people operate, but it should be managed like one, with urgency, professionalism, and lots of cash. The bad news is that a campaign focusing on history and morality that could begin to ground the Eagle by cracking the neo-imperial, liberal-conservative consensus would cost hundreds of millions of dollars. The good news is that this level of funding is available and currently misdirected on reform efforts. Financiers George Soros and Peter Lewis, the MoveOn.org network, and other fervent opponents of the war in Iraq ponied up hundreds of millions of dollars to try to defeat President Bush in the $4 billion 2004 presidential election.[1] In the usual conundrum of the left, success in that venture, while ending a reckless regime, would still have resulted in the White House being occupied by a neo-imperialist and supporter of the invasion of Iraq.[2] Anti-war donors spent even more supporting Obama, who was clear in his campaign that he would "win" the war in Afghanistan and continue the "war on terror" under a new name.

A sustained media campaign against American domination would require the support of just a few dot-com dons and donnas or hedge fund phenoms who want to head straight for structural change and skip the reformist way stations supported by philanthropic business leaders like Bill Gates, Warren Buffett, Ben Cohen, Gary Hirshberg, and the laterPaul Newman's family. It would take just a fraction of the money donated by

---

1 Total spending from a press release, Oct. 21, 2004, by the Center for Responsive Politics, from federally-reported data. According to data collected by Opensecrets.org, two anti-war donors alone, Soros and Lewis, gave $46 million to the effort to elect John Kerry. Moveon.org spent $21 million, of which $5 million came from those two donors. Also caught in the conundrum, the author contributed a more meager amount than the financiers (although perhaps a greater share of his income) to that cause.

2 See the depressing detailing of John Kerry's jingoistic campaign promises in Thomas Harrison's "The 2004 Elections and the Collapse of the Left," in *New Politics*, Volume X, Number 2, Winter 2005.

progressives to promote non-solutions, like the Kyoto Treaty and carbon taxes, to the non-problem of an uncertainly-projected climate crisis, or to the anti-poverty industry that illogically promises to "make poverty history" within the current system of domination of poor countries by developed nations and the dictators they maintain. Just the money Soros invests in attempting to decriminalize drug use could shock the foundations of exceptionalism.

Americans learn their myths about their role in the world at a dauntingly diverse array of settings: from neighborhood dinner tables to meetings of the Rotary, Veterans of Foreign Wars, and other community groups; from thin local newspapers and minute-long commercial radio newscasts to the bulky Sunday New York Times and the endless hours of National Public Radio discussion; from elementary schools to colleges; on television, from spy dramas to Face the Nation and from Good Morning America to Monday night football; from the websites of individual bloggers to those of corporate-sized think-tanks; from every time a politician says "God Bless America" to every time a soldier walks by in uniform. How could one possibly organize a response to all the neo-imperial propaganda about attitudes, actions, and purpose that emanate from these sources?

Ironically, this plaint is also heard from both types of Eagles, who believe that the public debate is unfairly dominated by the other, and have invested heavily and creatively in their ability to broadcast their perspective through magazines, radio shows, opinion articles, the web, and public events. Anti-imperialists have done the same, with books, bookstores, magazines, the web, and a smattering of radio shows and rallies, but they face the additional and perhaps the largest hurdle of the day-to-day drone of local and national acceptance of the necessity and the goodness of American power, a reality from which the Eagles benefit effortlessly. To attack that drone, well-funded Turkeys might be tempted to hit back, buying time to critique immediately Super Bowl patriotism, country music jingoism, ads for military recruitment, and imperial editorials in the *New York Times* and the *New York Daily News*. This would be a powerful campaign, but to redefine foreign policy, particularly for the next generation, it would be better to focus all resources on a new campaign that controls the debate, rather than reacts to others' tactics and appeals.

The campaign should seek to blanket national and local radio and television, the web, movie theater previews, and newspapers with a powerful sequence of advertisements that start at the beginning, by attacking America's glorious history as amoral, and wind up at the end, by attacking America's current domination as immoral. The content should be humorous and attractive, but brutal in its portrayal of the contradiction between the words of the exceptionalists and the reality of the suffering caused to others by America's self-interested domination. It should be short on scolding and long on respect for historical and current actors, who certainly believed they were moral because the mission was moral. Empire is inherently evil, but that doesn't mean that the people who make and have made American history while laboring within the context of domination are evil. They are simply human, usually as well meaning as can be hoped for, and presenting them as wicked hypocrites properly lacks credibility with the public. Nobody likes a whiner, children are told, and that is true in the public arena as well. Even without personal attacks, the ads will appear heavy-handed to some people, especially in older generations, but the target is the younger generation, who should enter political life with an awareness of an alternative history. Fruitful areas for historical mining might include:

Patriotism: The ads could quote Samuel Johnson on patriotism being "the last refuge of a scoundrel" or George Washington's admonition to "guard against the impostures of pretended patriotism." They could present images of presidents intoning about patriotism while young Americans kill and die, and then show how those conflicts were more relevant to political and economic fortunes of a few than to US security.

Freedom: Using graphic images of the victims of US wars and repression, the ads could take on the claim that soldiers, diplomats, and covert operatives are risking their lives for Americans' and others' freedom. They could show US Special Forces with their motto, "Free the Oppressed" in these conflicts, and then add lightly: "or oppress the free.... whatever."

Religion: The ads could show images of American flags in churches and religious leaders praying with US troops and blessing their bombs, juxtaposed with the devastation they bring. They could show American politicians and singers repeating "God Bless America," and then have religious leaders ask bluntly what God has to do with one country's domination of others, pointing out that God didn't ask America to invade Vietnam and Iraq, or support dictators for oil in Saudi Arabia, for CIA access in Ethiopia, for military bases in Somalia, and for Israel's sake in Egypt. They could show images of notorious foreign dictators and historical imperialists claiming God's blessing, or justifying race rule, and ask today's politicians to respect a rule about their personal faith: "we don't ask, you don't tell."

Exceptionalism: The ads could describe how it all started with a Massachusetts governor and preacher telling Americans they were "a city upon a hill" that should lead the world — and how he used that claim to justify stealing land from the Indians and believed that God spread small-pox among them just for that reason. They could update that belief through presidential speeches on America's global goals, such as Wilson on democracy, Kennedy on bearing any burden, Johnson and Reagan on the noble cause of Vietnam, Bush I on a New World Order, Bush II on spreading freedom, and Obama on the benevolence of America's post world-war II interventions. The ads could explain how thinking one is exceptional lead to the domination of others, and ask for America to stop being special and start being fair.

The American Revolution: The ads could portray it as a land-grab against the Indians and a bid to retain slavery, both of which were discouraged by the British. Like other historical ads, these would ask Americans to question their history and find that the United States is not an exceptional nation, but just another country.

The Constitution: The ads could portray it as land speculation for Jefferson, Madison, and Hamilton, and a selling out of black rights.

War of 1812: The ads could describe the war as a selfish, and failed, attack on Britain as it was leading a coalition of governments against the madman Napoleon, who invaded all of Europe from Italy to Russia, and from Spain to the Netherlands, and even devastated Egypt to add to his holdings. The tale would explain how the United States wanted to trade with Napoleon, and so declared war on Britain and tried to invade Canada, and how in 1814, with the Canadian adventure in ruins, Washington burning from a British assault and occupation, and coalition armies closing in on Napoleon, President Monroe thought better of it, and agreed to end the war without having achieved a single one of his aims.

Civil war and reconstruction: The ads could show how America has always valued its union above the rights of its black citizens: Lincoln went to war to save the Union, and offered to let the South keep its slaves if it returned to the fold; after the war, the so-called anti-slavery party agreed to remove federal troops from the South and let the whites rule again, in return for the presidency in a disputed election.

American Imperialism: The ads could show how having stolen continental America from the Indians, piece by piece, the newly powerful US government looked outward to join the European empires in exploiting the wealth of the colonized world, and at the start of the 20th century seized Cuba and the Philippines in brutal wars of counter-insurgency and began to install "our bastards" as dictators in Latin America.

World War I: The ads could describe the war as a struggle between European colonial powers in which Germany wanted to inspect American ships that it correctly suspected were carrying weapons to its enemies, and explain that US refusal led it into a war that Wilson said would make the world safe for democracy, but actually only made it safe for colonialism.

Munich: The ads could attack the myth that by being dominant and aggressive America is avoiding the "appeasement" of this meeting in Germany in 1938. They could show how Britain and France preferred to use their power to hang onto their colonies rather than reverse Hitler's violations of the treaty that ended World War I, such as rearming Germany and occupying the Rhineland, and argue that the bargain at Munich over the German-speaking areas of Czechoslovakia was no more important to Hitler's power than were American business activities in Germany. Finally, the ads could show how presidents exploit the myth of Munich to justify US wars from Korea to Afghanistan, and argue that in fact America is today's Germany, throwing its weight around to get its way all over the world.

World War II: The ads could show how the "Good War" in the Pacific started because the United States cut off Japan's oil to thwart its drive to take over Europe's Asian colonies. Similarly, they could show confront the belief that the United States fought Hitler to remove an evil man who killed Jews and seized European countries, when in fact it attacked Hitler only after he declared war on the United States. The ads could highlight the American practice of declaring cities military targets and destroying them with conventional, fire, and nuclear bombs, and describe the post-war practices of putting Nazis back in power to keep Germany from being unified as a neutral party in the Cold War, and welcoming dictators in Spain, Greece, Turkey, and Portugal into NATO.

Helping colonialism: The ads could tell the story of US aid to France, Britain, the Netherlands, and Portugal in their bloody efforts to hold onto their colonies after World War II.

Taking over for colonialism: The ads would show how European leaders asked the United States to take responsibility for managing the former colonial lands, and contrast that role with images of the murder and mayhem US-backed dictators used to maintain power, and of the poverty that has resulted.

Vietnam War: From bringing back the French to bombing the north to find a "decent interval" for withdrawal, the US record in Vietnam provides fertile ground for attack. It would be important to plow it fully and slowly, because the rehabilitation of the war into Reagan's "noble cause" is at the core of the neo-conservative agenda to expand US domination. The firepower, the assassinations, the Tiger Cages, the throwing of suspects from helicopters, the massacres, and the torture provide plenty of images to exploit.

US support for dictators in Africa: Algeria, Egypt, Liberia, Somalia, Congo and then Zaire, South Africa (and its invasion of Angola and support of rebels), Chad, Equatorial Guinea, Ethiopia, and Sudan are all countries deserving a spate of ads explaining through images the devastation brought about by US-backed dictators. Images of US politicians praising their "friends" could be contrasted with images of people jailed or killed, or in the case of the Congo in the 1960s, lynched by CIA mercenaries. The use of "terrorist" by American politicians to describe Nelson Mandela and his party could be featured, to discredit that word. Each country could have its own story told in separate ads, to provide a sense of the breadth of US domination.

US support for oligarchs and oil-igarchs in the long war for the Middle East: Iran, Saudi Arabia, Gulf emirs, Afghanistan, Pakistan could be featured in ads showing US support for dictators and its impact on their people.

US support for repression in Latin America: The ads could display disturbing images of slaughter and explain the role of US-backed thugs during the Cold War, from the 1954 coup in Guatemala through the military training of a continent of dictators in the 1960s to repression and civil war in the Central American countries in the 1970s and 1980s. Each country could receive its own significant exposure, to overwhelm Americans with the sheer number of countries they have oppressed. The ads could feature the recordings of the speeches and even the assassination of Archbishop Oscar Romero, whose appeal to the Catholics in the murderous, US-backed Salvadoran Army in 1980 should resonate with religious Americans today: "In the name of God, stop the repression."

Afghanistan: The ads could track the humanitarian results of US intervention from the start of US aid to Muslim radicals by Carter and Brzezinski, before the Soviet invasion, to today's occupation.

Iraq: The ads could review the sordid history of US support for Saddam Hussein, and then revisit the fraudulent claim that weapons of mass destruction required a US invasion. They could show the faces of the 4,000 US soldiers and over 100,000 Iraqi civilians who died as a result of the invasion.

After a substantial investment in starting this debate over history, the campaign would turn to placing today's policy of domination in a negative moral light. Having discredited the notion that an exceptionalist America conducts its foreign policy for the benefit of others, this second wave of ads could more credibly ask whether Americans have the right to dominate others for their own self-interest. Examples might include:

9/11 and the causes of terrorism: Counter-terrorism being the most potent argument for US domination at present, this would be an area for substantial advertising. The ads could include Bush saying that America was attacked for our freedoms, and Obama saying he is only seeking protection from attacks. They would explain that America was attacked for the freedoms it takes with other countries, particularly Saudi Arabia because of military basing and Egypt because of CIA rendition of government opponents, and won't be protected until it leave the Middle East to its people to work out their own destiny.

Nuclear weapons and Iran: The ads could toll off the decades since the United States pledged to negotiate away all nuclear weapons, and describe Iran's strategic situation as giving it as much of a right to nuclear weapons as any of the other nuclear powers, including the United States.

Counter-terrorism in Somalia: The ads could attack the current US military and covert involvement as the latest in the disastrous series of interventions from Carter's aid to a dictator in return for military bases through the 2006 US-backed invasion by Ethiopia.

Torture: The ads could revisit through videos, photos, and dramatizations the most heinous cases of abuse of prisoners in the past decade. The intent of the ads would be to leave Americans retching and asking how this could have been done on their behalf.

Foreign aid: The ads could contrast the dramatic pledges of 60 years of presidents with the horrific poverty remaining in developing countries. Separate ads could focus on the many reasons why foreign aid has been wasted, ranging from support for "friendly" dictators that led to waste and conflict to protectionism and "tying" to US purchases, which benefit specific companies at someone else's cost in the overall American economy.

Corruption: The ads could contrast Obama's call to combat corruption in Africa with the reality of continued arms transfer to corrupt governments and CIA bribes of foreign officials.

The World Bank and IMF: The ads could paint these institutions as a mix between a conspiracy to keep the developing world out of competition with Europe and the United States and an indirect way to maintain dictators that countries have a hard time aiding bilaterally. They could use the Bank and Fund's own studies to show their ineffectiveness in fighting poverty, and call either for their demise or for voting in them to be based on population, so as to end the developed world's control of lending decisions.

Aid to dictators: The ads could feature a transition from the singing of "We are the world" to a parody, "We arm the world," and be filmed in separate versions showing the actions of each of the repressive governments to whom the United States is currently providing arms and training.

Fear of Islam: The ads could show neo-conservatives railing about the current "present danger" of "Islamo-fascists" at home and abroad, and then place this fear-mongering in the context of their railings in the past 60 years, from Soviets to African "terrorists" like Mandela to Central American rebels who now hold elected power, and end with Colin Powell testifying that "I need enemies."

Global policeman: The ads could take on the hoary justification for US domination, and show a cop on the beat morphing into a mafia hit man, followed by images of people suffering under their US-backed regimes. They could highlight the nearly one thousand military facilities the United States maintains around the world, and call for the hundreds of thousands of US armed forces around the world to be brought home with their ships, tanks, and aircraft.

China: The ads could show clips of Eagles' acknowledging the US empire, but saying that if United States backs off, China would take over. The ads could dissect this illogical final line of defense of domination by explaining that China's record on aiding dictators is no worse than America's, and promise that if another empire arises to dominate, torture, invade, and rule, activists will go after that one as well.

A variation that would highlight the moral question would be to run ads for a few weeks in which people would simply read off the lines: "Do we have the right to.....?" After this period of anticipation, the next wave of ads would have the dots replaced with the endings of the sentence, such as "arm dictators," or "attack other countries," or "stop nations from building the weapons we already have," or "pick other countries' governments," followed by images and examples of that particular sin from today's policies. A final wave would feature people from developing nations saying: "No, you don't have the right to run my country. How would you like it if I tried to run yours?" In general, the ads focusing on current abuses and the moral choice should avoid policy debates about whether to arm or sanction a particular country, since the goal of the campaign is to attack the mindset that permits a policy of making deals with devils in pursuit of domination, rather than to block a particular deal. Similarly, while the ads should stress the need for cooperation over domination and hold out a demilitarized, more democratic world as a goal, they need not present a comprehensive vision of precisely what US policy should be or how the world would change.

It is always good, as George Washington said, to "raise a standard to which the wise and honest may repair." However, too much detail would distract the audience from the attack on exceptionalism. The purpose of the campaign is more to level the playing field for competing visions than to promote a particular one. When Eagles start bitterly complaining that Turkeys have failed to present a constructive alternative to today's policies, that is when the Turkeys will know that the advertising campaign is working, and should be stepped up, not diverted. After enough Americans are ready to consider a change, they could form a new party to provide the vision. It may be useful, though, to expend some resources countering Eagles' claims that reducing the US global military presence would put South Korea, Taiwan, and Israel at risk, since making the point that the reduction should be managed carefully only affirms the point that it is necessary.

ATTACKING EXCEPTIONALISM, WITH ACTIVISM AND AN ANTI-IMPERIAL PARTY

Important as a well-funded advertising campaign to discredit exceptionalism and domination is, it will not be enough. The anti-war novel *All Quiet on the Western Front* was among the best-selling books in Germany between the wars, yet the blustering Hitler was voted into power. The Cosby Show, featuring a black family, was wildly popular with white audiences in South Africa in the 1980s, yet they continued to support apartheid. Once the playing field has been leveled by the media campaign, bits of money from and bits of action by concerned individuals will still be, as in all successful movements, the driving force in changing attitudes and policies. When scholar Robert Browne and donor W.H. "Ping" Ferry placed the first advertisement protesting the Vietnam War in newspapers in 1963, they were overwhelmed with contributions and ideas for local initiatives.

A readiness to critique and a thirst for action was revealed in a populace thought to be unwilling to challenge the mavens of national security.[1] Exceptionalism has to be challenged and moral choices in foreign policy demanded in the thousands of local setting where domination is enshrined every day, from flag salutes at high school volleyball games to military recruiting booths at county fairs, from newspaper stories about a presidential speech to radio talk shows about foreign policy.

A successful campaign of activism would have to be coordinated at the national level by a planning committee that keeps the long-term goal, rather than short-term victories, in mind, and proposes slogans and ideas for related protests. Think-tanks like the Institute for Policy Studies and advocacy groups like Peace Action are full of people who could assist with that task. However, this committee should not, and indeed cannot, control the campaign. As public glorification of domination is being undercut by the media campaign, local activists who are re-energized by that effort need to dream up and carry out the thousands of acts, events, and bits of publicity needed to affirm its message with their fellow citizens, and particularly with secondary school students and recent graduates. The activists need to create a sense of urgency, indeed of competition between their communities, like the activists who spurred each other on when trying to outdo each other in creativity during protests against the Vietnam War, discrimination against black Americans, and US support for apartheid. The civil rights movement in particular showed that while there must be a shared vision of goals and strategies, and a big pot of money to fund action and publicity, success requires local actions undertaken with speed and impatience that take the initiative away from opponents and drive the debate. These movement's victories were, of course, not inevitable, and their strategies and tactics were not the work of genius. Countless other moral crusades, with equally fervent supporters and equally creative methods, have come and gone without much impact. The lesson is that engaging the national media and raising local awareness is necessary, but not sufficient.

There is no shortage of targets for local activism against exceptionalism and domination. Military publicity and recruitment is ubiquitous in America, generating the hundreds of thousands of recruits needed every year to sustain "full spectrum dominance" and global reach. Publicity and recruitment for the equally crucial components of empire, the covert agencies and the State Department, are also widespread. Schools, local media, and community organizations are constantly reinforcing the acceptance, and the celebration, of domination. Municipal pension funds and university consultants are linked to the imperial effort. The acts of education and protest will vary widely by community, from speaking up at community events to canvassing neighborhoods, from taking a visible part in holiday marches to holding separate marches aimed at symbols of domination. What is important is that they be frequent and noticeable, and encourage the average citizen to think about the issue and take a side.

Given the current makeup of local peace groups, creative, publicity-attracting challenges to the cultural promotion of the neo-imperial mindset and to local acts that sustain neo-imperialism would often have a pacifist flavor. Pacifism is a worthy philosophy, with

---

1   See Caleb Rossiter, *The Chimes of Freedom Flashing: A Personal History of the Vietnam Anti-war Movement and the 1960s*, Book 2, Chapter 4, TCA Press, Washington, DC, 1996.

demonstrably as much practicality in world affairs as armed resistance, let alone armed aggression. Its adherents must, of course, promote their belief that "war is not the answer" as they wish. However, they should recognize that most people do not agree, and never will, that war is never the answer, or that the military regimen is dehumanizing and dangerous to civil society. Similarly, activists must engage rather than antagonize. It is neither true nor credible to the American public that military, intelligence, and diplomatic service is immoral in itself. Moveon.org alienated more Americans than it attracted with its attack on David Petraeus as "General Betray-us" in 2007. There are many motives underlying decisions to join the armed forces, the covert agencies, or the State Department, but what appears to be common to all these decisions is a commitment to helping one's country and its people. It is not the service but its impact that should be questioned. Activists focusing on military recruitment centers, the widespread high school military training programs, or university programs producing military officers, intelligence analysts, or diplomatic officials should ask these potential shafts and points of the imperial spear to reconsider not the morality of service but its morality within the current policy of domination.

In the same vein, the reverence that many Americans hold for their flag as an embodiment of pride and aspiration should be respected, even as the foreign and military policies that are systematically wrapped in it are disputed. Activists can certainly protest against the use of military color guards at sporting and community events, but once the flag is being saluted, it is time to shut up. To attack this popular, powerful symbol is to cede its defense to the pro-imperial politicians, right-wing media, and veterans groups, with and without motorcycles, who use it to squelch debate. The flag represents the nation, and what that nation stands for is precisely what is up for grabs. Every time the flag is saluted or the anthem is sung, activists should salute and sing respectfully, and then start chants against domination, such as: Leave others alone; stop aiding thugs; empire — No!; bring the troops home; freedom for others. When troops are introduced at public events, activists should join in the roar of approval, and then start up the chants, to affirm that there is sentiment against domination but not those who carry it out.

Sometimes vocal protest may not be enough. Disruption can help force the average person, who usually can avoid thinking about, let alone challenging, the established order, to consider the arguments of the disaffected. America has a long history of creative disruption, with the United States itself moving from a concept to a possibility with the illegal destruction of goods at the Boston Tea Party and the unapproved stockpiling of weapons at Lexington and Concord. Armed resistance to the Fugitive Slave Act in northern communities spurred the South to secede. America only realized its promise of equality when the civil rights movement disrupted business and clogged streets in the South, in defiance of state segregation laws.[1] These non-violent protests spurred a violent reaction that brought the need to break the horror of the segregated police state to the national consciousness, and frequently led to armed self-defense by black activists protecting both

---

1 The civil rights movement was careful never to break a federal law or ignore an injunction from a federal judge. In one bizarre case, the Justice Department prosecuted the "Albany (Ga.) nine" for picketing the store of a white man who had been on a jury that acquitted a sheriff who had killed a black prisoner. See Taylor Branch, *Parting the Waters*, Touchstone: Simon & Schuster, New York, 1988, p. 866.

---

their communities and the non-violent civil rights workers. What motivated the panjan-drums of the American empire, such as Ford Foundation head McGeorge Bundy, to beg President Nixon in 1970 to suspend military actions like the invasion of Cambodia was not some concern for Indochinese peasants, but a fear that the universal campus revolt would shake the authority of government for a generation to come.

Violent disruption, though, is often counter-productive. Consider the dozens of po-litical bombings directed against infrastructure and symbolic targets by the "Con-Edison bomber" Sam Melville in the 1960s and the Weather Underground in the 1970s. The media ignored the reams of turgid rationalizations produced by the perpetrators, and presented the American public with an image of common criminals, who were duly imprisoned or, in the case of Melville, who was probably targeted for assassination in the Attica prison revolt, first imprisoned and then killed. Spates of violent protest tend to produce instinc-tive public rejection, whereas creative, long-running dramas of protest allow the public time to get comfortable with the issues and arguments. The ultimate act of violent pro-test against US imperialism came on September 11, 2001. The attacks that day, moreover, were a continuation of bombings over the previous 10 years by opponents of US support for dictators in Egypt, Saudi Arabia, and other parts of the Islamic world. This wave of violence by Islamist warriors led to intense discussion in the media, the public, congress and the executive branch, but only about how to attack and weaken them. One can search in vain through the memoirs of those in government for any analysis of why America was the target of such fury. Such a discussion would have led to a realization that our role in the Middle East had led to our own predicament. It could not take place, though, in the aftermath of a violent attack.

As an educational tool rather than a realistic bid to reverse domination in government, some local activists may decide that it is useful to back anti-imperial candidates among the Democrats or from the various Green parties. In general, though, it appears far too early to use this tactic. The Greens are hopelessly identified with the anti-growth mes-sages of global warming and the Democrats are hopelessly fixed as Soft Eagles. A new, an-ti-imperial party that is dedicated to international cooperation and an end to domination can and should eventually emerge, but only after the robust attack on exceptionalism has made its position credible. There is always a hope that population trends may make it safe for the Democrats to win as anti-imperialist party. By 2040 non-Hispanic whites will be a minority in America, and the ethnic groups that will then be in the majority are more fa-vorable toward a non-imperial foreign policy than whites. However, the Democratic Party has strongly supported America in its role of post-colonial policeman because its political survival is bound up in pro-imperial candidates, constituencies, and financial supporters. Turkeys should bite the bullet and finally recognize that they need to abandon it.

Despite most House seats being Gerrymandered by state legislatures into uncompeti-tive districts, a significant share of Democrats in largely white districts in the Midwest and the South depend on conservative Democrats and unaffiliated "swing" voters for vic-tory. The Democrats' need for swing voters is also true for nearly all Senate races and for every presidential race. As a result, the "Dixiecrats" in Congress, who have provided Republicans with the margin of support for wars from Vietnam through El Salvador to

Iraq, will for decades to come be a powerful force within the Democratic Party. Pressuring them into supporting the party's majority position against imperial adventures, in the same way that Republicans successfully discipline their few Northern dissidents to empire, would be political suicide, since they would jump to the Republicans. The overall financial health of the Democratic Party also requires obeisance to empire. Thanks to the strenuous efforts of House Whip Tony Coelho in the 1980s and President Clinton in the 1990s, military contractors and international corporations have become among the biggest funders of the Democratic Party. Neither they, nor the more traditional union and pro-Israel funders, will let it become a party that questions, let alone tightens down, the spigot of arms contracts at home and abroad.

For these reasons, the Democrats will likely always be, as noted in Chapter 7, Speaker Pelosi's "party of more body armor" for US troops in Iraq rather than the party that rejects the need to have enough troops to be in Iraq. The Soft Eagles that comprise the majority of Democrats find their awareness of domination's sometimes disastrous consequences muted by a belief that more thoughtful management could have alleviated the situation. In an understandable attempt to be relevant in Washington, even the most progressive of proposals from the most anti-imperialist of Democrats, such as the Congressional Black Caucus and the House Progressive Caucus, barely scratch the surface of the military budget, and of the issue of its role in empire. Like the policies of the "cheap hawks" of the 1980s, who became the ruling Democratic national security elite of the 1990s and 2000s, these proposals "support our men and women in uniform" with pay, training, and conventional weaponry, and cut only nuclear and space weapons, and a few high-profile combat systems. Even such modest proposals are supported by less than 20 percent of Congress. These progressive voices abhor the systematic torture built into the "war on terror" and call for the withdrawal of troops, but not financial support, from Iraq. Anti-war and anti-poverty activists looking for help from the Democrats have a long row to hoe, because the party cannot confront the fundamental cause of invasion and torture, as well a core component of the system of poverty, which is US military domination of the former colonial world.

Just as the success of anti-slavery agitation led to the creation of the Republican Party in the 1850s, the media campaign and local activism suggested in this chapter would eventually make anti-imperialists numerous enough to justify having their own party. This party would be motivated by respect for other cultures and a desire to cooperate with them, unlike the Anti-imperialist League of the late 19th century, which featured racist fears to mixing with foreign peoples. Libertarian isolationists who supported Ron Paul for president in the 2008 Republican primaries have such an aversion to foreign entanglement that it would hard to imagine them supporting the cooperative measures that it would be at the heart of the vision of a party founded by Turkeys. In any event, the anti-imperial left and right probably could not inhabit the same party because they agree so little on significant domestic questions. Turkeys will probably decide that they have no need to repeat the Soft Eagles' attempt to win over people within a party who fundamentally disagree with them. Particularly if the electoral system is reformed toward proportional representation, Turkeys may find that by forming a party that insists on a founding principle of replacing domination with cooperation, they can start to have a say at the national level in a decade or two.

Many governments with pretensions to global domination in the 20th century were unable to retain public support in the face of its costs. Britain, France, Germany, Japan, Russia, the Netherlands, and Portugal were all staggered by wars, and lost much of their willingness to pay the continuing price of foreign domination in blood and treasure. Something in their national character led them to aspire to regional and even global domination, but military sacrifice and especially defeat, seems to have exhausted the public's appetite for it. Part of the explanation of today's imperial character lies in America's good fortune of having to date avoided disastrous consequences. The chickens did not, to borrow from Malcolm X's controversial analysis of the assassination of President Kennedy, come home to roost until September 11, 2001. That attack had a clear, and clearly admitted, purpose of bringing the war for control of the Islamic world directly to the public of one of the belligerents. The planners of that attack, Osama bin Laden and Ayman al-Zawahiri, have repeatedly said that their goal is to raise the domestic price of US involvement in the Middle East until Americans demand that their government leave.[1]

Al-Qaeda's strategy is reminiscent of the bombardment of Belgrade in 1999 to stop ethnic repression in Kosovo, in which continuous attacks on economic infrastructure by the United States and its allies generated enough public discontent to force Yugoslav president Milosevic to order his Serbian forces home. At some point, when the domestic political price of foreign domination is too high, governments do indeed lose their taste for it. However, the loss of lives, money, and prestige on 9/11 was apparently nowhere near sufficient to shock the US empire into retreat. The Bush administration successfully portrayed the attack as an illogical act of hatred rather than a logical reaction to American policy, and its repetition as preventable only by more aggressive, rather than less aggressive, alliances and interventions.

Someday the American empire will end. Moving back through history, there are scores of states whose overwhelming power and drive led them to domination on a grand scale, and yet are today considered politically insular, with no pretensions to ruling anyone other than themselves. In the 19th century the sun never set not just on Britain's territories, but also on those of the other great mercantilist empires, Spain, Portugal, and France. The Fulani jihad of Usman dan Fodio spread violently from Nigeria across West Africa at the same time as, and to the same geographic extent that, Napoleon's France smashed its way across Western Europe.

Sweden was the scourge of 17th century Europe and the Netherlands was the global equivalent, controlling the seas and millions of subjects from Irian Jaya in the Pacific to New Amsterdam in the Atlantic. The great Muslim expansion of the 8th century saw the Umayyad Caliphate of Syria became the loose law of lands as far flung as France in the north, Mali in the south, and Persia in the east, and the caliphate's Almoravid successors in Morocco held power from Spain south to the Sahel. The empires march back through history as far as a record was made: Mayan, Chinese, Roman, Persian and Greek. The bod-

---

1 See *Messages to the World: The Statements of Osama Bin Laden*, edited by Bruce Lawrence, Verso Press, New York, 2005.

ies of their young men are buried in the farthest reaches of the globe for causes that must have seemed essential to them, but are confusing and alien to their descendants today. So, America is not unique in developing a taste for, and then an addiction to, foreign domination. What is universal may be set, but what is particular can be changed. At issue is not whether American domination will end, but whether it will end because of cost or conscience. The former would set the stage for just another in a series of global hegemons. The latter would inspire people around the world to make sure that it would not be theirs. In that case, America could, finally, rightly claim to be exceptional.

ACKNOWLEDGMENTS

I am grateful to the many dedicated public servants and foreign policy activists who befriended me as we wrote legislation and planned campaigns during my 30 years in and around Congress. Listed below are my happy few, my band of brothers and sisters, who took on odds as long as Harry's at Agincourt. I am proud to have been their colleague.

David Abramowitz, of the House Committee on Foreign Affairs

Charisse Adamson, of Demilitarization for Democracy

Nancy Agris, of Representative Mike Barnes' staff

President Oscar Arias, of Costa Rica

Cindy Arnson, of Representative George Miller's staff

Representative Howard Berman

Kathleen Bertlesen (Moazed), of Representative Sam Gejdenson's staff

Kai Bird, biographer of the Establishment

Willie Blacklow, of Representative George Miller's staff

Gary "Dr. Gloom" Bombardier, of Representative Matt McHugh's staff

Representative Barbara Boxer

The late Robert Browne, of Delegate Walter Fauntroy's staff, a founder of the Vietnam "teach-ins"

Cindy Buhl, of the Central America Working Group and Representative Jim McGovern's staff

Eileen Burgin, of Representative Marcy Kaptur's staff

Holly Burkhalter, of Human Rights Watch

Bruce Cameron, of the Americans for Democratic Action

Tom Cardamone, of the Council for a Livable World

John Cavanagh, of the Institute for Policy Studies

Gordon Clark, of Peace Action

Betsy Cohn, of the Central American Historical Institute

Richard Collins, of Senator Daniel Inouye's staff

The late Dick Conlon, of the Democratic Study Group

Greg Craig, of Senator Ted Kennedy's staff

Frick Curry, of the Center for International Policy

Representative Peter DeFazio

The late Dominique de Menil, of Houston's Rothko Chapel

Representative Bill Delahunt

Representative Rosa Delauro

Representative Ron Dellums

Selam Demeke, of Demilitarization for Democracy

Anne Detrick, of the Project on Demilitarization and Democracy

Bob Dockery, of Senator Chris Dodd's staff

Nabila Drooby, of Houston's Rothko Chapel

Reverend Joe Eldridge, of the Washington Office on Latin America

The late Father Ignacio Ellacuria, of the University of Central America

Margie Ellis, of the Arms Control and Foreign Policy Caucus

Frances Tarlton "Sissy" Farenthold, of the Institute for Policy Studies

Mark Forest, of Representative Bill Delahunt's staff

Jordana Friedman, of the Council on Economic Priorities

General Bob Gard, of the Vietnam Veterans of America Foundation

Representative Sam Gejdenson

Kathy Gille, of Representative Dave Bonior's staff

Natalie Goldring, of the British American Security Information Council

"Bubbling" Bill Goodfellow, of the Center for International Policy

Steve Goose, of Representative Bob Mrazek's staff and of Human Rights Watch

Monica Green, of Peace Action

Lise Hartman, of Representative Howard Berman's staff

Bill Hartung, of the World Policy Institute

Jerry Hartz, of Representative Dave Bonior's and Speaker Pelosi's staff

Senator Mark Hatfield

Tom Hayden

Richard Healey, of the Institute for Policy Studies

John Isaacs, of the Council for a Livable World

Raed Jarrar, of the American Friends Service Committee

The late Hugh Johnson, of Representative Mickey Leland's staff

Vic Johnson, of Representative Mike Barnes' staff

Representative Walter Jones Jr.

Representative Joe Kennedy II

Representative Marcy Kaptur

Lauren Kenworthy, of Representative Howard Wolpe's staff

Colonel Ed King, of Senator Robert Byrd's staff

Representative Peter Kostmayer

George Kundanis, of Speaker Tom Foley's and Speaker Nancy Pelosi's staff

Rob Kurz, of Representative Mike Barnes' staff

John Lawrence, of Representative George Miller's and Speaker Nancy Pelosi's staff

Representative Jim Leach

Senator Pat Leahy

The late Representative Mickey Leland

Bill LeoGrande, of Senator Robert Byrd's staff

Ed Long, of Representative Ted Weiss' and Senator Tom Harkin's staff

Lora Lumpe, of the Federation of American Scientists

Tara Magner, of the Winston Foundation

Mike Marek, of Representative Dave Obey's staff

Representative Ed Markey

Mike Matheson, of the State Department Office of the Legal Adviser

Dick McCall, of Senator Robert Byrd's staff

Representative Cynthia McKinney

Representative Jim McDermott

Representative Jim McGovern

Julie McGregor (Britti), of Senator Mark Hatfield's staff

Representative Matt McHugh

Representative George Miller

Representative Jim Moody

Bobby Muller, of the Vietnam Veterans of America Foundation

Scott Nathanson, of Demilitarization for Democracy

Kevin Nealer, of Senator Robert Byrd's staff and Brent Scowcroft's firm

Eric Newsom, of Senator Pat Leahy's staff

Sulayman Nyang, of Howard University's African Studies Department

Mike O'Neil, of the House Intelligence Committee

Sima Osdoby, of Women's Action for New Directions

Elisa Perry, of Representative Bill Delahunt's staff

Mark Perry, of the Vietnam Veterans of America Foundation

Bernie Raimo, with the House Intelligence Committee and Speaker Pelosi

Tim Rieser, of Senator Pat Leahy's staff

Rick Rolf, of Senator Mark Hatfield's staff

Jemera Rone, of America's Watch

Robin Sanders, of Representative Cynthia McKinney's staff

Laurie Schultz-Heim, of Senator Jim Jeffords' staff

Susan Shaer, of Women's Action for New Directions

Anne-Marie Smith, of the Center for International Policy

Nancy Soderberg, of Senator Ted Kennedy's staff and the National Security Council

Todd Stein, of the Arms Control and Foreign Policy Caucus

Representative Gerry Studds

Bill Tate, of Representative Jim Leach's staff

John Thomas, of Representative Walter Jones Jr.'s staff

The late Father Paul Tipton, of the Association of Jesuit Colleges and Universities

John Tirman, of the Winston Foundation and the Pimlico track

Marissa Vitagliano, of the Vietnam Veterans of America Foundation

Joe Volk, of the Friends Committee on National Legislation

Ambassador Bob White, of the Center for International Policy

Edie Wilkie, of the Arms Control and Foreign Policy Caucus

Danny Weiss, of Representative George Miller's staff

Jody Williams, of Medical Aid to El Salvador and the Vietnam Veterans of America Foundation

Representative Howard Wolpe

Emira Woods, of the Institute for Policy Studies

Billy Woodward, of Representative Gerry Studds' staff

Andrea Young, of Representative Cynthia McKinney's staff

Dan Zeitlin, of Representative Rosa Delauro's staff

My thanks to Andrea Secara and the editorial staff at Algora Publishing, who were skilled and supportive as they guided this book from manuscript to final product.

And as ever I am grateful to the professors at Cornell University who guided my graduate studies with a firm hand: the late Arch Dotson, the late Frank Golay, Jim Turner, and Jerry Ziegler.

I could not have even dreamed of writing this book without the support I received at home from my wife Maya Latynski and my son Tadzio Latynski-Rossiter. They make everything worthwhile. My deepest thanks go to them.

BIBLIOGRAPHY

Articles, hearings, letters, and reports

Barry D. Adam, "Nicaragua, the Peace Process, and Television News," *Canadian Journal of Communication*, vol. 16, no. 1, 1991.

Douglas Amy, "The Forgotten History of the Single Transferable Vote in the United States," *Representation*, v. 34, no. 1, Winter 1996/7.

Arms Control and Foreign Policy Caucus, U.S. Congress, "Barriers to Reform: A Profile of El Salvador's Military Leaders," May 21, 1990.

Arms Control and Foreign Policy Caucus, U.S. Congress, "The Contra High Command," March 1986.

Arms Control and Foreign Policy Caucus, U.S. Congress, "Contra 'Reforms': Are the Miami Agreements Significant?", June 18, 1986.

Arms Control and Foreign Policy Caucus, U.S. Congress, "Who Are the Contras: An Analysis of the Makeup of the Military Leadership of the Rebel Forces, and of the Nature of the Private American Groups Providing them Financial and Material Support," April 18, 1985.

Arms Control and Foreign Policy Caucus, U.S. Congress, "Police Aid to Central America: Yesterday's Lessons, Today's Choices," August 13, 1986.

David Armstrong, "Dick Cheney's Song of America: Drafting a Plan for Global Dominance," *Harper's*, October 2002.

Douglas Brinkley, "Democratic Enlargement: The Clinton Doctrine," *Foreign Policy*, Spring 1997.

Center for International Policy, "Arnold and Porter Legal Opinion Clarifies Landmine Treaty," International Policy Report, Washington, DC, September 2000, Revised December 2000.

Center for International Policy, "Commander in Chief; Contrasting Presidential Roles in the World Campaigns to Ban Chemical Weapons and Land Mines," International Policy Report, Washington, DC, November 1990.

Michael Alison Chandler, "School cancels Taliban debate," *Washington Post*, p. B1, December 15, 2009.

Noam Chomsky, "Modern-Day American Imperialism: Middle East and Beyond," a talk at Boston University, April 24, 2008, http://chomsky.info/talks/20080424.htm.

Coalition to Rethink U.S. Aid to the Middle East, "Toward a Safer Future for the Children of Abraham: A Proposal for Restructuring U.S. Aid to the Middle East," Washington, DC, January 1995.

Committee on Foreign Affairs, House of Representatives, hearing: "U.S. Policy on Conventional Weapons," November 9, 1993, U.S. Government Printing Office, 1994.

David Corn, "Elliott Abrams: It's Back," *The Nation*, June 14, 2001.

James S. Corum, "The Air War in El Salvador," *Air Power Journal*, Summer, 1998. http://www.au.af.mil/au/cadre/aspj/airchronicles/apj/apj98/sum98/corum.html.

Edwin Deagle, "Creating a Landmine Free Military," briefing, Vietnam Veterans of America Foundation, Washington, DC, February 2001.

Bill Delahunt and Donald Payne, Letter on AFRICOM from House Foreign Affairs subcommittee chairs to Secretary of Defense Robert Gates, September 16, 2008.

Demilitarization for Democracy (at the time of the report, the Project on Demilitarization and Democracy), "Abrams Tanks for Kuwait: A Sale in Search of a Mission," Washington, DC, January 15, 1993.

Demilitarization for Democracy, "Exploding the Landmine Myth in Korea," Washington, DC, August 1997.

Demilitarization for Democracy, "Fighting Retreat: Military Political Power and Other Barriers to Africa's Democratic Transition," Washington, DC, July 1997.

Demilitarization for Democracy (at the time of the report, the Project on Demilitarization and Democracy), "Making the World Unsafe for Landmines: A Timetable for Developing Military Alternatives and Implementing a Worldwide Ban on the Smallest Weapon of Mass Destruction," Washington, DC, June 1995.

Anne Detrick and Caleb Rossiter, "Guess Who's Selling Deadly Arms Now? Liberal Democrats Enter the Weapons Biz," *Washington Post*, Outlook Section, May 16, 1993.

John Feffer, "Crapshoot in Copenhagen," World Beat, *Foreign Policy in Focus*, Institute for Policy Studies, Washington, DC, December 8, 2009.

Robert G. Gard Jr., "Alternatives to Antipersonnel Landmines," Vietnam Veterans of America Foundation, Washington, DC, Spring 1999.

Thomas Harrison, "The 2004 Elections and the Collapse of the Left," in *New Politics*, Volume X, Number 2, Winter 2005.

Mark Hatfield, Jim Leach, and George Miller, "Bankrolling Failure: United States Policy in El Salvador and the Urgent Need for Reform," Arms Control and Foreign Policy Caucus, U.S. Congress, November 1987.

Mark Hatfield, Jim Leach, and George Miller, "U.S. Aid to El Salvador: An Evaluation of the Past, a Proposal for the Future," Arms Control and Foreign Policy Caucus, U.S. Congress, February 1985.

Mark O. Hatfield, Mickey Leland, and Matthew F. McHugh, "Danger Point: The Developing World and U.S. Security," Arms Control and Foreign Policy Caucus, U.S. Congress, August 1989.

Linda Haugaard, "Admissions and Omissions: the CIA in Guatemala," *In These Times*, July 22, 1996.

Andrew Higgins and Alan Cullison, "Saga of Dr. Zawahiri Sheds Light on Roots of al Qaeda terror," *Wall Street Journal*, p. A1, July 2, 2002.

Niklas Höhne, "Impact of the Kyoto Protocol on Stabilization of Carbon Dioxide Concentration," ECOFYS energy & environment, Cologne, Germany, 2005, available on: http://www.stabilisation2005.com/posters/Hohne_Niklas.pdf.

David Isenberg, "The Rapid Deployment Force: The Few, the Futile, the Expendable," Cato Policy Analysis No. 44, Cato Institute, Washington, DC, November 8, 1984. Available on the web at http://www.cato.org/pubs/pas/pa044.html.

Institute for Policy Studies, Citizens' Commission for a New U.S. Policy Toward the Developing World: "Fulfilling the Promise," Washington, DC, 1994.

Institute for Policy Studies, "Report of the Task Force on a Unified Security Budget, FY2010," Washington, DC, 2010, available at http://www.ips-dc.org/reports/usbfy2010.

Robert David Johnson, "The Unexpected Consequences of Congressional Reform: The Clark and Tunney Amendments and U.S. Policy toward Angola," *Diplomatic History* 27 (2003): 215-243, available on the web at http://academic.brooklyn.cuny.edu/history/johnson/clark.htm.

Jeane Kirkpatrick, "Dictatorships and Double Standards," *Commentary*, November, 1979.

Michael T. Klare, "The New 'Rogue State' Doctrine," *The Nation*, May 8, 1995.

Law Library of Congress, "Campaign Finance: An Overview," http://www.loc.gov/law/help/campaign-finance/.

Richard Lindzen, "Resisting Climate Hysteria," *Quadrant Online*, July 26, 2009.

Richard Lindzen, Yong-Sang Choi, "On the Determination of Climate Feedbacks from ERBE Data," *Geophysical Research Letters*, Vol. 36, August 26, 2009.

Mark Lynch, "Taking Arabs Seriously," in *Foreign Affairs*, September/October 2003.

John A. Marcum, "Lessons of Angola," *Foreign Affairs*, April 1976.

Joel Millman, "El Salvador's Army: A Force Unto Itself," *New York Times Magazine*, December 10, 1989.

Modernizing Foreign Assistance Network, "New Day, New Way: A proposal from the Modernizing Foreign Assistance Network," Washington, DC, June 1, 2008. http://modernizingforeignassistance.net/documents/newdaynewway.pdf.

Jeffrey Record, "Reagan's Strategy Gap," *The New Republic*, October 29, 1984, p. 18.

Robert Richie and Steven Hill, "The Case for Proportional Representation," *Boston Review*, February/March 1998; available on the Fairvote website.

Stephen Rosenfeld, "The Reagan Doctrine: The Guns of July," *Foreign Affairs*, Spring 1986.

Caleb Rossiter, "The Financial Hit List," International Policy Report, Center for International Policy, Washington, DC, 1984.

Caleb Rossiter with Anne-Marie Smith, "Human Rights: The Carter Record, the Reagan Reaction," International Policy Report, Center for International Policy, Washington, DC, September 1984.

Caleb Rossiter, "Winning in Korea without Landmines," Vietnam Veterans of America Foundation, Washington, DC, Summer 2000.

Caleb Rossiter, with Anne-Marie Smith, "Human Rights: The Carter Record, the Reagan Reaction," International Policy Report, Center for International Policy, Washington, DC, September 1984.

John Samples, "A Critique of the National Popular Vote Plan for Electing the President," Policy Analysis 622, Cato Institute, Washington, DC, October 13, 2008.

Students for a Democratic Society, *Port Huron Statement*, http://coursesa.matrix.msu. edu/~hst306/documents/huron.html

Subcommittee on International Organizations, Human Rights, and Oversight of the House Committee on Foreign Affairs, report: "The Decline in America's Reputation: Why?", June 11, 2008. The transcripts of the hearings that led to the report are available on http://foreignaffairs.house.gov under the Subcommittee's link.

Subcommittee on International Organizations, Human Rights, and Oversight, House Committee on Foreign Affairs, U.S. Congress, hearing: "Is There a Human Rights Double Standard? U.S. Policy Toward Equatorial Guinea and Ethiopia," May 10, 2007. Available on http://foreignaffairs.house.gov under the Subcommittee's link.

Vietnam Veterans of America Foundation, "The Dupuy Institute's Research Study: Military Consequences of Landmine Restrictions," Washington, DC, Spring 2000.

Vietnam Veterans of America Foundation, "Proposed Protocol to Address Explosive Remnants of War," briefing for the Geneva meeting of the CCW, Washington, DC, September 25, 2001.

Daniel Volman and William Minter, "Making Peace or Fueling War in Africa," Foreign Policy in Focus, March 13, 2009, at http://www.fpif.org/fpiftxt/5960.

Mark W. Zacher, "The Territorial Integrity Norm: International Boundaries and the Use of Force," *International Organization*, March 2001.

Fareed Zakaria, "The Previous Superpower," *New York Times*, July 27, 2003, a review of Simon Schama's *A History of Britain: The Fate of Empire, 1776-2000*.

Books

Aleyiwola Abegunrin, *Nigerian Foreign Policy under Military Rule, 1966-1999*, Praeger, New York, 2003.

Cynthia Arnson, *Crossroads: Congress, the President, and Central America, 1976-1993*, Pennsylvania University Press, University Park, PA, 1993.

Christopher B. Barrett and Daniel G. Maxwell, *Food Aid After 50 Years*, Routledge, New York, 2005.

Tom Barry, *Central America Inside Out*, Grove/Atlantic, New York, 1991.

Michael Beschloss, editor, *Reaching for Glory: Lyndon Johnson' Secret White House Tapes, 1964-1965*, Touchstone Books, New York, 2002.

Robert L. Biesner, *Twelve Against Empire: The Anti-Imperialists, 1898-1900*, University of Chicago Press, Chicago, 1968, 1985.

Kai Bird, *The Chairman: John J. McCloy, The Making of the American Establishment*, Simon and Schuster, New York, 1992.

Kai Bird, *The Color of Truth, McGeorge and William Bundy: Brothers in Arms*, Simon and Schuster, New York, 1998.

Sonja Boehmer-Christiansen and Aynsley John Kellow, *International Environmental Policy: Interests and the Failure of the Kyoto Process*, Edward Elgar Publishing, 2002, available on: http://archives.cnn.com/2001/WORLD/europe/italy/03/29/environment.kyoto/

John Booth, Thomas Walker, *Understanding Central America*, Westview Press, Boulder, CO, 1999.

Taylor Branch, *Parting the Waters: America in the King Years, 1954-1963*, Simon and Schuster, New York, 1988.

Robert Bryce, *Gusher of Lies: The Dangerous Delusions of Energy Independence*, Public Affairs, New York, 2009.

Anne Cahn, *Killing Détente: The Right Attacks the CIA*. Pennsylvania State University Press, State College, PA, 1998.

J.F. Cairns, *The Eagle and the Lotus: Western Intervention in Vietnam 1847-1968*, Lansdowne Press, Melbourne, 1969.

Bruce Cameron, *My Life in the Time of the Contras*, University of New Mexico Press, Albuquerque, 2007.

Dan T. Carter, *The Politics of Rage: George Wallace and the Transformation of American Politics*, Simon and Schuster, New York, 1995.

Stephen J. Cimbala, *Military Persuasion: Deterrence and Provocation in Crisis and War*, Pennsylvania State University Press, University Park, PA, 1994.

Christopher Clapham, Jeffrey Herbst, and Greg Mills, eds., *Big African States*, Wits University Press, Johannesburg, 2006.

John Cooney, *The American Pope: The Life and Times of Francis Cardinal Spellman*, Times Books, New York, 1984.

Terry Crawford-Browne, *Eye on the Money*, Umuzi Press, South Africa, 2007.

Robert J. Donovan, *The Presidency of Harry S Truman: Conflict and Crisis, 1945-1948*, University of Missouri Press, Columbia, MO, 1996.

Robert Dreyfuss, *Devil's Game: How the United States Helped Unleash Fundamentalist Islam*, Metropolitan Books, New York, 2005.

José Napoleón Duarte, *Duarte: My Story*, Putnam, New York, 1986.

William Easterly, *The White Man's Burden*, Penguin, New York, 2006.

Dwight D. Eisenhower, *Mandate for Change, 1953-1956*, Doubleday, Garden City, NY, 1963 and 1994.

Niall Ferguson, *Colossus: The Price of America's Empire*, Allen Lane, London, 2004.

Frances Fitzgerald, *Way Out There in the Blue*, Simon and Schuster, New York, 2000.

Lloyd C. Gardner, *Approaching Vietnam*, Korton, New York, 1988.

Robert M. Gates, *From the Shadows: The Ultimate Insider's Account of Five Presidents and How They Won the Cold War*, Simon and Schuster, New York, 2007.

Piero Glejesias, *Conflicting Missions: Havana, Washington, Pretoria*, Galago, South Africa, 2003.

James M. Goldgeier, *Not Whether, but When: The Decision to Enlarge NATO*, Brookings Institution Press, Washington, DC, 1999.

Amy and David Goodman, *The Exception to the Rulers: Exposing Oily Politicians, War Profiteers, and the Media That Love Them, Hyperion*, New York, 2004.

Doris Kearns Goodwin, *Team of Rivals: The Political Genius of Abraham Lincoln*, Simon and Schuster, New York, 2006, p. 206.

Tom Hayden, *Reunion: A Memoir*, Random House, New York, 1988.

A. Henderson-Sellers and K. McGuffie, *A Climate Modelling Primer*, John Wiley and Sons, New York, 1987.

Edward S. Herman and Noam Chomsky, *Manufacturing Consent*, Pantheon Press, New York, 1988, reissued 2002.

Engseng Ho, *The Graves of Tarim: Genealogy and Mobility across the Indian Ocean*, University of California Press, Berkeley, 2006.

George M. Houser, *No One Can Stop the Rain*, Pilgrim Press, New York, 1989.

Susanne Jones, *The Battle for Guatemala: Rebels, Death Squads, and U.S. Power*, Westview Press, Boulder, CO, 1991.

George McT. Kahin and John W. Lewis, *The United States in Vietnam*, Dial Press, New York, 1967.

Robert S. Kahn, *Other People's Blood: U.S. Immigration Prisons in the Reagan Decade*, Westview Press, Boulder, CO, 1996.

Stanley Karnow, *Vietnam: A History*, Viking, New York, 1991.

Scott Kaufman, *Plans Unraveled: The Foreign Policy of the Carter Administration*, Northern Illinois University Press, DeKalb, 2008.

Mohamed El-Khawas and Barry Cohen, *The Kissinger Study of Southern Africa: National Security Study Memorandum 39 (Secret)*, Lawrence Hill, Westport, CT, 1976.

Donna R. Jackson, *Jimmy Carter and the Horn of Africa: Cold War Policy in Ethiopia and Somalia*, McFarland, London, 2007.

Howard Jones, *Crucible of Power: U.S. Foreign Relations since 1987*, Scholarly Resources, Wilmington, DE, 2001.

Michael Klare, *Blood and Oil: The Dangers and Consequences of America's Growing Dependence on Imported Petroleum*, Metropolitan Books, New York, 2004.

Jean Lacoutre, *De Gaulle*, translated by Francis K. Price, Hutchinson, London, 1970.

Walter Laqueur, *The Changing Face of Anti-Semitism*, Oxford University Press, New York, 2006.

Walter LaFeber, *Inevitable Revolutions: The United States in Latin America*, Norton, New York, 1993.

Anthony Lake, *The 'Tar Baby' Option: American Policy Toward Southern Rhodesia*, Columbia University Press, New York, 1976.

Bruce Lawrence, editor, *Messages to the World: The Statements of Osama Bin Laden*, Verso Press, New York, 2005.

Michael Mandelbaum, *The Case for Goliath: How the United States Acts as the World's Government in the 21ˢᵗ Century*, Public Affairs, New York, 2005.

Michael Maren, *The Road to Hell*, The Free Press, New York, 1997.

John Mearsheimer and Stephen Walt, *The Israel Lobby and U.S. Foreign Policy*, Farrar, Straus and Giroux, New York, 2007.

Donald Morris, *The Washing of the Spears: The Rise and Fall of the Zulu Nation*, Simon and Schuster, New York, 1965.

Dambisa Moyo, *Dead Aid*, Allen Lane, New York, 2009.

Aryeh Neier, *Taking Liberties*, Public Affairs, New York, 2003.

Joseph Nye, *Soft Power: The Means to Success in World Politics*, Public Affairs, New York, 2004

George Packer, *The Assassins' Gate: America in Iraq*, Farrar, Strauss and Giroux, New York, 2005.

Richard Patterson and Richardson Dougall, *The Eagle and the Shield: A History of the Great Seal of the United States*, Office of the Historian, Bureau of Public Affairs, Department of State, 1976.

David Randall, editor, *General Circulation Model Development*, Academic Press, New York, 2000.

Caleb Rossiter, *The Bureaucratic Struggle for Control of U.S. Foreign Aid: Diplomacy vs. Development in Southern Africa*, Westview Press, Boulder, 1985.

Caleb S. Rossiter, *The Chimes of Freedom Flashing: A Personal History of the Vietnam Anti-War Movement and the 1960s*, TCA Press, Washington, DC, 1996. The book can be read online at www.calebrossiter.com.

Clinton Rossiter, *1787: The Grand Convention*, Macmillan, New York, 1966.

Clinton Rossiter, *Seedtime of the Republic: The Origin of the American Tradition of Political Liberty*, Harcourt, Brace, New York, 1953.

Mark Rudd, *Underground: My Life with SDS and the Weathermen*, William Morrow/HarperCollins, New York, 2009.

Jeffrey Sachs, *The End of Poverty*, Penguin, New York, 2006.

Leon V. Sigal, *Negotiating Minefields: The Landmines Ban in American Politics*, Routledge, New York, 2006.

Melvin Small, *Democracy and Diplomacy: The Impact of Domestic Politics on Foreign Policy, 1789-1994*, Johns Hopkins University Press, Baltimore, MD, 1996.

Richard Sobel, editor, *Public Opinion in U.S. Foreign Policy: the Controversy over Contra Aid*, Rowman and Littlefield, Lanham, MD, 1993 (including Cynthia Arnson and Philip Brenner, "The Limits of Lobbying: Interest Groups, Congress, and Aid to the Contras," and William LeoGrande, "The Controversy over Contra Aid, 1981-1990: A Historical Narrative").

Nancy Soderberg, *The Superpower Myth: The Use and Misuse of American Might*, John Wiley and Sons, Hoboken, New Jersey, 2005.

Elizabeth E. Spalding, *The First Cold Warrior: Harry Truman, Containment, and the Remaking of Liberal Internationalism*, University Press of Kentucky, Lexington, 2006, p. 88.

Glen Harold Stassen and Lawrence S. Winters, eds., *Peace Action: Past, Present, and Future*, Paradigm, Boulder, CO, 2007.

F.W. Taylor, *Elementary Climate Physics*, Oxford University Press, New York, 2005.

John Tirman, *Spoils of War: The Human Cost of the Arms Trade*, Free Press, New York, 1997.

Bill Turque, *Inventing Al Gore*, Houghton-Mifflin, New York, 2000.

Stephen Walt, *Taming American Power: The Global Response to U.S. Primacy*, Norton, New York, 2005.

Hanes Walton Jr., Robert Louis Stevenson, James Bernard Rosser Sr., eds., *The African Foreign Policy of Secretary of State Henry Kissinger*, Lexington Books, Lanham, MD, 2007.

Spencer Weart, *The Discovery of Global Warming*, Harvard University Press, Cambridge, MA, 2003.

Teresa Whitfield: *Paying the Price: Ignacio Ellacuría and the Murdered Jesuits of El Salvador*, Temple University Press, Philadelphia, 1994.

Cathy Wilkerson, *Flying Close to the Sun*, Seven Stories Press, New York, 2007.

Francis X. Winters, *The Year of the Hare*, University of Georgia Press, Athens, 1997.

INDEX

A

Abdnor, James (Senator), 237

Abrams, Elliott (State Department official), 84, 90, 114, 125,

Abu Ghraib prison, 14, 134, 137, 243

Abu-Jamal, Mumia (prisoner), 132

Acheson, Dean (Secretary of State), 30

Ackerman, Gary (Member of Congress), 139

Addington, David (White House official), 125

Aerospace Industries Association (AIA), 119-120, 122

Afghanistan, 3, 6, 11-12, 45, 53-55, 71, 86, 111, 128-132, 134, 138-144, 146-147, 160-161, 174, 179, 183, 196, 199, 222-223, 242-243, 265-266, 268, 272, 283, 286-287
    Soviet war in, 53-55, 71, 131-132
    US war in, 3, 11-12, 45, 54, 111, 128, 130, 132, 139, 142-144, 147, 160, 179, 183, 196, 222, 243, 265, 268, 272, 286-287
    "surges", 128-129, 141, 143, 146, 223
    women's rights in, 196

Africa, 5, 8, 10, 13, 15, 17-18, 28, 45-57, 59, 64, 66-67, 101, 105, 112, 121-122, 125, 141-142, 154, 156-163, 177-186, 188, 192-193, 198-199, 220, 222, 241-243, 249, 262, 266, 270, 272-275, 281, 287-289, 294

Africa Center for Strategic Studies (Pentagon), 158

Africa Partnership Station (Pentagon), 158

African Crisis Response Initiative (ACRI), 122, 157-158

African-Americans, 10, 19, 22, 39, 49, 141, 219, 221-222, 229, 240, 247-248, 274-275, 290

African-Americans, foreign policy views of, 222

African National Congress (ANC), 64, 66-67, 101, 121, 192, 222

African National Congress (ANC), "Spear of the Nation", 64, 142

AFRICOM (US African Command), 142, 156-158, 192-193, 263

Agency for International Development (AID), 55-56, 75, 77, 177
    AID IDCA (International Development Cooperation Agency), 56

AIDS, 177, 180-181, 185, 188, 197

Albright, Madeleine (Secretary of State), 93, 169, 195, 251-252

Alexander, Bill (Member of Congress), 64

Algeria, 28, 45, 101, 128, 287
    1991 civil war, 101, 128
    FIS election victory, 128
    independence war with France, 86

Al-Jazeera, 138

Allende, Salvador (Chilean president), 160

Almoravid dynasty, 294

Al-Qaeda, 3, 12, 125-126, 128, 130-131, 133-134, 136, 144-147, 181, 259, 265, 267, 272, 276, 294

Al-Zawahiri, Ayman (leader of Al-Qaeda), 131-132, 294

America's image abroad, 14, 18

America's self-image, 8-9, 19-22, 41, 172, 244, 249-253, 256-257, 265-267, 269-271, 277, 279-281, 283-285, 289-290, 292

American Civil Liberties Union (ACLU), 68, 115, 233

American Committee on Africa (ACOA), 49

American Enterprise Institute, 109, 146

American Friends Service Committee (AFSC), 137

American Indians: see Native Americans

American Israel Public Affairs Committee (AIPAC), 118, 121, 134, 139, 236-238

American Legion, 5, 164, 264

American University, 90, 258, 276, 281

Americans for Democratic Action, 114

Amnesty International, 67, 121-122, 151, 154

Anderson, Bill (singer), 265

Anderson, Kenneth (NGO lawyer), 167

Angola, 11, 28, 44-50, 52-54, 86, 123, 128, 152, 154, 159, 166, 179, 185, 193, 268, 287
 Cabinda oil enclave, 46, 48, 128
 civil wars in, 44, 46, 154, 159

Annan, Kofi (UN Secretary General), 177

Anti-apartheid Act, 66-67, 275

Anti-ballistic missile plan for Europe, 12, 143

Anti-imperialist League, 8-9, 293

Aoki, Steve (NSC staffer), 114

Arafat, Yasser (Palestinian President), 237

ARCA Foundation, 68

Argentina, 57, 60, 154

Arias, Oscar (President of Costa Rica), 4, 100, 102, 104, 120-121
 Arias peace plan, 104

Aristide, Jean-Bertrand (President of Haiti), 18

Arms Control and Disarmament Agency (State Department office), 115, 169

Arms Control and Foreign Policy Caucus (US Congress), 5, 44, 58, 62, 64-65, 73, 77-78, 84-85, 87, 89, 91, 95, 103, 156

Arms trade, 111, 113-114, 116-117, 119, 188
 Arms Trade Code of Conduct, 116
  Amendments based on, 116-117, 154

Arms trade, Conventional Arms Transfer (CAT) talks, 51

Arms Transfer Working Group (ATWG), 114-122, 195

Arnson, Cindy (House staffer), 4, 65, 71, 76, 98

Asner, Ed (actor), 69

Association of Jesuit Colleges and Universities, 92, 94-95, 171

Aspin, Les (Secretary of Defense), 87, 110

Asquith, Herbert (British Prime Minister), 225

Atlantic Charter, 27

Atwater, Lee (Republican strategist), 95, 282

Axelrod, David (White House official), 140

B

Bao Dai (Vietnamese emperor), 32, 44

Baker, James (Secretary of State), 15, 81, 100, 102-104, 111, 119, 127, 138, 221

Bagley, Smith (funder), 102

Bagram prison, 134, 243

Bahrain, 126, 159

Ball, George (State Department official), 36-37, 46, 77, 112, 244

Ban Ki-Moon (UN Secretary General), 198

Barnes, Mike (Member of Congress), 65, 73-76, 83, 86, 92

Barnet, Richard (anti-imperial author), 17, 146

Barré, Siad (President of Somalia), 45, 52, 54, 157, 179-180

Barrett, Christopher (economist), 186-187

BBC-Arabic, 138

Bell, Robert (administration official), 169

Bella, Ben (President of Algeria), 86

Bennis, Phyllis (anti-imperial author), 17

Bergsten, Fred (Treasury Department official), 153, 183

Berman, Howard (Member of Congress), 95, 113, 139, 187

Berrigan brothers (Dan and Phil), 257

Berry, Mary Frances (civil rights leader), 7, 66

Biden, Joe (Senator and Vice President), 134, 144

Bin Laden, Osama (leader of al-Qaeda), 15, 126, 131-132, 294

Bird, Kai (biographer), 25, 33-37, 51, 195, 257-258

Bischak, Greg (policy analyst), 113

Black Caucus (Congressional body), 67, 222, 293

Black Panther Party, 40-41

Blacklow, Willie (House staffer), 77

Blair, Tony (British Prime Minister), 121, 177, 181, 189

Blandon, Adolfo (Salvadoran General), 78

Block, John (Secretary of Agriculture), 85

Bloomberg, Michael (Mayor), 239

Blue Dogs (See also: Democratic Party, Dixies)

Blumenthal, Sidney (administration official), 282

Blutdenken (thinking with the blood), 257-258, 260, 263, 282

Boland, Ed (Member of Congress), 63, 82-84, 101

Bolivia, 161

Bombardier, Gary (House staffer), 65

Bond, Jim (Senate staffer), 77, 80

Bond, Julian (NGO leader), 222

Bonior, David (Member of Congress), 4, 63, 65, 84, 87, 90, 99-104

Bonner, Raymond (journalist), 72

Borders Books, 264

Bosnia, 17, 123, 152, 194-195

Bourgeois, Father Roy (peace activist), 120

Brady, Jack (House staffer), 75

Branch, Taylor (civil rights historian), 19, 222, 253, 291

Brazil, 18, 50, 155-156, 250, 281

Breslin, Janet (Senate staffer), 65

British anti-slavery movement, 275

British empire, 128, 152, 240-241, 253

British-American Security Information Council (BASIC), 12, 55, 182, 189, 201

Brookings Institution, 109, 146

Broomfield, William (Member of Congress), 75-76, 81, 92

Broomfield–Murtha amendment (Central America), 76

Browne, Jackson (singer), 69

Browne, Robert (economist), 289

Brunei, 85, 159

Brzezinski, Zbigniew (National Security Advisor), 15, 51, 53, 55, 287

Buffett, Warren (philanthropist), 283

Buhl, Cindy (activist and Congressional staffer), 4, 67-68, 90, 92, 98, 145, 156

Bundy, McGeorge (National Security Advisor), 25, 34-37, 64, 99, 257, 292

Bundy, William (State Department official), 25, 34-37, 257

Buonaparte, Napoleon, 8, 63, 89, 267, 285-286, 294

Burma, 31

Bush, George H. W.,
    foreign policy of, 13, 107, 190, 282
    and New World Order, 107-108, 128, 285

Bush, George W., foreign policy of, 13

Bustillo, Rafael (Salvadoran general), 91

Buthelezi, Mangostho (South African leader), 192

Burr, Aaron (Vice President), 228

Byrd, Harry (Senator), 49

Byrd, Robert (Senator), 50, 56, 64-65, 67, 135

Byrnes, James (Secretary of State), 253

C

Caesar, Julius, 8, 243

Cahn, Anne (historian), 261

Caligula, 13

Callahan, Sonny (Member of Congress), 171-172

Cambodia, 43-44, 86, 140, 164, 166, 292

Cameron, Bruce (Contra advocate), 86

Camp David Accords (Israel), 54, 118, 127

Campaign finance, reform of, 57, 217, 233, 239

Campaign finance, public financing, 233, 236, 239

Canada, 56, 172, 187, 218, 241, 249, 254, 285

Card, Andrew (White House official), 132, 229

Caribou Coffee, 264

Carmichael, Stokely (activist), 222

Carnegie Endowment for International Peace, 146

Carter Center, 162

Carter, Jimmy, foreign policy of, 6, 43-45, 51-59, 72, 105, 123, 154, 182, 258, 261, 287

Carter, Joanne (NGO director), 114

Casey, William (CIA Director), 82, 84, 100

Cassidy and Associates, 236

Castro, Fidel (President of Cuba), 41, 45, 86, 257

Cato Institute, 54, 146

Cavanagh, John (NGO director), 147

Center for American Progress, 146, 218
Center for American Security, 146
Center for International Policy, 35, 51, 63, 68, 75, 110, 140, 154, 166, 174, 183
Center for Security Policy, 262
Center for Strategic and International Studies, 146
Council for a Livable World, 58, 114
Central America, 2, 5-6, 13, 15, 17, 57-61, 63-65, 67-78, 81-85, 87, 89-92, 94, 97, 99-100, 103-105, 128, 139, 141, 145, 164, 262, 268
Central Intelligence Agency (CIA), 4, 13, 28, 37, 46-50, 55, 60, 68, 70, 72, 78, 81-82, 84, 96, 99-101, 108, 110-111, 125, 132-134, 137, 142, 160, 235, 258-259, 261-262, 266, 279, 285, 287-288
Cerna, Lucia (witness to Jesuit murders), 94-95
Cetshwayo (Zulu King), 9, 191-192, 244, 268, 273
Chad, 190, 196, 287
Chalabi, Ahmad (Iraqi politician), 259
Chamorro, Edgar (Contra leader), 85
Chamorro, Violetta (Nicaraguan President), 104
Champlin, Steve (House staffer), 99
Charney, Jules (scientist), 209, 212
Chechnya, 131
Chelmsford, Lord (British General), 177, 191-192, 196
Chemical weapons, 4, 83, 166, 258
Cheney, Richard (Vice President and Member of Congress), 11, 13, 84, 93, 108, 125, 130, 134, 145, 259, 268
Chile, 11, 51, 57, 62, 82, 154-156, 160
    US role in overthrow, and aid to Pinochet, 11, 160
China, 11, 16, 26, 31-32, 34-35, 46, 54, 107, 112, 147, 153, 159, 161, 165-166, 178, 181, 183-184, 190, 198, 200, 244, 249, 262, 269-271, 289
Chomsky, Noam (anti-imperial author), 10, 109, 241
Christic Institute, 69
Christopher, Warren (Secretary of State), 15, 99, 110, 138, 154
Church, Frank (Senator), 63, 101
Churchill, Wade (anti-war professor), 134
Churchill Winston (Prime Minister), 107, 158, 192, 225
Civil rights movement, 142, 290-291

role of violence in, 19, 134
Clark, Richard "Dick" (Senator), 49
    Clark Amendment (Angola), 49-50
Clark, Gordon (NGO leader), 120
Clark, Wesley (General), 173
Clear Channel radio network, 265
Cleveland, Robin (Senate staffer), 30, 174
Clinton, Bill (President), 60, 108, 111, 125, 146, 235, 238, 262, 282
    foreign policy of, 60, 108, 111, 146, 235, 238, 262
Clinton, Hillary (Secretary of State), 105, 137, 139, 181, 239, 269
Cluster bombs, 168, 174-175, 269
    campaign to ban, 174, 269
    efforts to control, 269
Coalition for a Democratic Majority, 57
Coalition for a New Foreign and Military Policy, 67
    Central America Lobby Group, 67
Coalition for Peace through Strength, 57
Code Pink, 272
Coelho, Tony (Member of Congress), 119, 235, 293
Cohen, Ben (political donor), 49, 283
Cold War, 6, 11, 26, 33-35, 37-38, 40, 45, 48, 51-56, 61, 65, 84, 107, 110-112, 115, 122-123, 128, 145, 151-152, 154, 161, 238, 244, 271, 276, 286-287
Collins, Richard (Senate staffer), 65
Colombia, 79, 90, 112
Colorado, University of, 96, 134, 245
Commission on US-Central American Relations, 68
Committee for the Liberation of Iraq, 262
Committee in Solidarity with the People of El Salvador (CISPES), 68
Committee on the Present Danger, 13, 57, 125, 261-262, 268
Common Cause, 57, 66, 68, 133, 199, 234, 236
Confucius, 161
Congo, Democratic Republic of (see also Zaire), 11, 16, 18, 45, 152, 162, 178-179, 191, 193-194, 196, 242, 287
    US aid to Mobutu (see also Mobutu), 50
    US role in 1960s, 11, 45, 193, 287
Congress (US), 1, 3-7, 9-10, 15-17, 20, 27, 32, 37-38, 44, 49-50, 55, 57-74, 76-79, 81-85, 87, 89-104, 107-111, 115, 117-122, 128, 130, 133-134, 136-139, 142, 146-148, 154-

155, 159-160, 169, 173, 182-183, 186-188, 192-193, 202, 206, 211, 217, 221-223, 225, 227-228, 230, 235-239, 242, 245, 247, 251, 260-261, 263, 271, 275, 281, 292-293
Congressional Research Service, 132, 142, 160, 182, 221
Conlon, Dick (House staffer), 66
Connelly, Gerry (Senate staffer), 65, 102
Connolly, Tim (Pentagon staffer), 169
Contras (Nicaragua rebels), 4, 60, 63-65, 77, 81-87, 89-90, 100-103, 108, 152, 262
Constitution (US), 31, 84, 126, 137, 159-160, 219-220, 224-230, 240-241, 243-244, 247-248, 263, 285
Convention on Conventional Weapons (CCW), 166-167, 172, 175
Conyers, John (Member of Congress), 81
Council for a Livable World, 58, 114
Council on Foreign Relations, 146
Council on Hemispheric Affairs, 68
Countdown '87, 101-102
Country Joe (McDonald) and the Fish ('60s rock band), 20
Craig, Greg (Senate staffer), 65, 109
Cranston, Alan (Senator), 156, 237
Crawford-Browne, Terry (South African activist), 67
Crichton, Michael (novelist), 204
Cristiani, Alfredo (President of El Salvador), 80-81, 91, 96
Croatia, 195
Crockett, George (Member of Congress), 80-81, 92
Crow, Sheryl (singer), 167
Cruz, Arturo (Nicaraguan politician), 82, 86
Cuba
    Guantanamo Bay, 9, 14, 134, 137, 139, 243
    and troops in Africa, 45-46, 49, 193
    US attack on, 1898, 99
Custer, George (General), 42
Czech Republic, 143, 226

D

D'Amato, Al (Senator), 80
D'Aubuisson, Roberto (Salvadoran leader), 72, 76
Dallaire, Roméo (Canadian General), 194
dan Fodio, Usman (Fulani leader), 8, 294
Danforth, John (Senator), 112

Davis, Nathaniel (State Department official), 46-47, 50
Davos meetings, 179, 256
Deagle, Edwin (NGO analyst), 168-169, 174-175
Dean, Howard (Chairman of the Democratic National Committee), 5, 15, 25, 30-31, 36, 114, 210
Declaration of Independence (US), 226, 240
De Gaulle, Charles, 26, 28-29, 31, 36, 43
Defense Department (See Pentagon)
DeLauro, Rosa (activist and Member of Congress), 102, 137
Dellums, Ron (Member of Congress), 4, 66, 69, 87, 117
Delta Council, 30
DeGrasse, Francois-Joseph (French Admiral), 248
Demilitarization for Democracy, 110, 114, 122, 163, 168-169, 272
De Menil, Dominique (NGO leader), 96
Democracy, promotion of, 13, 111, 115-116, 127, 159
Democratic Congressional Campaign Committee, 119
Democratic Leadership Council, 15, 87, 108, 139
Democratic National Committee, 15, 61, 119, 239
Democratic Party, foreign policy of, 1, 15, 39, 58, 95, 108-110, 118, 139, 292
Democratic Party, Conservatives (Dixies or Dixie-crats, see also Blue Dogs), 2-3, 59, 61-65, 74, 76-77, 85-87, 97, 100-103, 134, 260
Democratic Party, Liberals, 1-2, 4, 21, 26, 32, 40, 61-62, 73, 85, 87, 100-101, 103, 108, 113, 115, 222
Democratic Study Group (US House), 58, 66
Delahunt, Bill (Member of Congress), 1, 59, 131, 137-138, 192, 223-224, 252
Demilitarization for Democracy, 110, 114, 122, 163, 168-169, 272
Derian, Patt (State Department official), 51, 57, 140, 154
Detrick, Anne (NGO staffer), 113, 116
Development, international (See also foreign aid), 55-56, 157, 186-187
Dickens, Charles (author), 177, 183
Disunion (of US), 233, 240-241, 246-248

Dixie Chicks (singers), 265-266
Djibouti (Afars and Issas), 52, 142, 157
D'Louhy, David (State Department official), 79
Dockery, Bob (Senate staffer), 65, 94
Dodd, Chris (Senator), 65, 79, 81, 94, 97, 102, 113, 116, 119, 160
Doe, Samuel (Liberian President), 179
Doha trade round, 16
Dole, Robert (Senator), 67, 171
Dominican Republic, 8, 11, 35, 62, 64
    US policy in, 19th century, 8
    US invasion 1965, 62
Dorgan, Brian (Senator), 117-118, 121
Douglas, Michael (actor), 264
Douglass, Frederick, on agitation, 6
Drone attacks, 128, 141, 144-145, 259, 262, 268, 284
Duarte, Jose Napoleon (President of El Salvador), 72, 76-77, 80, 99
Dubai, and world ports, 16
Dubois, W. E. B. (activist and sociologist), 221, 252-253
Duffendach, Sarah (House staffer), 99
Dukakis, Michael (Governor), 108, 276, 282
Duker, Laurie (NGO lobbyist), 69
Durand Line, 144
Dylan, Bob, 42, 256

E

Eagle, the (as symbol of foreign policy), 7-8, 11-22, 29, 51, 55-56, 58, 60, 62-65, 67-68, 70-71, 75, 80-83, 86-87, 89-90, 98-99, 104-105, 109, 111, 119, 121-123, 125-129, 133-134, 136-140, 145-147, 151-154, 156-157, 159-163, 177, 187-188, 191, 193, 195-196, 200, 217-218, 222-223, 233-236, 239, 246, 250, 252, 260, 266-272, 274, 276-277, 279-280, 283-284, 289, 292-293
Eagles (advocates of US domination), beliefs and policies of, 8, 13, 16, 18, 20, 62, 64, 104, 109, 122, 125-126, 152-153, 191, 193, 195-196, 200, 239, 246, 250, 260, 274
Eagles, Hard Eagles, 12-14, 16-17, 22, 58, 63, 82, 87, 104-105, 119, 125-129, 134, 137, 146, 152-154, 159, 177, 187, 266, 268-269
Eagles, Soft Eagles, 14-18, 20, 22, 55, 58, 60, 62-65, 67-68, 70-71, 80-83, 87, 89-90, 98-99, 109, 121, 123, 127-129, 133-134, 136-138, 140, 145-147, 152, 154, 156-157, 159,

161-162, 187-188, 191, 193, 196, 200, 218, 222, 233-235, 246, 260, 268-270, 274, 280, 292-293
Eagleton, Thomas (Senator), 138
Easterly, William (economist), 180
Easum, Donald (State Department official), 46
Eavis, Paul (NGO leader), 121
Egypt, 3, 11-12, 51, 112, 118, 125-127, 131-133, 145, 156, 159, 165, 190, 238, 243, 269, 285, 287-288, 292
    US aid to, 12, 112, 118, 127, 132, 156, 159, 190, 238, 287-288
Einstein, Albert, 204-205
Eisenhower, Dwight, 26, 29, 32-34, 48, 70, 126, 238
    foreign policy of, 26, 32, 126, 238
    as general, 29
El Salvador, 5, 11, 35, 44, 51, 60-62, 64, 68-82, 87, 89-99, 105, 113, 135, 147, 154-155, 160, 171, 179, 183, 237, 243, 262, 270, 292
    civil war in, 44, 69, 90, 154, 270
        Atlacatl Brigade, 91
        Tandona (The Big Class), 91, 94-98
    US aid to, 5, 44, 60, 62, 68-78, 80-82, 87, 89-95, 97-99, 147, 154, 160, 171, 179, 183, 237, 262, 270
Electoral "college", reform of, 19, 228
Ellacuría, Ignacio (Jesuit priest and rector), 60, 90-95, 98
Emanuel, Rahm (Member of Congress), 2, 135
Empires, historical, 153, 243-244, 246, 250, 286, 294
Engle, Elliot (Member of Congress), 105
Enough Project (NGO), 193, 196
Environmental Defense Fund, 57
Equatorial Guinea, 59, 158, 185, 192, 268, 287
Ethiopia, 45, 51-55, 59, 128, 142, 158, 162, 166, 180, 192-193, 199, 285, 287-288
    civil wars in, 51, 54, 59, 128, 142, 162, 180, 192-193, 287
    Derg ruling council, 52
    invasion by Somalia, 45, 51-55, 59, 128, 142, 158, 180, 193, 285, 287-288
European Union, 121, 226
Evans, Lane (Member of Congress), 171
Exceptionalism, 8-9, 19-22, 41, 172, 244, 249-250, 252-253, 256-257, 265-267, 269-271, 277, 279-281, 283-285, 289-290, 292

American belief in, 9, 14, 19-20, 22, 27, 33-34, 41, 57, 70, 105, 145, 161, 172, 198, 200-201, 203, 206-207, 219, 223, 233, 243, 247, 250-252, 255-256, 267, 269-270, 274, 280-281, 285-286, 291, 293
  cultural pump of, 19, 249, 257
  plan to discredit, 277, 280, 289
Exposure to American values (Pentagon claim), 157-158
Export–Import Bank (US), 116

F

Fagin, Daryl (NGO lobbyist), 114
Falwell, Jerry (minister), 255
Farenthold, France Tarlton "Sissy" (peace activist), 96
Farrell, Mike (actor), 69
Fascell, Dante (Member of Congress), 75, 92
Faulkner, Daniel (murdered policeman), 132
Fauntroy, Walter (Member of Congress), 66
Federal Communications Commission (FCC), 239
Federal Election Commission (FEC), 234-235
Federalist Papers, 244
Federation of American Scientists, 111, 117
Feffer, John (NGO author), 199-200
Feingold, Russ (Senator), 193, 223-224
Feinstein, Lee (NGO and State Department staffer), 115, 169, 173
Feith, Doug (Pentagon official), 125, 259
Ferguson, Niall (historian), 132-133, 276
Ferry, W. H. "Ping" (political donor), 289
Finland, 165
Fischer, Bram (South African lawyer), 281
Fitzgerald, Frances (historian), 261
FMLN rebels (See El Salvador)
FNLA rebels (See Angola)
Foley, Tom (Member of Congress), 4, 62, 64-65, 68, 87, 92-93, 102
Ford, Gerald, foreign policy of, 13, 27, 43-45, 47-48, 50, 52-54, 108, 261, 292
Foreign aid, 1, 6, 10, 17, 33, 45-46, 49, 55-57, 73-75, 77, 86, 97-98, 104, 112, 117-120, 160, 162, 164, 171, 177-181, 186-190, 198-199, 217, 271, 273, 288
  food aid, 179-180, 186-187
  tying of, 158
Forsberg, Randy (arms control analyst), 66

Fox News, 12, 240, 265
Franken, Al (Senator), 260
Friends Committee on National Legislation (FCNL), 58
France, 7, 10, 16, 18, 25, 27-33, 40, 45, 52, 105, 111, 132, 188-189, 195, 218, 238, 244, 253, 255, 286, 294
  American citizen protests against, 189
  policy in Africa, 28, 45, 294
  policy in Indochina (including Vietnam), 25, 27-29, 31-33, 40, 45, 52, 105, 132, 195, 218, 255
Franklin, Benjamin, 7-8, 10-11, 18, 28, 30, 32, 61, 126, 160, 203, 226, 253
  proposes Turkey as symbol, 7-8, 11, 253
Franklin, John Hope (political scientist), 30
Freedom House, 13, 162, 218, 262
Freeze campaign (nuclear weapons), 17, 66
French fries (Freedom fries), 18, 132, 138
Friedman, Thomas (columnist), 109
Fukuyama, Francis (historian), 107, 110
Fuerth, Leon (Senate and White House staffer), 108
Funes, Mauricio (President of El Salvador), 105

G

Gabon, 185
Gaffney, Frank (NGO director), 262
Galbraith, Peter (Senate staffer), 195
Gard, Robert (General, NGO analyst), 169, 174
Garvey, Marcus (activist), 222
Gates, Robert (Secretary of Defense), 84, 140, 175, 177, 186, 192, 283
Gates, Bill (philanthropist), 84, 140, 175, 177, 186, 192, 283
Gaza strip, 238
Gejdenson, Sam (Member of Congress), 75, 121
Geneva Conventions, 16, 166, 243
Geno's (Philadelphia restaurant), 132
Gephardt, Richard (Member of Congress), 112, 160, 235
Gere, Richard (actor), 69, 87
Germany, 9-10, 18, 33, 144, 157, 188, 200, 220, 286, 289, 294
Gerry, Elbridge (Governor), 65, 71, 75-76, 92, 99, 102, 219

Giap, Nguyen Vo (Vietnamese General), 29, 31, 43-44

Gille, Kathy (House staffer), 4, 63, 65, 99

Gilman, Ben (Member of Congress), 115, 120

Gingrich, Newt (Member of Congress), 104, 171

Glenn, John (Senator), 235

Global war on terror, 6, 11, 15, 20-21, 131, 136, 140, 147, 156, 179, 189, 276, 283, 293

Global warming, 18, 129, 198-202, 207-211, 217, 274-275, 282, 292
  claims of impact, 198, 200
  climate models, 18, 201, 274
  Copenhagen meeting, 198
  Kyoto Treaty, 200
  "off-sets", 154

Goland, Michael (political donor), 237

Goldring, Natalie (NGO staffer), 117

Goldwater, Barry (Senator), 35-36, 47, 84, 282

Gómez, Leonel (Salvadoran activist), 93, 98

Goodman, Amy (anti-imperial radio commentator), 12

Goose, Steve (NGO staffer), 167, 175

Gordon, Brad (House staffer), 118

Gore, Al (Senator and Vice President), 108, 125, 170, 173, 199, 201-208, 210-211, 217, 227, 229-230, 262, 275, 282

Government Accountability Office (GAO), 18, 78, 186

Grand Old Opry, 254

"Great White Fleet", 9

Greece, 115, 160, 241, 286

"Green" (actions and policies), 57

Green Party, 20, 54, 91, 132, 155, 199-200, 202, 236, 266, 274, 292

Greenpeace, 57

Grenada, 62, 83, 105, 183

Group of 8 (G-8), 179, 185

Guam, US seizure of, 8, 225

Guantanamo Bay prison, 9, 14, 134, 137, 139, 243

Guatemala, 11, 60-62, 68, 74, 82, 99, 161, 287
  US aid to, 60, 62, 68, 74, 82, 99, 287
  US overthrow of, 11

Guevara, Che, 21, 246

Guinier, Lani (legal theorist), 221-222

H

Hadrami people, 131-132

Haggard, Merle (singer), 255, 265-266

Haig, Alexander (Secretary of State), 63-64, 71, 183

Haiti, 112, 122-123, 195, 251

Halberstam, David (author), 33, 258, 270

Halperin, Mort (NGO and administration staffer), 68, 115

Hamilton, Alexander (Secretary of the Treasury), 228

Hamilton, Lee (Member of Congress), 86, 101, 127, 138

Hammer, Armand (business executive), 207

Hansen, James (scientist), 210

Harkin, Tom (Senator), 50, 65, 77-78, 81-82, 117, 153
  Harkin Amendment (human rights), 50, 81-82, 117

Harriman, Averell (diplomat), 53

Harriman, Pamela (diplomat), 195

Harris, Emmy Lou (singer), 167, 201

Hartman, Lise (House staffer), 95

Hartung, Bill (military author), 117

Hartz, Jerry (House staffer), 99

Hasenfus, Eugene (Contra supplier), 89, 100

Hatfield, Mark (Senator), 4, 21, 37-38, 44, 65-66, 77-78, 80-81, 95-96, 116-118, 121, 156, 171

Hawaii, 8

Hayakawa, S. I. (Senator), 50

Hayden, Tom (anti-war activist), 4, 38-39, 50

Helms, Jesse (Senator), 117, 153

Helsinki Accords, 57

Helsinki Watch, 57-58

Herblock (cartoonist), 270

Heritage Foundation, 146, 183, 262

Hernandez, Maria Julia (Salvadoran activist), 79, 96

Hersh, Seymour (journalist), 134

Hewson, Paul "Bono", 177, 183, 185

Hilliard, Earl (Member of Congress), 237

Hinchey, Maurice (Member of Congress), 235

Hirshberg, Gary (political donor), 283

Hiss, Alger (State Department official), 31

Ho Chi Minh, 26, 28-31, 33, 36, 41, 181

Holbrooke, Richard (State Department official), 51, 109, 140, 143, 154

Holmes, Oliver Wendell (Supreme Court Justice), 75, 226

Holum, John (State Department official), 115, 169

Honduras, 83, 85, 96, 101, 103, 112-113, 156

Horton, Willie (prisoner), 282

House of Lords, 224-226

House of Representatives (See Congress, US)

Hull, Cordell (Secretary of State), 28

Human Rights bureau (State Department), 55, 57, 78-79, 99, 114-117, 122, 140, 154, 166, 183, 272

Human Rights, promotion of, 20, 112, 116, 153, 158, 191

Human Rights Watch, 4, 58-59, 78, 90, 122, 151, 165-167, 175, 193-195
    Americas Watch, 67, 79, 90, 99, 103
    Arms division, 59, 165

Humphrey, Hubert (Vice President), 49

Huntington, Samuel (political scientist), 110, 130

Hussein, Saddam (Iraqi President), 14, 20, 48, 102, 107, 111, 126, 128-129, 133, 137, 196, 218, 262, 268, 279, 287

Hyde, Henry (Member of Congress), 237

I

India, 8, 16, 18, 165, 178, 183-184, 192, 234, 244, 249, 276

Indians: see Native Americans

Indonesia, 11, 18, 60, 112, 116, 140-141, 153-154, 189-190, 250
    Dutch role in (Java), 25, 28-29
    US role in, 153-154, 189

Inkhata Party (South Africa), 192

Inouye, Daniel (Senator), 63, 65, 101, 135

Institute for Policy Studies, 17, 57, 110, 146, 155, 193, 199, 272, 290

Inter-American Defense College, 158

Intergovernmental Panel on Climate Change (IPCC), 198-200, 203-204, 208-213

International ANSWER, 21

International Committee of the Red Cross (ICRC), 165-166, 171

International Court of Justice (World Court), 84, 173

International Criminal Court (ICC), 14, 152

International Military Education and Training (IMET), 155-156

International Monetary Fund (IMF), 145, 153, 179-180, 182-184, 189-190, 223, 288

Iran, 11-12, 15-16, 20, 54, 69, 78, 85, 89-90, 100-102, 126-128, 138-140, 143, 147, 161, 238, 241, 258-260, 269, 272, 276, 287-288
    House of Pahlavi, 126-127
    nuclear program, 12, 15-16, 139, 269, 276, 288
    US overthrow, 11

Iran–Contra scandal, 60, 68-69, 78, 83-87, 89-90, 97, 100-103, 105, 126, 128, 140, 259

Iraq, 2-4, 6, 10-11, 13-15, 17-18, 21, 48, 78, 102, 109, 111, 117, 127-136, 138-139, 141-143, 145-148, 159, 161, 174, 177, 179, 181, 195-196, 203, 207, 211, 218, 222-223, 227, 238, 242-243, 246, 252, 256, 259-260, 262-265, 268, 270, 272, 281, 283, 285, 287, 293
    1991 Gulf War, 114, 119, 127-128, 259-260
    2003 US war in, 3, 30, 126, 152, 252, 256
    2002 resolution, 9, 18, 38, 50, 75, 84, 134-135, 137-139, 153, 159, 192-193, 196, 259, 268
    Abu Ghraib prison, 14, 134, 137, 243
    Congressional response, 2-4, 6, 10-11, 15, 17, 78, 102, 109, 111, 117, 128, 130, 132-136, 138-139, 142, 146-148, 159, 211, 222-223, 227, 238, 242, 252, 260, 263, 281, 293
    "surge", 128-129, 135-136, 141-143, 145-147, 222-223, 256
    UN Mandate and, 138
    US withdrawal agreement, 21, 139, 142, 293

Iraq, Parliament, 3, 117

Isaacs, John (NGO leader), 114, 116

Isandlwana (battle of), 191-192

Islam, 11, 128, 130-132, 134, 140-141, 255, 288

Islamist militants, 12

Islamic Jihad, Egypt, 125, 132

Israel, 13, 16, 31, 46, 54, 60, 108, 113, 118, 125-129, 134, 141-142, 145, 161, 165, 190, 234, 236-238, 251, 255, 269-271, 285, 289
    "Clean Break" memo, 125
    Likud Party, 13, 125
    role in US politics, 31, 127, 161, 237-238, 271

J

Jackson, Henry "Scoop" (Senator), 21, 31-32, 48-49, 51, 53, 63-67, 77-80, 86, 94, 102, 112-113, 116-117, 138, 155-156, 171, 193, 206, 217, 223, 237, 246, 260

Jackson, Jesse Jr. (Member of Congress), 229

Right to Vote amendment, 69, 86, 229
Jackson, Samuel (actor), 266
Jackson, Shirley (author), 48, 51-55, 69, 86, 109, 229, 247, 265-266
Japan, 8-9, 25-26, 29-30, 33, 130, 286, 294
  empire of, 26
Jarrar, Raed (Iraqi peace activist), 137-138
Jefferson, Thomas, 7, 228, 244, 251, 285
Jeffords, Jim (Member of Congress), 65
Jepsen, Roger (Senator), 50, 237
Johnson, Andrew, 254
Johnson, Joel (arms industry lobbyist), 120
Johnson, Lyndon, 26, 32, 35-38, 41-42, 145, 147, 170, 181, 245, 247, 282
  foreign policy of, 26, 32, 35, 42, 145, 147, 170
Johnson, Samuel, 285
Johnson, Victor C. "Vic" (House staffer), 65, 73, 75, 92-93, 98
Johnston, Bennett (Senator), 97
Joint Chiefs of Staff (See also: Pentagon), 11, 110, 167-169, 173, 195
Jolie, Angelina (actress), 177
Jones, David (General), 169
Jones, James (National Security Advisor), 140
Jones, Walter Jr. (Member of Congress), 132, 138, 218
Jordan, 118, 238
Joulwan, George (General), 174

K

Kagan, Don (historian), 13, 262
Kaptur, Marcy (Member of Congress), 182
Karzai, Hamid (Afghan President), 142-144, 270
Kasten, Robert (Senator), 77, 80, 95
Katzenbach, Nicholas (Attorney General), 35
Kaye, Walter (political donor), 239
Kazakhstan, 268
Keith, Toby (singer), 260, 265
Kemble, Penn (Contra advocate), 86, 262
Kemp, Jack (Member of Congress), 76
Kennan, George F. (State Department official), 163
Kennedy, Edward "Ted" (Senator), 51, 65, 109, 113, 155
Kennedy, John, foreign policy of, 5, 32, 34, 134, 251, 255, 268
Kennedy, Joseph "Joe" II (Member of Congress), 4, 116, 120

Kennedy, Patrick (Member of Congress), 116
Kennedy, Robert (Attorney General), 25, 34
Kenya, 52, 54, 59, 162, 185-186
Kerry, John (Senator), 81, 121, 134-135, 231, 246, 283
Khalilzad, Zalmay (State Department official), 109
Khmer Rouge (Cambodia), 43-44, 54, 86, 140, 164, 166, 292
King, Edward Lavoise (Senate staffer), 4, 65
King, Martin Luther Jr., 30, 40-41, 222, 247, 272
Kipling, Rudyard, and "White Man's Burden", 9, 61, 255, 267
Kirkland, Lane (President of AFL-CIO), 73
Kirkpatrick, Jeanne (State Department official), 20, 251
Kissinger, Henry (Secretary of State), 16, 44-50, 56, 72-76, 78, 81, 94, 108, 115, 126, 140, 160, 268
  Kissinger Commission on Central America, 72, 76, 78, 81, 94
Kitchener, Herbert (British General), 192
Klare, Michael (political scientist), 110, 127
Klaus, Vaclav (Czech President), 226
Koh, Harold (State Department official), 115
Kondracke, Mort (columnist), 81
Korea, need for landmines (See South Korea, landmines)
Korb, Larry (Pentagon official), 272
Kornbluh, Peter (activist and archivist), 160
Kosovo, US attacks in, 123, 125, 141, 152, 195, 294
Kostmayer, Peter (Member of Congress), 80-81
Kristol, Irving (neo-conservative), 13
Kucinich, Dennis (Member of Congress), 218
Kundanis, George (House staffer), 65, 68, 99
Kurz, Rob (House staffer), 65
Kutuzov, Mikhail (Russian general), 267
Kyoto Treaty: see Global Warming

L

LaFeber, Walter (historian), 9, 69
Lake, Anthony "Tony" (National Security Advisor), 49, 109-113, 140

Landmines, campaign against anti-personnel, 5, 14, 108, 116, 152, 165-169, 171-173, 175

Landmines, campaign against anti-personnel, tactics and search for alternative weapons, 152, 166, 168, 170, 172-173

Laqueur, Walter (historian), 129

Laos, 34, 43

Latin America, 8-9, 51, 57, 67-68, 71, 79, 84, 90, 93, 105, 120, 154, 156-158, 160-161, 163, 188, 192, 239, 244-245, 266, 270, 286-287

Lawson, Robert (Canadian diplomat), 172, 174

Lawyers Committee on Human Rights, 67

Leach, Jim (Member of Congress), 44, 77-78

Leahy, Patrick (Senator), 65, 81, 97, 116, 122, 156, 164-166, 170-175

Lebanon, 129, 238

Ledeen, Barbara (NGO leader), 260

Ledeen, Michael (neo-conservative author), 259

Lee, Barbara (Member of Congress), 134, 218

Lee, Robert E. (Confederate General), 248

Lee, Spike (film director), 234

Lehman, Bill (Member of Congress), 70

Leiken, Robert (Contra advocate), 86

Lenin, V.I. (Soviet leader), 243, 256-257, 274

Letelier, Orlando (Chilean official), 155

Levin, Carl (Senator), 113, 136, 223, 260

Lewis, Peter (political donor), 25, 29, 32, 283

Liberia, 54, 59, 157, 179, 242, 287

Libya, 18, 238, 259

Lieberman, Joe (Senator), 119

Lincoln, Abraham, 8, 22, 30, 101, 126, 219, 226, 247, 251, 254, 282, 286

Lincoln, Abraham, and Mexican War, 8

Lindzen, Richard (scientist), 206, 209, 212

Live Aid, 180

Lockheed Martin Corporation, 109

Long, Ed (congressional staffer), 65, 78

Lopez-Nuila, Reynaldo (Salvadoran officer), 78

London, Jack (novelist), 254

Lord, Winston (State Department official), 153

Lord's Resistance Army (Acholi resistance group, *See* Uganda)

Lowry, Mike (Member of Congress), 65

Lumpe, Lora (NGO analyst), 117

Lyman, Arthur (Iran-Contra lawyer), 102

M

MacArthur, Douglas (General), 25, 29

Mack, John (House staffer), 104

MacNeil-Lehrer Newshour, 113

Madison, James, 224, 228, 244-246, 248, 285
at Constitutional Convention, 224, 228
and War of 1812, 285

Mahdi Army (Sudan), 16-18, 51, 54, 59, 112, 132, 142, 152, 179, 192-193, 196, 199, 242, 287

Malawi, 162

Malcolm X, 134, 222, 234, 294

Maliki, Nouri al- (Iraqi Prime Minister), 135-138

Mandela, Nelson (South African President), 64, 66-67, 142, 158, 222, 257, 281, 287-288

Mandelbaum, Michael (advocate of US dominance), 15, 132-133, 265

Manolis, Spiro (Pentagon official), 155-156

Mansfield, Mike (Senator), 37-38

Mao Tse Tung, 31, 41, 86, 180

Marcos, Ferdinand (President of the Philippines), 54

Marek, Mike (House staffer), 65

Maren, Michael (author), 180

Marine Corps League, 264

Markey, Ed (Member of Congress), 64, 87

Marshall, John (Chief Justice), 8, 26, 30-31, 126, 238, 247, 266-267

Marshall, George (General and Secretary of State), 8, 26, 30-31, 126, 238, 247, 266-267

Marshall Plan, 26, 30-31, 266

Marx, Karl, 256

Massachusetts Bay Colony, 250

Matheson, Michael (State Department official), 173

McCain, John (Senator), 4, 97, 146-147, 280

McCall, Dick (Senate staffer), 65

McCarthy, Joseph (Senator), 31, 35

McChrystal, Stanley (US General), 143-144

McCloy, John J. (administration official), 36, 257-258

McConnell, Mitch (Senator), 67

McCurdy, Dave (Member of Congress), 83, 86-87, 97

McFarlane, Robert (National Security Advisor), 86

McKinney, Cynthia (Member of Congress), 4, 117-122, 237

McNamara, Robert (Secretary of Defense), 36-37, 55, 99

McGovern, Jim (Member of Congress), 65, 92, 94, 97-98, 145, 156, 193
El Salvador role, 92-94, 97-98

McGrath, Rae (NGO activist), 165

McGregor, Julie (Senate staffer), 65, 95

McHugh, Matt (Member of Congress), 4, 65, 70, 81, 92, 97, 156

McKinley, William, and war with Spain, 9

Mearsheimer, John (political scientist), 236-237

Meeks, Greg (Member of Congress), 252-253

Melville, Sam (prisoner), 257, 292

Members of Congress for Peace through Law (See Arms Control and Foreign Policy Caucus)

Mengistu, Haile (head of Ethiopian Derg), 52, 180

Menjivar, Milton (US officer), 96

Metzenbaum, Howard (Senator), 113

Mexico, 8, 27, 86

Middle East, long war for, 3, 11-15, 17, 20-21, 28, 110-111, 113, 118-119, 125-127, 130, 133, 139-140, 159, 161, 181, 238-239, 243-244, 259, 266-267, 272, 277, 287-288, 292, 294

Midway Island, 8

Mikva, Abner (Member of Congress and Judge), 138

Milankovich cycles, 209

Millennium Challenge Corporation, 190

Millennium Challenge Goals (UN), 180

Miller, George (Member of Congress), 5, 44, 64-65, 68-69, 73, 83, 89, 92, 97, 223

Miller, Judith (journalist), 259

Millman, Joel (journalist), 96

Mills, C. Wright (sociologist), 38, 162

Miranda, Roger (Nicaraguan officer), 103, 262

Mitterand, François (French President), 18

Moakley, Joe (Member of Congress), 65, 91-98

Mobutu, Joseph (President of Zaire), 46-47, 50, 54-55, 117, 128, 179, 190, 269

Modernizing Foreign Assistance Network, 188

Moffit, Ronni (NGO staffer), 155

Moi, Daniel (President of Kenya), 59

Monaco, 159

Monroe, James, 8, 70, 286
Monroe Doctrine, 8, 70

Moore, Michael (film director), 207

Moratorium committee (Vietnam War), 37

Morocco, 45, 51, 53-54, 159, 294

Moskowitz, Shelly (NGO lobbyist), 81

Moveon.org, 136, 240, 283, 291

Moynihan, Daniel Patrick (UN Ambassador and Senator), 50

Moyo, Dambisa (economist), 178

Mozambique, 166

MPLA rebels (See Angola)

Mubarak, Hosni (President of Egypt), 12, 127, 132, 142, 269

Mugabe, Robert (President of Zimbabwe), 56

Muhammed (the Prophet), 8, 134

Muhammed, Elijah (Nation of Islam leader), 134

Muller, Robert "Bobby" (NGO leader), 163-170, 174-175

"Munich" analogy, 27, 32, 36, 286

Muravchik, Joshua (neo-conservative), 89

Murtha, Jack (Member of Congress), 21, 62, 75-76, 81, 92, 94, 96-97, 135

Muslims (See Islam)

MX missile, 51, 66, 108, 199

N

NASCAR, 200, 254

Nathanson, Scott (NGO lobbyist), 112, 117

National Collegiate Athletic Association (NCAA), 239

National Democratic Institute, 159, 162-163, 281

National Endowment for Democracy, 104, 162

National Football League (NFL), 132, 264-265

National Popular Vote Plan, 229-230

National Public Radio, 12, 284

National Rifle Association (NRA), 120, 236

National Security Archive, 96, 160

Native American nations, 8

NATO, 46, 71, 109, 142-143, 147, 286

NATO, and NATO expansion (Committee to Expand NATO), 109

Nazi, Nazi-ism, 27, 30-31, 40, 207, 250, 258, 286

Nazi, Nazi-ism, and analogies, 207

Neier, Aryeh (NGO leader), 52, 58, 79, 103, 158

Neighbor to Neighbor, 68
Neo-conservatives, 13, 48, 103, 109, 125-126, 145, 196, 280, 288
Netherlands, 29, 84, 131, 244, 285-286, 294
Netherlands, Dutch empire, 244
Network in Solidarity with the People of Guatemala, 68
Neumann, Janos von "John" (mathematician), 209, 213
New York Post, 18, 87
New York Times, 30, 77, 84, 87, 96-97, 101, 103-104, 143, 169, 182, 192-193, 240, 259, 284
Newman, Paul (political donor), 283
Newport, Gus (Mayor of Berkeley CA), 68
Newsom, Eric (Senate staffer), 156, 170
Newton, Isaac, 204-205
Nicaragua, 51, 55, 60-61, 63-64, 68-71, 73, 77, 81-86, 89-90, 97, 99-100, 102-105, 154, 162, 173, 262, 268
    Contra war in, 60, 90, 100, 102
    and MiG fighters, 64, 103
    and Sandinista rebellion, 105, 162, 268
Nicaragua Network, 68
Nigeria, 162, 178, 185, 294
Nimeiry, Gaafar (Sudanese President), 54, 179
9/11 attack, 262, 292, 294
Nitze, Paul (State Department official), 261
Noblesse oblige (obligations of the nobility), 257, 263, 282
Nolan, Janne (arms trade analyst), 119
Non-governmental organizations and advocacy groups (NGOs), 4, 49, 56-58, 60, 62, 64-66, 89, 113-114, 161, 168, 170, 248, 290
Noriega, Manuel (Panamanian General), 105, 128
North, Oliver (NSC staffer), 86, 100
North Korea, 15-16, 44, 169, 241, 244
North Vietnam, 25-26, 35-36, 43
Nuclear attacks (Hiroshima, Nagasaki), 204, 282-283
Nuclear Non-proliferation treaty (NPT), 16, 133
Nuclear power, 15, 274
Nye, Joseph ("soft power" strategist), 15

O

Obama, Barack, 2, 4, 11-12, 15-16, 21, 65, 105, 125-126, 128-129, 137, 139-148, 152, 159, 181,
193, 196, 198, 208, 223, 239, 242, 245-246, 252, 263, 268, 272, 280, 283, 285, 287-288
    and 2002 anti-war position on Iraq, 11, 137, 139, 159, 196, 223, 268
    and 2009 trip to Middle East, 11-12, 15, 21, 125-126, 139-140, 159, 181, 239, 272, 287-288
    and campaign promise to add 100,000 troops to military, 12
    and Afghanistan "surges", 128-129, 139, 141-147, 223
    foreign policy of, 4, 11, 21, 65, 105, 129, 139, 145, 147-148
    and Nobel Peace Prize, 11, 263
Obey, David (Member of Congress), 70, 92, 135
Obiang, Teodoro (President of Equatorial Guinea), 158
O'Connell, Janice (Senate staffer), 65, 79
O'Donnell, Tom (House staffer), 171
Oliver, Spencer (House staffer), 61, 86, 100, 226
Oman, 54
Omang, Joanne (journalist), 86
O'Neil, Mike (House staffer), 65, 93
O'Neill, Paul (Treasury Secretary), 4, 62, 69, 74, 82, 85, 130, 134-135, 185, 222
O'Neill, Paul (Treasury Secretary), and Iraqi oil field claim, 134, 185
O'Neill, Thomas P. "Tip" (Member of Congress), 4, 62, 69, 74, 82, 85, 135, 222
OPEC (Organization of Petroleum Exporting Countries), 126-127
OPEC, and oil embargo by, 126
Ortega, Daniel (Nicaraguan President), 83, 86, 105
Ortega, Humberto (Nicaraguan official), 104
Open Society Institute, 158
Oslo Treaty (cluster bombs), 168, 174-175, 269
OSS (US intelligence agency), 28
Ottawa Treaty (landmines), 5-6, 14, 69, 108, 116, 152, 163-175, 199, 248, 269, 272
Oxfam (NGO), 177, 187

P

Pacifica Radio, 12, 240
Palestinians, 14, 129, 131, 141, 160, 237-238
    Hamas Party, 160
    Palestinian Authority, 160

Palin, Sarah (Governor), 147, 183

Pakistan, 3, 15-16, 51, 55, 60, 128-129, 132, 140-141, 144, 146, 161, 165, 242, 244, 287
    FATA areas, 144-146
    ISI (intelligence service), 144
    Pakistani Taliban, 3, 129, 144, 146

Panama, 9, 62, 97, 105, 122, 155
    Panama Canal, 9, 105, 155

Paraguay, 57

Paralyzed Veterans of America, 163

Parks, Hays (Pentagon lawyer), 67, 171

Paul, Ron (Member of Congress), 218, 293

Pax Americas, 87

Peace Action, 17, 66, 117, 120, 147, 272, 290

Pell, Claiborne (Senator), 65, 86

Pelosi, Nancy (Member of Congress), 4-5, 15, 21, 68, 135-136, 138, 145, 222-223, 260, 293

Pentagon (Department of Defense), 11, 33, 39, 43, 70, 90-91, 95-96, 108-111, 113-114, 130, 133, 142-143, 145, 147, 154, 156-158, 167-175, 189, 194-195, 207, 222-223, 235, 258-263, 270-272, 279

Pentagon Papers, 33

Percy, Chuck (Senator), 72, 113, 237

Perle, Richard (neo-conservative strategist), 48, 125, 207, 261-262, 268

Perry, Mark (NGO staffer), 167

Perry, Oliver (Admiral), 8

Perry, William (Secretary of Defense), 16, 110, 168

Peru, 112, 155, 161

Peru, and Sendero Luminoso (Shining Path) rebels, 156

Peter, Paul and Mary (singers), 62, 77

Petraeus, David (US General), 136, 291

Philippines, US war in, 9, 27, 51, 54, 60, 112, 140, 154, 267, 286

Pickering, Thomas (State Department official), 79

Pinochet, Augusto (Chilean President), 160

Plato, 161, 256

Podhoretz, Norman (neo-conservative), 13

Poland, 12, 143, 241

Political action committees (PACs), 119, 161, 234-236

Ponce, René Emilio (Salvadoran general), 91, 97

Portugal, 10, 44, 46, 244, 271, 286, 294

and African colonies, 8, 26, 28, 30, 46, 184, 241, 246, 250-251, 271, 286
    Portugal's empire, 244, 294

Posada, Luis (CIA agent), 4, 78

Potsdam conference, 29

Potter, Paul (SDS president), 39-40

Poverty, efforts to reduce, 16, 51, 56, 69, 177-181, 184-191, 197, 199, 242, 247, 269, 273, 284, 286, 288, 293
    and Big Plan, 180, 181, 183-186, 191
    Make Poverty History, 180-181, 184, 186, 191

Powell, Colin (Secretary of State), 10-11, 102, 110, 181, 195, 256, 259, 288

Powers, Gary (US aerial spy), 100

Powers, Thomas (historian), 272

Prendergast, John (NGO leader), 196

Presidential elections, rules for, 72

Presidential election, 2000, 34, 139, 142, 203, 211, 226, 231, 253, 283

PRODEMCA, 13, 262

Professional "wrestling", 266

Progressive Caucus (Congressional body), 134-136, 222, 293

Project for the New American Century, 13

Project on Demilitarization and Democracy (See also Demilitarization for Democracy), 111, 169-170, 195

Proportional representation (for US House), 217-221, 224, 230, 250, 293

Puerto Rico, 9, 225

Q

Qatar, 126, 159

Quakers (see also American Friends Service Committee, Friends Committee on National Legislation), 58, 67, 137, 166-167, 175

Qutb, Sayyid (Islamic theorist), 132

R

Rademaker, Stephen (House and State Department staffer), 139

Raimo, Bernie (House staffer), 65

Raitt, Bonnie (singer), 69

Rankin, Jeannette (Member of Congress), 130

Rapid Deployment Force (US Central Command), 54, 59, 123, 126

Raskin, Marcus (NGO founder), 146, 249

Reagan, Ronald, foreign policy of 6, 10, 51, 59, 61, 63, 67, 80, 85-86, 100, 105, 107, 140, 148, 154, 159, 261-262

Reagan, Ronald, and "constructive engagement" with South Africa, 10, 67

Redford, Robert (actor), 69

Reid, Harry (Senator), 135-136, 138

Rendition, 4, 125, 131-132, 137, 223, 288

Republican Party, foreign policy of, 12, 14, 20, 35, 47, 95, 138, 140, 146, 219, 247, 293

Reserve Officers Training Corps (ROTC), 266

RESULTS organization, 114

Revelle, Roger (scientist), 206

Rhodesia (see also Zimbabwe), 48-50, 56-57

Rice, Condoleezza (Secretary of State), 181, 259, 270

Rice, Susan (State Department official), 157, 193

Ridgway, James (columnist), 69

Ridgway, Matthew (General), 32

Rieser, Tim (Senate staffer), 4, 65, 164, 167, 170-174

Robertson, Pat (minister), 177, 255

Robinson, Jackie (sports star), 49

Robinson, Randall (anti-apartheid leader), 18, 66

Rochambeau, Jean-Baptiste (French General), 248

Rohrabacher, Dana (Member of Congress), 117, 119

Rolf, Rick (Senate staffer), 65

Rolling Stone magazine, 260

Roman empire, 227

Rome Treaty (See ICC)

Romero, Oscar (Archbishop), 70, 287

Romero, Peter (State Department official), 98

Rone, Jemera (NGO lawyer), 4, 79, 90

Roosevelt, Theodore
and belligerent foreign policy of, 9
and The Winning of the West, 9-10, 32

Roosevelt, Franklin, 10, 28, 32, 61, 126, 226
foreign policy of, 10, 28, 32, 61

Rosenberg, Tina (journalist), 79

Rosenfeld, Stephen (journalist), 80, 86

Ross, Dennis (State Department official), 140, 183, 229

Rothko Chapel (Human rights NGO), 66, 96

Rove, Karl (administration official), 203

Rubin, Barnett (administration official), 144

Rumsfeld, Donald (Secretary of Defense), 109, 156

Rusk, Dean (Secretary of State), 25, 31, 36, 47

Russell, Richard (Senator), 246

Russia, 16, 40, 50, 109, 111, 126, 131, 133, 143, 165-166, 253, 267, 285, 294

Russo, Marty (Member of Congress), 236

Rwanda, 17, 152, 157-158, 191, 193-196

S

Sachs, Jeffrey (economist), 177, 180, 183-186

Sadat, Anwar (President of Egypt), 54, 127, 132

Sadler, Barry ('60s singer), 20

Saferworld, 116, 121

Samuelson, Robert (economist), 200

Sandinista party (See also Nicaragua), 69, 81, 86, 104-105, 162, 268

SANE (Commitee for a Sane Nuclear Policy), 37-38, 68-69

Sasser, Jim (Senator), 97

Saudi Arabia, 3, 11-12, 85, 112-114, 116, 122, 126, 131, 142, 145, 159, 165, 185, 237, 243, 251, 269, 285, 287-288, 292

Sauri (Kenyan village), 185-186

Save the Children, 177

Savimbi, Jonas (Angolan leader), 159, 179

Saxon, John D. (Iran-Contra lawyer), 102

Schneider, Mark (State Department official), 51

School of the Americas (US Army), 120, 155-157

Schultz, Laurie (congressional staffer), 65, 86

Schwartz, Bernard (arms manufacturer), 119, 142

Scott, David (Member of Congress), 51, 53-55, 57, 112, 117, 235

Scowcroft, Brent (National Security Advisor), 15, 108

Segregation, 19, 27, 30, 38, 61, 141, 221-222, 227, 247, 291

Selassie, Haile (Emperor of Ethiopia), 52

Sellers, Peter (actor), 261

Sen, Amartya (economist), 63, 179

Serbia, 131, 140

Shah of Iran (Pahlavi), 126-127, 258

Shaik, Shabir (South African financier), 121

Sheehan, Neil (journalist), 270

Sherman, William T. (General), 254
Shinpoch, Jan (House staffer), 65
Shultz, George (Secretary of State), 16, 64
Sigal, Leon (journalist), 164-165, 167-169, 171-173
Silber, John (university president), 73
Simon, Paul (Senator), 22, 25, 32, 34-37, 84, 113, 134, 192, 222, 237, 257-258, 261, 291
Singapore, 161, 184
Singer, Fred (scientist), 206, 255
Skelton, Ike (Member of Congress), 146
Sklar, Barry (Senate staffer), 65
Slaughter, Louise (Member of Congress), 37, 40, 60, 69-70, 87, 95, 97, 154, 164, 193-194, 207, 287
Slave trade, 225, 253-254, 275
Slavery, 7-8, 19, 22, 27, 30, 184, 219, 226, 245, 247, 254, 275, 282, 285
Socialist Workers Party, 27, 38
Soderberg, Nancy (Senate and NSC staffer), 113-115, 169-170, 173, 193
Sofaer, Abraham (State Department official), 84, 173
Soft power, 15, 55, 136, 139, 269
Solarz, Steve (Member of Congress), 71, 74-75, 237
Somalia, 11, 16-17, 45-46, 51-55, 59, 110, 112, 122, 128, 141-142, 144, 157-158, 170, 179-180, 191, 193-195, 242, 285, 287-288
   civil war in, 46, 54, 141, 157
   invasion by Ethiopia, 2005, 128, 158, 179, 194
   invasion of Ethiopia, 1977, 52, 54-55, 193
   US aid to, 59, 112, 180
   US troops in, 1992-1994, 52, 112, 122, 128, 141, 193-194
Somoza (family of Nicaraguan presidents), 60, 63, 69, 81-82
Soros, George (NGO founder), 158, 165, 283-284
South Africa, 17-18, 27, 45-50, 57, 64, 66-67, 101, 112, 121, 141, 154, 160, 178, 182-183, 188, 193, 198, 220, 222, 241-242, 262, 281, 287, 289
South Korea, 32, 140, 169, 190, 270-271, 289
South Vietnam, 25-26, 33, 36-38, 43-44, 47, 181
Soviet Union, 10-11, 15, 34, 46-48, 50-54, 57, 61, 66, 73, 83-84, 107, 111, 131-132, 145, 209, 213, 238, 240, 244-245, 251-252, 261, 269, 276
   policy in Africa, 10, 15, 46-48, 50-54, 57, 66
Spain, 8-9, 90, 244, 285-286, 294
Spanish–American War, 245
Spellman, Francis (Cardinal), 255
St. Germain, Ferdinand (Member of Congress), 182
Stalin, Joseph (Soviet leader), 256
Steele, James (Colonel), 78, 96
Stennis, John (Senator), 80
Stimson Center, 146
Strategic Arms Limitation Talks (SALT), 51, 53
Studds, Gerry (Member of Congress), 65, 71, 75-76, 92, 99
Student Non-violent Coordinating Committee (SNCC), 39
Students for a Democratic Society (SDS), 4, 27, 38-42, 50, 256-257
Students for a Democratic Society (SDS), and Port Huron Statement, 38
Subsidies (for crops), 16, 77, 85, 186-187
Sudan, 16-18, 51, 54, 59, 112, 132, 142, 152, 179, 192-193, 196, 199, 242, 287
   and Darfur rebellion, 147, 191, 193, 196
Suez Canal, war for, 126
Summers, Larry (Treasury Department official), 129
"Support the Troops" campaign, 136, 260
Swaziland, 15
Sweden, 131, 188, 294

T

Taiwan, 113, 270-271, 289
Taliban, 3, 12, 129-130, 134, 143-147, 196, 265, 268, 270, 272
   Afghan, 12, 129-130, 134, 143-145, 147, 196, 265, 272
   Pakistani, 144
Talleyrand, Charles Maurice de (French foreign minister), 63, 69
Tanzania, 185
Taylor, F.W. (scientist), 19, 204-205, 208-209, 211, 222, 253, 291
Team B (CIA planning exercise), 13, 47, 108, 261
Temperance movement, 275
Tenet, George (CIA Director), 259

Terzano, John (NGO staffer), 167, 170
Thurmond, Strom (Senator), 61
Torricelli, Robert (Member of Congress), 98
Thamotheram, Raj (NGO leader), 116, 121
Tillman, Pat (athlete), 265
Tipton, Paul (Jesuit priest), 92, 94-95, 171-172
Tirman, John (political scientist), 20, 113, 252-253
Tobin tax, 189
Todman, Terence "Terry" (State Department official), 51
Tolbert, William (President of Liberia), 54
Tolstoy, Leo (novelist), 249, 267
Torture, 3-4, 12, 14, 16, 84, 96, 115, 121-122, 125, 131-132, 134, 137, 139, 147, 152, 154-155, 157-158, 164, 190, 223, 242-243, 248, 262, 269, 280, 287-289, 293
"Toys for Tots" Marine program, 263
Treasury Department, 78, 130, 134, 153, 183, 185, 187
Trenberth, Kevin (climate modeler), 213
Trident missile, 108
Truman, Harry, foreign policy of, 10, 25-26, 28-32, 43-44, 61, 126, 238, 271, 282
Tunney, John (Senator), 49-50
Turkey, the (as symbol of foreign policy of cooperation), 7-8, 11-12, 19-20, 51, 55, 115-116, 123, 134, 163, 195, 217, 253, 286
Turkeys (anti-imperialists), beliefs and policies of, 9, 16-22, 38, 51, 58, 60, 62-65, 81, 86-87, 89-90, 98-99, 105, 107, 109-111, 114, 122-123, 129-130, 133-136, 139, 146-148, 151-153, 159-161, 163, 178, 188, 191-193, 195-196, 199-200, 217-218, 222, 224, 233-234, 238-241, 246, 248, 250, 256, 260, 266, 271-274, 276-277, 279-280, 282-284, 289, 292-293
Tutela Legal (Legal Protection), 79, 96

U

Uganda, 142, 193-194
Ulundi (battle of), 191, 248
Umayyad dynasty, 294
UNITA rebels (Ovimbundu resistance group: See Angola)
Unitarian Universalist Service Committee, 68
United Arab Emirates (UAE), 126

United for Peace and Justice (anti-war coalition), 21, 133
United Kingdom, 16, 170, 187, 226
United Nations (UN), 12, 14, 17-18, 20, 50, 52, 54, 79, 90, 98-99, 107, 109, 112, 116, 125, 133, 137-138, 152, 157, 162, 166, 177, 180, 185, 188, 191, 193-196, 198, 243, 251, 256, 259, 272
  Childrens Fund (UNICEF), 177-178
  and Millennium Village, 185
  and Register of Conventional Arms, 116
  Security Council, 14, 17-18, 68, 84, 86, 112, 119, 133, 137, 160, 169, 188, 194
United Service Organizations (USO), 266
Universal Declaration of Human Rights, 115
University of Central America (UCA), 60, 91-92, 94-95, 105
Uruguay, 57
US foreign policy
  cooperation, 11, 19, 217, 279, 281
  domination, 4, 6, 11, 16, 18-19, 21, 52, 61, 72, 181, 189, 217-218, 222, 240, 243, 266-267, 270-272, 275-276, 279, 281, 283, 287-289, 293
  primacy, 15, 130
US Jobs Now (arms sales campaign), 112
Uzbekistan, 165, 251

V

Vance, Cyrus (Secretary of State), 51, 53, 55
Veterans for Peace, 68
Veterans of Foreign Wars, 164, 264, 284
Victoria (Queen of England), 105, 128, 177, 191
Vietnam, 2, 6, 11, 13, 15, 17, 20-21, 25-29, 31-50, 52, 54-56, 59-60, 62-63, 65, 76-77, 83, 105, 126, 129-130, 132, 140, 143, 145-147, 159-161, 163-165, 169-170, 174-175, 179, 181, 183, 195, 200, 218, 240, 243, 248, 252, 255, 257-258, 260-261, 263-266, 268, 270, 272, 285, 287, 289-290, 292
  US role in French war in, 26-27, 29, 36, 287
  US war in, 252
  and Rolling Thunder bombings, 25, 35-36
  and POW/MIA myth, 264
Vietnam Syndrome, 45
Vietnam veterans, 163-164, 169, 175, 264
Vietnam Veterans of America Foundation, 164, 169, 175

Vitagliano, Marissa (NGO staffer), 167
Voting Rights Act, 221

W

Wahabism, 131
Walker, William (State Department official), 81, 92, 94-95, 98
Walt, Stephen (political scientist), 15, 237
Walter Reed Hospital, 264
War Powers Resolution, 50, 138, 153
  and 1973 debate, 138
  and 2008 review in Congress, 138
  and Baker-Christopher review, 102, 138
War Victims Fund, 164
Ward, Kip (US General), 157
Wareham, Mary (NGO staffer), 167
Warsaw Pact, 57-58, 69, 107, 109, 111, 151, 200
Waruingi, Macharia (doctor), 186
"Washington Consensus" on growth, 180, 182-184
Washington Institute for Near East Policy, 139
Washington, George, 248, 285, 289
Washington Office on Africa (WOA), 49
Washington Office on Latin America, 57, 68
Watt, Mel (Member of Congress), 221
Wayne, John (actor), 266
Weathermen (See also SDS), 256-257
Weiss, Ted (Member of Congress), 65
Wellesley, Arthur (Duke of Wellington), 8
West Bank, 13, 190, 238
Western Hemisphere Institute for Security Cooperation (See School of the Americas), 156
Weymouth, Lally (columnist), 221-222
White, Robert (State Department official), 35, 64, 70
Whitfield, Teresa (journalist), 91, 93-95
Wilkie, Edith "Edie" (congressional staffer), 4, 64-66, 73
Williams, Jody (NGO activist), 69, 165, 167
Williams, William Appleman (anti-imperial author), 17
Wilson, Woodrow, 9-10, 139, 256, 285-286
  foreign policy of, 10, 139, 256
Winthrop, John (Governor), and "City upon a hill" sermon, 250-251
Witness for Peace, 68
Wohlstetter, Albert (nuclear strategist), 109, 261

Wolfensohn, James (World Bank President), 185
Wolfowitz, Paul (neo-conservative strategist), 13, 48, 108-109, 125, 130, 140, 154, 177, 179, 261
Wolpe, Howard (Member of Congress), 83, 182
Women's Action for New Directions (WAND), 271
Women Strike for Peace, 68
Women's rights, promotion of, 127, 154, 161, 191, 250, 268
"Woodstock nation", 260
Woodward, Bill (House staffer), 65, 92-93, 98
World Bank, 51, 55, 117, 153-154, 177, 179-180, 182-184, 189-190, 198, 257, 288
World Policy Institute, 117
World Trade Organization, 153
World War I, 9, 30, 86, 166, 258, 286
World War II, 1, 6, 10, 26, 28, 31, 33, 41, 52, 111, 148, 184, 196, 209, 213, 242, 244-246, 252, 261, 267, 286
Wright, Jim (Member of Congress), 4, 38, 62, 72, 74-76, 82-83, 100, 102-104, 132, 272
Wurmser, David (neo-conservative), 125

Y

Yemen, 55, 128, 131, 144
Yom Kippur War, 46, 126, 238
Young, Andrew (State Department official), 54, 257
Yugoslavia, 107, 140, 152, 195

Z

Zablocki, Clem (Member of Congress), 83
Zaire, 11, 45-48, 50-51, 54-55, 59, 117, 190, 251, 269, 287
  and Lunda rebels, 55
  US role in, 1970–1996, 47-48
Zenawi, Meles (Ethiopian prime minister), 142, 158
Ziegler, Jerry (Cornell professor), 5
Zimbabwe, 56, 190-191
Zinn, Howard (anti-imperial author), 17, 280
Zulu empire, 244
Zulu War (1879), 191, 193, 268
Zuma, Jacob (President of South Africa), 121